Ewing Galloway

Parthenon, Athens

HELLAS AND HELLENISM

A SOCIAL AND CULTURAL HISTORY OF ANCIENT GREECE BY

NICHOLAS P. VLACHOS, PH.D.
PROFESSOR OF GREEK AND LATIN,
TEMPLE UNIVERSITY

MAN IS THE MEASURE OF THINGS.— PROTAGORAS

GINN AND COMPANY
BOSTON · NEW YORK · CHICAGO · LONDON · ATLANTA
DALLAS · COLUMBUS · SAN FRANCISCO

836.1

The Athenæum Press
GINN AND COMPANY · PROPRIETORS · BOSTON · U.S.A.

PREFACE

THE only justification for *Hellas and Hellenism* lies in the attempt here made to co-ordinate the political, social, and cultural elements of Hellenic history and to present these as so many aspects of what is after all an indivisible whole. Hellenic civilization is interpreted as the product of the Hellenic mind and therefore as the product of a distinct type of social environment. This book holds with John Dewey that environment is "the great conditioner of mind" and that "the kind of mind they [that is, the instincts] become, depends upon the kinds of objects of attention and affection which the specific social conditions supply." Hellenism and all its works can be rightly understood only when viewed as having sprung from a common social matrix — the Hellenic city-state. Thus interpreted the history of Greek civilization becomes a social study; as such only is this book offered to the public. The chapters on religion, education, literature, art, and philosophy are not so many abbreviated histories on these topics, nor do they aim to offer complete catalogues of factual material; the pertinent facts in all these fields are presented as so many social phenomena, serving to illuminate the central problem, the character and the history of the Hellenic polis.

The chapter on the city-state therefore contains the heart of the book. Its comparative lateness may reasonably be justified by the necessity of first disposing of the preliminaries. The polis has its roots in the past; without the Heroic Age and Homer it must remain an enigma. And a sketch of the political history of Hellas gives the reader the needed opportunity for surveying the entire field; only after he has grasped the reasons for the tragic failure of the city-states to achieve national union, is he prepared to consider the other side of the question, why this same polis was yet to become the greatest factor in human progress that the world had seen. Such a study of Hellenic society may well serve as an introduction to all social science; for the human problems remain the same throughout the ages, but only in the history of the Hellenic polis can they be examined in their simplest setting and in sharpest outline.

The present book is the fruit of many years of teaching. Experience has shown that in order to present the material most effectively a certain amount of schematizing is unavoidable. The tree of Hellenism as painted in these pages has been severely trimmed, and much of its luxurious growth has been pruned away, in order to accentuate the chief configuration. Orphism, for instance, finds no place in the book, and philosophy closes with Plato. Aristotle's distinction lies admittedly in his great powers of analysis, while Hellenism proper is the achievement of creative artists, among whom the great Stagirite is not to be numbered; his mode and outlook stand in sharpest contrast to those of Plato, "wie der anatomische Atlas zur plastischen Menschengestalt."[1]

Possibly some may object to the closing of the account with the extinction of Hellenic independence; for Greek genius certainly did not die with the Greek city-state. As a social study, however, the book finds its logical conclusion with the death of the typical social organization which is its theme. Again, it may be asked, Why so much space to literature and so little to art and architecture? The answer must be sought in the practical needs of the student. The material for the teaching of Greek literature is abundant and readily at hand; it is otherwise with art and architecture, for neither photographs nor lantern slides will ever serve as satisfactory substitutes for the originals in the teaching of these subjects.

It goes without saying that in writing such a book as this one draws constantly on the work of others; the debt I owe is beyond acknowledgment, for although footnotes and bibliographical appendices may indicate whence most of

[1] W. Jaeger, *Aristoteles*, p. 397.

the material was garnered, I have in many years of teaching and reading unconsciously absorbed much (even in the way of a happy phrase) the source of which it was impossible to trace.

I wish to express my thanks to the publishers who have allowed me to quote from their publications: G. Bell and Sons, Carnegie Institution, Clarendon Press, Columbia University Press, Harcourt, Brace and Company, The Macmillan Company, Methuen and Company, Charles Scribner's Sons; to the President and Fellows of Harvard College and the Harvard University Press for permission to quote from the Loeb Classical Library; and to colleagues and friends who have toiled unselfishly to refashion my English into something more nearly resembling a conventional English prose style; they are not to be blamed for the many blemishes that remain.

In conclusion, my fondest hope is that this book may prove a timely one. We ourselves are passing out of our Heroic Age and are entering upon a period of transition which will bring us perhaps the need for a new orientation toward life and a new interpretation of human values. May a dispassionate inquiry into the Hellenic social experiment help to stimulate the minds of our youth, and may it assist them to a clearer perception of the true character of the problems we are facing.

N. P. VLACHOS

CONTENTS

HELLAS AND HELLENISM

CHAPTER I

INTRODUCTORY

Egypt and Babylon

THE cultural history of ancient Hellas forms but one chapter, though a very important one, of what is usually called ancient history. To see the Hellenic achievement in its proper perspective, and to evaluate its true significance in the history of human progress, some degree of acquaintance with the phases of ancient history is indispensable. Before the coming of the Greeks, Egypt and Babylonia had made great strides in the arts of civilization which have had their share in laying the foundation of Western culture. It is, therefore, important to know not only what these civilizations accomplished, but also what they failed to do.

The story of the ancient world begins in the fourth millennium B.C. in two centers, Egypt and Babylonia; in each, like geographical conditions led to strikingly similar results.

The rich soil of the Nile valley presented the dwellers of ancient Egypt with an opportunity for more than merely satisfying their daily wants: the bounty of the river made possible the accumulation of a surplus. But, for the full exploitation of these great natural resources, some form of organization was imperative. The long narrow valley easily supported hundreds of thousands of human beings, who, not being divided by natural barriers, were forced to learn to live together in peace in order to take full advantage of the annual overflow of the river.

We know that originally the settlements on the Nile were separate units, nomes; but we know also that the great advance in civilization made by Egypt took place only after the political unification of these independent nomes. What form did this organization take? The great pyramids of

Gizeh supply the answer. The greatest of them covers some thirteen acres. It is a solid mass of masonry containing over two million blocks of limestone, each weighing on an average two and a half tons; the sides at the base of the pyramid are seven hundred and fifty-five feet long; its height rose to nearly five hundred feet. We are told that a hundred thousand men toiled for twenty years at the building of this monument, and we believe the report. Now what purpose did the pyramid serve? It was the tomb of the king. Herein lies the answer to the question we asked above: the political organization of united Egypt took the form of a despotism. We find the inhabitants of the thirty or so communities united *and* enslaved; for a hundred thousand of them worked for years to build the monarch a monument suitable to house his soul, and we do not hear of any rebellion. Plainly these people saw some connection between their own interests and the tomb they built for their king. And here is the first major problem confronting us in ancient history: by what mysterious means had these kings succeeded in converting the people to this extraordinary view of their own interests?

Before attempting to answer this question, let us inquire first into the character of that despotism — for such it was — which flourished in Egypt in the third millennium B.C.

At the head of the government stood the king, who was believed to be the son of a god and was himself, in the eyes of the people, divine. His power was unlimited. He ruled the country in the god's name, as its sole master and lord; he commanded his armed subjects in war, directed their industry, prescribed the course of labour necessary for irrigation, and disposed of all the resources of the country at his own discretion. In religious matters he was assisted by the priests . . . In secular affairs [he] was assisted by officials, who carried out his commands and directed the people in their occupations of peace and war — [but] they, like the priests, were merely personal servants and agents of the king and the god. Side by side with the priests and high officials an army of scribes, overseers, artisans and policemen was employed. They all received maintenance from the king. The population was absolutely at the mercy of the king and his officials. In the political life of the country they took no share whatever; they had no right of private property, especially in land.[1]

Such was the political organization of the earliest people whose history is known to us. We return to our question: What had made possible this exploitation of an entire people at the hands of its king? This does not mean: How had the common people lost their political rights and the right to own land? For the probability is that they had never possessed either. Now, whatever be the variety of facts which anthropologists have collected concerning the organization of early society, one fact stands out clearly, the solidarity of tribal life. Early man was essentially a herd animal; the individual was completely submerged in the group, ruled by the lore and the accumulated traditions of the past. His life was governed by a network of taboos, which precluded the possibility of any liberty of movement on his part; and the prerogative of administration, with the exclusive possession of the tribal wisdom, was usually in the hands of the old men of the tribe.[2] Nothing is more characteristic of tribal life than its conservatism. Life becomes a routine when a state of equilibrium has been reached, that is, when the group has arrived at some state of adjustment to its environment; nothing is allowed to disturb the precarious hold on life that has been gained. Amid such conditions human life continued for thousands of years. Progress was necessarily slow, and must be measured by millennia. It is only when some great crisis presents itself that the opportunity for change occurs.

Such a crisis may have been the cause of the rise of des-

[1] M. Rostovtzeff, *A History of the Ancient World*, Vol. I, Chap. V. (Quoted by permission of the Oxford University Press.)

[2] There can hardly be any doubt that, for instance, the Spartan *gerousia* and the Roman *senatus*, political institutions of civilized peoples, had their roots in the tribal traditions of the dim past (both words mean "council of elders").

potic power in Egypt. It well may have been that amid the perpetual discord of the warring nomes these early Egyptians lived in actual want and starvation in a land of plenty, through the lack of that larger organization which alone would enable them to take proper advantage of their natural resources. When conditions become intolerable, the crisis is there, and with it the opportunity for leadership.

Now to us the quality of leadership may defy analysis, but we do not regard it as something supernatural. Early man found it both uncanny and supernatural, for he lived habitually in a twofold world, of visible and invisible forces, and of these the latter were incomparably more powerful. Very soon he found it necessary to establish satisfactory relations with these unseen powers; that made his religion and his magic. Of all the nations of the ancient world none was more magic-ridden than the Egyptian.[1] It was inevitable that a leader, arising in a society impregnated with such ideas, should himself become Chief Magician, and that the means he employed should take a magical form. As the safety of each clan, or nome, in prehistoric Egypt had depended upon the totem and the magic power wielded by the priest, so the safety and well-being of the united kingdom depended upon the king, the incarnation of totemic powers and the master of magic spells, to whom Toth himself had revealed his secret. Nay, the king identified himself with the two great divinities upon whose favor the very life of Egypt depended: the Sun-god and Osiris, the god of the fructifying waters. The king became the King of Harvests. In fine, he held the prosperity of the people in the hollow of his hand. In the unshaken belief that such was the case lies the secret of the Pharaoh's power.

This, then, was the type of monarchy which prevailed in Egypt and held its people enslaved; as such it lasted, with interruptions, from the days of the great pyramids (2900 B.C.)

[1] The so-called Book of the Dead is nothing but a collection of magical formulas supposed to ensure the felicity of the departed in the Great Beyond.

until the twelfth century B.C., when, after a career of conquest, Egypt gradually sank into a state of coma.

There is, however, another side to the picture. The concentration of all Egypt's rich resources in the hands of one man was not without its advantage. It made possible the erection of such monuments as the pyramids and the great temple-complex at Karnak, which are still accounted among the wonders of the world. Moreover, it stimulated the activity of artisan and artist alike; all toiled for the king, sculptor and painter, jeweler and lapidary, weaver, metal-worker, and worker in wood — all alike rivaled one another in their zeal to serve the king. However, when all is said, the refinement and elegance of Egyptian art remains as the beauty of a poisonous flower blooming in the turbid waters of a stagnant pool. Egyptian art moved along fixed lines and through patterns prescribed by the tyrannical combination of priest and king; therein lies the secret of its excessive stylization, which is perhaps, to the modern beholder, its most striking quality — the same patterns are repeated *ad nauseam*, the same ideas expressed in the same formulas. It was not a free art vigorously developing under the stimulus of a changing social life, but the highly artificial product of a society where no fresh winds were allowed to cleanse the stifling atmosphere of ancient traditions and even more ancient superstitions.

When we turn to Babylonia, we find a set of conditions strikingly similar to those of Egypt: a rich alluvial plain, the inundations of a mighty river, a network of canals, and therefore the same eventual necessity for centralized power. Here too we meet with the same alliance between government and religion; the authority of the state was summed up in the person of the priest-king, and the people were held as firmly in the grip of superstition. The priest, master of spell and incantation, predictor of the future by the course of the stars and the livers of sacrificed beasts, held undisputed sway over the minds of the populace. There were minor differences, attributable to local conditions, and especially to the more exposed situation of Babylonia. The struggle to safeguard the wealth gained from the rich plain against raids of less favorably situated neighbors in the mountains and desert led to a more highly developed military art, and eventually to the tradition of conquest and tribute-levying for which the career of Sargon of Agade (*c.* 2600 B.C.) laid the foundation. The part of conqueror was then essayed successively by a number of rulers or would-be rulers of the great plain until, with the coming of Hammurabi (*c.* 1950–1900 B.C.), the entire plain was united under the rule of Babylon. About 1700 B.C. the invasion of the Kassites put an end to the supremacy of the mighty city. With the beginning of the first millennium B.C. the Assyrians succeeded to the imperial ambitions of their Babylonian kinsmen, but they did not reach the acme of their power until the eighth century B.C., from which time the dominion of the Near East remained undisputed until the fall of Nineveh in 612 B.C. The Assyrians were masters of the military arts; in the refinements of cruelty and methods of terrorization practiced upon their unhappy victims they were without rivals. It is not too much to say that no single dynasty has contributed so greatly to the sum total of human misery as did the powerful and energetic rulers of Assyria in the heyday of their glory.

With the fall of Nineveh we are already well advanced in the era of the Greek city-states. In summing up, then, the part played by the Near East in the history of civilization, we note that in spite of certain solid contributions[1] to the progress of civilization which may rightfully be credited to it, we look as yet in vain for a form of social organization that shall make a free and vigorous development of the arts of civilization possible. The truth is, of course, that the combined dominion of despot and priest characteristic of the Near East is incompatible with any such spontaneous development.

[1] For a summary of these see J. H. Breasted, Ancient Times, §§ 368–371.

It was reserved for Hellas to discover, in the city-state, the political and social formula that should release the creative ability of the race; this not only became the determining factor in the evolution of Hellenic culture, but also furnished the world with a new ideal, that of political liberty. And yet it might be maintained that precedents for the Greek city-state are found elsewhere. That, outside of Greece, these aspirations to liberty and citizenship did not reach fulfillment cannot be ascribed entirely to the peculiar genius of the Hellenic race; a great deal was due to certain geographical conditions, which it now becomes our duty to examine.

SUGGESTIONS FOR READING. A clear and concise summary of the ancient history of the Near East may be found in HAMILTON and BLUNT, *An Outline of Ancient History*, Part I (Oxford, 1924).

For a fuller account consult J. H. BREASTED, *Ancient Times* (Ginn, 1935), or the authoritative work of Rostovtzeff quoted above (p. 5).

On early civilization see J. L. MYRES, *The Dawn of History* (Holt, 1911), and A. A. GOLDENWEISER, *Early Civilization* (Knopf, 1922).

The Geographical Setting: Mountains and Sea

The Balkan Peninsula, homeland of the ancient Greeks, projects far into the Eastern Mediterranean. The sea itself here both separates and unites three continents, Europe, Asia, and Africa, whose coastlands form a true geographical unit. A group of islands links Greece with Asia, and the long island of Crete serves as a steppingstone to Egypt.

The Balkan Peninsula itself is divided by mountain chains into a number of distinctly separate regions. This fact invited the growth of independent political entities; hence the history of Hellas does not treat of a national unit, but remains to the end a history of a multiplicity of small states. Herein, as we shall see, lies the secret at once of the greatness of Hellas and of its weakness.

This entire system of mountains and valleys, with a coast line all out of proportion to its size, with its bays and headlands and innumerable rocky islands, stands, viewed from the sea, boldly outlined in the clear atmosphere; if later we shall discover in the Hellenic race a certain gift of imagination, a sensitiveness to beauty, and a love of independence, we cannot fail to observe that here, if anywhere on earth, nature had provided the appropriate setting for a race thus endowed. We are tempted to ask how far environment affected racial gifts, and how much Greek genius owed to the stimulus of its surroundings.

Mountains and sea — they have always been the home of daring and doing, of liberty and the love of adventure; human progress never has made great strides on the vast plains, where nature and life are equally dull and depressing. The sea is a challenge and a stimulus to the enterprising spirit of man, and has never failed to leave its mark on the pages of history; and the mountains have ever sheltered the love of liberty. The settlers in the Balkan Peninsula, a rude but vigorous race, were doubly fortunate in that the sea brought them into contact with the advanced civilizations of the Near East; for the Balkan Peninsula turns distinctly in that direction.

There was another incentive to embark upon the dangerous sea. The homeland of the Hellenic people was poorly endowed for the sustenance of human life. Its bones are but thinly clothed with flesh: the soil is mostly thin and poor and rocky; even the valleys are rarely productive or truly fertile. The proof is that of the cereals not wheat but barley formed the staple food of the Greeks; wheaten bread remained a luxury. The common people lived on porridge the basis of which was barley. Their domestic animals are a further index to the poverty of the soil. Rich meadows are rare. Navigable rivers are few, most Greek "rivers" being mountain streams in winter and stony ravines in summer. Goats, sheep, and swine can find a living on the hillsides, but rarely cattle; as for horses, the possession of these constituted throughout Greek history a privilege of the rich.

But if the soil is poorly adapted for the growing of cereals, it lends itself very well to the cultivation of the grape and the olive, and in the end it was these which transformed Greece, at least partly, from a land of farmers and shepherds into a land of traders and merchants. Both the olive and the grape play a large part in the economy of Mediterranean lands. Not only did the olive furnish food and a substitute for butter-fat, but its oil did duty as ointment for the body and fuel for lamps. Wine was the national drink of Hellas, a most precious gift of their most beloved god, and drama itself is the most glorious offspring of his worship.

Lastly we must not forget the wild flowers of Greece, which made the countryside gay with color in the spring; for without them there would have been no bees, and without bees no honey, a real necessity to the Greeks, as it was their only substitute for sugar.

Of mineral wealth Greece is almost destitute; of the precious metals silver was dug from the mines of Laureion in Attica, and there was some iron ore in the Peloponnesus and elsewhere.

The climate of the Aegean basin is kindly to man. The winters are mild and rainy, the summers hot and dry. The northeast winds sweep unhindered from the plains of southern Russia over the Black Sea into Greece; their bracing quality has prevented the climate from becoming enervating in the heat of summer. Even though the rainfall in ancient Greece may have been somewhat greater than it is at present, now that its mountain sides are entirely denuded of their forests, still even in those far-off days Greece reveled in sunshine. This is of greater importance for the understanding of its history than might at first be surmised. For the Greek lived his life in the open, with his fellows. His home was but a poor place, good enough to sleep in and, to his mind, good enough for the women; but men needed a larger sphere. Perhaps the most gregarious creature the world has ever seen, the ancient Hellene craved the company and the approval of his fellows. He who did not mix with his kind was under suspicion; to live to oneself without sharing in public life was an anomaly. The history of the term *idiotes*, originally meaning a private person, one not holding public office, indicates with what feelings the lack of interest in common affairs was regarded.

In this way both geography and climate favored the growth of the city-state. For the mountains separated these Hellenes; the sea again united them; the immemorial civilization of the Near East was at their very door. Above all, in each community they lived in perpetual comradeship, bound together by common interests. Public opinion would prescribe conduct; in fact, nothing could survive there which did not enjoy social approval. The ideal of life itself would be a completely social one. But it would be also a life of sober habits and frugality; theirs would never be the ideal of the comfort that wealth brings. In material things the Greeks remained poorly equipped to the end. Perhaps that may account partly for the miracles they performed in the realm of the spirit.

SUGGESTIONS FOR READING. J. L. MYRES, *Greek Lands and the Greek People* (Oxford, 1910).

A. E. ZIMMERN, *The Greek Commonwealth*, Part I, "Geography" (5th ed., Oxford, 1931).

MARION I. NEWBIGIN, *The Mediterranean Lands* (Knopf, 1924).

E. C. SEMPLE, *The Geography of the Mediterranean Region* (Holt, 1931), especially Chapters I, IV, and V.

The Bronze Age in the Eastern Mediterranean

Not so very long ago the history of Greece began with Homer and the Trojan War. That any degree of civilization worthy of the name existed in the Greek area before 1000 B.C. was totally unsuspected by scholars until well beyond the middle of the nineteenth century. It is true that Homer described the decorations of the palace of Menelaus, king of Sparta and husband of the famed Helen, in extravagant terms; that same poet had much to say of the wealth of Mycenae, the home of Agamemnon, leader of the host that besieged Troy for ten weary years. But, then, who was Homer? Did he ever live? And if he did, were the Iliad and Odyssey his work? Was the siege of Troy a fact or a fable? Scholarship, in a decidedly skeptical mood, banished Homer's world and Homer himself to the realm of fancy.

Thus matters stood when in the seventies a rank outsider, Heinrich Schliemann by name, a man without scholarship of the approved type and naïve enough to believe Homer, began to excavate the supposed site of Troy. From Troy he turned to Mycenae and Tiryns, and to the amazement of the world vindicated his beloved poet, the supposed realm of fancy turning into a real world indeed. But even then the full significance of Schliemann's discoveries was not realized until the excavations of Sir Arthur Evans and others on the island of Crete (begun in 1900) showed that this "Mycenaean" civilization, revealed by Schliemann, was but an offshoot of a much older civilization centering in Crete. An interesting story might be told of the successive finds made by archaeologists in the Aegean area and on the mainland; but we shall have to content ourselves with a brief glance at the results of all this labor.

We know now that, contemporary with the civilization of Egypt and Babylon, there flourished in Crete an indigenous civilization, the development of which can be traced from the Late Stone Age through the Bronze Age, and which ends with the coming of the Iron Age. The beginning of the Bronze Age can be dated at approximately 3400 B.C. The end came about 1200 B.C., when the island was overwhelmed by the great folk-wandering, traditionally known as the Dorian invasion. But the chief period of Cretan power and splendor fell between 2400 and 1400 B.C. Soon after 1400 B.C. supremacy in the Aegean world was transferred to the mainland, and the remaining two hundred years form a period of decline and stagnation in Crete.

We should like to write a history of the thousand years or so when Crete was supreme in the Aegean. Thucydides, the historian of the so-called Peloponnesian War, tells us that Minos, king of Crete, built a war fleet and was the first to establish a *thalassocracy* (empire of the sea). But even in his day (end of the fifth century B.C.) all recollection of Minos' empire had faded, and only picturesque legends survived. However, the archaeological data now at our command enable us to form a fairly just estimate of Cretan culture.

The ruins of the palace at Knossos clearly proclaim that city as the administrative center of the island and the residence of its kings. The absence of fortifications admits of only one explanation: the island itself was politically united, its fleet serving to protect it against the only quarter whence an enemy might make his appearance.

The type of civilization was already urban; more than twenty town sites have been laid bare on the island. The houses, sometimes of more than one story, stood in streets in which even drains were not missing. Clearly here dwelt a populace not dependent solely on agriculture; here potter and weaver, trader and merchant, lived and worked together, all under the watchful eye of the king, who dwelt with his official family in the great palace, which combined the functions of administrative building, royal warehouse, and residence of the chief himself — a veritable labyrinth. However, we can find no evidence of the king's living in a splendor and majesty which separated him from his subjects; the rooms of the great palace are many in number, but remarkably small in size.

Of the Cretan arts the most striking is that of the frescoes with which their walls were adorned. Not only do these reveal to us the artist's unusual skill in drawing and his feeling for design, but the choice of subject and the manner of treatment are most revealing of the character and habits of this long-forgotten race. Even the lapse of more than three thousand years cannot rob these wall paintings of their freshness and their charm. The cupbearer, the boy gathering crocuses, or the cat fresco from Hagia Triada will serve well as a pertinent illustration. The scenes are taken from daily life and evidently spring from a delight in the simple facts of home life. Hence the naturalism of these artists; they observed the life about them with loving interest and rendered it with painstaking care.

We can follow the development of the Cretan potter's art through the centuries. Even in the beginning of the millennium under discussion the potter's wheel and kiln were in use. Polychrome ware of high artistic excellence, sometimes called Kamares ware, after the place where it was first found, is a feature of the earlier period. The style is light on dark, and the motifs are curvilinear and floral. Of all prehistoric pottery this polychrome ware of Crete is perhaps the most beautiful. Later the style changed to dark on light, and a new set of decorative patterns appear, among which marine life, represented by octopus, sea urchin, and shellfish, plays an important part, without, however, superseding the floral motifs of the past.

The faïence plaques and figurines (a branch of art undoubtedly of Egyptian origin) from the palace shrines at Knossos are further evidence of the artistic skill of the Cretans. Such figurines as the snake-goddess and the plaque of the wild goat with the two kids are among the most amazing of Cretan productions that have reached us; the latter especially will compare favorably with similar work of any time or place.

These figurines, as well as the frescoes, give us an idea of Cretan garments; the dress worn by the fashionable court ladies of Crete, with its tight-fitting open bodice and bell-shaped flounced skirt, will seem to the student of Cretan culture perhaps the most surprising feature of that civilization.

Specimens of the jeweler's and metalworker's art are naturally less abundant. As an example we may cite the so-called Harvester vase of Hagia Triada. Though made of steatite, it is obviously an imitation of metalwork. The decoration represents a procession of tipsy(?) harvesters; the movement and spirit, the life of the thing, is wholly admirable. The leaping boy, an ivory figurine from Knossos, well illustrates another aspect of Cretan art, and the justly famous Vaphio cups, probably the work of a Cretan artist, again prove the mastery of the Cretan in his naturalistic rendering of observed facts.

Of their religion we have only the mute witnesses of their monuments, so that we shall have to speak with caution. We note the absence of temples, that most conspicuous feature of Hellenic religion. The Cretan gods were worshiped in mysterious caves, — apparently they were approached with awe and fear, — or their shrines were placed in sacred groves or in rock sanctuaries; again, the royal palace had its own chapel. But what was the nature of the powers worshiped? With what rites were they appeased? It seems on the whole quite likely that Crete shared the immemorial worship of a goddess of nature, with whom there was associated a male companion. This may have been the goddess often represented accompanied by various forms of animal life, ranging from lions to doves; she would be the divine embodiment of the life-giving and propagating force of nature. The true significance of the numerous cult objects, such as the "horns of consecration," the double ax, tree, and pillar, we may guess at, but cannot affirm, in the absence of written documents.

Did the Cretans, then, lack the art of writing? Indeed not. They developed their own script; we can follow its evolution from the early pictorial signs to the linear script of later times. But very little progress has been made in the deciphering of this writing. Even if it ever should be read, it seems doubtful if it would greatly add to our knowledge of

Cretan civilization. Most of the Cretan documents consist of inscribed clay tablets which have the appearance of state records and inventories, although an occasional larger document may contain a state paper of historical value. The important fact remains that the inhabitants of Crete had developed a system of writing long before the Greek world was ever suspected of possessing such an art. Indeed, there is a possibility that the Phoenicians, from whom the historical Greeks borrowed their alphabet, in turn may have derived theirs from the Cretans.

Who were the creators of this ancient civilization? Could we but read their documents, we might be nearer a solution of this problem. So much seems certain: they were a non-Hellenic race, nor did their language belong to the Indo-European family. They formed a branch of that race which, for want of a better name, has been called the Mediterranean race, and they were akin to the inhabitants of Caria in Asia Minor. Indeed, while there is much in Cretan art which is suggestive of Hellenic art, the total impression made by the remains of Cretan civilization is un-Hellenic. The Cretan shared love of life and close observation of the facts of nature with the later Hellene; the spontaneity and vivacity of the Cretan's work makes him look like a kinsman of the Greek. But was he? Or was it geographical and climatic conditions that produced a superficial resemblance in the character of the products of two racially different peoples?

In fact, the dissimilarity between Cretan and Hellenic work is often as marked as the similarity. Let us look once more at Cretan architecture. The palace at Knossos, with its maze of rooms and passages, might well have given rise to the legend of the labyrinth; but can we detect here the faintest promise of the clear-cut and austere quality of Doric architecture? The sanity and rationalism which are pre-eminently Hellenic traits are not in evidence in the much-vaunted pillared hall at Knossos, for do we not see its pillars tapering downward? Again, in the Cretan sport of bull-baiting, profusely illustrated in the art of Crete, we may find the origin of the myth of the Minotaur; but can we discover here any indication of the clean athletic sports of Hellas? Even the elaborate dresses of the Cretan ladies strike us as barbaric and foreign when compared with the graceful draperies of the Hellenic world.

In short, there is an alien, Asiatic cast about prehistoric Crete which shows unmistakably that the true elements which were to produce Hellas were still lacking.

Wherein, then, consists the real significance of the discoveries in Crete? They have revealed to us the existence of an island civilization, individual and strikingly different from the contemporary civilization of the Near East. The true meaning of this civilization, therefore, lies in the contrast which it presents to that of the Near East; we have discovered a prehistoric parallel to the eternal warfare of ideas that divides the East from the West. In the East geographical conditions made possible and invited the growth of empires, large political entities ruled by absolute monarchs who were an object of reverential awe to their distant subjects and who lived in unapproachable grandeur in mighty palaces; they were the creators of the vast edifices — palaces, tombs, and temples — which still excite the wonder of the world. But on the Aegean Islands a totally different type of civilization arose; though these islands had access to the storehouse of ancient culture in the Near East, the sea saved them from being drawn into the political orbit of the East. Crete, especially, was near enough to Egypt to learn from it and large enough to create a culture of historical importance. It was, however, too small to allow the rise of royalty of the Asiatic type; Cretan kings lived in close communion with their subjects, who swarmed about their master in the streets of their tiny towns. In short, Cretan society had a more democratic flavor, enjoyed a greater liberty of movement, than its neighbors of the East; its spontaneity seems not to have been unduly repressed by the heavy hand of the priest. In so far Crete has a rightful claim to being considered the forerunner of Hellas.

SUGGESTIONS FOR READING. C. H. and H. B. HAWES, *Crete, the Forerunner of Greece* (Harper, 1916).

H. R. HALL, *The Civilization of Greece in the Bronze Age* (Methuen, 1929). Richly illustrated.

J. D. S. PENDLEBURY, *A Handbook to the Palace at Knossos* (Macmillan, 1933).

For a lively account of the subject see James Baikie, *The Sea Kings of Crete* (A. and C. Black, 1910).

CHAPTER II

THE HEROIC AGE

Introduction

THE preceding pages contain a short account of that pre-Hellenic civilization which, having its center in Crete, thence spread through the Aegean to the mainland. It was not a Greek creation, but the work of an indigenous Mediterranean race which spoke a non-Hellenic language. The overthrow of Cretan power dates from about 1350 B.C. We now enter upon Hellenic history proper.

For the first six hundred years, however, we move in a darkness which is only partly illuminated by legendary material surviving in Hellenic poetry of later days (Homer is the earliest example), by archaeological data, and by stray references to Hellenic doings in the contemporary records of Egyptians and Hittites. The story which we are trying to piece together from this scanty material is that of the gradual settlement of Greece by the Hellenic people, and of their amalgamation with the prehistoric inhabitants whom they found in possession. The Hellenic peoples of historical times, therefore, are a blend of northern (Indo-European) and Aegean (Mediterranean) stocks.[1] The constituents vary among the ethnic groups of Hellas; relatively speaking, the Dorians were of purer northern stock than the Ionians. But it remains true for all the Hellenes that they were a mixed race.

The invasions of the northerners occupied centuries; successive waves of major proportion were so far apart in time that they have left their impress on the Greek language in the three main dialects which form the most important linguistic divisions among the Greek-speaking peoples.

[1] "Indo-European" is a linguistic term; "Mediterranean," an anthropological term.

Homer

National Museum, Naples

These six hundred years of Hellenic history we may conveniently divide into two periods, each ushered in by an important migration. To be sure, the earliest invasions antedate the province of our study and fall in the days when Cretan power was still supreme.

The first period, extending from 1350 to 1150 B.C., is marked by the invasions of the Achaeans (an Aeolic-speaking race) and the overthrow of Crete. The heroic deeds of these Achaeans, that is, of their chieftains, were celebrated by Homer, who lived some three hundred years after the events which he described. Toward the end of the era there occurred the famous expedition of the Achaean chieftains against Troy.

The second period extends from 1150 to 750 B.C. It is opened by the Dorian invasion and the overthrow of Achaean power. During these four centuries Greece slowly settled into the divisions of historic times; toward their close a new Hellas emerges, with its city-states. But the process of this change and growth is completely hidden from us, except in so far as Hesiod's poetry gives us a glimpse of the conditions of his time (750 B.C.).

The first period forms the Heroic Age of Greece. In the following pages we shall take up the material for its study; the legends, the archaeological data, and Homer.

The Legends

To the ancient Greek the story of Hellenic origins and beginnings presented no such problems as it does to us. He could give a remarkably full account of the early days of his native land, and, what is more surprising, it was on the whole a chronologically consistent one. The tale was replete with names and personalities. There were founders of races (most of these rather shadowy); founders of cities, such as Cadmus of Thebes, who slew the dragon and sowed the dragon's teeth; founders of dynasties, such as Pelops, who won his bride in a famous chariot race. Then there were the "culture heroes," such as Triptolemus, who taught men the art of plowing and the cultivation of grain; Orpheus, the first musician, whom even the beasts followed; Daedalus, the great craftsman, who built the labyrinth and made himself a pair of wings in order to escape from his bondage to the king of Crete. Furthermore, the common man of Greece knew of such heroes as Herakles, the hero par excellence, whose superhuman feats of strength and daring covered the extent of the world known and unknown; or of Theseus, the Athenian counterpart of Herakles, slayer of the Minotaur. Perhaps more impressive even than the careers of the individual heroes were the stories of the great enterprises in which they joined forces to win everlasting glory among men. Such were the Calydonian boar hunt and the quarrel that arose over the spoils, the two successive sieges of Thebes, the voyage of the Argonauts in quest of the Golden Fleece, and above all the siege of Troy.

The average Greek accepted these stories, with the persons and events they described, as historical facts. But what is the modern historian to make of men who were sprung from gods and conversed with gods; who engaged in battle, as Bellerophon did, with a monster (the Chimera) which is gravely described as being shaped like a lion in front, a dragon behind, and a goat in the middle?

Let us examine the career of one of these heroes, that we may become aware of the character of the problem confronting us. The story of Perseus will serve our purpose.

Acrisius, king of Argos, was warned by prophecy that he would meet his death at the hands of a son of his daughter Danaë. Hoping to prevent the fulfillment of the prophecy, Acrisius shut his daughter in a tower or an underground chamber (the story has variants). But Zeus, the supreme god, visited the maiden in the guise of a golden shower; and in due time she bore a son, whom she named Perseus. Upon discovering the birth of the child, Acrisius put both mother and babe into a chest and cast them adrift on the sea.[1] But the waves carried them safely to an island in the Aegean where they were rescued by the brother of the local king. There, in Seriphos, Perseus grew to manhood. Long afterward he returned to Argos, having persuaded his wicked old grandfather that he had no designs on his life. However, at an athletic contest Perseus, in throwing the discus, accidentally hit Acrisius on the head; the ancient prophecy was fulfilled.

But this forms only a small part of the story, for the tale of Perseus is embellished with two great adventures which carry us into fairyland. We hear that Polydectes, king of the island where Danaë and Perseus had found shelter, fell in love with Danaë and, to get her son out of the way, sent him off to fetch the head of the Gorgon Medusa. The goddess Athena favored Perseus, and with her counsel he succeeded in his dangerous task. First he visited the Graeae — three sisters, Terror, Shuddering, and Fear. They had only one eye among them, and by stealing this Perseus forced them to aid him. After telling him where to look for the Gorgons, they gave him the "Cap of the Unseen," which rendered him invisible, the winged "Shoes of Swiftness," and a wallet in which to carry the head of Medusa safely. Now the Gorgons were winged spirits of the Dark; snakes were entwined in their hair, and their aspect was dreadful enough to turn the beholder into stone. But Perseus, flying close and gazing fixedly at the reflection in his shield, by a dexterous blow of his sword severed the head of Medusa. The other Gorgons thereupon gave pursuit, but the magic cap saved the hero.

Perseus' second great adventure befell him on the homeward journey. While flying along he espied a maiden of great beauty chained to a rock in the sea. She was Andromeda, daughter of Cepheus, king of the Ethiopians. Because her

[1] See the beautiful poem of Simonides, in Howe and Harrar, *Greek Literature in Translation*, p. 122.

mother had offended the sea-goddesses by boasting that her own beauty was greater than theirs, Andromeda must fall a sacrifice to a hideous sea monster. Perseus, like all true heroes, comes in the nick of time, kills the monster, and makes the rescued princess his bride. On reaching Seriphos with Andromeda, he finds his mother a suppliant at the altar, seeking to escape the insistent wooing of Polydectes; with the aid of the head of Medusa, Perseus rescues Danaë too, and all sail homeward to Argos.

Now it is plain that the career of Perseus is made up of elements and motifs that belong not at all to history, but to the realm of fairy tale and folk tale. The theme of a hero narrowly escaping death in his early days, only to fulfill a dire prophecy involving the murder of a parent or grandparent, is repeated in countless tales; there is a Greek parallel in the story of Oedipus ("Swelled-foot"), who undoubtedly belongs to the folk tale. The motif, too, of a valiant hero rescuing a fair maiden from imminent death belongs to all times. And fairyland is the home of the Graeae, who share one eye, the Gorgons, the magic cap, and the winged shoes.

Shall we then conclude that there never was such a person as Perseus? There are one or two considerations which may well make us pause. First there is the parallel of Teutonic saga. Here we meet with historical characters whose careers are overlaid with myth and folk tale. In the second place, what *is* a folk tale? A folk tale is a story told to amuse, to entertain, perhaps to thrill. In all ages man has hankered after the marvelous; his imagination, starved by the even flow of his humdrum existence, loves to feast on the exploits of heroes, and to wander in the fabulous land of Nowhere, where anything and everything is possible. Such tales are accepted at their face value; they make no pretense to truth, and the invariable mark distinguishing them is that they are without name, date, or place — "once upon a time." If the hero has a name, it is a nickname, suggested by the adventure itself, like "Swelled-foot." And as for place and date, the true folk tale knows them not.

But (1) Perseus has a real name, which stubbornly refuses to be explained away on the basis of his adventures; (2) he is consistently associated with Argos and Mycenae; (3) he is pretty definitely dated. The only conclusion at which we can arrive, therefore, is that at one time in prehistoric Greece, in Argolis, a prince called Perseus won great renown by his exploits; but the record of his actual achievements has been buried under a mass of folk-tale material which somehow became associated with his name. And that does not take us very far.

Happily Perseus' case is an extreme one. When we examine the earliest literary document dealing with that legendary age, we find a different story; for the Iliad purports to be a straightforward account of an episode of the Trojan War. The fairy-tale element is conspicuously absent: Homer's heroes do not rely on magic caps or winged shoes but on the strength of their arm; and even though gods intermingle freely with Homer's humanity, still there is no incident in the story which does not admit of a rational explanation. Homer describes a definite world, with a definite geography. His heroes are Achaeans of a definite generation, which he is careful to distinguish from its elders. They are "bronze-clad" Achaeans; that is, he describes a stage of civilization known as the Bronze Age (although iron is just beginning to be known), and he describes it pretty consistently. And whether or not the second half of the second book of the Iliad belongs to the original Iliad, the poet who composed it was not afraid to supply us with statistical information concerning the allied forces that lay before Troy.

Granted the plausibility and consistency of the Homeric narrative, how can we be sure that this Achaean world corresponds to an actual stage in Hellenic history? We have no other literary evidence; archaeology alone can vindicate

Homer. It is therefore the archaeological evidence to which we must now turn.

In doing so there is one consideration which deserves notice. It is this, that while we are no doubt interested in ascertaining the truth concerning the Heroic Age, we must not be unmindful of the fact that for our present purposes it is even more important to find out what the Greeks believed to be the truth. For during the entire historical period of Hellas the Greeks lived literally in the shadow of that Heroic Age as the collective mind of Greece had conceived it. It exercised an influence on Greek religion, literature, and art that has no parallel in the world's history. In the Teutonic world the heroic tradition was interrupted by the conversion to Christianity and, in England, by the invasion of an entirely new ethnic group. Not so in Greece; even the Dorian invasion could not block the stream of heroic tradition which flows uninterrupted through Greek history. Secondly, among no other people has the heroic saga found a poet who could so fully reveal its very essence and life as Homer did. Homer is unique. "The poet" became the educator of Greece, which had neither religious prophet nor priest to guide it.

Every bit of Greek life furnishes abundant evidence of the immense prestige which the Heroic Age enjoyed at all times. The personages and events of that age are illustrated by Greek vase paintings and sculptures alike. The temple of Zeus at Olympia was undoubtedly the most august shrine in Hellas. On the east pediment the artist had portrayed in stone the start of the famed chariot race between Pelops and Oenomaus; the twelve metopes on this same temple illustrated the twelve labors of Herakles. In poetry it is a like story. Pindar gives up the greater part of his victory odes to the heroic saga. The tragic poets took their themes almost invariably from the same storehouse of literary treasure: of the thirty-one extant tragedies a majority deal with the Homeric heroes or their offspring; the remaining are chiefly taken from the heroic saga.

We repeat, the Greek world lived in the shadow of the Heroic Age, and since Homer is our chief clue to the understanding of that age, let us not begrudge him the space he is to occupy in this book.

First, however, we must ask what confirmation of the heroic saga has been brought to light by the spade of the archaeologist.

The Archaeological Evidence

Our discussion in Chapter I showed that the civilization discovered by Schliemann at Mycenae and Tiryns proved to be a branch or an offshoot of an island civilization of much greater antiquity. Subsequent excavations on the mainland have revealed the fact that this "Mycenaean" civilization was by no means confined to the site from which it received its name.

And now at the outset we may state one significant fact: it is the legendary sites of the heroic saga that have yielded the most important remains of the "Mycenaean" civilization; in other words, the geography of the Heroic Age has been substantially vindicated by the labors of archaeologists. Orchomenus in Boeotia is the home of the original Argonauts; Herakles was born in Thebes and ruled in Tiryns; the legend of Troy centers in Argos, Sparta, and Troy; Minos ruled Crete; Thebes figures prominently in the heroic legends. Now Mycenae, Tiryns, Thebes, Orchomenus, Mycenaean Sparta, Troy, Crete, and numerous other sites mentioned in the legends are precisely the spots where archaeological labors have found their richest rewards in the quest for this prehistoric culture. The only major legend that has not been similarly confirmed is the Calydonian boar hunt, the scene of which is laid in Aetolia, a region not yet sufficiently explored by archaeology.

The work was begun by Schliemann, whose object, as we saw, was to uphold Homer. There were at Mycenae visible remains which held out a certain promise of success: there were the ruins of mighty walls; there was the Lion Gate,[1] which formed the main entrance to the fortress; there was the "Treasury of Atreus," a circular tomb with a dome-shaped top, excavated into the hill and measuring roughly some fifty feet in diameter and fifty feet in height. Even so, Schliemann himself had no inkling of the wealth he was to bring to light. The excavations on the site were begun in 1876. After clearing out the Lion Gate and partly excavating the "Tomb of Clytemnestra" he began work on a mound within the fortress which proved to be the ancient royal cemetery of Mycenae. This consists of a circular enclosure, eighty-seven feet in diameter, surrounded by a ring of lime-stone slabs set vertically in a double row; this circular row of slabs, filled in with earth and small stones, forms a wall three to five feet high which enclosed the burying ground of the Mycenaean rulers. The graves, six in all, of which Schliemann opened five, are shaft graves, oblong pits sunk vertically in the ground; some of the graves lay at a depth of thirty-three feet below the surface of the mound.

Let us glance at the contents of the first grave which he opened. It measured some sixteen feet in length and ten feet in breadth; the depth varied with the irregularity of the rock surface. Herein were found three bodies which, to judge from the character of the trappings, must have been women; they lay three feet apart on a bed of pebbles and were "literally laden with jewels." Here is the inventory of the wealth with which these Mycenaean princesses were buried, as enumerated by Tsountas and Manatt in *The Mycenaean Age* (p. 88): there were six diadems, among them the splendid gold crown with the flower crest, which still encircled the head of one of the women; a gold comb with bone teeth; a gold-

[1] The name originates from the fact that two rampant lions are carved on a triangular slab which rests on a lintel; the lions are carved in relief, and guard a sacred pillar between them; the lintel consists of a single block measuring eighteen by eight by three feet.

headed hairpin; six gold spirals, fifteen gold pendants, eleven gold necklace-coils; six gold bracelets; eight gold crosses and stars; ten gold grasshoppers hung from gold chains; a gold butterfly; four gold griffins, one flying; four gold lions couchant; twelve gold ornaments, each with two stags reposing upon branches of a date palm; ten ornaments with lions, one with two lions attacking an ox; three gold intaglios with vigorous figure subjects; fifty-one gold ornaments embossed with cuttlefish, butterflies, swans, eagles, hippocampi, and sphinxes; four female idols in gold, including two of Aphrodite with doves; eighteen gold wheels and tubes; two pairs of gold scales; a gold mask of a child; a gold goblet embossed with fish swimming; five gold vases with lids; and finally seven hundred and one "large, thick, round, plates of gold, with a very pretty decoration of repoussé work in fourteen different designs — spirals, flowers, cuttlefish, butterflies, etc." In addition to this profusion of gold there were four silver vases and goblets, two silver rods plated with gold, a magnificent alabaster vase and cup; a bronze vase and three large bronze caldrons; several engraved gems; and "an enormous quantity of amber beads." Such is a rapid inventory of the funeral outfit of these Mycenaean ladies. Homer had called Mycenae "rich in gold," and we are now inclined to agree.

We cannot follow Schliemann as he came upon one grave after another, and as, in Tiryns, he laid bare the ground plan of the chieftain's palace; nor can we enumerate the excavations carried on in the wake of the pioneer all over Greece and the islands where Homeric fame seemed to hold out the promise of success. Suffice it to say that while subsequent discoveries have greatly enlarged our knowledge of "Mycenaean" civilization, no other archaeologists have had the good fortune to light upon an entirely untouched and forgotten series of graves so richly endowed as those brought to light by Schliemann's epoch-making discoveries.

What, then, is the total result of these excavations, and

what light do they throw on the Heroic Age of Greece? While there is still a great deal of uncertainty concerning the relations between the older Cretan civilization and that called after Mycenae, especially in regard to the ethnic problems involved, we may summarize the chief facts that have been established, as follows:

1. The Greek mainland had passed out of the Stone Age before 1600 B.C. By that time Cretan influence began to penetrate and soon became predominant. Of this there is no doubt: the similarity of the oldest fresco paintings to the corresponding ones on Cretan walls, the recurrence of the same peculiar religious symbols (double ax, sacred pillar, and doves), the striking likeness in the elaborate court dress of the women, the popularity of the Cretan potter's ware, the products of metalworker and jeweler, all proclaim the close dependence of the "Mycenaean" world upon Crete.

2. But there are marked differences. The chief centers of "Mycenaean" culture are to be found on hilltops which were *fortified.* For instance, Mycenae itself occupies the side of a lofty hill, from which the chieftain could survey the greater part of the Argive plain. Massive walls are a feature of the fortress. Here, it seems, ruled the dynasty which was buried in the shaft graves and which was followed by a dynasty that built the monumental beehive tombs outside the fortress. Such a *tholos*, or beehive tomb, was the "Treasury of Atreus," to which we have made reference; its location may indicate that the power of Mycenae over the Argive plain was no longer challenged. A similar fortress occupied the low hill at Tiryns, to the south of Mycenae and nearer the sea. Here, on the higher citadel, was found the best preserved of the prehistoric palaces of Greece. Its ground plan can be traced with ease: a strong gateway, a well-proportioned *propylon* (vestibule) which opens into a paved court with colonnades, and next a large *megaron*, the chief hall of the palace, such as Homer describes, with a hearth in the center and four wooden columns supporting the roof; then a separate apartment for

the women and a bathroom paved with one large limestone block. Here we meet with a type of architecture which, widely departing from Cretan work, seems to point in the direction of the Hellenic architecture of historical times.

This type of civilization, of which the hill fortress and the tholos tomb are the most characteristic features, spread over the Peloponnesus and central Greece and penetrated into southern Thessaly (the home of the Homeric Achilles).

3. About 1350 B.C. Crete was overrun by invaders, and Knossos was sacked. To be sure, the palaces were rebuilt. but the supremacy passed from Crete to the mainland. Cretan art became stagnant, and Mycenae appears to have headed a loose confederacy of the mainland states, and of the islands as well. The palace and citadel of Mycenae were rebuilt; gigantic "Cyclopean" walls now surrounded the whole of the fortress, which served both as royal residence and as the seat of administration. But the impression made by the remains of Mycenae and its very site is not so much that of a governing center of a well-ordered kingdom, such as Knossos had been, but rather that of a stronghold of the chief robber-baron and pirate, whose roving expeditions carried him and his doughty companions far beyond the confines of Argolis.

4. This turbulent society of warriors, who rudely interrupted the life of the Creto-Mycenaean world and appropriated its accumulated wealth, can be none other than Homer's Achaeans. Their last great exploit probably was the sack of Troy (*c.* 1200 B.C.); the magnitude of that event reverberated through the Hellenic world for many generations and became the subject of a cycle of sagas, one of which Homer made the theme of his Iliad.

Fortunately we are not reduced to Homer as the sole witness to the authenticity of these Achaeans. First there is the Egyptian evidence. An Egyptian document dating from King Merneptah (*c.* 1225 B.C.) mentions "Northerners coming from all lands" to attack Egypt and mentions among these the "Akaiwasha" — plainly the Egyptian version of Achaeans. They are described, graphically enough, as "fighting to fill their bellies daily." Apparently the Egyptian was well acquainted with these roving bands of adventurers. A second document, dating from 1194 B.C., speaks of a much more formidable invasion which came from the Aegean and Asia Minor; the marauders came by land and sea and were beaten off with difficulty. Whether these were Achaeans or those who had been dispossessed by the Achaeans and had joined the Phrygians, whose inroads contributed to the downfall of the Hittite empire, does not greatly matter. "The isles were restless," the document states; so restless apparently that even Egypt felt the consequences of the turmoil in the Aegean, in which no doubt the Achaeans had the lion's share.

Secondly there are the data which have lately come to light in Asia Minor. Asia Minor is an Asiatic highland enclosed by a European coast. That fact has dominated its history throughout the ages. Even as early as the twenty-seventh century B.C., King Sargon of Agade, the great Semitic conqueror hailing from the Euphrates valley, had penetrated into Cappadocia. From the third millennium on, a mixed population inhabited the highlands, stimulated by its contact with the civilization of the Euphrates valley and periodically disturbed by invaders from the north. In the second millennium a great empire arose in the heart of Asia Minor, the empire of the Hittites. Politically they formed a large and powerful confederacy of peoples of mixed descent, united into a feudal empire by 1500 B.C. This new and formidable political power slowly extended its dominion until it penetrated northern Syria and there clashed with the rival ambition of Egypt. The Hittite capital was at Boghaz-Keui, which was strongly fortified by a wall some four miles in circumference; within there were interior strongholds, a palace, several temples, and large storehouses. Inside the palace and one of the temples the German excavators found thousands of tablets of baked clay covered with inscriptions, which are slowly yielding their secrets to the persistent attempts at interpretation made by competent linguists.

Here again we meet with the Achaeans and even with the names of some of their kings; several famous names of the heroic saga are passing out of the realm of myth into that of history. Again our tentative chronology of the Heroic Age is being confirmed, for the documents which have a bearing on our problem date roughly from 1330 to 1230 B.C. They mention a kingdom of Achaea; its head is recognized as a "great king" and "brother" of the Hittite king. Another prince, who is referred to as the ruler of "Achaea and Lesbos," seems to stand to the Hittite king in the relation of a potential vassal, and the name he bears in the Hittite document has been identified with Eteocles, whom the Greek legend knows as the founder of Orchomenus. (Another and more famous Eteocles plays a heroic and tragic part in the legend of the Labdacids of Thebes.) Another of these Achaean princes, who has been somewhat doubtfully identified as Atreus (according to Homer, Agamemnon's father), is said to have invaded Caria (in southern Asia Minor) from the island of Rhodes and to have been driven off by the Hittite king. The most puzzling feature of this Hittite evidence is that it seems to place Achaea on the western coast of Asia Minor rather than in Greece; but, then, we remember that Greek legend will have it that Pelops, the founder of the most powerful Achaean dynasty, was born in Sardis, where he consorted with the gods, which probably means with the Hittite rulers.

Finally there is the evidence found in Troy. There in the northwest corner of Asia Minor, close to the Hellespont, on the hill of Hissarlik, the traditional site of ancient Troy, excavations have laid bare a formidable fortress flourishing contemporaneously with the Achaean strongholds. The place was very strongly fortified, but its area is too small (about five acres) to accommodate a city; its extent puts it in the same class as the fortresses of Mycenae and Tiryns, large enough to hold a splendid royal residence and to accommodate in times of war a garrison of some three thousand warriors. The pottery is mostly a native product, but enough Mycenaean ware was discovered to date the fortress as contemporary with the Achaean strongholds. Homer tells us it was sacked by the Achaeans, and the existing remains seem to confirm him. The traditional date of its fall was 1192 B.C., which again agrees with the archaeological evidence.

To sum up, we may regard the historical character of the Homeric Achaeans as proved. To the strenuous careers of these princes, which fell somewhere between 1350 and 1150 B.C., both sides of the Aegean bore witness. Their exploits form the historical kernel of the heroic legends. From the last of their enterprises Homer, some three hundred years after the event, chose the themes for the Iliad and the Odyssey.

The Iliad

The scene of Homer's Iliad is laid on the plain of Troy. Here the Achaeans have gathered under their chieftains to avenge the wrong done by Paris, the Trojan prince, to Menelaus, king of Sparta; for Paris has carried off Helen, Menelaus' wife, famed for her beauty. The authority of Menelaus' brother, Agamemnon, king of Mycenae, who seems to have exercised a certain overlordship over the other Achaean chieftains, brought the fighting barons in his train; also, they may have been lured by the prospect of the booty to be gained from the sack of wealthy Troy.

It is the tenth year of the war. For the struggle proved a protracted one; the formidable walls of Troy, still partly standing, may well have held the assailants at bay for many weary years. And now a new affliction has befallen the Achaean host: a pestilence rages in the camp, and men and beasts are perishing.

At this point the Iliad opens. The poem, then, does not tell the story of the siege of Troy, but only of a dramatic episode in that siege; it is not a chronicle, but an epic poem. The episode it celebrates is the quarrel that arose between Agamemnon, the leader of the host, and the greatest of his vassals, Achilles, the foremost fighter on the Achaean side. This is the nucleus of the Iliad, and as such it is announced in the opening lines of the poem: the wrath of Achilles and the countless woes that came upon the Achaeans in consequence of that wrath.

Presently the seer Calchas discloses that Apollo has sent the plague in punishment for the wrong done to his priest; for Agamemnon holds the priest's daughter captive, refusing to surrender her to her father's pleas. When he finally yields to the greater might of Apollo, it is with bad grace; he demands compensation for his loss and seizes the maiden Briseis, the prize of Achilles. Achilles' anger knows no bounds. He refuses to fight Agamemnon's battles any longer; nay, he prays to his mother Thetis, a sea-goddess, to prevail on Zeus, lord of the gods, to give victory to the Trojans. May Agamemnon taste the bitterness of defeat and discover to his cost that he cannot with impunity insult the bravest of the Achaeans!

Zeus yields to the entreaties of Thetis in spite of misgivings as to the consequences of his promise. For well he knows that Hera, his consort, the bitter enemy of Troy, will not abide by his verdict. At length the promise of Zeus, though he is thwarted again and again by the rebellious gods, is fulfilled: the leading Achaean chieftains are disabled, one after another, and the victorious Trojans attack the very rampart which the Achaeans, now on the defensive, had built around the camp. Hector, foremost of the Trojan heroes, bursts through the ramparts and attacks the ships with fire; only the valiant Ajax remains to defend them.

At this critical moment Patroclus, the dear friend and companion of Achilles, begs him to have pity on the Achaeans in their sore plight: if he will not go to the rescue himself, at least he should permit Patroclus to wear his well-known armor and appear at the head of the Myrmidons. Achilles grudgingly assents; but Patroclus is to do no more than drive the Trojans back from the ships. Patroclus then dons the armor of Achilles and sallies forth. His appearance has the desired effect: the Trojans, thinking that Achilles has returned to the battlefield, flee. But Patroclus forgets the injunctions of his friend. He pursues the fleeing Trojans through the plain up to the walls of Troy, and there Hector, with the aid of Apollo, slays him. Achilles' armor falls into the hands of Hector, but, after a heroic fight, Patroclus' body is saved.

Now grief at the death of his dear companion and thirst for revenge rage in the savage heart of Achilles. He renounces his wrath and makes his peace with Agamemnon. Hephaestus, the divine artisan, makes him wonderful new armor, and Achilles goes forth seeking Hector. At last he finds him, alone outside the walls of Troy. Here, in the twenty-second book of the Iliad, comes the climax. Three times Achilles pursues the fleeing Hector around the walls of Troy, "and all the gods beheld." Even Zeus is moved to pity, but, knowing that Hector's fate has been weighed in the balance and that his doom is upon him, he gives Athena a free hand. She deludes Hector by a false promise of aid; he is prevailed upon to face Achilles, and soon the relentless hero exults over the death of the man who robbed him of his friend.

This is the nucleus of the Iliad. But Homer was more than a writer of ballad or lay. Possessing the true instinct of an epic composer he gradually enlarged the canvas; in his hands the slight theme grew into epic proportions. To bring out the surpassing prowess of his hero it was necessary to portray more fully the other characters, Achaean and Trojan heroes who fill the background. In a number of telling scenes, which, if the Iliad were a drama, would only delay the denouement, but which in an epic poem serve a legitimate purpose, he introduces that whole galaxy of warriors who henceforth were to live in the imagination of Hellas. Menelaus and Paris meet in single combat; so do Hector and Ajax; Diomedes, who defies the god of war himself, Odysseus, Agamemnon, Idomeneus, all perform prodigious feats of valor. The modern reader may well grow a little weary of the incessant fighting. But Homer knew the audience he addressed; the glee of battle was the very breath of its nostrils.

However, the Iliad is not all battle and carnage. There are scenes of the Achaean princes assembled in council, where Nestor, the wise and aged king of Pylos, holds forth at great length and is heard amid respectful silence. Or the common folk, convoked by the king, are gathered in the turbulent assembly and are addressed by one of their number, Thersites, the base calumniator of the noble lords, who is reduced to silence by the firm hand of Odysseus, and there is great merriment at Thersites' discomfiture. We meet in the tent of the sulking Achilles; eloquent pleas are made to the hero, that he may relent, but he vehemently rejects the terms of peace. Presently we see the gods assembled on Olympus after the pattern of the princes in council; following the painful silence caused by the domestic quarrel between the father of gods and men and his rebellious spouse, there is great hilarity on the part of the Olympians when limping Hephaestus breaks the tension by serving as cupbearer among them. Again, we come upon scenes of profound pathos, revealing the universal range of the poet of the Iliad. Foremost among these is Hector's justly celebrated farewell to Andromache, his dearly beloved wife, a scene of exquisite beauty; to it belongs the palm. Scarcely inferior is the close of the Iliad, the ransom of Hector's body after the appeal of the aged Priam to the man who slew his son, and the lamentation over the body, led by Andromache, by Hecuba, the mother of Hector, and by Helen herself. A great poet, Shelley, speaks of "the high and solemn close of the whole bloody tale in tenderness and inexpiable sorrow . . . wrought in a manner incomparable with anything of the same kind."[1]

[1] *Letters from Italy*, No. XLIV.

Such, then, is the Iliad. Beginning as an Achilleid, a lay or ballad dealing with a fatal quarrel between two Achaean princes, it grew in the hands of its maker into the epic which we possess today.

The Odyssey

The other great poem dealing with the Heroic Age is the Odyssey. It tells of the adventures of Odysseus, how he wandered for ten years on his homeward journey, how he returned in disguise and delivered Penelope, his faithful wife, from the wooing of her insolent suitors. The whole epic falls readily into six divisions of four books each.[1]

The first four books deal with conditions in Ithaca, Odysseus' home, during the absence of its master. The central figure is Telemachus, the youthful son of Odysseus. Unable to assert himself amid the lawless doings of the suitors, he goes forth to visit Nestor in Pylos and Menelaus in Sparta, hoping to gain information concerning his long-lost father.

Books V–VIII contain the story of Odysseus' escape from the isle of Calypso, the nymph who had hidden him from the world for seven long years, and of his entertainment at the court of the Phaeacians.

In books IX–XII Odysseus relates his adventures to Alcinoüs, king of the Phaeacians. Here occur the famous tale of the lotus-eaters; the adventure in the cave of the Cyclops; the story of Aeolus and the bag of winds; of Circe, the sorceress who turned his men into swine; of the descent into Hades, where Odysseus conversed with many spirits of the departed; of his escape from the perilous song of the sirens; of Scylla and Charybdis; of the slaughter of the sacred oxen and the consequent fate of Odysseus' comrades; and finally of his landing, the sole survivor of all his crew, on the island of Calypso.

[1] The division into twenty-four books is the work of scholars of a later age, as is the case with the Iliad.

Books XIII–XVI tell of Odysseus' arrival in Ithaca, whither the Phaeacians conveyed him in the enchanted ship. He is hospitably entertained by the faithful swineherd, Eumaeus, who does not know his master. He meets Telemachus returning from his fruitless quest and makes himself known to his son; they plan for the coming revenge on the suitors.

In books XVII–XX Odysseus, disguised as a beggar, returns to his home and is a witness of the riotous proceedings of the suitors.

The last four books bring the climax. Penelope, who has kept her suitors waiting by the famous device of the unfinished web, undoing every night what she had woven during the day, now proposes a trial of skill among them: let them bend the bow of Odysseus and show their skill in archery; she promises her hand to the victor. All in vain they try to bend the mighty bow. Then the despised beggar performs the feat with ease; and, casting off his disguise, Odysseus stands revealed among them. Revenge is followed by a recognition scene between husband and wife. Thus all is well that ends well.[1]

The Iliad and Odyssey Compared

Even from such a hasty examination of the poems as we have made, it is yet evident that, though both poems are epics, narrative poetry, they are fundamentally different.

The material of the Iliad belongs to the heroic saga. It tells a straightforward story of the doings of its heroes and remains throughout on a purely human level. To be sure, the Iliad is full of gods, but, as we shall see, they have very little to do with the course of the purely human events. The Iliad would not be complete without the gods, for the human careers it depicts would lose in splendor; the greater the

[1] An excellent résumé of the Odyssey may be read in H. R. James, *Our Hellenic Heritage* (Macmillan, 1927), Vol. I, pp. 133–193.

Harbor of Corfu (Ancient Corcyra, Traditionally Identified as the Island of the Phaeacians)

concern of the gods with the heroes, the greater are the heroes themselves. The climax comes in the combat between Achilles and Hector, when all the gods, spellbound, watch Hector fleeing before swift-footed Achilles. But the story is essentially a human story. Only once a true miracle interrupts the natural flow of events, when the horse of Achilles predicts the early doom of its master; but the Erinyes swiftly close its mouth, vindicating the laws of nature.

The Odyssey, however, takes us into a different world. The central motif of the story, that of husband or lover returning in disguise after many years of absence to rescue wife or bride, belongs to the folk tale. So does the device of Penelope, the web that never was finished; for thus do the weak trick the strong in the folk tales of the world. The faithful dog who alone recognizes his master, the test of skill successfully met by the disguised hero — these and many like features of the story belong not at all to the heroic saga, but rather to the folk tale.

The adventures of Odysseus frankly take us into fairyland itself. The one-eyed giant, the sorceress, the fair maidens luring the sailor to his death, the perils of the passage between Scylla and Charybdis, the bag of winds, the enchanted ship — these belong to the realm of Nowhere. It is quite evident that, as was the case with Perseus, the career of the hero of the saga has been overlaid with borrowed motifs. And we can readily understand why Odysseus should have been the name around which these mariner tales clustered, for he was by common consent the most resourceful and the most cunning of all the legendary heroes; here, then, was the very man to extricate himself from the manifold dangers of the unknown seas, to outwit the wiles of the sorceress and the cruelty of man-eating giants. The epithet that constantly accompanies his name is "of many devices."

However, this difference between Iliad and Odyssey does not prevent them both from belonging to the type of poetry which we, after the Greeks, call epic poetry. They are narrative poems, planned and executed on a large scale, containing numerous episodes which all fit into the larger whole. And both exhibit the same remarkably high degree of skill in composition and finish in workmanship. This brings us to a special problem they present, which is known as the Homeric question.

The Homeric Question[1]

We find, in fact, the literature of Europe opening with two masterpieces. Neither of them bears the faintest resemblance to what we should expect of the first, crude efforts at poetical composition. The inevitable conclusion is that both poems, far from being the first, are rather the last and crowning work of a long succession of poets.

There is, happily, abundant internal evidence to confirm us in that conclusion. There is the evidence of Homer's language: it is a mixed dialect in which countless archaic dialect forms have survived from earlier times; there are certain descriptive epithets used over and over again, the meaning of which Homer does not always seem to understand himself; there are phrases, metrical formulas, and

[1] The unwary reader should be warned that the title of this section suggests to the professional philologist the problem not of the existence but rather of the authorship of the poems. Was there such a person as Homer? Was he the author of both the Iliad and the Odyssey, or are they the products of several hands? And in what form did these epics leave the hands of their maker(s)? An immense literature has gathered on the subject since F. A. Wolf first published his *Prolegomena ad Homerum* in 1795. An almost infinite variety of answers to the question he raised have been suggested by a succession of writers; most of the answers, however, are imposing structures based on the slenderest of foundations. Today the general sentiment is veering in the direction of the point of view represented in this book, namely, that the Homeric epics are the work of an individual poet, who lived and worked in Ionia sometime in the ninth century B.C., although the possibility is not excluded that interpolations, some of considerable proportions, have added to the bulk of the Iliad and Odyssey. The interested reader may consult Florence M. Stawell, *Homer and the Iliad* (Dent, 1909) or John A. Scott, *The Unity of Homer* (University of California Press, 1921) or the pertinent chapters in M. P. Nilsson's *Homer and Mycenae* (Methuen, 1933).

verse endings whose frequent occurrence points to days when memory was not yet assisted by the art of writing. In short, it is quite evident that in Homer's day an agelong convention was ruling the utterance of the bard. The meter itself, the heroic hexameter, is much too stately and long a verse to be in any sense primitive. Finally Homer himself refers to minstrels who recite at the palaces of Alcinoüs, Odysseus, and Menelaus; to him the minstrel was an institution, an indispensable part of heroic society, and the minstrel's song a thing of immemorial antiquity, as it undoubtedly was.

The Iliad and the Odyssey, then, seem to mark the end of a long creative period which saw the gradual evolution from the crude lays of the earliest minstrels to the finished epic of Homer. Can we approximately date this period? We have seen that most likely the Heroic Age begins with the coming of the Achaeans and the fall of Knossos, and ends somewhere in the twelfth century; it extends in that case from about 1350 to 1150 B.C. Tradition placed the fall of Troy at the beginning of the twelfth century, and an equally credible Greek tradition assigned Homer to the ninth century; Homer, then, was separated by some three hundred years from the glories he described. These three hundred years, more or less, cover the period of the evolution of epic poetry. In the course of these centuries the minstrel song, which had originated in the Aeolic-speaking homeland, was carried by the migrating tribes across the Aegean into Ionia, where it found a new home; for the archaic dialect forms embedded in Homer's Ionic are Aeolic, the language of the Achaeans. These migrations, as we shall see, were owing to the upheaval caused by the Dorian invasion.

So much, then, for the internal evidence concerning the history of epic poetry, contained in the Homeric poems themselves. It leaves us still very much in the dark as to the fundamental causes that produce a heroic age and the minstrel song as its accompaniment. Professor H. M. Chadwick in his illuminating book *The Heroic Age* (Macmillan, 1912) has made most valuable contributions to the solution of the problem. For one thing he has drawn attention to the interesting parallel between the Greek and the Teutonic epic. The Teutonic *Heldenalter* is in some ways better attested than the Hellenic Heroic Age, because the former belongs to historical times. In fact, it coincides with and is largely the product of the disintegration of the Roman Empire, and roughly covers the period of 350–550 A.D. These were the years of the historical folk-wanderings, the migrations which caused the overthrow of Roman power. And even as the conquering Achaeans in the fourteenth century B.C. found in Creto-Mycenaean Greece a rich and highly developed civilization, so the invading Goths and Huns found a rich prey in the treasures and culture of the Roman world of the fourth century A.D. It is such sudden access to wealth and power on the part of a rude but vigorous people at the expense of an ancient civilization which makes the Heroic Age. For these turbulent times call for great leaders, men of forceful personality, whose prowess and magnificence stamp themselves deeply on the imagination of their contemporaries and of posterity. In the newly won kingdoms the new rulers establish courts where, surrounded by their faithful followers, they dwell amid the splendor of the civilization they have appropriated. And their feats of arms, their irresistible progress from victory to victory, become the inspiration of song and story. Hence we find that the minstrel gains admission amid the courtiers, for on him rests the task of celebrating in song the heroic deeds of the lords. That such was the case in 400 A.D. we know from reliable sources; princes had their praises sung by minstrels during their lifetime and in their very presence. We may safely infer, therefore, that the singer's traditional presence in the royal halls of the Achaeans, as attested by Homer, is true to fact. This is the first stage in the history of the epic.

The second stage is reached when, on the basis of the poetic output of these early bards, the different lays, which after all move within a remarkably circumscribed field, are gathered into poems of larger scope. The lay or ballad is now succeeded by the epic proper. The Homeric epics belong to this second stage. Of the Teutonic epics *Beowulf* in many ways furnishes an interesting parallel to the Iliad. For consider: *Beowulf* was composed three hundred years after the events it reports; so Homer describes an episode of the Trojan War which was fought three hundred years before his time. *Beowulf* is written in the language of the Anglo-Saxons, but deals with material of Scandinavian origin; so the Iliad is written in Ionic, but treats of material concerning the Aeolic branch of the race. In both cases the theme and the poetry were carried across the sea, and neither author so much as mentions the new homeland: England is utterly ignored in the one case, and Homer gives no inkling of his acquaintance with his own Ionia.

Further comparison between Greek and Teutonic epic poetry reveals the fact that in both cases the element of the folk tale and myth intrudes. But if the Teutonic analogy proves anything, it shows that the early epic poets had no freedom to invent either historical characters or historical events. Homer could no more have invented the siege of Troy than Agamemnon or Menelaus or Helen. The minstrels were severely restricted within the traditional field; they might embellish and enlarge, they might introduce new matter of subordinate character, but the central historical events and primal agents were data which could not be lightly tampered with.[1]

We are now in a better position to appreciate Homer's poetry; we know its function, the purpose it served. We

[1] Was Hector one of these primal agents? Scholars have justly doubted his authenticity as one of the ancient figures of the Trojan saga, for he, the chief defender of Troy, bears a good Greek name which means "Stayer." Evidently, Paris not being available for the part, Hector was introduced to fill an indispensable role in the drama of the fatal quarrel and its dire consequences. This may show how far the minstrel was allowed to enlarge upon his material. See J. A. Scott, *The Unity of Homer*, Chap. VII.

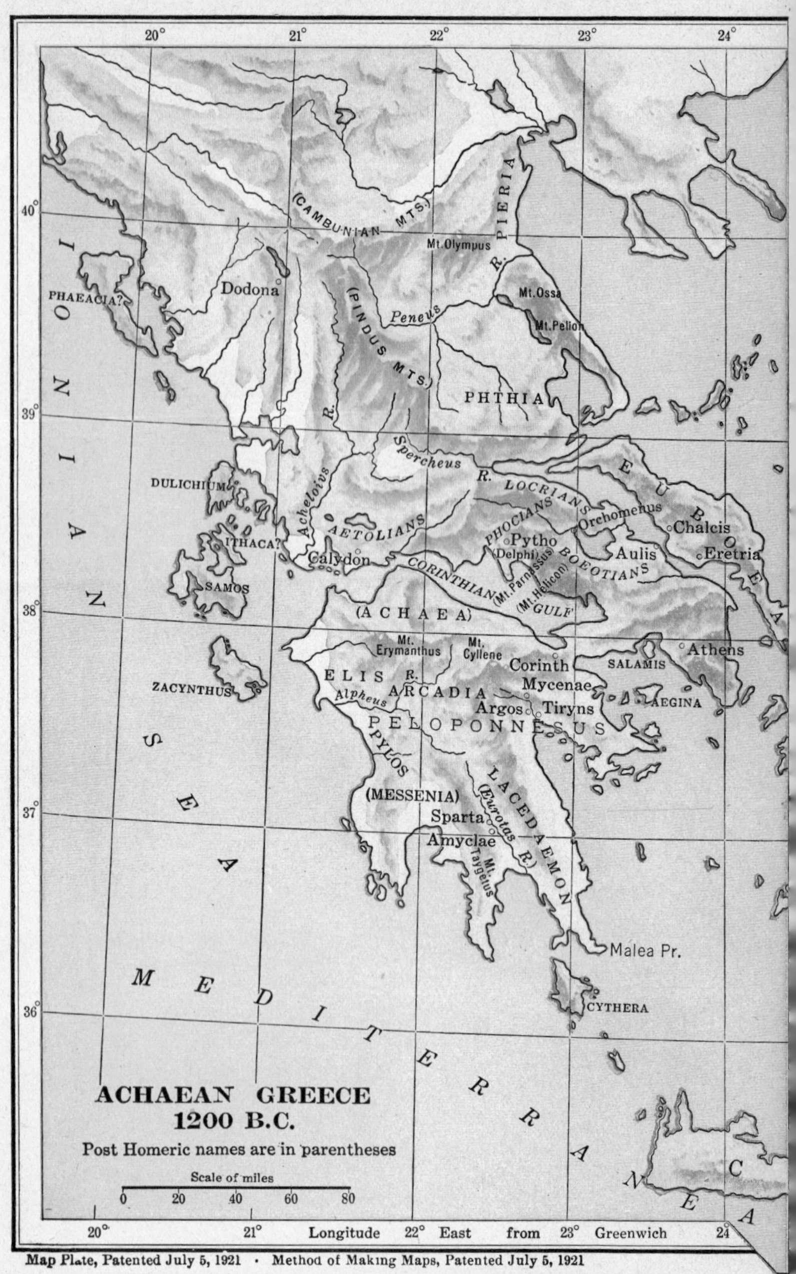

Map Plate, Patented July 5, 1921 · Method of Making Maps, Patented July 5, 1921

IMBROS
LEMNOS
TENEDOS
Troy
Scamander R.
DARDAN-IANS
Mt. Ida
Granicus R.
(Halys R.)
MYSIANS
LESBOS
ÆGEAN SEA
CHIOS
Hermus R.
MAEONIANS
(SAMOS)
Mt. Mycale
Miletus
Maeander R.
CARIANS
DELOS
LYCIANS
COS
RHODUS
CARPATHUS
Knossos
Phaestus
CRETE
SEA
25°
26°
27°
28°
29°
40°
39°
38°
37°
36°

recognize in Homer one of the last representatives of those court poets who composed for the entertainment of nobles in an age when that type of patriarchal society was slowly dying. We know also that these epics were destined to become the chief factor in the education of the later Hellenic world. It therefore becomes necessary to inspect more closely the character and the temper of the Homeric world. But first let us take a look at its geography.

The Geography of the Homeric World

The Peloponnesus contained the center of the Achaean power; Agamemnon, from his stronghold at Mycenae, and his brother Menelaus, ruling in Sparta, divided a large part of the Peloponnesus between them. Agamemnon ruled part of Argolis; he had a firm grip on the northern coast (which perpetuated the Achaean name in historical Hellas) and on the isthmus connecting it with central Greece. The entire southern part of the peninsula (the later Laconia and Messenia) was under the joint dominion of the two sons of Atreus. Argos itself was ruled by Diomedes and two other princes, while Nestor was king of Pylos on the western coast. Arcadia plays no great part in the epic.

In central Hellas the strongest and most important group was that of the Boeotians, who had twenty-nine towns; but the fortress of Thebes, which had played so prominent a part in the legends of Boeotia, had evidently not been rebuilt; the royal house of Thebes is not represented among the Achaean leaders. Of the heroes of central Greece we mention the "lesser" Ajax, who ruled the Locrians, and the "greater" Ajax, who hailed from the island of Salamis. The Phocians and Aetolians were settled in the territory which was theirs in historical times, while at the eastern extremity of central Greece the Attic peninsula, Eleusis excepted, was ruled by Menestheus from his Athenian stronghold; but its political importance was small.

In northern Greece there was Phthia, the home of Achilles, ruled by his father, Peleus. Of the other principalities of Thessaly, mentioned by Homer, none call for special comment.

Of the islands, in addition to Salamis, Ithaca, one of the Ionian Islands (we do not know which), comes first to mind, the home of Odysseus. Crete, with its hundred cities, is represented in the Iliad by its hero Idomeneus. Nor is Homer unacquainted with the cities of Euboea. Finally, Rhodes was the site of an important Homeric principality.

This Homeric world, we cannot help observing, presents a picture strikingly different from the political map of historical Hellas. Mycenae, an insignificant hamlet in historical times, holds the central place, while Athens, the leader of Hellas in the fifth century, has an inferior position. Indeed, neither the Pylos of Nestor, nor the Ithaca of Odysseus, nor the home of Achilles, plays any considerable part in the history of later Greece, and even the Homeric Sparta probably did not occupy the site of the historical Sparta.

Homeric Society

It would be vain to look in the Iliad or Odyssey for a full description of the society in which Homer's heroes play the most important part. Homer's task was to glorify their exploits, not to give an account of the political, social, and economic phases of their world. However, in reading between the lines we discover that Homeric society belongs to an early order of social organization. The political power centers in the king or chieftain (and there are all kinds of kings; Homer uses the word in the comparative degree, as if we should speak of one ruler as being "king-er" than another). He is the leader in war, priest, and judge. But he feels constrained to consult the nobles, the lesser princes who are his vassals; occasionally he even summons the assembly of the common folk to hear his word, though these gatherings have a purely fortuitous character.

The resources of this world are pastoral and agricultural; its wealth consists of cattle and land. Achilles affirms he has no personal quarrel with the Trojans; they never carried off *his* cattle or *his* horses, nor yet did they destroy his crops. War and piracy add to the revenues of the barons.

It is still mostly a society in the tribal stage; its economy is still largely that of the household which tries to be self-sufficient. But skilled workers have their place. On the whole it is a surprisingly democratic society in which a lord does not disdain to build his own house or boat or bed; in which princesses, like Nausicaa, attend in person to the family wash; and in which Odysseus, upon his return, finds his old father, in peasant's togs, tending the vines.

The chieftains are largely occupied in war and hunting, and, if we may judge from the character of the heroic legends, they needed to be strong men to maintain their place. The legends of the royal houses are filled with tales of horror and bloodshed. Agamemnon, upon his return from Troy, is slain by Aegisthus, his cousin, who took revenge for the wrong Atreus had done to Aegisthus' father, Thyestes. Aegisthus in turn is killed by Orestes, Agamemnon's son. It is a violent age in which the chief must rely on his strong right arm to command respect for his rights. Yet it is not a lawless society. The stranger is under the protection of Zeus, the god of the suppliant. To the love of husband and wife Hector and Andromache, Odysseus and Penelope, bear eloquent witness, while the maiden Nausicaa will always remain the very incarnation of beauty and charm, of the unspoiled freshness of youth. In general the women of the noble houses seem to have enjoyed a greater degree of freedom and to have commanded greater respect than in historical Hellas. Yet, we repeat, it is a violent and ruthless age. We do not forget that Briseis is the "prize" of Achilles; that she is seized by Agamemnon; that Hector anticipates no better lot for his beloved wife when he shall be gone; that the hero of the Iliad, Achilles, in his worst moments is little better than a savage — the modern reader invariably sides with Hector against Achilles.

This brings us to another subject: plainly, if the modern reader favors Hector above Achilles, he does something which Homer never intended him to do. In fact, he judges by a different standard. But if we are to appraise ancient Hellas aright, it is important that we should gain a better understanding of the Homeric point of view. For Homer is the Greek poet par excellence; his interpretation of life lies at the basis of all that is Hellenic.

The Homeric View of Life

What, then, is that ideal of life that Homer has embodied in his epic? We may answer the question at once by defining it as a purely pagan and youthful conception of life; that is, it is the kind of ideal for which we should naturally look in a youthful world that has broken through the crust of tradition and is launched upon a new career. These Homeric princes lived in an age that knew as yet of no conflict within man, no divided self in which the flesh wars against the spirit; no misgivings as to the destiny of man and his place in the universe troubled them. If the tendency of an early and uncompromising Christianity was to deny the intrinsic value of life, to look upon it as a test and a trial, to regard the world as a battling ground between the divine forces and Satan and his legions, and to regard the present life valuable only as a preparation for the life to come, the pagan attitude was exactly the reverse; it was the affirmation of life, its eager acceptance, and it expressed spontaneous delight in life as such. The pagan is a true child of nature, whose promptings he follows without question. True, he discovered that certain social obligations impede the full exercise of his powers; but the unregenerated pagan chafes under these restraints, and his ideal resembles the schoolboy's longing for a world in which it would be possible to indulge every desire and every whim, without suffering any unpleasant consequences.

Indeed, the Homeric man is not far removed from the schoolboy. The world of Homer is essentially an adolescent world. Observe these heroes a little more closely. They love life, and they love action. And what are their motives? Whence springs their restless activity? First there is the desire for glory. This is the urge that moves Achilles, that most typical of the heroes. Having the choice of a long but uneventful life at home or a short but glorious career abroad, Achilles does not hesitate. And the fame he anticipates is a personal one; so far he thinks in purely selfish terms. In their thirst for glory the Homeric warriors are in a class by themselves. The heroes of more mature races have been figures of social significance; such was the Roman Romulus, who founded a city, and such are all the great national heroes, including Washington and Lincoln. But Achilles is so far removed from being concerned for the welfare of the Achaeans that, when he does not get his due, he prays for their defeat. The most conspicuous characteristic of the Homeric heroes is, as Professor Chadwick remarks, their "reckless individualism." To be sure, they must be brave and loyal friends and generous. These too are qualities that youth admires. But they must be equally unrelenting in their hatreds; thirst for revenge, the desire to "get even," drives them to unremitting efforts until their overmastering passion is stilled. Their pleasures too are those of youth. They delight in action for its own sake; they enjoy feats of strength and contend with one another strenuously in exhibitions of physical prowess and skill. Achilles institutes athletic contests at the funeral of Patroclus, and Alcinoüs does the same in honor of his unknown guest. It is no accident that *athlete* and *athletics* are words Greek in origin.

In short, life is a glorious adventure, and old age and death come soon enough. The gods are capricious, and, while they live free from care, to man they send woes innumerable.

Even so they send blessings too, fame and wealth. And when Odysseus, on his visit to Hades, tries to console the shade of Achilles, the hero indignantly replies, "Nay, speak not comfortably to me of death; rather would I live on earth as the hireling of another, with a landless man who had no great livelihood, than bear sway among all the dead."

Such is the Homeric world, an adolescent world with all the charm and all the crudity of youth. Reflection is foreign to it; it does not question life seriously; all the more ardently it strives for the prizes life has to offer. And it is Homer's art that has revealed to us the genius of the Heroic Age; in him and through him the whole range of the human world in the vitality of its youth lies open to our vision. In all this pageant of humanity there is no character described in detail; but by seizing the essential in every portrayal, Homer has made each figure true to life. He does not describe the beauty of Helen, but he tells us in a few words the effect she produced among men. We see her on her way to the walls of Troy, passing the old men who sit by the Scaean gate, and we overhear their comment, "Small blame that Trojans and Achaeans should suffer for many years for such a woman; for wonderfully in face does she look like the immortal gods." Helen, contrite, yet willful, charming in her irresponsibility, well aware that her lover is unworthy and that the husband she deserted was a better man, yet trembling at the thought of Paris' facing the wrath of Menelaus, Helen, paying touching tribute to the memory of Hector, who had never given her a word of reproach — she is a type belonging to all time.

Let us watch her, as the poet portrays her for the last time, when, the war over, she is back in her old home with Menelaus (Odyssey, Book IV). Telemachus, the son of Odysseus, accompanied by Nestor's son Pisistratus, has arrived at the palace at Sparta. Menelaus entertains them, unaware of the identity of his young guest, although he marks the grief the mention of Odysseus' name causes the

Menelaus and Helen

From a drinking bowl by Macron; early fifth century. (Courtesy of the Museum of Fine Arts, Boston)

youth. And now Helen enters; "she came forth from her fragrant vaulted chamber like Artemis of the golden arrows." To her quick eye the identity of the young man is immediately revealed; he looks like Odysseus! No doubt he is that Telemachus "whom Odysseus left a newborn child in his house, when for the sake of me, shameless woman that I was, ye Achaeans came up to Troy with bold war in your hearts." Then the slower-witted Menelaus too marks the likeness. He assures his young guest of his high regard for Odysseus; it had always been his dream, upon his return from Troy, to settle Odysseus and his household on his own domain, that they might dwell as friends together; but some envious god has prevented the happy consummation of his plan. By this well-meant but somewhat tactless remark he "stirred the desire for lamentation in the hearts of all"; "the son of Nestor bethought him in his heart of noble Antiochus," his brother, who also had never returned from that fatal expedition. Thus the entertainment of the visitors in the palace of Menelaus is in danger of turning into a dismal occasion indeed, when Helen comes to the rescue. Homer says, "She cast a drug into the wine whereof they drank, a drug to lull all pain and anger and bring forgetfulness to every sorrow." That is Homer's way of saying that once more her radiant self cast its spell over them, and soon the conversation was turned into more cheerful channels. And so we leave Helen, serene as ever, in the role of the gracious hostess in the palace of Menelaus, restored to her husband and daughter, and wondering at "the blindness that Aphrodite gave me, when she led me thither away from mine own country, forsaking my child and my bridal chamber and my lord." We have singled out Helen, but every Homeric figure, from Agamemnon to Thersites, from Odysseus to the insolent beggar, — the cowardly braggart whose quarrel with the disguised Odysseus arouses the mirth of the suitors, — proves anew the unfailing touch of the master.

As for the society of gods, it is, if possible, even more

human than that of mortals. It is the divine counterpart of human society. Of a moral order of the world Homer had no conception. His gods differ from men in the greater power they possess; they are above the limitations that beset humanity. They do not grow old, nor do they die. But in a moral sense they differ not one whit from man. Indeed, far from being morally superior to man, even the best of them (for example, Athena) on occasion will stoop to acts of meanness and trickery which we fancy an Achilles would disdain. They are swayed by the same kind of motives that operate among men. Hera, Athena, and Poseidon further the Greek cause as best they can; Aphrodite, Ares, and Apollo are on the Trojan side; and nothing divides these gods into opposite camps except grievances and prejudices, favors received or refused, likes and dislikes. Paris is Aphrodite's protégé, Odysseus the favorite of Athena. Zeus presides over his household of warring gods and exercises a kind of fitful control, against which the gods and goddesses are prone to rebel; it is only by his superior power, and especially by the fear inspired by the thunderbolt he wields, that Zeus is able to enforce his will at all.

There is nothing more human in Homer than the domestic squabbles on Olympus. Achilles has begged his mother, Thetis, a sea-goddess, to ask Zeus to give victory to the Trojans. What is to be the basis of Thetis' appeal? Shall she remind that august deity that her son has been treated unfairly, that it is Zeus's duty to uphold the cause of justice among men? Nothing of the kind. Achilles knows better: let Thetis remind Zeus of that famous occasion when the other immortals (he mentions Hera, Athena, and Poseidon by name) had plotted to bind him, from which humiliating experience Thetis had saved him by the timely summons to lofty Olympus of the hundred-handed monster, whose terrifying aspect had cowed the conspirators. Thetis promises to make the appeal to Zeus, that is, when he returns to Olympus, for it appears that the whole company of gods is at present feasting with the Ethiopians and will not return until the twelfth day. The reader may well wonder what, in the meantime, is to become of the government of the world. Upon the return of the Olympians, Thetis makes her modest request to Zeus, and begins, as Achilles had bidden her, with a reminder of her services in the past. Will Zeus in return honor her son? The ruler of gods and men is greatly perplexed. But Thetis presses for an answer and a definite promise. Then the god, angered, explains his dilemma: a sorry business this is; if he grants her request he will anger Hera, fierce champion of the Achaean cause, who without reason is forever chiding him among the immortals and asserts that he is aiding the Trojans; Thetis had better go now, lest Hera see her; he, Zeus, will attend to the matter. Then he nods in confirmation of his word, and great Olympus trembles. In spite of this last indication of the majesty of Zeus, the modern reader can hardly refrain from smiling at the secretive plottings of these immortals; it is so strangely reminiscent of the deals engineered by contemporary politicians.

Zeus now returns to the bosom of his family and is received by the gods with all outward marks of respect. But Hera had seen after all, and with a woman's intuition had guessed the truth. At once she assails her lord and master. Who has been plotting with him? Why does he delight in deciding matters apart from her? Zeus tries to evade the issue by loftily asserting his masculine superiority: there are matters of statecraft she cannot understand, even though she be his wife; whatever it is fitting for her to hear, she will hear before anyone else; but let her not inquire into his secret councils. Hera makes the time-honored reply: she *never* inquires; let him be at ease; but *now* she fears that Thetis has persuaded him to honor Achilles and to destroy many Achaeans. Such accurate guessing at the truth, which he is so desirous of hiding, rouses the anger of Zeus. He warns her that by harboring these suspicions she will be even farther estranged from him; let her be quiet or not all the gods in Olympus will be of any avail to her when he shall come to chastise her. The tense situation is relieved by the intervention of Hephaestus as peacemaker. But the entire episode, which might easily have sunk to the level of the comic strip, is reported by Homer in the same stately and dignified verse and in the same exalted tone which marks the entire Iliad from beginning to end.

It would be committing a grave error to draw conclusions from the relations between gods and men as portrayed by Homer that would be valid for the actual relations between gods and men in Homer's day. Because Achilles is insolent toward Athena, and Helen actually insulting in her address to Aphrodite, it would be absurd to suggest that the ordinary mortals of Homer's day indulged in like outspoken language to their gods.

As was observed above, the entire Olympian world is brought in as an indispensable setting and background to the human action that goes on in the foreground. These are mighty heroes and to the blows they deal the whole universe reverberates; in their quarrels the gods themselves are involved. But as evidence for the actual religion of his own time Homer's account is of little value. There can be no doubt that the common folk of his day observed in their daily habits innumerable taboos, that they performed paltry rites to appease and win the favor of the gods of field and farm, of home and hearth, of springs and woodland; there can be no doubt that they had their humble cults of family gods and clan gods. But for these petty details there is no room in Homer's epic.

Yet this much is a legitimate conclusion we may draw from the epic: the faith it describes was a living faith of men. In this adolescent age the world was still replete with miracle and mystery; man's sense of wonder had not yet been dulled. His imagination clothed with human form and human life the invisible powers that encompassed him. This transformation of an alien universe into a world akin to man "made him at home in the world."[1] To this same transformation the beauty of the poetry is due in no small degree. The raging thunderstorm becomes an angry Zeus hurling his thunderbolt; the earthquake, Poseidon striking the earth with his trident. In the ravages of blight and pestilence man saw an offended god shooting his death-dealing arrows, who, however, were he properly approached might be prevailed upon to cease his cruel sport. The madness of love is interpreted as the power of Aphrodite made manifest, and the inspired song of the poet was the gift of the gracious Muse. Even when Achilles, deeply wronged by Agamemnon, yet refrains from drawing his sword, the imagination of Homer sees the goddess of wisdom, Athena herself, seizing him by his yellow hair; and, indeed, was this not a veritable miracle that the high-spirited Achilles, under such provocation, should yet stay his hand?

But Homer did not invent these divine figures any more than he invented Achilles or Odysseus. He did exactly the same thing for the gods that he did for his human characters; his truly extraordinary gift of imagination permitted him to portray the gods in so vivid a manner that they have lived forever after. This vision has remained one of the most precious heritages the Hellenic world has bequeathed to us.

All these gods and goddesses are of the world; they dwell in the very heart of nature. There is no august figure among them, no Jehovah, creator of the universe, who causes the sun to rise and the stars to shine. Helios (the sun) is a god, and the constellations are mythical beings. Here we meet with the fundamental difference between the Greek and the Hebrew. In the Hebrew the moral sense is supreme; in the Greek, imagination and the love of beauty and poetry.

The interpretation of Homer, then, reveals the natural world as divine, and therefore divine action is never intro-

[1] See G. Lowes Dickinson, *The Greek View of Life*, Chap. I. Doubleday, Doran, n.d.

duced, at least in the Iliad, to cause events that would not naturally follow from their precedents. When Hector meets Achilles, he is doomed, and not all the gods can save him. When Achilles withdraws from the battlefield, the Trojans are victorious; there is neither mystery nor miracle in this. It would be hard to find in the entire Iliad a single incident, ostensibly brought about by divine intervention, that cannot be accounted for on purely human or natural grounds.

It remains to consider Homer as a factor in the cultural history of Greece. We have no means of appraising adequately the influence for good and ill that his poetry has had on the mentality of Hellas. But in all that is to follow we must never lose sight of the fact that Homer was the chief teacher of Hellas; as such he is acknowledged by the generations that came after him. It is with his purely pagan philosophy of life that the youth of Hellas were imbued in their schooldays; it was he who taught them that life was glorious and beautiful; he exhorted them to be brave fighters and loyal friends, and no less to be good haters; his poetry served to stimulate that innate desire to excel, "ever to be the best and to stand out among the others," which is so prominent a characteristic of the Hellene.

This whole view of life was adolescent in spirit; and if we find that the Hellenic world never grew into full maturity, that the Greeks remained children through the best part of their history, we shall note that they never quite outgrew Homer. In the post-Homeric world of city-states there was no room for the reckless individualism of the Homeric hero. But the love of doing, the desire to excel and to win the praise of one's fellows — that remained. Therein consists the Homeric quality of Greek life.

Even the gods were to suffer the consequences of Homer's vivid portrayal. Neither the art of Aeschylus nor that of Phidias could transform the father of gods and men into the majestic figure of a supreme ruler of the world; in the Hellenic imagination he was forever the distracted ruler of a rebellious household and the husband of the wily Hera. Even so, Homer's gods and Homer's poetry proved one of the strongest factors in fostering a national consciousness in Greece, where particularism, invited by geographical conditions and perpetuated by social traditions, was the rule.

To sum up, then, the continued hold of Homer's poetry upon the imagination of Hellas proves the continuation of a pagan and youthful ideal of life in historical Greece.

SUGGESTIONS FOR READING. The Homeric passages quoted in this chapter by permission of the Macmillan Co. are from the translation of the Iliad by LANG, LEAF, and MYERS (Macmillan, 1911), and the translation of the Odyssey by BUTCHER and LANG (Macmillan, 1912).

In addition to the works of CHADWICK and STAWELL, referred to above, the reader will find A. LANG, *The World of Homer* (Longmans, 1910), of great interest. See also J. A. SYMONDS, *Studies of the Greek Poets* (American edition, 2 vols. in one, Harper; n. d.).

CHAPTER III

THE TRANSITION

The Dorian Invasion

THE end of the age of Achaean dominion may be set tentatively at 1150 B.C. The Achaeans had lived gloriously, but they had lived on their capital. Perhaps it was the Trojan expedition which drained their last resources. So much is certain: the Creto-Mycenaean culture, to which they had contributed little, swiftly declined, and the age-old splendor of Mycenae and other cultural centers was submerged beneath the waves of a new immigration. The "Mycenaean" civilization, which had gradually lost its vitality during the stormy career of the Achaeans, now received its death blow at the hands of the Dorians.

Who were these Dorians, and what was their relation to the Achaeans? We are confronted here with a series of problems that still await solution. The ancients preserved the tradition of the coming of the Dorians under the guise of a "Return of the Sons of Herakles." Their legends are confusing and throw little light on the problem; such light as there is must be supplemented by linguistic and archaeological evidence.

Now historical Greece is pretty well divided between two racial and linguistic groups, which are known as Dorian and Ionian. They bear marked racial characteristics and in Hellenic speech and literature are represented by two distinct dialects. But they by no means exhaust the varieties of Hellenic race and language. The Doric and Ionic dialects form the two linguistic extremes; between these stands at least one dialect which also is represented in Greek literature, Aeolic, originally the speech of the Achaeans. But Ionic, Aeolic, and Doric are, after all, only varieties of a language which is fundamentally one. These varieties, then, probably mark three successive stages of the Hellenic invasion of the Balkan Peninsula.

The Ionic-speaking Greeks may have been the first; they penetrated into central Greece on both sides of the isthmus. The Aeolic-speaking Achaeans were next in succession; they occupied part of Thessaly, the isthmus, and the greater part of the Peloponnesus, and drove the Ionians into less fertile Attica, whence they overflowed to the islands and finally reached the central coast of Anatolia. The last comers were the Dorians. Their first arrivals date from at least 1100 B. C. They conquered the Achaeans, who, exhausted by continuous warfare, were driven out of Thessaly into its southeast corner, which in historical times still bore their name (Achaea Phthiotis), and across the sea into northern Anatolia. The Dorians then turned into central Greece; they left their impress on Boeotia but seem to have passed by Attica. They dislodged the Achaeans from their strongholds in the Peloponnesus and confined them to the strip of land on the Corinthian gulf, which, again, in historical times was called Achaea. The Dorians gained control of the isthmus and settled the entire western Peloponnesus (Argolis and Laconia), to which they later added Messenia. And they too crossed the Aegean, and by way of Crete and Rhodes reached the southern coast of Anatolia. There the strength of the invasion at last spent itself. The central part of the Peloponnesus, the Arcadian highlands, escaped the Dorian; but another division of the Dorians seems to have invaded Aetolia from the north and thence to have crossed into Elis.

The result of these migratory movements was a Greece greatly differing from Homeric Greece; in its main divisions it is the Greece of historical times.

We have no means of measuring the time occupied by these successive settlements; doubtless centuries passed before a well-established order emerged from the chaos and confusion. We know that Dorian Sparta was settled by about 1000 B.C.

The Achaean empire had fallen, and with it had gone the "Mycenaean" civilization. This had never been anything but a civilization of the upper class, the "kings"; gradually spreading over an ever widening area, it became more and more diluted, until, finally, in its debased form it approached the native art and culture. Pottery passed into the "geometric" period; the freer forms and curving lines of plant and marine life, products of an art which delighted especially in rendering nature's oddities, disappeared before a new art, primitive and stiff, which was content to fill the surface of a vessel with straight-lined decorations. There is here a real break and a reversal to primitive methods.

From the Bronze Age we now pass into the Iron Age. Even in Achaean times iron was not unknown, but now it definitely supplants the earlier metal for swords, knives, and other cutting implements.

On the whole the Dorian invasion caused an upheaval from which the Greek world did not recover for a long time. This is the age of darkness from which historical Hellas does not emerge until well into the eighth century B.C. It was during this age of darkness that Homer, somewhere in the territory gained by the Ionians across the Aegean, composed his Iliad and Odyssey. His theme was not the life of his own time, but the glories of an age that had passed. However, toward the end of this period, about 750 B.C., a poet arose in Greece as a witness to the changing conditions and as the prophet of a new faith.

Hesiod

Hesiod was born in Ascra, a village lying at the foot of Mt. Helicon in Boeotia. His father, who, like many others, had migrated across the sea to Aeolia, had found life there as hard as in the homeland, to which he returned at last. There, in Boeotia, Hesiod lived the life of the ordinary peasant and, prematurely aged by bitter experience, composed his peasant songs. Later ages coupled his name with

Homer's, which means that he was traditionally regarded as a poet of ancient times. That is all we know about his date, although the very evident fact of Hesiod's dependence on at least the form of Homeric poetry, together with other internal evidence, leads us to place him about a century after Homer. If Homer lived about 850 B.C., Hesiod's floruit cannot be far from 750 B.C.

A stronger contrast than that between Homer, the court poet, and Hesiod, the peasant, can hardly be imagined. It is not only that their interests differ but that their outlooks on life are strikingly dissimilar. The splendor of the past has little appeal to the peasant, overwhelmed with the misery of his lot in life. He looks upon the glowing world of romance described by Homer as a tissue of lies, the beautiful lies with which the Muses sometimes delude the singer when they are in the mood to beguile men. But the Muses can also teach the truth, and he, Hesiod, is the mouthpiece of the Muses, but only to tell of things that are true. Here we meet with an entirely new conception of the part assigned to the poet: he consciously assumes the task of teacher, and a new type of poetry makes its appearance, didactic poetry. Hesiod belonged to an age which knew of no other medium of expression but Homeric verse, and hence we witness the strange spectacle of a disgruntled peasant addressing his fellows in the polished verse of the court poet.

It is in the poem known by the picturesque title of *Works and Days* that we can catch a glimpse of the author's personality. The poem consists of three parts: the first is a sermon on justice, addressed to the poet's wayward brother, Perses; the second is a farmer's guide, or handbook, to which is appended a treatise on trading by sea (interpolated is a medley of precepts, mostly proverbial lore); the third part deals with the interesting subject of lucky and unlucky days. It is in the first section, the poem on justice, that Hesiod stands revealed as a distinct personality, the first literary character in the Western world. His voice comes to us as the first to demand social justice. He shows little patience with those who can sing only of the glories of kings. The "kings" whom he knows and whom he regularly adorns with the epithet "gift-devouring" are little deserving of admiration or respect. Here is the strongest evidence of the break with the past: kings are no longer objects of almost religious awe; no longer are they wielders of scepters that have descended from Zeus himself; they are only human beings and singularly frail in their humanity. Only greed and desire for power distinguish them in the eyes of the peasant poet, who accuses them of abusing their prerogatives with utter disregard of justice — overbearing beings forgetful of Aidos and Nemesis.[1] How have the mighty fallen! These "kings" of Hesiod, successors of the Achaean chieftains, are no more than petty nobles, owners of the best lands, who in the absence of a written code of laws oppress the peasantry with impunity. Hesiod himself had suffered at their hands, for, bribed by Perses, they had robbed him of his just heritage. It was the bitterness of this experience that prompted Hesiod's denunciation: *facit indignatio versum.*

But there is more than this. The poet demands justice on earth and confidently asserts it to be an issue in heaven. Zeus has become its guardian; his eye sees all and understands all; he watches over the conduct of the city, to see what sort of justice it keeps within its walls. Let the kings beware: there is a maiden goddess, daughter of Zeus; Dike (Justice) is her name; she has her seat in heaven beside her father and tells him of the wickedness of men, that they may pay for the folly of their princes who pronounce sentence crookedly. Nay more, there are thirty thousand deathless spirits watching over the deportment of men.

Truly we have traveled far from the carefree Olympian society of Homer! The Boeotian peasant in no uncertain

[1] Two telling words that hardly admit of translation: the first indicates the sense of shame that attends or ought to attend an unjust act; the second, the righteous indignation that demands retribution.

terms postulates a moral government of the world, justice upheld by divine power. What impresses us most about this man is his downright moral earnestness. Again and again he utters words that make us rub our eyes and wonder whether perhaps one of the Hebrew prophets has wandered among the blithe Hellenes. "Evil abounds and is ready at hand; the path to it is smooth and it dwells near." "Before virtue" (and here for the first time *arete* bears a moral implication) "the immortals have placed sweat of the brow"; "long is the path leading to it and steep; it is rough at first, but, when one has reached the top, then it is easy." "You, Perses, heed the right and do not increase violence — better to go on the other side to justice; for justice prevails over violence. Justice, when wronged, follows the wicked into their haunts and brings mischief with her. But the city of the righteous flourishes; peace dwells within it; the earth bears abundant livelihood and the sheep are weighted down with their woolly fleeces." "For the animal kingdom Zeus has ordained this law, that fishes and beasts and birds devour each other; for among them justice dwells not. But to man Zeus gave justice, which is by far the best." "Work, foolish Perses, work the work that the gods have appointed to man. Work, that hunger may hate thee. Work is no disgrace; it is idleness which is a disgrace."

But not all in Hesiod is on the same high level. Much of the wisdom he teaches is only the proverbial wisdom of the peasant and betrays an unpleasantly practical and even niggardly turn of mind. He has the peasant's attitude toward woman, a creature suspect and only too likely to ruin a man's life; indeed, we find in his story of Pandora an echo of the ancient belief which connects the origin of evil with woman. He knows also of the succession of the ages, for at one time man was happy and mingled with the gods; but through the succeeding ages he has gradually deteriorated, until now the golden age is far off and we live in an iron age in which there is no rest from toil or sorrow; now men live in hatred of one another, children dishonor their parents, the oath is disregarded, and Aidos and Nemesis flee from the earth and man.

Hesiod's poetry makes no cheerful reading. Yet it is precious to us, for we find in it the first clearly formulated demand for social justice coupled with the assertion that such is the concern of the gods. We are now prepared for the story of the awakening of the Hellenic world, of the gradual realization of a new idea — the rule of law before which all men shall be equal.[1]

[1] There have come down to us under Hesiod's name two other poems: the *Theogony*, which may be his, and "The Shield of Herakles," which certainly is not. The *Theogony* contains a genealogy of the gods; here the author has brought order into the chaotic world of gods and goddesses. Such information was useful and in demand. We know of other poems attributed to him, one containing an enumeration of heroic women, and similar catalogues seem to have been a feature of that Boeotian school of poetry of which Hesiod is regarded as the founder. Into some of these it became the fashion to introduce romantic episodes. One of these has come down to us under the name of "The Shield of Herakles." The hero arms himself for combat with Cycnus, and the greater part of the poem consists of a description of the shield Hephaestus made for Herakles — evidently an imitation of the famous description of Achilles' shield in the Iliad (Book XIX). There is one passage (lines 237–269) which is in notable contrast to the battle glee of the Iliad. In it the horrors of war are painted with an imaginative power never surpassed in later Greek poetry.

CHAPTER IV

THE POLITICAL HISTORY OF HELLAS

The Beginnings

THE repeated shocks of the Dorian invasion and the migratory movements attending it had left the Aegean world in a state of unsettlement from which it took centuries to recover. When finally, about the middle of the eighth century, the light of history breaks upon Hellas, even though at first we can only dimly discern shapes and outlines, we come upon a world that is literally teeming with life. Perhaps in all the world's history there is no more fascinating spectacle than this first glimpse we get of the awakening of the Greek world. We witness, in fact, the birth of man and the beginnings of Western civilization.

With the eagerness and energy of youth these early Greeks reached out in every direction, setting their minds and hands to all the several tasks ever attempted by man. And the hour was theirs. There was no great imperial power near to blight the free growth of Hellas. The Hittite empire was no more than a memory, and the Assyrian hardly reached the borders of the Greek world. The Lydian kings, nearest neighbors of the Anatolian Greeks, had their own troubles. The Mede and the Persian were as yet below the horizon of history. These first one hundred and fifty years (from 750 to 600 B.C.) constituted a time of stirring activity, and in the main the foundations were laid and the framework erected. And the Greeks were eager learners as well as originators; whatever suited their purpose they appropriated, but, in doing so, made it over into something entirely their own.

The age of the awakening of Hellas begins, as does the modern era of Europe, with a series of voyages of discovery.

The Greeks explored their seas, the Mediterranean Sea and the Black Sea. It was their season of swarming. They sent out settlement after settlement. They penetrated into the Hellespont and through it found their way into the Black Sea. They explored the northern Aegean, always on the lookout for a good harbor, that they might dwell within sight of the sea while cultivating their plot of ground. Presently the peninsula of Chalcidice, the coast of Thrace, the Hellespont, and the entire circuit of the Black Sea were dotted with Greek settlements. With equal boldness they sailed westward and discovered their America. The greater part of Sicily became a Hellenic island, the richest of them all, and Hellenic towns sprang up along the southern coasts of Italy, which became a "Greater Greece"; and to this day the noble ruins of Paestum stand in the midst of the desolate plain as witnesses to the creative genius of a departed race. They founded Naples. They went farther northward and founded Marseille as well; and Hellenic influence penetrated southern France, never to be entirely obliterated by the Romans, who came after them. But in that part of the Mediterranean world they met with the stubborn resistance of the Etruscan pirates, who found willing allies in the Carthaginians; both were equally desirous of keeping the Greeks out of territory which they claimed as their own.

These Greek settlements were not colonies in the modern sense of the word. The Greek name denotes them as "off-dwellings," dwellings away from home where the more enterprising citizens, in search of land and wider opportunities than the straitening conditions at home afforded, could found a new center of Greek life. Many a revolution at home was forestalled by encouraging the surplus population and those discontented with existing conditions to seek a new environment where they could make a fresh start. But the ties uniting the mother city with her daughter were of a sentimental nature only; when, as occasionally happened, the mother city attempted control of her offspring, the friendly relations between them might change into bitter enmity, as was the case, for instance, between Corinth and Corcyra.

This colonizing movement contributed more than any other factor to breaking the bonds of tradition and releasing the springs of creative work among the Greeks; their horizon was immeasurably enlarged, their knowledge increased; their confidence grew, and in the new centers many of the old restraints ceased to operate. In their manifold activities, no matter where carried on in this new world, which they had made their own, they displayed the same spirit which distinguishes all their work from that of any other race. Whatever they did bears the stamp of their peculiar genius.

The two most marked traits of the Greek genius are its intellectual temper and its sensitiveness to beauty. The first shows itself as a need to see clearly and to set forth clearly, as a passion for sharply outlined forms, for order and balance. Whatever it be, a vase, a poem, a temple, a philosophy, or a political constitution, if it is Hellenic, it is a thing rationally designed. The second characteristic of the Greek genius, its esthetic quality, may be an Aegean inheritance. It is in the combination of these two that the unique character of Hellenism must be sought. It led to an identification of order (*kosmos*) with beauty. The union of these two marks the products of Hellas.

Thus the energy of the opening epoch in the history of the ancient Greeks was directed in every field toward the achievement of a rational order which should satisfy equally their instinct for beauty and their feeling for form and design. In their poetry we shall find it in the reshaping of folk song into the ordered choral melic of strophe and antistrophe. Next they turned the ecstatic song of Dionysiac revelry into the stately majesty of their drama. In architecture they created the order and balance, the simplicity of design, of the Doric temple. Their early sculpture and vase-painting betray the same innate feeling for the decorative effect of design and

The Temple of Poseidon and the "Basilica" at Poseidonia (Paestum)

form. In religion they re-formed the crude village rite into a solemn ritual of beauty and joy. Their earliest philosophers sought for a formula that should reduce the infinite variety and multiplicity of phenomena to an intelligible order.

The intellectual temper of Hellenism, then, reveals itself in the attempt to impose the tyranny of rational analysis on all phases of human life. It is not to be wondered at that "scheme," "system," "method," "logic," "analysis," "canon," "symmetry," "harmony," "rhythm," "synthesis," are all of Hellenic origin.

In the political field this intellectual bias shows itself as clearly as in other phases of Hellenic culture. To this we must turn first in an orderly account of Greek civilization; for, as we shall see, the form of political and social organization adopted by the Greeks was to prove a dominant factor in the shaping of their civilization.

Now it may be stated at once that the creation of the city-state, the polis, as a political, social, and religious unit was the particular achievement of the ancient Greeks. Its history illustrates both their political genius and their political ineptitude. To them political problems were intellectual problems, even if they were not consciously aware of this. Here they are in startling contrast to the Romans, who possessed the political sagacity which the Greeks lacked. The Greek instinctively seeks an analysis of his political difficulties; the Roman proceeds with the give-and-take method and muddles through.

The individual city-state, then, was the Hellenic form of political organization; and it remained so to the end. Hence the Greeks never attained national unity. And it cannot be said that such unity was ever a desirable thing to them; quite the reverse, the subordination of the individual polis to the combined will of all would have seemed to them an intolerable infringement upon its liberty of action.

We should like to be able to trace the growth of the city-state; but when we catch our first glimpse of the polis, it has already assumed a definite shape. Its development was by no means uniform; indeed, it may be said that each Greek polis had its own political individuality and that no two were exactly alike. The conditions under which each developed determined very largely the particular character of its political growth. Yet it is possible to generalize about certain aspects of the development of the polis.

The first thing to grasp is that, as we have seen, in consequence of geographical conditions these political units were small. A small river valley with its outlet upon the sea, a little island, or again an inland valley enclosed by hills — there the group clustered and worked out its salvation by adapting itself to its environment.

Secondly, in most cases, the group united for common defense on a neighboring hilltop; this became a place of refuge which was fortified. The word *polis* itself was applied originally to these citadels, which served also as the abode of the gods and as a religious center (Homer calls the polis "sacred"). Very many of these citadels had served as such from immemorial times, and some had been heavily fortified in the Achaean days.

Thirdly these communities had ceased to be monarchies. Monarchy never had struck root in Greek soil. The scepter-bearing kings of Homer had departed and were replaced by Hesiod's "gift-devouring" nobles. Magistrates chosen from the aristocracy divided the royal power among themselves; but, being elected for a definite term only, they came under the domination of the ancient council of nobles, which had survived the death of monarchy. Council and magistrates enjoyed a monopoly of the administration of the law, whose sole keepers they were. In short, family prestige, proud of its privilege, ruled and invariably abused its power.

Finally, wherever urban conditions developed around the base of the citadel, the polis, now becoming a city, was the center of the administration of the territory; and the inhabitants, whether or no they dwelt within its limits, or its walls, if such there were, became citizens (*politai*) of the city (*polis*). Gradually the geographical principle began to assert itself alongside the tribal conception of society as based on kinship; local units of administration were superimposed upon tribal organization.[1]

Such urban development of the city as the civic center of a district was not a universal phenomenon in the Greek world. Sparta was rather a territorial state than a city; neither Arcadia nor the western part of central Greece (Aetolia and Acarnania) nor Thessaly adopted the system; so that in something like half of Greece proper the ancient ways of village life continued. On the other hand, across the Aegean in Anatolia, and in all the new territory occupied by the colonies east and west, the system was universal. The reason is not far to seek: the settlers in these distant regions had only a precarious hold on their new possessions, and urban life, preferably in walled towns, proved a better safeguard against the surrounding perils.

Local conditions governed political developments, and, as usual, economic changes brought political changes in their train. On the whole, Greece remained on an agricultural basis. The old way of life demanded that each group be self-sustaining; it lived on the land and off the land. But two modifications of the old system made their appearance. First the Greeks turned more and more to the cultivation of the vine and the olive, for which most of their land is better adapted than for the growing of cereals. This had the added advantage of providing them with the materials for trade and barter. Secondly industry followed in the wake of trade. Miletus, for instance, inherited a textile industry which had utilized the excellent wool produced on the central plateau of Anatolia. New sources of wealth, then, were added to the old ones; and the noble landholders shortly found a new aristocracy of wealth, born of trade and industry, competing with them. Accompanying these changes there was a rise in the level of life; especially in the new colonies the peasant

[1] See W. R. Halliday, *The Growth of the City State* (Small, 1923), Lecture IV.

or hireling of the past found greater opportunities for bettering his lot. Moreover, in consequence of a growing trade, in turn facilitated by the new coinage, the greater abundance of metal, especially iron, brought the possession of arms and armor within the reach of ever increasing numbers. In the old days the defense of the community was entirely in the hands of the aristocracy. This now changed, and city after city was forced to adapt its methods of warfare to the new conditions; the hoplites, spearmen clad in armor, carrying metal shields and fighting in serried ranks, took the place of the nobles fighting from the war chariot or on horseback.

Now, when men are called upon to defend their country at the peril of their lives, they are not slow in demanding the right to a share in the government. Yet the first demand was not for political rights, but for social justice. What these commoners, like Hesiod, wanted in the first place was a "square deal"; and as a first step they demanded the codification and publication of the laws. The century falling between 650 and 550 B.C. saw the appearance of lawgivers all over Hellas. This much was gained. The first taste of victory was a spur to further efforts, and soon warfare between aristocracy, or oligarchy, and democracy arose in a majority of the city-states. The question was, Should the few rule or the many?

Of representative democracy the Greeks had no notion. Theirs was a direct democracy, or perhaps we should call it a democracy of the town meeting. The citizen in person attended the assembly on stated days and demanded to be consulted or, at least, to be asked for his approval. This vision of a commonwealth governed by its citizens, who are all equal and subject to the law expressing the common will, was not easily realized. The first difficulty was to unite the citizens, who were divided by ancient loyalties — first to the family, then to the clan, and finally to the tribe, remnants of an earlier social order of which they could not readily divest themselves. Next there was the difficulty, inherent in all society, of reconciling the clashing interests of rich and poor, of the few and the many. In a number of city-states no lasting compromise was ever reached, and in their history civil war is chronic. And lastly, even if these difficulties were overcome, there remained the problem of training for the duties of citizenship men who had never known either political rights or political responsibility. In many centers democracy failed for this reason.

It was owing to such obstacles in the path of self-government as these that in the transition between aristocracy and democracy we meet with a peculiar political phenomenon which the Greeks called "tyranny." Briefly stated, it means that in despair of finding a solution of their troubles the commoners were content to allow a man of will and daring (usually someone from the ranks of the nobles) to seize the reins of government by force and to set himself up as the dictator of the destinies of his state. The word *tyrannos* had originally no such connotation as our *tyrant* has for us; it is probably of Lydian origin, and the Anatolian Greeks knew it first as a term designating the king ruling in Sardis. The Greek "tyrants" did not abolish the existing laws but acted as chief executives, not responsible to either nobles or commoners. Usually they had the support of the poor, in whose interests they were supposed to rule, and were hostile to the nobles. Rarely did they succeed in establishing a dynasty and bequeathing their power to their descendants; more commonly, if a tyrant managed to retain power through his lifetime, his death ended the tyranny. Frequently such a tyrant proved a boon to the city, furnishing it with a stable government and contributing greatly to its prosperity and progress. There were many picturesque personalities among the tyrants, of whom Herodotus tells us a wealth of anecdotes.[1] The age of the tyrants falls between 650 and 500 B.C.,

[1] Consult Herodotus on Periander of Corinth, Cleisthenes of Sicyon, Pisistratus of Athens, and Polycrates of Samos, for the type of stories current in Hellas of the fifth century concerning the careers of these supermen.

although they are never altogether absent from the stage of Greek politics and are likely to make their appearance in any major crisis.

But the institution of tyranny, although helpful in bridging the gap between the old days of aristocratic rule and the new days of the democracy, was abhorrent to the Greek mind. Liberty in our sense they never knew, for a man always belonged to the city whose walls sheltered him. They knew liberty as freedom from the rule of kings and irresponsible despots; and tyranny too easily degenerated into despotism. And so the ancient strife between the many and the few continued, sometimes ending in the establishment of an oligarchy, sometimes in democracy. Few Greek cities enjoyed a really stable government. There was, however, at least one exception, and to this we now turn.

Sparta

Sparta furnishes us not only with the spectacle, rare in Hellas, of a constitutional state enduring unchanged for centuries, but also with a telling illustration of that ruthless logic with which the Hellenic mind was wont to attack its political problems. Situated in the Eurotas valley, where the conquering Dorians had established themselves as masters, it gained by further conquest the western half of the southern Peloponnesus, Messenia. Thus the Spartans solved their land problem, but they found themselves ruling a sullen population which outnumbered its conquerors ten to one.

The peculiar political and social institutions of Sparta, which aroused the admiration of the greatest political thinkers of Greece, and which we are now about to examine, probably did not reach their final form until after Messenia's desperate attempt to regain its independence had been finally crushed (sometime before 600 B.C.). At the conclusion of this life-and-death struggle the Spartans seem to have recognized that no alternative was open to them but resolutely to turn aside from all other objects in life and to convert their state into an armed camp, in which all citizens should be soldiers, dedicated from the day of their birth to the organized defense of their overlordship in the territory they controlled.

Spartan society was divided into three classes. First came the real Spartans, descendants of the conquering Dorians. Political rights belonged exclusively to them, and the social institutions, described below, pertained only to them. Next came the Perioeci (the "neighbors"), inhabitants of the scattered little towns of Laconia and Messenia, who, although not enjoying any political rights, were yet free to pursue their own ends. Of them, mostly artisans and traders, with a sprinkling of small farmers, the state asked nothing but occasional military service. Finally there were the Helots. They formed the bulk of the population, and were kept in a state of serfdom, attached to the soil, which they cultivated for their Spartan masters. The burden thus imposed upon them was not inordinate; it was the moral degradation involved in their position which made their lot so hard. They lived under the constant vigilance of their lords, watched over by a secret police; it is said that every year the Spartan magistrates declared war upon them so that it might be lawful to kill them upon any provocation. The most energetic and enterprising among them often disappeared mysteriously.

Such was the social organization of the Spartan state. Of its origins nothing can be affirmed with certainty; the phenomenon of a serf class is found elsewhere in Greece and dates from the days of the great migrations.

We turn now to the political organization of the Spartans. The oldest element in their constitution was undoubtedly the council of elders, the *gerusia*. It was made up of twenty-eight men, over sixty years old, and, as we saw, was a relic of tribal days; for tribes are ruled by an iron tradition of which the elders are the keepers. This survival of tribal ways in the Spartan state largely contributed to making it the most hidebound conservative political community in Hellas. These elders not only were a governing council but also sat as a supreme criminal court.

The two kings of Sparta date from the time of the migrations. They traced their descent through Herakles to Zeus. Members of the two royal houses were traditionally held to have led the Spartan hosts to victory; to dispense with these acknowledged recipients of divine favor would have seemed to the Spartan equivalent to challenging the power of the gods. Thus kings survived in Sparta; but it was a much attenuated royalty, for even in conservative Sparta the claims of democracy did not go entirely unheeded. A town meeting (it was called the *apella*) was convened once a month to listen to such matters as the council might see fit to lay before the citizens and perhaps to vote as well, although a quaint provision in the Spartan constitution seems to have allowed the council to "secede" and to ignore the will of the assembly if it did not square with its own preference. At any rate, the assembly never became a potent factor in the government of Sparta. The really democratic element in the Spartan state consisted of the five *ephors* (overseers), chosen by the assembly from the body of the citizens. Their office, like the Roman tribunate, grew in importance until they formed a check on the power of the kings, whom they accompanied upon their campaigns, and upon the gerusia itself. They undertook the presidency of the council and the apella; they guided the foreign policy of the state; they supervised the morals of the citizens, who were bidden to "shave their upper lip and obey the laws"; and they presided over the civil courts.

Plainly the Spartan constitution was a compromise between different historical elements, and, as is usually the case, as such it proved more workable and enduring than those wonderful constitutions which result from abstract thought. Although it had unusual features (especially in its retention of royalty), it was not this that gave the Spartan commonwealth its rare physiognomy; for this we must look to the social institutions governing the life of the Spartans.

These were based upon the Hellenic axiom that the individual belongs to the state; but only in Sparta was this axiom followed to its logical conclusion, so that there the life of the individual citizen became one of complete subservience to the ends of the state. Now the supreme end of the state, surrounded as it was by a potential enemy numerically far superior, was to safeguard its existence. This, then, was the most pressing duty, and became in fact the only duty of the citizen. As one historian puts it, what was originally a military necessity became eventually a political ideal.[1]

State supervision began for the Spartan with the day of his birth. He was duly inspected, and if he did not give promise of physical fitness, he was rejected; the babe was left to perish or perhaps to be reared by a charitable Helot. If he passed this first test, the state claimed him at the age of seven to rear and educate and mold him for its service. The boys were organized into troops and lived and trained together under public masters. This training lasted until they were twenty years old. It was mostly physical instruction, but aimed at character as well; the qualities chiefly admired were courage, power of endurance, and unquestioning obedience to authority.[2] At the age of twenty military service began; and although after reaching the age of thirty the Spartan could attend and vote at the assembly and enjoyed other privileges, yet his life continued to be spent mainly in the barracks and in camp until he reached the age of sixty. He could marry after his twentieth birthday, but of home life he was to know little. He was not permitted to engage in any gainful occupation; he could not even handle silver or gold coins. His leisure might be spent in

[1] See M. L. W. Laistner, *Greek History* (Heath, 1932), p. 141.

[2] For a sympathetic account of Spartan education see J. K. Freeman, *Schools of Hellas* (Macmillan, 1912), pp. 11–34.

training or hunting, and the product of the chase would vary the monotony of the daily menu. Or he might listen to the discussions of the elders and even take part himself; but verbosity was frowned upon, of which our word *laconic* as applied to speech still reminds us.

Thus the Spartan was denied indulgence in two of the most fundamentally human instincts, those associated with the family and acquisitiveness. Yet the Spartan state endured for centuries! It was a kind of aristocratic communism under which the Spartan lived, which rigorously excluded those who were not of the true blood. The authority of the state stood between the young Spartan and all that seemed desirable in life to ordinary men: his food was mean, his clothing scanty; winter and summer he went barefoot, clad in a single garment; his bed was hard; to the amenities and luxuries of life he remained a stranger. And yet he was proud of being a Spartan and was ready to make the supreme sacrifice for the greater glory of Sparta. A more completely social ideal has never ruled the minds and hearts of men, but it made of the Spartan at the same time something greater and something smaller than man.

The possession of so superbly trained an army made Sparta the military leader of Greece. At first the Spartans seemed to have had the thought of subjugating the Peloponnesus; in the end they were satisfied with wresting the leadership in the Peloponnesus from their ancient rivals in Argos. Slowly Spartan supremacy in military affairs was recognized, and there was formed the Peloponnesian League, a loose confederacy of states, acknowledging the leadership of Sparta in times of war.[1]

[1] See Xenophon's essay "On the Lacedaemonian Polity" and Plutarch's "Lycurgus."

Athens

At the eastern extremity of central Greece the peninsula of Attica juts out into the sea. Shut off from central Greece by a high mountain range, it looks naturally toward the east. A string of islands connects it with the Ionian seaboard of Anatolia and invites to trade and industry, an invitation which the people of Attica were rather late in accepting.

The early history of Attica, which had escaped the Dorian invasion, does not differ greatly from that of other Greek lands. There is only one important exception: the various geographical districts (and there are four of these) were early united to form a political whole. The rock of the Acropolis became the civic center of Attica; there the people met for the common worship of their divine protectors, and there they rallied for defense; the city that grew up at the foot of the sacred rock became the center of the political life of Attica. And so it happened that in historical times the dwellers in any of the townships scattered through Attica yet were citizens of Athens.

Otherwise the early history of Attica shows no divergent features from those we have observed elsewhere. Here too royalty gave way to annually elected magistrates (the Athenians called them *archons*, leaders). The name of king survived only as the title of the chief priest, himself one of the archons. Here too the nobles (*eupatrids*), the leaders of the ancient clans, monopolized the political administration and jurisdiction. The Athenian aristocracy, ambitious for wealth and power, governed with a harsh and stern rule. It was a real class government; the small landholders of Attica had as much reason to complain of their "kings" as Hesiod had in neighboring Boeotia. And many new causes contributed to aggravate the burdens of the poor. The appearance of coinage, which always works hardship among a people accustomed to barter; the introduction of the olive and the vine, withdrawing an increasing extent of land from the raising of foodstuffs; the growing scarcity of available land (Attica had taken no part in the colonizing movement); the harshness of the laws governing the relations between creditor and debtor, which permitted the creditor to lay hands on the person of the debtor, with the added circumstance that the keeping and the knowledge of these laws was confined to the creditor class — through all these causes the poor man of Attica suffered no less than his fellows elsewhere in Greece. And the same causes led to the same results: in Attica too the lawgiver made his appearance,[1] and an attempt was made to establish a tyranny.

By the beginning of the sixth century matters had reached such a pass that only a miracle, it seemed, could prevent the outbreak of civil warfare. Many of the small landholdings had passed into the hands of the rich, and the remainder were largely pledged for debts; many Athenians were homeless wanderers, eking out a miserable living abroad; many had become enslaved to their creditors. Athens itself was a backward state, lagging behind the others in the diversified activities of an awakened and enlarged Greece; even its little neighbor Megara had successfully defied it on more than one occasion.

And then the miracle happened. At the critical hour there appeared a man who was to prove the savior of his country, and whose name was revered by later generations in Athens in much the same way as national heroes are remembered by a grateful posterity. This was Solon. Within the space of the two following generations he was succeeded by two others, Pisistratus and Cleisthenes; and it may be asserted with truth that these men laid the foundation for the greatness of Athens. Within the space of eighty years (roughly between 590 and 510 B.C.) Athens was transformed from an ailing, backward state, misgoverned and apprehensive of its

[1] Draco was his name, and although his code may have been no harsher in its terms than the age warranted, yet *Draconian* is still proverbially used to indicate the kind of law that knows no pity.

future, into a flourishing democracy, confident of its power and ready to assert its right to a leading part in the activities of Hellas. All three men were radicals in the best sense of the word, bold enough to apply the ax to the root of existing evils, and all three were men of vision. There is no better example in the world's history of the solution of national problems through the unflinching application of human intelligence to them. In brief, what they did was this: Solon gave the Athenians social justice; Pisistratus raised the prestige of Athens in Greece at large — in ordinary parlance he put Athens on the map; Cleisthenes established the democracy, a "government of the people, by the people, for the people." Of the three the first and the last were magistrates; Pisistratus was a "tyrant." Their work is a credit both to them and to the intelligence of the people who accepted it.

Solon, chosen as a magistrate and "reconciler," cut the Gordian knot by abolishing all debts secured by land; and Mother Earth, who had been groaning under the burden of numerous mortgage stones, was freed. In addition he freed those who had been enslaved for debt. This revolutionary measure became known as the *Seisachtheia*, the shaking off of the burdens; and, revolutionary as it was, it saved Athens from the immediate danger of civil war. Why did the rich tamely submit to a measure that not only deprived them of a goodly portion of their wealth but may have entailed actual hardship on some? The answer must be found in the Greek conception of the state: the state does not exist for man, but man belongs to the state. Solon evidently persuaded the recalcitrants that no half measures would ensure the survival of the commonwealth; but he refused the demands of the extremists whose program included a complete redistribution of the land.

Then he rewrote the Athenian constitution. His legislation was partly economic in character and partly political. Slavery for debt was abolished forever, and limits were set to the amount of land that could be held individually; the exportation of grain was forbidden, which served to encourage the raising of other crops, better adapted to Attic soil and likely to furnish material for export. Industry and trade were encouraged; the currency was adjusted to a new standard, which promised to facilitate Athenian commerce abroad; artisans from elsewhere were made to feel that Athens welcomed them and needed them. Moreover, the door to Athenian citizenship was opened to the resident alien; by this and similar measures he strove to wean his fellow Athenians away from the ancient tribal concepts to a new idea of citizenship.

But the most momentous of his legislative measures concerned the political reforms he inaugurated. To establish a democracy never entered his head; nevertheless, his reforms would inevitably lead to democracy. The old council of the Areopagus, stronghold of the aristocracy, was not abolished, but, restricting its function chiefly to a judiciary one, he made it the guardian of the law. By its side a new council was created, consisting of four hundred members, one hundred representing each of the four historic tribes; the new council was to prepare the business to be voted on by the assembly. The landless and the poor, who had been grouped into one class as the Thetes and who had been excluded from political rights, were now admitted to the assembly. This, a measure of simple justice, was unmistakably democratic in character. But the two councils, the Areopagus and the Council of Four Hundred, were to be the anchors, holding the ship of state safe from political storms. Finally, Solon created a new court, the Heliaea, as a popular court of appeal. This court, on which anyone could serve, became the true cornerstone of democracy: from now on, the magistrates, even though they continued to be chosen from the ranks of the nobles, were responsible to an ordinary jury for their conduct while in office. This measure broke the back of the rule of the nobles.

His work done, Solon retired voluntarily from Athens. It

is difficult to say what we should praise most in this extraordinary man — his fairness and personal integrity, his moderation and understanding of life, or the originality and audacity of his political thinking. The Greeks canonized him as one of the Seven Wise Men; and the more we think of the "solons" that came after him, the greater our admiration for the original Solon.

But Solon's work suffered the defects of its greatness. Precisely because it was the product of rational thought, the political machinery he had set up refused to work smoothly in the beginning. The old rancors reappeared, and in consequence of the internal discords Athens lost control over the island of Salamis, which she had wrested from Megara, and without which she could never hope for free access to the sea.

It was plain that what Athens needed was a strong man who should control the situation, by force of arms if necessary, and, allowing the new constitution to work, accustom the people to its use. Pisistratus probably first drew the attention of his fellow citizens by the prominent part he took in the recovery of Salamis. Then, after two unsuccessful attempts, he finally established himself as tyrant (546 B.C.) and maintained himself, as many tyrants had done before him, by embracing the cause of the dispossessed against the more fortunate. Without making any change in Solon's work, he satisfied the demands of the poor by dividing among them the estates of some of the nobles, his personal enemies, whom he drove into exile. But Pisistratus was not content to establish a political truce in Athens. A man of vision, the first to realize the possibilities of Athens' future place in Hellas, he embarked on a new policy which was to place Athens in the front rank among Greek powers. He transformed Athens from a stay-at-home farming community into an active participant in the trading life of Hellas; its pottery and its olive oil became the staples of the new trade. He secured for the Athenians safe access to the grain-raising lands around the Black Sea, whence they might import the grain that Attica could not supply for its growing population. He undertook an ambitious building program, to add to the city's prestige. He made over the rustic celebrations in honor of Dionysus, god of the vine, into a splendid dramatic festival. He reinstituted the civic festival of Athens' own goddess, Athena, on such a scale that it became a powerful stimulus to civic pride. Lastly he conceived the idea of elevating Athens to the place of the mother city and leader of the Ionians, even as Sparta held the leadership among the Dorians. He had found Athens a relatively obscure town; when he died (527 B.C.) he had given it a "place in the sun."

The work of Solon, the wise man and political reformer, had been supplemented by the work of the practical man, who combined forcefulness with far-reaching vision. The Athenians had received their training in the elementary principles of self-rule and had become aware of their part in the career of a great, forward-striding state. It now remained for Cleisthenes to complete the work of his predecessors.

Pisistratus' sons, Hippias and Hipparchus, continued their father's enlightened rule; but in 514 B.C. a private grievance caused Harmodius and Aristogiton to form a conspiracy for the overthrow of the tyranny. The plot only partly succeeded: Hipparchus was slain, and the two conspirators paid the penalty of death. It is only human that later ages should have elevated them in song and story to the rank of martyrs in the cause of popular liberty.

After the murder of his brother, Hippias was a changed man, and his rule degenerated into the kind of despotism so abhorrent to the Greek mind. The inevitable end came four years later (510 B.C.), when he was driven out of Athens with the help of the Spartans. In the civil strife that followed, Cleisthenes, a member of the noble Alcmaeonid family, which had been exiled by Pisistratus, came forward as the champion of democracy and gave Athens a democratic constitution which continued to function, with little interruption, for some two centuries.

The constitution devised by Cleisthenes furnishes another illustration of the relentless logic of Greek political thinking. To understand it aright, we shall have to go back to the earliest forms of Greek social organization. The Hellenic polis was made up not of individuals but of kindreds. The oldest social units date from days when men could conceive of no other ties uniting them than those of kinship. The handicap with which each Hellenic state started consisted of this heritage of the past, hallowed by time and inextricably interwoven with social custom and religious rite. Brotherhood, clan, and tribe, and the ancient loyalties they commanded, kept the Athenian state divided against itself; the four tribes especially constituted a permanent obstacle to union. These divisions sheltered further antagonisms, for local interests clashed as well: we hear of the Men of the Plain, the Hill Men, and the Men of the Coast as conflicting forces within the state.

Cleisthenes, with one bold stroke, broke up the whole system. The old brotherhoods, indeed, were allowed to remain, but only as centers of religious activities. The four old tribes were done away with as political institutions, and in their stead ten new ones were created. The formation of these new tribes shows the radicalism of Cleisthenes in the clearest light. He took the existing demes, or townships, of Attica as elements out of which to make his tribes; the city of Athens itself was divided into demes. The demes were then grouped, according to their location, into three groups: demes of the city, the plain, and the coast. These three groups were now divided each into ten trittyes (thirds), each third, or trittys, to be of approximately equal population. Finally, each of the ten new tribes was made by combining three trittyes, one from each of the three groups. As one historian puts it, "a system more artificial than the tribes and trittyes of Cleisthenes it might well pass the wit of man to devise."[1]

[1] E. M. Walker, in the *Cambridge Ancient History*, Vol. IV, p. 143.

The new tribes, which Cleisthenes, with the help of the wise and kindly god at Delphi, obligingly provided with substitutes for the "ancestors" once worshiped, cut across the ancient lines of division and compelled the citizens of different localities to agree upon common representatives in the new council.[1] The old council, based as it was upon the four old tribes, went by the board; the new council was made up of fifty representatives from each of the ten tribes. But Cleisthenes rightly saw that five hundred is too unwieldy a number to work efficiently; so, nothing daunted, he now proceeded to divide the year into ten artificial units of thirty-five or thirty-six days each, and allowed one tenth of the council to act as an executive committee (this was called a *prytany*), the chairmanship rotating among the members of the prytany day by day. In this way, since the selection of the members of the council in the course of time came more and more to be determined by lot, and since the law forbade the same person to serve on the council more than twice, a large minority of Athenian lads could confidently look forward to becoming president of the Athenian republic for a day.

The sovereign assembly, made up of all citizens and called together at stated intervals, passed on all matters laid before it by the prytany. Thus the Athenians practiced representative government in their council and the referendum in their assembly. It was democracy with a vengeance! The only free men not enjoying political rights were the *metics*, or settlers from other parts of Hellas; and as the political and economic importance of Athens increased, their numbers grew.

[1] To understand the boldness of Cleisthenes' innovation, the American student might imagine that at a critical period of our history some bold reformer, in order to suppress the activities of political machines within the states and, furthermore, to reconcile conflicting interests between the East, South, and West, should abolish the historic states within the Union and carve artificial states, one of which, for instance, might be made up of part of Pennsylvania, part of Georgia, and part of Nebraska, the voters of the new "state" to elect common representatives to a new congress.

In addition, there was a slave population, employed principally in domestic service and in the workshops of the artisans who could afford them. Their number too increased; but to regard the Athenian democracy for that reason as an aristocracy based upon slave labor — as is still occasionally done — is to misconceive completely its real character.

The only element lacking in the constitution of Cleisthenes was leadership, without which democracy is likely to be a sorry affair. While Cleisthenes made no provision for this, he tried to guard against the danger of individual ambition for power by one of the strangest measures ever written into any constitution. Once a year the sovereign people were to vote on the desirability of removing a citizen dangerous to the democracy. If a majority of the assembly agreed upon a certain name, — and at least six thousand votes had to be cast, — this man would go into honorable exile for ten years. This procedure was called *ostracism*, after the *ostraka*, or potsherds, which were used as ballots. This institution, a further example of Greek radicalism and of the subordination of the rights of the individual to the interests of the state, in the end proved harmful, and after a century of trial was allowed to fall into desuetude. But Cleisthenes knew his Athenians: he knew there would never be a lack of candidates for leadership; the Homeric motto "ever to be the best" was as potent a spur among the Athenians as elsewhere in Hellas. The real danger was rather the other way, and ostracism was probably as good a curb on individual ambition and as good a safeguard to the young democracy as could be devised.

The new tribes were also made the basis of the military organization. Each tribe contributed a regiment of hoplites and elected its general. The office of general, *strategos*, remained an elective office and gained in importance until in the days of Pericles it was the board of strategi which furnished the Athenian republic its prime minister and a directing hand.[1]

[1] On the constitutional development of Athens see W. R. Halliday, *The Growth of the City State* (Small, 1923), Lecture V.

The Persian Wars

The first two decades of the fifth century are marked by a great crisis which threatened to make an end of Hellas and reduce it to the status of a province of a mighty Eastern empire, Persia. What were the geographical and political divisions of Hellas in the opening days of the fifth century?

Geographically it falls into three main parts: Greece proper; to the west, Greater Greece (southern Italy) and Sicily; to the east, the cities of the Anatolian seaboard. Greece proper was divided into northern Greece, central Greece, and the Peloponnesus. Macedonia was not considered as belonging to the Greek world. Thessaly is the chief district of northern Greece. It is securely boxed in by mountain ranges which divide it from Macedonia to the north and the equally backward Epirus on the west; on the southern side Mt. Othrys blocks easy communication with central Greece. Protection on the sea side is afforded by the huge mountain wall of which Mt. Pelion and Mt. Ossa form the peaks; farther north Mt. Olympus, rising to a height of ten thousand feet, stands guard over the northeastern boundary of Thessaly. Thus isolated from the rest of Hellas, Thessaly, which boasts the largest and richest plain in Greece and its largest river, never played in Greek history the part to which its natural wealth entitled it. Its four cantons formed a confederacy, governed by an aristocracy of large landowners whose fields were tilled mostly by a serf class, the *penestae*.

In central Greece the chief state was Boeotia, which formed a loose confederacy headed by Thebes; but it was not politically united as Attica was under Athens. Boeotia, moreover, lacked good harbors, and to be excluded from the sea spelled backwardness in Hellas. The Athenians, between whom and the Boeotians there was no love lost, were wont to indulge their wit at the expense of their supposedly slow-witted neighbors. The territory of the Phocians and Locrians separated Boeotia from Thessaly. In Phocis was situated the oracle of Apollo, undoubtedly the most frequently visited Panhellenic shrine. The shrewdness of its college of priests, who profited by the information brought to them by visitors from everywhere, enabled Apollo to exert a deep influence over the affairs of Greece. No enterprise of any consequence was undertaken without consulting Apollo, who had taken a leading part in directing the Greek expansion. Attica formed the peninsula at the eastern extremity of central Greece, and by its favorable situation, which we have noted above, was destined soon to take the lead in Hellas. The western districts of central Greece, Aetolia and Acarnania, broken up by irregular mountain formations and without easy access to the sea, need not detain us; their role was a negligible one. The large island of Euboea, which flanks the eastern coast of central Greece, had on its seaboard no safe harbors affording protection against the prevailing northeast trade winds; and the Euripos, flowing between the island and the mainland, in ancient times proverbial for its treacherous currents, did not encourage seafaring. Nevertheless its two chief cities, Chalcis and Eretria, had taken an active part in the colonial expansion, and many cities of Chalcidice (off Macedonia), as well as in Greater Greece and Sicily, were founded by the seafarers of Euboea.

Finally there were the Peloponnesus and the isthmus which connected it with the body of Greece. It was owing to their favorable geographical location, giving them access to both the East and the West, that Corinth and Megara played a role in Greek history out of proportion to their territorial extent or their natural resources. They had taken a leading part in the colonial expansion. The most important of Megara's colonies were undoubtedly the settlements on the Bosporus, Byzantium and Chalcedon; but the Megarians had been active in the west as well. Corinth had found an outlet for her energies chiefly in the west, along the coast of western Greece, where the island of Corcyra held her most important colony, and in Sicily, where Syracuse was her chief foundation.

In the Peloponnesus itself, Sparta, as we have seen, had gained the hegemony after she had added Messenia to Laconia. Elis, with its large fertile plain, was among her oldest allies. Here was situated Olympia, where every four years the Greeks united to honor Olympian Zeus and celebrate the Olympic games. Inland Arcadia, home of shepherds and the great god Pan, was next to join the Spartan alliance. Only Argos held aloof, and the narrow strip of land, on the northern coast of the Peloponnesus, which preserved the ancient name of the Achaeans. These Achaean towns had done their share in the colonization of the west, where some of the most flourishing of the towns of Greater Greece, like Sybaris and Croton, testified to the shrewdness of the Achaean fathers in choosing a favorable site for the dwellers-away-from-home.

When we now turn to the west, we shall find Greater Greece the home of a large number of city-states. Farthest to the north were Euboean Cyme (Cumae) and its daughter Neapolis (Naples). From there southward the Greeks had established themselves along the coast down to the toe of Italy and in the heel as well. These colonies were chiefly Achaean, although the longest-lived of all was Laconian Taras (Tarentum). They profited from their favorable location to amass a wealth that became proverbial: Sybaris at one time was the last word in luxury and refinement as the Greeks understood it. Sheep-raising and agriculture went hand in hand with a vigorous trade with the less civilized tribes of Italy, who shared with the Etruscans the eager desire for Greek wares.

Sicily was almost equally divided between the Chalcidian colonies of the northeastern half and the Dorian colonies of the southeastern half. The western extremity of the island remained under the control of Carthage, the great Phoenician trading center in the western Mediterranean. Had these western Greeks formed a national union they might have driven the Carthaginians out of the waters of Greater Greece; but these western cities were as quarrelsome as their mother cities in the homeland, — perhaps even more so, for there was here much more to quarrel about. The ancient rivalry of Sybaris and Croton, to cite but one instance, had ended in the complete destruction of the former. As we have remarked, this western world became the America of ancient Greece and far surpassed the homeland in wealth. But its position was a precarious one: the jealousy of the Carthaginian traders, the daring of Etruscan pirates, and the dangerous proximity of the Samnites and other native hill-dwellers, to whom this Greek wealth was a standing temptation, combined to render their position far less safe than that of their brethren in the homeland.

Even more precarious was the position of the Greek towns in the east, on the Asiatic side of the Aegean. Settled there since the days of the migrations which had forced the Ionic and Aeolic-speaking Greeks to found new settlements across the sea, they too had flourished exceedingly, and in the course of time had expanded by way of the Hellespont and the Propontis into the Black Sea, the shores of which were dotted with Greek colonies, chiefly of Ionian origin. Miletus alone is known to have founded no less than forty of these. In their Asiatic home these Greek towns were faced by a more pressing danger than those in the west, and were no more able to present a united front against that danger. Here was an ancient country, and most of the oldest Greek settlements occupied the site of earlier strongholds. The Hittite empire, once mistress of central Anatolia, had long since passed away; but with the beginning of the eighth century a new power, the Lydian kingdom, grew into being, and its capital, Sardis, was only a day's journey distant from the coastland held by the Greeks. From its earliest days the Lydian kingdom pursued an aggressive policy against the Greek towns, which occupied all outlets to the sea; and gradually the Greek towns became tributary to the Lydian kings. But the Lydian overlordship seems not seriously to have impeded the political and economic development of the Greek towns. On the

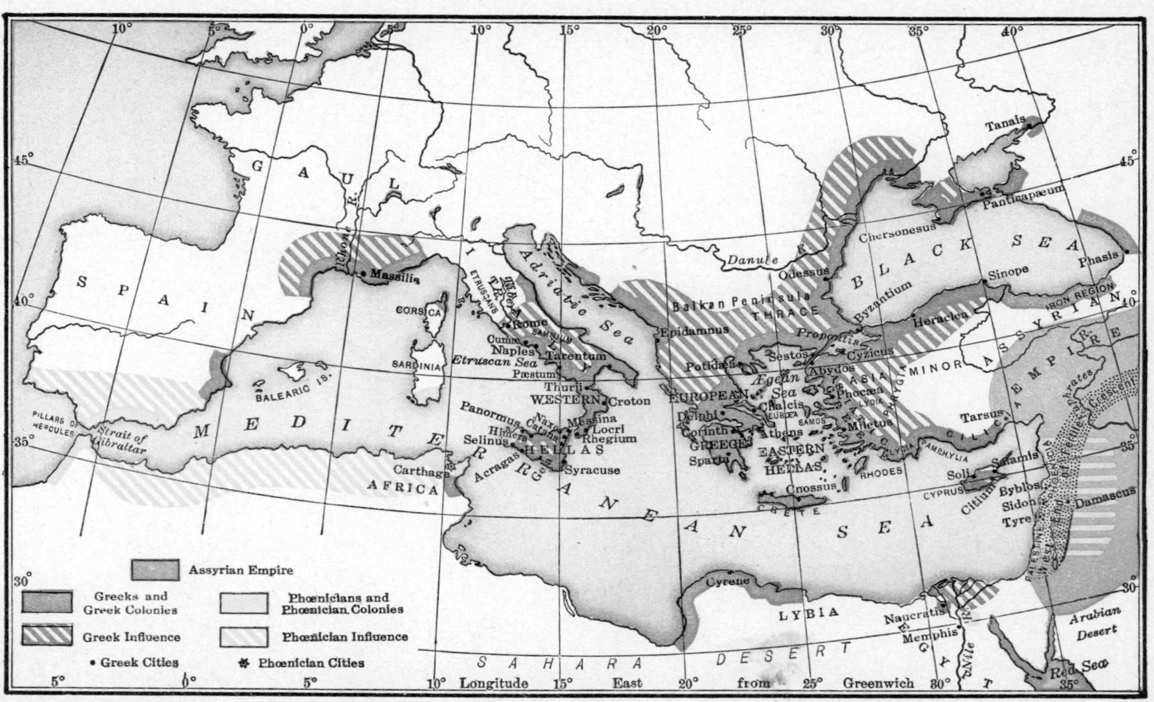

Colonial Expansion of the Greeks and Phœnicians down to the Sixth Century B.C.

contrary, there is no question that the close proximity of the ancient East and the free intercourse with the rich hinterland stimulated not only the industrial and commercial life of the Ionians but their intellectual and artistic development as well. Miletus, for instance, not only took a large share of the manufacture of textiles, metalwork, and dyes, but also formulated the first of Hellenic philosophies. Moreover, Lydian proximity does not appear greatly to have hampered the Greek city-states in their favorite pastime of fighting among themselves; Miletus, again, carried on an intermittent warfare with the neighboring island of Samos to its heart's content. Nor did the Lydians interfere greatly with the internal political evolution in these Greek towns. Here too the rule of the ancient aristocracies was challenged by new groups, and here too tyrannies formed the intermediate stage between aristocracy and democracy. Indeed, the process of intercourse between Greek and Lydian was in a fair way to obliterating racial differences: Lydia grew increasingly Hellenized, and the ambition of its last king, the famous Croesus (560–546 B.C.), whose wealth is proverbial, was to have his kingdom enter the family of Hellenic polities, whose superiority to the rest of the world he plainly perceived.

In the meantime an event of momentous significance had taken place. The Assyrian Empire, which for a century and a half had held the Asiatic world at its mercy, had fallen. The Medes took Nineveh in 612 B.C. The Chaldeans fell heir to the western half of the Assyrian Empire. Egypt received a new lease of life, during which the Greeks found a welcome within its territory in the settlement of Naucratis. The Medes and their kinsmen, the Persians, consolidated the northern and eastern possessions of Assyria, including Assyria itself. This brought the Medes into close proximity to Lydia. A clash between them, according to Greek tradition, was averted only by a solar eclipse which halted the armies as they faced one another. The Halys River was agreed upon as the boundary line between Mede and Lydian; and an alliance was made between the two parties, confirmed by the marriage of Astyages, the Mede, to a Lydian princess (585 B.C.). The fall of Lydia was postponed for another generation.

By the middle of the century the ruling Median dynasty was overthrown by the Persian Cyrus. Croesus thought his opportunity had come, and, misled by an ambiguous reply from the god at Delphi, crossed the Halys River. His overthrow followed in 546 B.C. and produced a sensation in Hellas, the echo of which we hear in the story of the meeting of Croesus and Solon. Lydia was reduced to the status of a province of the Persian Empire, and the Greek cities whose sympathies had been with Lydia were conquered in turn until, by 540 B.C., all the Anatolian Greeks, including the islands of Lesbos and Chios (Samos alone seems to have maintained its independence for a time, under the tyrant Polycrates), had passed under the control of Persia.

In 538 B.C. Cyrus took Babylon, and the Chaldean Empire was added to the dominion of the Persians. Cyrus' son and successor, Cambyses, conquered Egypt (525 B.C.). Thus Persian rule united the territories extending from the Greek littoral of Anatolia in the west to the Indus in the east and from the Persian Gulf to the Caspian Sea. Far-away Bactria as well as Parthia, the Armenian highlands, the Phoenician coast towns, Egypt, and Babylon — all paid tribute and rendered military service to the "King of Kings."

The Persians and their kinsmen, the Medes, belong to the Iranian branch of the Indo-European race, which includes the Greeks and Romans as well as the conquerors of India. In fact, the Persians in their dominant characteristics bear a close resemblance to the Romans. A practical people with a genius for organization, great conquerors and great road-builders, tolerant (on the whole) and enlightened, their methods in empire-building shine in comparison with those of the Egyptians, Babylonians, and Assyrians.[1]

[1] On the subject of the ancient empires see the illuminating discussion of Rostovtzeff, *Ancient History*, Vol. I, Chap. X.

The consolidation and organization of this vast empire was completed by the third of the Persian kings, Darius (522–486 B.C.). It was divided into some twenty *satrapies* (provinces, governed by a satrap); and the Asiatic Greeks, now, under the supervision of a Persian satrap, responsible to a king dwelling some fifteen hundred miles away, felt themselves lost. Moreover, the Persian satrap was only too much disposed to check the democratic aspirations of the Greeks; he preferred to deal with tyrants, who should feel under obligation to Persian power for the positions they occupied. Hence a general state of suppressed indignation, of restlessness and discontent, prevailed among the Anatolian Greeks; and the spectacle of their forlorn condition called forth feelings of sympathy in the hearts of their kinsmen in the old country. Was the most flourishing and most progressive section of the Greek world to remain subject to an Oriental despot? That this despot was probably a more humane and enlightened ruler than Croesus had ever been, made little difference to them, even if they were aware of it. But Croesus had sent rich offerings to Apollo in Delphi; he had helped to build the great temple at Ephesus. Darius did none of these things, and seemed singularly insensible to Greek superiority over ordinary barbarians.

Now this same Darius undertook a campaign that carried him into Thrace and to the Danube, which he crossed. He entered the territory of the nomad Scythians, and if he aimed at Scythian conquest his campaign was a dismal failure (512 B.C.). The occasion and the real object of the campaign remain obscure. The facts that matter are these: first, that he did gain a foothold in the Balkan Peninsula; second, that the Asiatic Greeks took the campaign to be a failure, — it proved to them what they were only too eager to believe, that even the "King of Kings" could be successfully challenged. Their courage revived, and when the opportunity came they rose in rebellion against the galling Persian yoke (499 B.C.). This rebellion, in the beginning of which the

Athenians assisted with twenty ships, and the Eretrians of Euboea with five, opened with an assault upon Sardis, which was accidentally set on fire and burned. Had the Greeks remained united, as they were in the opening year of the war, the event might have been different. But at the crucial sea fight at Lade (a small island near Miletus) part of the Greek fleet deserted without striking a blow, and the battle was lost. After a heroic resistance Miletus was taken and all but completely destroyed (494 B.C.). The sack of Miletus made a profound impression in Hellas, especially at Athens; and when Darius, two years later, sent another expedition into Thrace and gained the submission of Macedon, which made him a neighbor of Greece, Athens duly apprehended the significance of his policy and its danger to her own existence.

Now we come to that heroic struggle which diminutive Hellas waged against the organized might of Persia, and which ended in the complete victory of Hellas and, in particular, gave Athens a faith in herself that was to carry her to a position of unprecedented power and influence in Hellas. The story of this momentous conflict has been told so often and so well that it would be a work of supererogation to set forth at length the details; yet no student of ancient Hellas can afford to remain ignorant of these details. Above all, he should consult the accounts the Greeks themselves have left us. Our two chief witnesses are the contemporary Aeschylus, writer of tragedies, who himself fought in the Athenian ranks, and Herodotus, oldest of the historians, who, while not a contemporary, was not too far removed in time from the events to be able to consult eyewitnesses and participants in the great war.[1] Here we must content ourselves with the barest outlines of the story.

[1] Aeschylus' *Persians* and Herodotus, Books VII and VIII, ought to form the minimum reading, to which might be added Plutarch's *Themistocles*. The best account in English remains that of G. Grote in his *History of Greece* (especially Chapters XL and XLI). For a more recent account see the *Cambridge Ancient History*, Vol. IV, Chaps. VIII–X, and H. R. James, *Our Hellenic Heritage*, Vol. I, Chaps. XII–XV, pp. 279–377.

In 490 B.C. Darius sent a new expeditionary force, this time aimed at Athens. The fleet crossed the Aegean and landed in Euboea. Eretria was sacked. The Persian army now landed on Attic soil near Marathon. The Athenians, aided only by a loyal band from Plataea, a neighboring Boeotian town, went out in force and, although outnumbered, proved once for all the superiority of the Greek hoplites over Eastern infantry. The Athenians were ably led by Miltiades, who, himself at one time a tyrant on the Thracian Chersonese, where he had furthered Athenian interests until driven out by the Persians, gave the Athenians the benefit of his experience of Persian warfare.

Darius did not live to avenge the ignominious defeat of Marathon. His son Xerxes was prevented by the rebellion of Egypt from carrying out his father's plans against Greece for some years. The Greeks thus gained a ten years' respite. In Athens, meanwhile, there appeared a man who was destined to become the savior of Hellas, — Themistocles, perhaps the most gifted and versatile of all the statesmen ancient Greece produced. He combined a high order of intelligence with vision and incredible resourcefulness, and possessed a gift for persuasion in an eminent degree; moreover, he was not particularly scrupulous about the means he employed to gain his ends. One fact was clear to him beyond all others: that the future of Athens was on the sea and that only on the sea could a decision be sought between Persia and Hellas. Once masters of the Aegean, the Athenians not only could safely defy the Persians but could wrest from them control of the Anatolian coast as well. First of all he persuaded the Athenians to make the Piraeus their harbor, rather than the open bay at Phalerum. Then a quarrel with Aegina, the Dorian island in the Saronic Gulf, which had been a thorn in the side of Corinth as well, gave him his opportunity. The discovery of a new and rich vein in the Laureian silver mines had unexpectedly enriched the Athenian treasury. Upon his urgent advice the Athenians devoted the money to shipbuilding, ostensibly against the Aeginetans (482 B.C.). The result was that when the crisis came the Athenians had at their disposal some two hundred war vessels, a greater fleet than the combined total of the rest of the Greek continental states. Next Themistocles tried to organize the Greek states for common defense. The preparations of the Persians, well known to the Greeks, were planned on such a large scale that many of the Greeks, including the well-informed Apollo at Delphi, despaired of offering successful resistance. The Persian king evidently proposed to crush Hellas by sheer weight of numbers. Herodotus gives us fantastic figures: the land army alone numbered one million seven hundred thousand fighters, and a huge fleet of war vessels and transports in proportionate numbers was to accompany the army. Even after discounting Herodotus' exaggerations we cannot question that the Persian hordes were coming in so overwhelming numbers that the Greek states could not hope to overcome them in open battle.

In the spring of 480 B.C., when all preparations for the equipment and the safe conduct of the expeditionary forces had been made with Persian thoroughness, the march began. The Hellespont had been bridged, and the fleet sailed along the coast, accompanying the army.

The first plan of the Greeks, to hold the pass leading from Macedonia into Thessaly at the vale of Tempe, had to be abandoned; for the coast offered no shelter or base to the fleet, and the enemy was coming by both land and sea. Thessaly, then, had no choice but to submit to the invaders. The mountain ranges dividing Thessaly from central Greece offered a better opportunity for resistance. At the narrow pass of Thermopylae, Leonidas, one of the Spartan kings, with three hundred Spartans and some thousands of allies, took his stand while the Greek fleet rode at anchor at the northern end of Euboea, at Cape Artemisium. The plan of defense, in which the land forces and the fleet would cooperate, was excellent, and it might have succeeded in blocking the Persian advance, if the Spartans and the other allies had seen fit to occupy Thermopylae in sufficient numbers. But the Spartans, interested chiefly in the defense of the Peloponnesus, were not minded to take great risks beyond the isthmus. Their shortsightedness caused the position eventually to be turned, and the three hundred Spartans died a heroic death. They had failed to save Greece, but it cannot be denied that they had set an example of stubborn courage worthy of the Spartan name.

The defeat at Thermopylae meant the loss of central Greece and Attica. Boeotia followed the example of Thessaly and Medized. The people of Attica left their beloved Athens and had to stand by helpless while Athens went up in flames. The Greek fleet gathered in the waters of Salamis. And now divided councils prevailed among the Greeks. Spartans and Corinthians insisted that the isthmus be defended, and that the Greek fleet gather there. Themistocles saw that the Greek ships would be no match for even the diminished numbers of the Persian fleet (it had suffered from more than one disastrous storm) in the open waters by the isthmus. When, in spite of his remonstrances, the opposing view threatened to prevail and the tragic fiasco of Lade seemed about to be re-enacted, he outwitted both friend and foe by sending a secret message to Xerxes, urging him to close the entrances to the bay of Salamis and prevent the Greek fleet from escaping. Xerxes acted upon this advice, and on the following day, in the narrow waters of Salamis, where the Persians could derive no advantage from their numbers, the Greeks won a complete victory.

This victory proved decisive. With the control of the sea lost, affairs wore an entirely different aspect to the pusillanimous Xerxes and his counselors. An immediate retreat to Asia was determined upon. The most able of the generals, however, with the best part of the army, remained behind to renew the attack in the spring of the following year (479 B.C.). Although even then the Spartans were slow in the performance of their duty, allowing Attica to be overrun a second time, they finally went out in full force with their Peloponnesian allies, and on the battlefield of Plataea Spartan valor dealt a death blow to Persian ambition for dominion in Europe. In the same year a Greek fleet which had crossed the Aegean offered battle at Mycale, and once more Greek arms prevailed. From then on the tables were turned, and Greece became the aggressor.

In western Greece, on the island of Sicily, a similar drama was enacted, with the Carthaginians taking the part of the invaders. The Carthaginian armament was defeated at Himera, in a bloody battle which, according to Greek fancy, took place on the very day the battle of Salamis was fought. Did the Carthaginians, whose Phoenician kinsmen fought in the Persian fleet, act in collusion with Persia or was the fact of the double invasion a mere coincidence? We do not know, but it is certain that the Greek victory in the western part of Hellas was no less decisive, and that the danger of another Carthaginian invasion could be discounted for a long time to come.

The Athenian Empire

Marathon, Salamis, Plataea — these are names of great historic significance. These battles had settled the question whether an Eastern monarch was to rule the Mediterranean. For there can be no doubt that if Greece had been converted into a Persian satrapy western Greece in turn would have fallen under the same Persian dominion. Persia might have anticipated Rome by some centuries and converted the Mediterranean, geographically a unit, into a political unit as well. It may well be doubted, however, whether Persia, in spite of certain outward resemblances to imperial Rome, would have succeeded in permanently maintaining its hold on the Mediterranean. The Persians labored under too many Eastern handicaps. Eastern habits of life and government were too deep-rooted to allow any group within their geographical limits to escape the Oriental influence. The Persian may have sprung from the same ancestral stock as the Roman and Greek, but his habitat in the East had made an Oriental out of him. And the ways of the East can live and flourish in the East only.

Another question is how Persian overlordship would have affected the development of Greek civilization, and here it is beyond all doubt that the free play of creative forces which found their release in the free city-states of Hellas, and first and foremost in Athens, would have been stifled under Persian dominion. Indeed, it was from the defeat of mighty Persia that Athens drew her inspiration; and if the Western world owes its civilization to the pioneer work of Hellas, it must acknowledge its debt of gratitude to these Hellenic sailors and soldiers who would not suffer their country to be smothered under the Eastern avalanche.

The years separating the victory of Plataea (479 B.C.) from the outbreak of the Hellenic World War (431 B.C.), known as the Fifty-Year Period, saw the rise of Athenian imperialism, a new phenomenon on the political horizon, which threatened to make an end of Greek particularism. The success Athens achieved in spite of some setbacks seemed to forecast the doom of the city-state system of Greece; in fact, she came near achieving national union for Hellas. But in the end she failed. It is our task now to trace the growth of Athenian imperialism.

After Plataea and Mycale there remained the task of liberating the Hellenic cities still under Persian control. When Sparta showed herself unfit to lead in this enterprise (she was essentially a land power, and a Peloponnesian power at that, lacking the resources for oversea campaigning), the part of leading the Greeks in their war on Persia naturally fell to Athens. Her patriotism had triumphantly passed the severest tests, and she seemed to have a greater fund of intelligence as well. A confederacy of Aegean cities and islands was formed. It was resolved that they should contribute, for the common defense, men, ships, and money. But it so happened that many of the towns were too small to furnish any appreciable military forces, and were allowed to assist with money only. The towns were duly assessed by the incorruptible Aristides, the most just of all Athenians, and presently some half-million dollars in our money (an immense sum for those days) was annually poured into the common treasury. This was placed for safekeeping on the sacred island of Delos, which had long been the central site of the worship of Ionian Apollo. The larger islands, such as Naxos, Chios, Lesbos, and Samos, placed their ships and men at the disposal of the confederacy; the rest were almost uniformly content to contribute money. The result was that the confederacy practically financed Athenian sea power. The Athenians did their work rapidly and thoroughly. The northern Aegean, the Hellespont, and the coast of Anatolia were freed. The battle of the Eurymedon, in 468 B.C. (?), cleared the Persians out of their last strongholds on the Greek littoral.

The leader in the Athenian enterprise had been Cimon, the son of Miltiades. Themistocles had seen to it that the walls of Athens were rebuilt in spite of Spartan obstruction, and that the Piraeus was fortified. Then the usual penalty of eminence in Athens had overtaken him: he was ostracized and eventually ended his days as the pensioner of the Persian king! Cimon had pursued a consistent policy: war on Persia, and peace and friendship with Sparta. There was, however, an opposing faction which believed Cimon's policy of peace with Sparta to be based on pure self-delusion. Sparta, the erstwhile leader of Greece, they held, could not but view the sudden rise of Athenian power with uneasiness and chagrin; the hope of permanently reconciling her to Athens' new position seemed to them chimerical. Subsequent developments appeared to bear them out. Disaster overtook Sparta; an earthquake, attended with great loss of life, laid the city in ruins; the Messenians rose once more in armed rebellion, and their resistance proved more stubborn than was expected. Finally Sparta invited the assistance of Athens, still nominally her ally as she had been since the days of Xerxes' invasion. The Athenians under Cimon responded with alacrity, only to be curtly dismissed when their first attempts to take the Messenian stronghold had failed. That was Cimon's undoing: he was ostracized (461 B.C.), and the opposition, headed by Ephialtes and (after his assassination) by Pericles, now directed Athenian policies.

The ensuing thirty years (461–431 B.C.) are known as the Age of Pericles. There was inaugurated an ambitious program which included (1) aggressive warfare on Persia, on what heretofore had been admittedly Persian territory; (2) extension of Athenian power in central and northern Greece; (3) a more thoroughgoing application of the democratic principles of the constitution of Cleisthenes.

The first half of the Periclean Age marked an outburst of energy on the part of Athens that must have amazed the rest of Hellas. At one time Persia was attacked in Cyprus and Egypt; Thessaly, Phocis and Locris, Boeotia, Megara, Aegina, and Achaea, — all were for some time during these years willing or unwilling allies of Athens. But this part of the program ended in eventual failure. Except for Aegina, which became a member of the Delian League, Athens, at the peace concluded in 445 B.C., was forced to renounce her claim to leadership on the Greek continent; and the disaster which overtook her attempts in Cyprus and Egypt led to a peace with Persia which limited the activities of the Athenian fleet to Aegean waters (448 B.C).

The Delian Confederacy, which from its beginning had been a confederacy in name only, the logic of events had converted into an empire, and some two hundred cities paid tribute to Athens. To these it had been made abundantly clear that attempts at withdrawal from the league would not be countenanced; assertions of independence on the part of individual members had only called forth stern measures of repression on the part of Athens. Thus even in Cimon's day Naxos and Thasos had lost their fleet and independence, and others had since experienced the strong hand of Athens. In other ways too Athens began to adopt the ways of imperial powers. Most galling was her custom of establishing groups of her own citizens as "lot-holders" on territory of the confederate states, where they formed in effect Athenian garrisons. Even in their domestic politics these cities were bidden to adopt a system modeled after the Athenian democracy — a measure by no means unwelcome to the majorities in these towns. Finally, the "allies" were constrained to bring their important lawsuits to Athens, to be tried by the Athenian lawcourts. Although this may have ensured a more even-handed and uniform administration of justice within the empire, and although these visits to Athens by men from all parts of the Aegean must have contributed to making the allies "empire-conscious," yet this exercise of Athenian power provoked a great deal of resentment.

The democratization of the Athenian commonwealth was carried out to the letter. (We postpone a discussion of it until a later chapter.) Meanwhile, especially after the conclusion of the peace in 445 B.C., Pericles executed a grand building program. The Athens which the Persians had left a heap of smoking ruins was now, in its public buildings and monuments, to present an appearance worthy of its imperial role. The confederate treasury, which had been transferred to Athens (454 B.C.), furnished the money.

Thus in 431 B.C., the year of the outbreak of the Hellenic World War, Athens occupied a unique position in Hellas. The most populous town in Greece (the inhabitants of Attica may have numbered some three hundred thousand, half of whom formed the citizen population), it was the center of commercial and industrial Greece as well as the center of its artistic and intellectual life. Some fifty thousand aliens (including their families) had been attracted within its borders, and the slave population may have amounted to one hundred thousand. This city united under its rule the Aegean Islands, the littoral of the northern Aegean, the Hellespont and Propontis, and the coast towns of Asia Minor. The empire had been divided first into five and later into four districts for administrative purposes, and contained more than two hundred city-states, with a total population of perhaps two million. These cities derived a certain economic advantage from their inclusion in the empire, in which a brisk commercial intercourse, across waters rendered safe by the Athenian navy, enabled all to find markets for their products. It was an impressive demonstration of what sea power meant and means. Athens itself by this time was united to the harbor of Piraeus by long walls, which rendered the city impregnable on the land side. In command of the sea it could safely defy any Greek power or combination of powers.

The Hellenic World War

The fifty years separating the Persian Wars from the suicidal conflict of the Greek states, which has been misnamed the Peloponnesian War, had seen Athens, under the inspired leadership of Pericles, become the focal point of Hellenic life. But the same period had witnessed the birth and growth of a new political phenomenon which loomed in startling opposition to the prevailing sentiments of Hellas — the new imperialism of Athens. The question was how long the rest of Greece would allow Athens to go her way in disregard of the public opinion of Greece.

The one political achievement of Hellas was the creation of the city-state, a community in which, by a nice balancing of conflicting interests, the members might live governed by laws of their own making; but the essential condition of its being was its autonomy, its political and economic independence. Thus Hellas had become a land of numerous independent city-states. Under the stress of the Persian Wars they had been forced into some sort of a union, and even before 500 B.C. some kind of interstate organization had been attempted by Sparta and the Peloponnesian League. But Sparta claimed no more than leadership in war; except for a penchant she had for favoring the rule of the few over the rule of the many, she professed to leave the members of the Peloponnesian League complete independence.

The imperial policy of Athens, however, ran counter to Greek political ideals in that it abrogated this right of independence for the members of the Delian League. In fact, the city-states within the league were tributary to Athens, who held over them the whip hand of her naval power. It was this circumstance which made her Ionian daughters look upon the mother city as a tyrant rather than a parent; the Dorian cousins beheld the spectacle with dismay and horror, as a phenomenon un-Hellenic and subversive of Hellenic principles. And indeed, given the Greek political ideal, with particularism as its cardinal principle, the rule of one over many was a self-contradictory thing. There was the added fact that Athens, in the ruthless Greek way, had taken no trouble to sugar-coat the bitter pill; nay, for some time now she had been giving herself airs, posing as a superior being and talking of her mission in Hellas. When, now, we remember that Athens had been a comparatively obscure state until Marathon and Salamis had given her supreme self-reliance, we shall begin to understand what feelings of indignation this upstart city aroused among neighboring Megara, Corinth, and Boeotia, until even slow-moving Sparta was stirred to fear and anger. The restless ambition of Athens, her high-handed methods, her self-righteousness and calm assumption of superiority, had finally produced among the states of Hellas that same dangerous state of mind that Germany at one time aroused among the European states: they lived in a constant state of apprehension, fearful of the sudden moves that their energetic neighbor was wont to make. Gradually the rest of Greece drew closer to Sparta, until insensibly Hellas was divided into two opposing camps, the

Spartan and the Athenian. Thus a precarious balance of power was established, as it was in prewar Europe; but once the peace was broken, it was clear that all the Hellenic states would be drawn into the maelstrom of the war. It was only a question of time when the breaking point would be reached and the pent-up feelings of hatred and fear vent themselves in the fury of war.

In 433 and 432 B.C. a series of events brought on the crisis. Corinth, once more at war with Corcyra, found herself baffled by the "defensive" alliance that Corcyra had concluded with Athens. The Corinthian colony of Potidaea, which had been forced to enter the Athenian Empire, received harsh treatment at the hands of Athens. To cap the climax, Athens excluded her little Dorian neighbor, Megara, from all the harbors of the empire. At this last most wanton display of Athenian power, we may imagine, the indignation of the Greeks knew no bounds. The Peloponnesian League convened at Sparta in the fall of 432 B.C. and heard, with emphatic approval, the Corinthians denounce the Athenians and blame the Spartans for their indifference to the wrongs inflicted on Hellas. Thucydides, the historian of the war, reports their speech, which admirably reflects the exasperation and the general state of alarm prevailing in Greece at the time. We cannot forbear quoting part of the speech.

You have never even fully considered what sort of men the Athenians are with whom you will have to fight and how very, how utterly different they are from you. For they are given to innovation and quick to form plans and to put their decisions into execution, whereas you are disposed merely to keep what you have, to devise nothing new, and, when you do take action, not to carry to completion even what is indispensable. Again, they are bold beyond their strength, venturesome beyond their better judgment, and sanguine in the face of dangers; while your way is to do less than your strength warrants, to distrust even what your judgment is sure of, and when dangers come to despair of deliverance. Nay more, they are prompt in decision, while you are dilatory; they stir abroad, while you are perfect stay-at-homes; for they expect by absence from home to gain something, while you are afraid that, if you go out after something, you may imperil even what you have. If victorious over their enemies, they pursue their advantage to the utmost; if beaten, they fall back as little as possible. Moreover they use their bodies in the service of their country as though they were the bodies of quite other men, but their minds as though they were wholly their own, so as to accomplish anything on her behalf. . . . In this way they toil with hardships and dangers, all their life long; and least of all men they enjoy what they have because they are always seeking more, because they think their only holiday is to do their duty, and because they regard untroubled peace as a far greater calamity than laborious activity. Therefore if a man should sum up and say that they were born neither to keep quiet themselves nor to let other men have peace, he would simply speak the truth.[1]

The Lacedaemonian League voted that the Athenians had broken the treaty.[2] Thus responsibility for the outbreak of hostilities was laid upon the Athenians; the Spartans maintained their hand was forced, but that they could not ignore their plain duty in the matter. This gave them a moral issue; and though they did not find the happy phrase that might express their lofty purpose, it was no doubt their intention "to make the world safe for the city-state."

Pericles, who saw that the war would inevitably come some day, advised against any compromise and bade the Athenians accept the challenge. What was to be the outcome of this conflict, which soon was to involve nearly all the Greek states of the continent and the Aegean, and finally to involve the distant west as well? On land the allies were undisputed masters. On the sea the power of Athens was equally beyond dispute, and the Athenians had the necessary financial resources to remain in control. They could afford to allow the Spartans and their allies to lay waste Attica, themselves secure behind their walls, and retaliate by sudden attacks

[1] Thucydides, Book I, Chap. 70. The translation is that of C. Forster Smith, Loeb Library.

[2] This was the thirty-year treaty of peace concluded in 445 B.C.

Map Plate, Patented July 5, 1921 · Method of Making Maps, Patented July 5, 1921

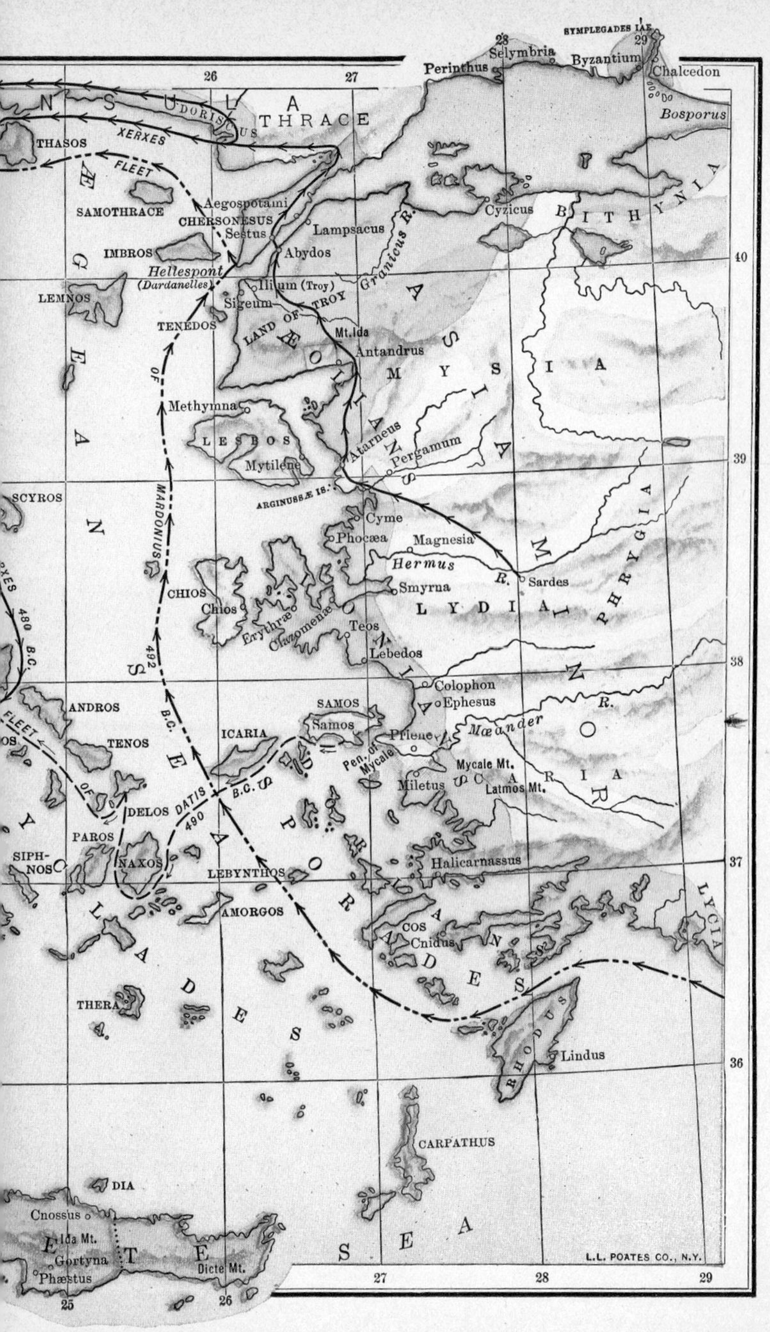

on the Laconian coasts from the sea. It seemed to Pericles and other clear-sighted men that the war would end in a stalemate. And so it might have done if the Athenians had followed Pericles' advice to hold on firmly to their possessions and to make no attempt to extend their dominion.

In the opening years of the war the Athenians suffered irreparable loss through the outbreak of the plague and the death of Pericles. The plague robbed Athens of between one fourth and one third of its population; what was worse, it made havoc with the Athenian morale. Thucydides has given us a famous description of the disease itself, its symptoms and its course, and in unforgettable pages has described the frightful demoralization it caused among the people.[1] Athens never recovered from this blow, against which not even the foresight of Pericles could have guarded. But Pericles himself died in 429 B.C., and with him the steadying hand was lost to the Athenian ship of state. For more than thirty years the Athenian democracy had enjoyed the blessing without which any democracy is at a disadvantage in comparison with a state governed by a single will or a strongly intrenched minority — an enlightened leadership. Under his guidance Athens had pursued a consistent course that had placed the city in a position of eminence such as he thought she deserved in Hellas, both on account of the heroic sacrifices she had made and the services she had rendered to the cause of Hellenic freedom in the conflict with Persia, and on account of her citizens' devoted patriotism, of which the rest of Hellas had been of late years the amazed beholder. Pericles had known how to enjoy the continued favor and the loyal support of his fellow citizens without ever surrendering his own convictions of right and wrong. Always in command of the situation, he was at the same time the master and the servant of his people; his personal integrity had been beyond question. The Athenians never found one to

[1] Thucydides, Book II, Chaps. 49–54.

take his place.[1] But for the calamities that overtook Hellas (that Spartan king who, upon invading Attica, said, "This day will be the beginning of great evils to the Greeks," had little conception of the full meaning of his words) neither the plague nor the death of Pericles can be blamed. The fact is that within the Greek world at large there had accumulated the fuel for a conflagration which, when once started, was well-nigh unquenchable.

First, there was the racial cleavage which divided Hellas into two main groups, the Dorian and the Ionian, a racial division which may remind us of that between Teuton and Latin in modern Europe. The deep-seated animosity between Dorians and Ionians had its origin in a fundamental difference in temperament. In the comparison between the two drawn for us by Thucydides (quoted above) we may find the explanation of this antagonism. The stolid Dorians, conservative to the extreme, slow-moving but sure of themselves, aristocratic in temper, looked with a combination of contempt and dislike on the volatile Ionians, versatile, enterprising, and resourceful, but lacking that stability of character which the Dorians prized above all other things — a race whose turbulent democracies offended the Doric sense of order. The war gave an opportunity for these smoldering animosities to burst into flame; indeed, it was the chronic antagonism between Dorians and Ionians in Sicily which provided the Athenians with the pretext for intervening in the affairs of that distant island.

But there was another, more grievous division which ranged Greek against Greek throughout Hellas. This was found within the individual city-states. As we have seen, it was only in rare cases that the wisdom of the lawgiver and the spirit of compromise had brought about a lasting reconciliation between the interests of the many and the privileges

[1] See Thucydides, Book II, Chap. 65, a sober tribute of a great historian to a great statesman. For a touching example of Pericles' integrity see Thucydides, Book II, Chap. 13.

of the few. Not many cities had had a Solon; in most of them there was a chronic division between the party of the oligarchs and that of the democrats. *Stasis*, that is, party strife, was a standing evil in Hellas; and the smaller the individual political units were, the more intense was the party feeling. Through the outbreak of the war, with the Spartans the acknowledged supporters of oligarchic factions and the Athenians the defenders of democracy, this party passion found its release. The hour had come at last for ancient hatreds, for the sense of wrongs long endured, for the desire of revenge, to burst forth in all their naked ugliness. As the war went on, the savagery of Greeks against Greeks increased until their very senses were dulled by the spectacle of the atrocities committed, and until, as Thucydides says, the very meaning of words changed: to be honest and frank was to be a simpleton and a fool; to be moderate and level-headed in the midst of a distracted world was to be a traitor and a coward; to be utterly reckless was accounted true bravery; and to divest oneself of all sense of honor and all scruple was held to be the most convincing proof of cleverness. The entire passage in Thucydides,[1] with its searching analysis of the demoralization caused by the war, should be read by every student of ancient Greece and, let us add, of modern Europe as well. A more damning indictment of war would be hard to find, and Thucydides is not a "pacifist." The brutal doctrine of the right of the stronger was proclaimed and acted upon throughout Hellas until the most gifted people the world had seen were in danger of sinking to the level of savages. War, said Thucydides, is a rough schoolmaster, and, he might have added, the Greeks were apt pupils.

A detailed account of this war lies beyond the scope of the present work. We shall be content to summarize its principal phases. The first ten years of warfare proved indecisive and led to a stalemate, signalized by a peace patched up be-

[1] Book III, Chaps. 82–83.

tween Athens and Sparta (421 B.C.). But the hopes of those who thought that this bitter warfare could end thus were as futile as the hopes of those moderates in the World War who prayed for a "peace without victory." The passions unleashed could not be stilled so easily. The allies on both sides refused to abide by the peace terms. The Athenians themselves only awaited leadership to engage in some new enterprise. That it was Alcibiades who proved the mischief-maker was but an accident; had there been no Alcibiades, posterity would have blamed some other Athenian for taking the lead. The important fact is that the impulse to action came from the people itself.

Alcibiades, a nephew of Pericles, was as distinguished for his family connections and his own undeniable talents as he was notorious for his reckless manner of life and his lack of principle. Peace denied him the opportunity for distinction which he craved. Athenian imperialism had greatly changed in temper since the days of Pericles. Cleon, the "tanner," who after Pericles' death had been most successful in catching the ear of the assembly, had bidden the Athenians to cast aside all specious pretense and frankly to recognize their empire for what it was in fact, — a despotism based upon the right of the stronger. When Lesbos, aside from Chios the only real confederate state within the empire, had revolted, and Mytilene, the chief Lesbian city, had surrendered, he had advocated setting an example to the other states within the empire by putting to death the entire male adult population and selling the women and children into slavery. The measure was actually passed by the enraged Athenians (427 B.C.). Fortunately, it was rescinded on the following day, when saner councils prevailed; but the Athenians had received their first training in methods of terrorism.

Now Alcibiades, bent upon breaking the peace of 421 B.C., first embroiled Athens in war through an alliance with Argos, Sparta's ancient foe in the Peloponnesus. When this experiment failed of its objective, he urged an attack upon Dorian

Melos. This little island alone, among the group of islands known as the Cyclades, had contrived to remain outside the Athenian Empire. Without provocation it was attacked, and when it was conquered its male population was put to the sword and the women and children were enslaved. The horror of this wanton act served only to deepen the resentment of Athens' foes (416 B.C.).

The following years brought the crisis of the war. The Athenians had made many attempts to extend their influence to western waters. Now, upon the advice of Alcibiades, they decided to make a bid for power by a determined attack upon Syracuse, the chief Dorian stronghold in Sicily. To argue that the conquest of Syracuse in itself was not impossible is beside the point. The fact remains that the carrying out of such a grandiose scheme of conquest within the confines of Hellas, immediately after her conduct at Melos had brought upon Athens the odium of ruthless despotism, could be interpreted only as a final challenge to public opinion. It was the very thing Pericles had warned against.

In 415 B.C. an armament such as Hellas had not seen since the days of Xerxes left the harbor of Athens. A second armada was dispatched in 413 B.C. The whole expedition upon which the power and resources of Athens had been lavished ended in complete disaster. Thucydides has told the dramatic story once for all.[1] The failure was largely due to the Athenians themselves. Alcibiades, the heart and soul of the enterprise, was recalled through the machinations of his enemies at home to stand trial; he escaped to Sparta and turned traitor.

We come now to the third and last phase of the Hellenic World War. That it lasted so long (412–404 B.C.) was due more to the blundering and incompetence of Athens' enemies than to her own inherent powers of resistance. During all these years Athens was on the defensive, and her empire

[1] See Thucydides, Books VI and VII. For an English version cf. H. R. James, *Our Hellenic Heritage*, Part III, Chaps. VII and VIII, pp. 177–231.

was rapidly disintegrating. Persia now returned to the scene and supplied Sparta with the gold needed for the maintenance of a fleet. Even the temporary return of Alcibiades could not mend matters; he was forced a second time to go into exile. Yet even as late as 406 B.C. the Athenians managed to keep control of the Hellespont and maintain communications with the Black Sea, the source of their grain supply. In that year, near the Arginusae Islands, the Athenian fleet for the last time defeated the Peloponnesians. This, the greatest naval battle ever fought between Greeks, had a sequel which proves how deeply the cancer of corruption had eaten into Athenian character. For upon their return the generals were accused of having failed to rescue such of the Athenian combatants as were struggling in the water and to recover the bodies of the dead for burial. Six of the generals stood trial, were condemned — contrary to all law — by a single vote, and were actually executed. The monstrous iniquity of this verdict, one of the darkest blots on the history of Athens, was followed by an equal demonstration of folly when an offer of peace from their enemies was peremptorily dismissed. The measure was full; the following year saw the destruction of the last Athenian armament in the Hellespont (battle of Aegospotami, 405 B.C.). A Peloponnesian army now invaded Attica, a Peloponnesian fleet blocked the harbor, and in 404 B.C. Athens was starved into submission.

Thus the end had come. Her exasperated enemies would not consider anything short of the utter destruction of the city. The good sense of the Spartans prevailed, however. Athens had to renounce all pretense to empire; her fleet was reduced to twelve ships; and the harbor fortifications and the walls connecting the Piraeus with the city were pulled down, to the accompanying music of flutes. Thus Hellas celebrated its victory over the tyrant city.

But Athens' sufferings were not yet over. The last and most frightful chapter of the story remains. The Spartans had insisted on abolishing the democracy and left the city in control of a board of thirty men, all oligarchs. Political exiles were recalled, and the door was opened wide to that party strife of which, in its extreme form, Athens had been remarkably free. The "white terror" which followed took a further toll of Athenian lives; and when, after eight months of systematic murder, the democracy was finally restored, Athens was completely exhausted.

The Aftermath

The most fatal consequences of the war are to be sought in the realm of the spirit. The material damage was easily repaired; it was in other ways that the aftereffects of the war showed themselves. This is a fact of outstanding importance in the cultural history of Hellas; for the spiritual change that comes over postwar Greece is reflected in her arts and literature.

Here we are concerned with the political consequences. Just as in these days we have discovered that, when a conflict has assumed such proportions as the World War did, it cannot suddenly be terminated by a treaty of peace (least of all by a peace conceived in hatred), so Hellas discovered that the peace of 404 B.C. had settled nothing. The document proclaiming liberty to Hellas and victory over the tyrant city in point of fact spelled the common doom.

For the evil of "tyranny" had not been rooted out. One "tyrant" had been deposed, but in the process of overthrowing Athenian rule Sparta had been trained in imperialism. The Greek world discovered that it had only exchanged one master for another, and the new master proved a far harsher one than the old one had ever been. For, after all, the Athenian Empire had had its beginning in a union for liberty; its origin dated from the glorious days when the Hellene had vindicated his freedom against the Persian. And even when Athens had laid her strong hand on those recalcitrant cities which wished to withdraw from the common organization, there was an intelligent purpose behind her display of strength. The Athenian Empire was at least the fruit of a consistent policy, dictated by the logic of events.

When, after the war, Sparta was left in the undisputed position of leadership in Hellas, what use did she make of her opportunity? Had she learned to avoid the mistakes of Athens? Was her conduct to be more generous, more enlightened? War does not train men to be generous, nor does it leave them amenable to the counsels of reason. The desperate struggle for power which had covered a period of twenty-seven years had stifled all better impulses in Hellas. The lust for power ruled supreme in Sparta, and while she paid lip service to the principle of autonomy, in fact she interfered with the "self-determination" of the "liberated" states in a more high-handed manner than Athens had ever done. In the course of her self-appointed career as arbiter of Hellas she first fell foul of her ancient ally, Persia. The campaign against Persia was stopped short when her former allies, Thebes and Corinth, combined with her former enemies, Argos and Athens, to set a limit to her wanton aggressions (395 B.C.). Eight years of desultory warfare convinced Sparta of the impossibility of maintaining her supremacy on both land and sea, and under the presidency of a representative of the king of Persia a general peace was proclaimed (386 B.C.). The king proclaimed the freedom of all Hellenic states except those in Asia Minor, which now, nearly a century after the battle of Salamis, again fell under Persian dominion. But such "self-determination" as they had enjoyed the last fifty years under Athenian and Spartan rule they may well have been willing to sacrifice for the advantages of trade that would be theirs through incorporation in the Persian Empire.

In fact, Sparta had struck a bargain with Persia by which she sacrificed the Anatolian Greeks in return for a free hand at home. She interpreted the terms of the peace in her own way. Wherever there was any sign of a combination of Greek cities that might threaten her own supremacy (for the old Peloponnesian League remained in force, though with modifications), she sternly suppressed such attempts on the ground that they violated the peace terms guaranteeing autonomy to all. Thus the Arcadians, who had formed a new civic center in Mantinea, were compelled to dismantle the new city (385 B.C.); the league of Chalcidian cities under the leadership of Olynthus was considered another infringement of the peace terms, and the new confederacy was broken up (379 B.C.). In 382 B.C. Sparta had treacherously seized the citadel of Thebes, forestalling a similar movement for union in Boeotia. But she had not been able to prevent Athens, which by 390 B.C. had rebuilt her walls uniting her with the Piraeus, from reviving her old maritime alliance in defense of Greek liberty, this time, however, aimed at Spartan encroachment.

The blow that would finally lay Sparta low was not to come from Athens. It was outraged Thebes that proved Sparta's nemesis. There a newly awakened patriotism found two great leaders in Pelopidas and Epaminondas. Once the citadel of Thebes had been freed (379 B.C.), the political genius of Epaminondas effected a union of all Boeotia under the presidency of Thebes. Epaminondas was a great strategist as well, and the originator of new military tactics. From 378 until 372 B.C. he avoided open battle with the Spartans, unwilling to lose all by a premature effort. When he thought his country ready, he boldly challenged the power of Sparta. His faith was justified on the battlefield of Leuctra (371 B.C.), where in open battle the Spartan army was defeated by inferior numbers. Thus the legend of Spartan invincibility was exploded once for all.

For nine years Thebes held the hegemony in Greece. But Thebes no more than the others had a constructive policy for Hellas. The chief object of the Theban leaders was to destroy the Spartan power. In that they succeeded admirably: not only did Thebes break up the Peloponnesian League but she also broke Sparta's stranglehold on Messenia, which at last recovered her independence. The speedy collapse of Sparta was due chiefly to the fact that her population, depleted by incessant warfare and prevented by the rigidity of Spartan institutions from refilling its ranks, had dwindled to such a degree that at this time it was doubtful whether Sparta could put an army of fifteen hundred real citizens in the field. The armed forces with which she had terrorized Hellas had been made up mostly of allied troops. Once the Peloponnesian League was disbanded and Messenia restored to independence, Sparta fell back to the position of a second-rate power.

On the battlefield of Mantinea (362 B.C.) Thebes gained her last great victory; for Epaminondas was among the slain, and with his death the Theban hopes for dominion in Greece ended.

Macedonia

Since the conclusion of the peace of 404 B.C. Hellas had been the scene of a suicidal conflict which makes the history of fourth-century Hellas melancholy reading.[1] After the death of Epaminondas the power of Thebes on the mainland of Greece waned as rapidly as it had risen. And the second Athenian confederacy, disrupted chiefly through the fault of the Athenians themselves, after 355 B.C. ceased to be a controlling factor on the sea. The Peloponnesian League, which had exercised a steadying influence on Hellenic affairs ever since the days of its origin in the sixth century, had ceased to exist. By the middle of the fourth century, complete anarchy prevailed among the Hellenic states, and, what was worse, the last generations of the Greeks had grown up under conditions that made them familiar with their homeland as the scene of perpetual conflicts. They began to accept this state of affairs as the order of the day; an increasing number left their fields and farms to serve as mercenaries in the pay of the latest Hellenic state to make a bid for power. Thus Greece, divided

[1] Cf. the account in Laistner's *Greek History*, Chap. XVII.

against itself, would fall an easy prey to any strongly organized foreign power. Persia was the traditional enemy to Hellenic independence; but recent events had shown that the Persian Empire itself was disintegrating. The real danger came from a totally unexpected quarter, and Hellas was slow to realize it.

Beyond the northern mountains forming the boundary of Thessaly and Greece there lay a country of great possibilities, Macedonia, which formed a geographical unit exceeding any of the individual Greek states in extent of territory and in potential resources. Its large river valleys were well adapted for the growing of wheat and for pasture lands. It had plenty of forest lands on its mountainsides. But it was a backward country and had never been accounted as part of Hellas; its inhabitants spoke a dialect difficult for a Greek to understand. Its relation to Hellas was not unlike that of Czarist Russia to the European states. Politically and socially Macedonia was still living in the Homeric Age. Kings ruled, largely dependent on the loyalty of their vassal nobles for the safe tenure of their power, and liable to be suddenly dispatched by dynastic intrigues. Not only did Macedonia lack strong political organization; foes from without had beset it since immemorial times. The warlike tribes dwelling on its borders — Illyrians, Paeonians, and Thracians — habitually made inroads on the rich lowlands. The seacoast, with the three-pronged peninsula of Chalcidice, had been seized long before by the colonizing Greeks, who had thus shut the Macedonians off from free communication by sea. On the other hand, these same Greek towns, which bought the products of Macedon (chiefly timber and pitch) in exchange for Greek wares, had served to acquaint the Macedonian hinterland with certain features of Hellenic civilization. But this process of Hellenization was at best slow enough. To the Greek mind the Macedonians were barbarians, heavy drinkers, unacquainted with the refinements of Hellenic life.

It was not until the end of the fifth century that Archelaus, a great rogue but an ambitious one, had tried to effect a more stable union in his domains. Amyntas, the father of Philip, had followed in his footsteps, and when, in 359 B.C., Philip was called upon to rescue his country from internal discord and foreign invasion, he found the ground not entirely unprepared.

Philip was well acquainted with Hellas. For three years he had lived as a hostage in Thebes and, gifted with unusual talents, had been an apt learner. He had studied not only the superior civilization of Hellas but also its weaknesses; and when he left Thebes for his native country, not only was he initiated into the secrets of Greek politics but he had had an opportunity to observe at close range the superior military organization of the Thebans, effected by Epaminondas. The task awaiting him was an enormous one; that he accomplished all his objects within a decade shows him to have been a man of genius. In an incredibly short space of time he imposed order on Macedon, knitted its constituencies into a compact whole, reorganized the military forces, increased the revenues of the state by the annexation of the gold mines of Mt. Pangaeus, and extended and rendered secure the boundaries of Macedon. Then he managed to open the windows of his house by conquering the peninsula of Chalcidice, and made his entrance on the Greek political stage in full panoply. The opportunity for this he found in another of those miserable quarrels, now chronic in Hellas — the so-called "Sacred War," which had involved all central Greece and Thessaly. Philip, although rebuffed at first, rendered his Greek allies the services they expected from him. But he came to stay. In 346 B.C. a general peace was concluded in which all the advantages were on Philip's side. Only Phocis, the storm-center of the Sacred War, was excluded from the benefits of the peace. It was subdued by Philip, and to him was awarded the vote in the Sacred League which had belonged to the Phocians. At the following celebration of the Pythian games at Delphi, in the land of the Phocians, Philip presided. The Athenians stayed away in disgust. But Philip now "belonged"!

It was only now that Hellas began to suspect the ulterior designs of the Macedonian. In Athens, Demosthenes had lifted his warning voice ever since Philip had attacked Chalcidice; but he had long pleaded in vain for a return of the old patriotism, the old spirit of sacrifice for Athens' sake. Now, at last, the people of Athens experienced a change of heart, and for a few years the Anti-Macedonian party, led by Demosthenes, had the upper hand. Philip, however, knew all the tricks of the political game as it was played in Greece. In every important Greek center there was a Pro-Macedonian party, financed by Philip; siding with these were such idealists as Isocrates, the foremost rhetorician of Hellas, who, weary of the spectacle of the incessant strife among Greeks, preferred to see Hellas united against the common enemy, Persia, even if such union were presided over by the Macedonian.

For some time Athens bestirred herself to oppose Philip, and his latest enterprise against the Thracian Chersonese was turned into failure. But it was too late to avert the common doom now overhanging Hellas. The Greek states, half-hearted and weary of war, could not be aroused to a sense of their danger, and on the battlefield of Chaeronea, in Boeotia, the fate of Hellenic independence was decided for all time (338 B.C.). The military genius of Philip prevailed over the heroism of the Thebans, who fought valiantly by the side of the Athenians. From this time on, Greece was an appendage to Macedon until the Roman Empire finally absorbed both.

Philip had realized his ambition; now he united the Hellenic states in a league, the presidency of which belonged to him. He placed Macedonian garrisons at strategic points in Greece and called a Panhellenic Congress at Corinth, which should decide all disputes between the Greek states; otherwise, the Hellenic polities were to be governed by their own laws. But the only defensive or offensive alliance they were allowed to make was with Macedon.

Philip was now ready to lead the Greeks in his supreme enterprise, the attack on Persia. Before he could carry out his plan, he was assassinated (336 B.C.). His death made no difference in the position Hellas occupied relatively to Macedonia; for he was succeeded by his even more famous son Alexander, who carried out his father's plans.

In justice to Philip we may add that he was not only a great statesman and military leader but a genuine Phil-Hellene, who to the end of his days stood somewhat in awe of Athens and the accumulated treasures of Athenian culture. He treated the city with a consideration which is in strange contrast to the savagery he exhibited on many other occasions; even Demosthenes was perfectly safe at Athens after the battle of Chaeronea.

Epilogue

Looking back over the story of the last century of Hellenic independence, we wonder at the perversity displayed by a people otherwise so sane and rational in their outlook upon life. Can we discover the causes that drove them relentlessly to pursue a path that could lead only to disaster?

The prime cause was inherent in the very political ideal embodied in the city-state. The Greeks, in their search for a social and political organization which should promote the common good, ensure social justice to all, and be governed by the common will as expressed in laws, had found in the city-state the only solution of their problems. It was a new departure, and we hail it as a most important political experiment.

But this achievement, momentous as it was and full of promise, bore in itself the seed of its own destruction; for the Hellenic ideal of self-government was necessarily narrow and confined by the very walls of the city-state. The Greek citizen had a clear conception of his duty to his own city; he recognized that his own interests were best served by promoting the common weal. But even the most enlightened citizen had no idea whatever of his duty to man; nay, more, he could conceive only faintly and fitfully of his duty to Hellas. Only under the stress of national peril had the several states managed to unite for a short time, and even then the union was not all-inclusive. The leaders in the city-states acted upon the principle that the purely selfish interests of their own polis, its glory and power and aggrandizement, were the only considerations to guide their conduct. The political ideal incorporated in the polis was, accordingly, narrow, selfish, and shortsighted. It made Hellas into a house divided against itself.

As long as the individual city-states were small, while their mutual jealousies and rivalries could and did lead to frequent warfare, this petty warfare, not often passing beyond the stage of perennial border raids, was not likely to inflict mortal wounds upon Hellas. It was the gradual formation of larger groups, for common defense or for the furthering of common interests, that brought the need for the establishment of an equilibrium among them; with it came the constant fear of disturbing the "balance of power," and the possibility of wars of larger proportions.

The ultimate cause of the downfall of Hellas we may trace to the outbreak of the Hellenic World War. It stimulated the mutual jealousies and suspicions to a degree unknown before and left Hellas in a state of utter demoralization. It converted local patriotism into a ruthless lust for power and into a fury of hate for all that stood in its way. The story of postwar Hellas is the record of the aftermath of the war, and its continuation under various guises until all hope of union was lost forever and the exhaustion and anarchy resulting from this endless warfare rendered Hellas an easy prey to the uncouth Macedonian. That the Greeks themselves foresaw that this continued strife would lead to their destruction is pathetically attested by the fact that between 387 and 366 B.C. we hear of no fewer than seven peace conferences, at which the representatives of the Hellenic powers met in the hope of establishing lasting peace among themselves. But these congresses, instead of bringing peace, served only to accentuate the causes of the mutual distrust. In fine, the several states were incapable of surrendering their selfish and shortsighted policies to the greater interests of the whole.

The true tragedy, therefore, of the political history of Hellas consists in this: the polity, originally the only possible form of political organization, had a career long enough to make the dogma of the sovereignty and autonomy of the city-state a political axiom. Tradition had made it sacred; and when the time came that only surrender of the sovereignty of the particular state to the greater sovereignty of a united Hellas could ensure the survival of the whole, it was found that the ideal of separatism had become an article of faith which it was sheer blasphemy and treason to question. Down to the end, Greek political thinking operated with an antiquated formula which appeared the more sacred the more out-of-date it became, as such things are wont to do; and even the keenest minds of Hellas could conceive of no other formula.

More than two thousand years have passed since the Greek political experiment ended in failure, but the lesson contained in its history cannot escape the thoughtful reader. The place of the polity has been taken by the nation; but the parallel between the history of Hellenic "politism" and that of European nationalism is all but complete. The sovereignty of the national state is as sacred a principle today as the sovereignty of the city-state was in Hellenic days. The inevitable crash has come in our time, and the Hellenic World War has had its counterpart in our own World War. The history of postwar Europe remains to be written. So far it has run true to form: the dream of uniting the European states in a political confederacy today seems as little likely to be turned into reality as were the speculations of the political theorists of fourth-century Greece, who strove for a united Hellas.

But there is another side to the story of the Greek polity. To this we shall turn in our next chapter.

SUGGESTIONS FOR READING. The interested reader may compile a political history of Greater Greece and Sicily (a topic treated very cavalierly in our sketch) from the pertinent sections in the *Cambridge Ancient History*, and discover for himself parallels to the trends observed in Greek political history.

On the subject of Greek political history GEORGE GROTE, *History of Greece* (Everyman's Library), is the English classic; ERNST CURTIUS, *History of Greece* (Scribner's), the German classic.

The best modern work in English is J. B. BURY, *A History of Greece* (Macmillan).

The first volume of M. ROSTOVTZEFF, *History of the Ancient World*, contains (in Chapters XII–XXIII) a finely illustrated account of Hellenic history.

BOTSFORD and SIHLER'S *Hellenic Civilization* (Columbia, 1920) contains interesting source material.

CHAPTER V

THE CITY-STATE

The Greek Concept of the State

WE OPENED the sketch of the political history of Hellas, contained in the previous chapter, with the remark that the form of political and social organization adopted by the Greeks was to prove a dominant factor in the shaping of their civilization. So far the contention may seem hardly justified, except in the case of Sparta; and even here, though her political and social organization exercised a preponderant influence on her development, the influence was chiefly negative, in that it gave the Spartans a single interest in life and practically excluded all concern with other cultural aspects. We shall need to examine afresh the character of the polis and the social ideals which it implied. For if we should imagine that the difference between the Hellenic polis and the modern national state is merely quantitative, the polis differing from the national state only in size, we should make a grievous mistake, and the significance of the historic development of Hellenic culture would escape us.

The Greek conception of the state and of group life in general was an inheritance from tribal days. There is no question that for uncounted millenniums man's mode of life approached that of the herd animal. Only within the group was there safety. After the family, the clan and the tribe are the earliest forms of social organization of which we have knowledge. Now, as was remarked above,[1] the most striking feature of tribal life is its solidarity; it is governed in all its details by the force of tradition, which it would not occur to any tribesman to challenge. Thus human survival was made possible by the complete absorption of the individual in the

[1] Chap. I, p. 5.

Pericles

group. This is true even of the Homeric Achaeans; only rarely does a Thersites emerge from the undifferentiated mob. In the Hellenic polity also we have met with the actual survival of tribal organization. Cleisthenes abolished the four old tribes of Athens, but his ten new tribes were clearly a concession to a sentiment that could not be ignored.

Secondly, we find that the Greeks never quite succeeded in freeing themselves from the superstitious awe with which tribesmen regard the sacred traditions governing their conduct. The Hellenes also had their "unwritten laws"; their commands might be as irrational as Polynesian taboos, but "they were born in Heaven and their father is Olympus; the god is mighty in them nor does he grow old."[1] Even the admittedly man-made laws of his own day the Greek invested with the sanctity attaching to the older customs and folkways which he still observed. In short, the law was something sacred to the Hellene, and he speaks of it as his master, with an emotion that will always surprise the modern reader. Let him consult Plato's *Crito* and discover for himself the extent to which even a rationalist like Socrates shared the common Greek attitude toward the laws of his state.

Thirdly, as in tribal life social and religious customs and ritual are practically identical, so in Hellenic life they are inseparable and are not readily distinguished. Therefore the Greek polity is not simply a political unit but a religious organization as well. Political gatherings scrupulously observe the unwritten laws governing religious gatherings. No one in Periclean Athens would dream of opening political discussion in the assembly until the proper religious ceremony had been performed and the evil spirits had been driven out by the magical property of the blood of sacrificial pigs. Religious sentiment and religious emotion had an important part in holding the political community together. As a great writer has remarked, Hellenic patriotism regarded from this point of view assumes the form of "municipal piety."

[1] See Sophocles, *Oedipus Tyrannus*, lines 863 ff.

The Greek therefore inherited from the tribal past the habit of thinking of himself not as an isolated individual but as a member of a group bound together by a common descent, common traditions, and a common worship. The Greek city-state was built against this background of experience and ideas. Our memories have a much more varied and richer political experience to draw upon, and, accordingly, we carry into our political thinking the ideas and theories which our cultural past has bequeathed to us. We speak glibly enough of man's "natural rights," although historically speaking there is scant justification for such; and we demand of the state that it guarantee to the individual the free exercise and enjoyment of these natural rights — that is, so far as they do not clash with the common interests. But the state is carefully watched in the discharge of its functions; for we regard it as a limitation upon the liberties of the individual. We hold that state to be the ideal one in which such interference with individual liberties is reduced to a minimum. We may be patriots where "our country" is concerned; toward the state we are rather cool and may be a little wary. In brief, then, (1) we conceive of the state as something external to ourselves, and (2) we sharply distinguish between the state and society, and, of course, between the state and the church.

In Hellas political thought moved in the opposite direction. It began with the state as a concept including political, social, and religious organization. Far from being external to the individual, the state was regarded as the primary fact in human experience, outside of which human life could not realize its true destiny. It was conceived as a living organism, of which the individual was an integral part, useless outside of it, as much as a foot or a hand is useless when severed from the body. It is not easy to see the full implications of the Hellenic idea of the state. If the Greek concept of the state be that of a living organism, in which all the parts serve the end of the whole, we cannot escape the conclusion that the ideal implicit in the polis was nothing short of a *completely integrated society*, all members of which co-operate, according to their various abilities, toward promoting the interests of the whole.

Now it is undoubtedly true that the real significance of this concept of the polis was not consciously present in the common mind of Hellas; for the explicit statement we shall have to wait until we reach Plato and his ideal commonwealth. But that it was none the less operative in Hellas, of this the facts of Greek political history leave no doubt.

Secondly, these implications were never fully realized in any Hellenic states; the ideal would have ceased to be such had it been converted into a historic fact. But the individual Hellene was well aware of the prior claim the state had on him; that personal liberty which is our most highly prized possession was not for him. He knew of only two alternatives: submission either to the will of the group to which he belonged or to the arbitrary will of a despot. The latter he accounted slavery, unworthy of Greeks, but befitting barbarians, such as the subjects of the Persian king; the former, under the guise of equality under the law, was the kind of liberty he knew and gloried in.

To find a modern parallel for this archaic notion of the state, we shall have to go to the Russia of today. Here too a complete integration of social life is aimed at, a subordination of all individual activity to the aims of the state; and with it comes a state tyranny, which extends to the realm of the mind and the spirit as well. In Russia there is only one political doctrine which is right; it is treason to entertain any other. Even art and literature must serve the ends of the state, as they did in Periclean Athens. We find, therefore, in the Russian Soviet and in Soviet ideals a curious reversion to the primitive political ideals of a bygone age. But there is an important difference. It is most clearly revealed in the fact that in Russia the state carries on an active propaganda in behalf of its ideas and an equally vigorous warfare on heterodox opinion, whereas in Sparta or in Periclean

Athens the great mass of the people never questioned the validity of the state's claims, indeed supported it with a loyalty and ardor that left no room for doubt on the subject. The reason is that in Hellas the solidarity of the polis was a natural product of historical conditions, whereas the present order in Russia is the result of a revolution by which a doctrinaire minority imposed its will on the majority.

When we keep in mind the fundamental difference between the modern conception of the state and the Hellenic one, a great deal of what we have noted in the history of the Greek polis becomes more intelligible. First of all, there is the callous disregard of personal rights. Here the outstanding example is furnished by Sparta; we have seen that community forcibly suppressing two of the most vital instincts in human life — those relating to the family and to private property. But although Sparta was in a class by itself and provides an extreme illustration of the axiom of the supremacy of the state, the rest of Greece will prove to have shared the Spartan view, differing only in its application. The institution of ostracism alone proves it for Athens, the most enlightened of Hellenic states. The interests of the state were paramount; compared with these the individual rights of even the most distinguished of its citizens counted as nothing if the position he occupied seemed to endanger the well-being of the state. Thus Athens sent its foremost citizens, such as Aristides, Themistocles, and Cimon, into honorable exile. True, the institution went into the discard in the fourth century B.C., but only because by that time the entire outlook upon life had undergone a profound change.

Secondly, the Greek state and the Greek statesman were equally obtuse toward the rights of private property. The Greek axiom seems to be that, since the accumulation of wealth in the hands of private individuals is possible only under the aegis of the state, the state therefore has primary rights as well. Solon's famous *seisachtheia*, which abolished all debts, is a case in point. This, to be sure, was an emergency measure; but examine the methods of taxation in Athens, and Solon's measure will appear to be only an extreme application of a principle that was valid at all times. The chief financial needs of Athens centered in the public worship and in the defense of the state. The cost of both was defrayed by taxation in the form of capital levies on the richest citizens: the "liturgies" paid for the religious festivals; the trierarchies, for the equipping of the fleet. In short, Athens not only conscripted the bodies of the citizens for the good of the state; it conscripted their wealth as well.

Finally, there is the peculiar attitude of the Greek toward political parties. The conflict between "the few" and "the many," between oligarchic and democratic factions within the polis, he regarded as a standing evil of city life, never ceasing to lament its presence. Here again we differ widely from the Greeks; such differences appear to us as essential to the very existence of political liberty, which a political orthodoxy imposed by the state would extinguish. If it seemed otherwise to the Greek, it was because division among the citizens, especially along political lines, was incompatible with his ideas of state solidarity. And, indeed, in a fully integrated commonwealth there is no room for political parties; to the logical Hellenic mind, party loyalty meant disloyalty to the polis.

The solidarity of the state, then, was an article of faith among the Greeks, as the solidarity of the tribe had prevailed among their forebears. And precisely the same causes that had led to the one produced also the other. The tribe could not survive unless united. What chance for survival would a Greek town have had, no matter where situated, if it could not present a united front to the surrounding world? In a nationally united Hellas municipal loyalty would have become obsolete; in the Greek world of city-states it was a condition indispensable for survival.

Such, then, were the Greek ideas of the state and of the relation between the state and the individual. We cannot help viewing with misgiving a political doctrine which seems to demand the complete subordination of the individual to the state. Would it not result in stifling all individual initiative? Will any man show the best there is in him if his actions are judged by a purely social standard? Will he strive to do his utmost when he is promoting not his own private interests but rather those of the group to which he belongs?

We cannot answer these questions better than by an examination of the actual working of a Greek polity. As our example we shall take the Athenian democracy in the days of Pericles, because it is best known to us and because, admittedly, Periclean Athens presents us with the most fully developed case of the Hellenic polis.

Periclean Athens

Since the days of Cleisthenes (*c.* 510 B.C.) the further development of the democratic principles embodied in his lawgiving, and their extension into increasing spheres, had kept pace with the rising power of Athens. The Areopagus, the old stronghold of conservatism in Athens, had been robbed of its control over legislation and had been relegated to the rank of a criminal court; it remained the most august religious tribunal of Athens, but its political significance had largely disappeared. Next, the introduction of pay for the performance of certain political duties enabled even the poorest citizen to hold office and to sit on the jury. Thirdly, the lot came to determine more and more who was to serve in a public capacity, until all officeholders and magistrates and councilors owed their position to the lot, with the exception of the ten generals (elected every year) and those other servants of the public whose tasks demanded a specialized technical skill. Otherwise one man was accounted as competent as another for the holding of public office. Finally, while it evidently had been Cleisthenes' intention that the burden of government should be upon the representative

Council of Five Hundred, developments during the fifth century had tended to shift the center of political gravity from the council to the assembly. The assembly met three or four times each prytany, which means that there were between thirty and forty regular meetings of the people every year; with possibly additional meetings called by the leading "general" (prime minister we should call him) in times of crisis.

Now, in the words of Zimmern,[1] "democracy is meaningless unless it involves the serious and steady coöperation of large numbers of citizens in the actual work of government." Let us now see how the citizens of Periclean Athens co-operated.

Upon the attainment of his majority, at the age of eighteen, the Athenian youth took a solemn oath, the civic oath that the Hellenic city-state demanded of its citizens. At the shrine of Aglauros, in the presence of the august Council of Five Hundred, the new citizen received his armor and, standing at the altar, recited the following oath:

> I will not dishonor these sacred arms. I will not abandon my comrade in battle. I will fight for my gods and my hearth. I will not leave my country smaller but I will leave it greater and stronger than I received it. I will obey the commands of the magistrates. I will submit to the existing laws. I will respect the worship of my fathers.

In some such words (for the exact form of the Athenian oath in the Periclean Age is not known to us) the prospective citizen dedicated himself to the cause of his city. It was an impressive ceremony, which cannot have failed to leave its mark on the mind of the youthful aspirant to citizenship.

The next two years he spent in military training, for which gymnasium and palaestra had prepared him. From his twentieth year on he was a defender of his country, and that remained the first and most sacred duty of citizenship. What it implied is shown by an Athenian record that has been preserved from 459 B.C. On the stone are engraved the

[1] A. E. Zimmern, *The Greek Commonwealth*, p. 160.

names of the citizens of *one* tribe (there were ten of these), who fell fighting for Athens "in Cyprus, in Egypt, in Phoenicia, at Halieis, in Aegina, at Megara in the same year"; and one hundred and seventy-two names follow.[1]

But other duties soon began to make demands upon his time. There were the meetings of the assembly, where the political leaders debated questions of public policy. How exciting these political contests could be, where ambitious men strove with one another for the glory of leadership, we learn from the pages of Thucydides. There the young citizen could get his political education. And he had the right to vote. The local interests of his own deme brought him into contact with his fellow demesmen, and in sharing the deliberations on the tiny interests of his own township he was further preparing himself for a share in the consideration and management of the larger concerns of the state.

After reaching the age of thirty the lot might appoint him a member of the council for one year, in which case he would be in continued attendance upon the duties of his office for one tenth of the year, fed and housed by the state. He would take a hand with his forty-nine colleagues in preparing matters for the consideration of the people at one of the meetings of the assembly; he would receive in audience envoys from all parts of Hellas; he would dispose of current state business; he would supervise the details of financial and military and naval administration. This office the law would allow him to hold only twice.

Again, he might find himself allotted to one of the numerous committees to which the Athenian democracy entrusted its routine matters. Some seven hundred citizens were annually picked by lot to serve as committeemen. After a year's service each would have to give a full account of his public acts; for the democracy was suspicious, and, especially when the committeemen handled public moneys, the people were not in the habit of taking anything for granted.

[1] J. B. Bury, *History of Greece*, p. 355.

Furthermore, there was jury duty to be performed. Annually about six thousand citizens, mostly elderly men (six hundred from each of the ten tribes), were placed on the jury panels for service in the popular courts. The juries were large, consisting of from two hundred and one to two thousand and one jurors. There was neither presiding judge to expound the law nor lawyers to argue cases; the citizen in person pleaded his case before these courts, which, on the whole, rendered fair verdicts.

In addition, the state, being a religious organization as well, made incessant demands on the time of the citizens for public worship. The number of festival days amounted to about seventy a year. They were marked by contests, which were by no means confined to athletics but included "musical" contests, in one of which, for instance, five choruses of men and boys (each chorus consisting of fifty dancers and singers) competed for a prize. There were recitations of Homer; above all, there were dramatic contests in honor of Dionysus. It has been computed that upward of two thousand Athenians annually were in training for these "musical" contests.

The state had made it possible for even the poorest to take an active share in civic life; it was no less insistent that the rich assume the obligations their wealth imposed on them. As we have seen, these assumed the form of "liturgies" and trierarchies. One of the "liturgies" was the *choregia*, which gave the rich man an opportunity to serve the state by equipping and training a chorus for one of the numerous musical and dramatic contests; or he might defray the cost of arrangements for a horse race or a torch race. In this case, too, the state encouraged the spirit of emulation: it offered a prize not only to the successful playwright but also to the *choregus*, who mounted the play and paid for the training of the chorus. Never has a state more systematically exploited man's inborn love of distinction than the Athenian state did. We hear of public contests in every sphere of life:

Horsemen in the Panathenaic Procession, Parthenon Frieze

contests between potters, contests in drinking, contests between prytanies. The Greek word for contest is *agon*; in the Greek sense Athens was in a perpetual state of agony. Here we must keep in mind what we observed in an earlier chapter concerning Homer as a witness to Hellenism and the Hellenic view of life. Greek society, in its best days, retained the characteristics of that adolescent world revealed by Homer. That Egyptian priest who said to Solon "You Greeks are ever children" was a shrewd observer; for the Greeks displayed throughout their history that desire for praise, that love of glory, which is characteristic of Homer's humanity and upon which we look rather as the innocent vainglory characteristic of youth.

The Hellenic ideal of life was therefore a completely social one; to the Greeks the most desirable life was that which gained the prize of public acclaim. To be distinguished in the eyes of one's fellows was the common ambition. It pursued them even beyond the grave; for we have many an epitaph bearing witness to this desire for public approval, from that of the woodcutter, who, "by Zeus, never saw a better woodsman than myself," to that of Aeschylus, the poet, who boasts of his valor proved on the battlefield of Marathon.

There is a celebrated story in Herodotus in which the historian makes Solon, the wisest man of his day, visit Croesus, the richest. Croesus, after showing the sage his wealth, asks him, "Now, tell me, whom do you deem the most happy of all?" confidently expecting that Solon will answer, "You, Croesus!" The actual reply of Solon provides an excellent commentary on the Greek view of life. He picks out an obscure Athenian, "first, because his country was flourishing in his days"; secondly, "because he was happy in his family life, being blessed with sons and grandsons"; finally, because "he died in battle, most gallantly. The Athenians gave him a public funeral on the spot where he fell and paid him the highest honors." [1] What, then, are the

[1] See Howe and Harrar, *Greek Literature in Translation*, pp. 134–136.

components of a happy life? First, a prosperous community; next, a happy family life; third, public approval. What is all the wealth of Croesus compared with these?

Such, then, was the commonwealth of Athens in the days of Pericles, a society governed by amateurs who received their only civic training in the school of life. It was a society which gave almost unlimited scope to individual ambition and the desire for distinction, and yet inculcated at the same time a public spirit which subordinated the interests of the individual to the common good. This was no doubt attributable largely to the inspired leadership of Pericles who would have his fellow citizens be "lovers" of Athens, as if she were their mistress, on whom they might lavish their wealth and to whose service they might dedicate their very lives. He preached a form of civic patriotism which had become a consuming passion in his own person and which was strong enough to kindle the imagination of his fellow citizens until they came to share his vision of Athens as the most glorious achievement of the human spirit. "We shall be the wonder of the ages," he proclaimed triumphantly, and they believed him.[1] Perhaps this society would be found at fault when judged by the standards of efficiency which our own age has learned to venerate. We know only that no other period in the history of man, before or since that age, leaves us with so overwhelming an impression of human happiness achieved in spite of material poverty and physical hardship, and that no other age has witnessed an equal release of creative energy.

We shall never find the formula for human happiness. But if we were to compose such a formula on the basis of the experience of Periclean Athens, it would run somewhat as follows. It would postulate a comparatively small society, homogeneous and firmly bound together by a common aim and a common way of life, — a society which would have as its object not individual comfort and individual security but

[1] The *locus classicus* on the subject is found in the famous funeral oration of Pericles as reported by Thucydides, Bk. II, Chaps. 35–46.

the well-being of the group. It would seek this object by assuring to each man the opportunity to do his part according to his talents and to find public recognition for the services rendered. It would preach the strenuous life; it would urge the citizen to spurn the prudent course of safety and to court adventure; it would embolden him to proud self-assertion; and finally — strangest of all — it would offer him abundant opportunity to die gallantly for the cause he had supported with his life.

There remains one question: What part was allotted to the noncitizens of Athens in the common enterprise? There were thousands of resident foreigners, chiefly in the Piraeus, and the number of slaves was even larger. Was not this Periclean society based upon slave labor, and does not this explain why the Athenian was free to take part in public life?

As for the slaves, — although this is not the place to discuss the part slavery played in the economy of fifth-century Athens, — we may admit that in industrial life (which was largely in the hands of the resident foreigners) slavery played no inconsiderable role. Any man with a trade or a shop who did not have, in addition to his son, at least one slave as a fellow worker would have been considered poorly equipped. Moreover, there were a large number of slaves employed in domestic service. But the economic basis of Athenian society was still agricultural, and here the rule was small farms, worked by their owners. The grape and the olive were the chief products, and the owner tended the trees and the vines with his own hand; in fact, in the rural parts of Greece slavery was almost unknown.

But we do not need slavery as an explanation of the apparently greater leisure enjoyed by the Hellene as compared with the much harassed modern citizen, who can barely find time to compute his income tax or to vote. The real explanation is far simpler. The Mediterranean lands have always been the home of leisure and *dolce far niente.* Nature is kind to man and makes no great demands on him; he needs little in the way either of shelter or of clothing. It seems, indeed, as if Dame Nature herself invites him to possess his soul and lead the simple life. For she is niggardly as well as kind (at least in Greece): she will not reward man's efforts in such a degree as to spur him to excessive toil. It is easy enough to keep body and soul together, and what more does one want? The life of the Greek tiller of the soil who labors in a climate that knows hardly any rainfall from the middle of May until the middle of September is vastly different from that of the American farmer whose one hundred and sixty acres demand unremitting toil from sunrise to sunset the greater part of the year. In fact, as has been observed, Mediterranean man is not a farmer: he is a gardener. The traditions of life and the standards of life in such a country are necessarily simple. The Athenians of the fifth century dwelt in houses built of clay, which the sun had baked into bricks (a Hellenic house-breaker was a "wall-digger" and presumably plied his trade with a shovel); and the house of a Miltiades could not be distinguished from that of the humbler citizen. Of all the conveniences and contraptions with which we clutter up our dwellings to ensure our comforts the Hellene knew nothing; of the "tyranny of things" that has assumed such alarming proportions in our times he was completely free. Herein we must seek the secret of that leisure which left him greater freedom to participate in public life. There is a good story in Herodotus[1] which well illustrates the simplicity of Hellenic life as compared with Persian standards. After the battle of Plataea, when the Persian camp, with all its sumptuous wealth, had fallen into the hands of the Greeks, Pausanias, the Spartan king, ordered the Persian cooks to prepare a dinner in the best Persian style while his own men prepared a Spartan supper. When both tables had been set side by side, Pausanias called in the Greek captains, saying, "Men of Hellas, I have called you in to show you the folly of the

[1] Bk. IX, Chap. 82.

Persian, who, having such fare as this, came to rob us of such miserable fare as that."

To sum up. In our sketch of the political history of Hellas, contained in Chapter IV, the evils inherent in the Greek system of city-states were exposed. In the present chapter it was shown that there was another side to this story: that same polis sheltered a social ideal of life which, rightly applied, could bear the richest fruits; it furnished a powerful incentive to human ambition and human activity. Through the civic pride and civic loyalty which it fostered, it became the most potent factor in shaping the civilization of Hellas.

But this ideal of life did not remain unchallenged. The Hellenic World War undermined the fundamental principles of Greek life; it was that war and the disillusion which followed it that dispelled the faith upon which Hellas and, above all, Athens had built. It is a pity that with the passing of the old ideals much of the zest of life went as well.

In the following pages we shall duly note the influence of political developments upon the other aspects of Greek culture. For the sake of clarity we shall roughly divide the cultural history of Hellas into three periods. First, the period of formation, lasting from 750 B.C. to 500 B.C. The second period, 500–431 B.C., is ushered in by the Persian Wars; it is the age of faith par excellence. The last period, 431–336 B.C., begins with the Hellenic World War; it is the age of disintegration.

SUGGESTIONS FOR READING. For the Greek city-state see A. E. ZIMMERN, *The Greek Commonwealth* (5th ed., Oxford, 1931), and G. GLOTZ, *The Greek City* (Knopf, 1930).

For a description of the working of the Athenian state in the Age of Pericles cf. the excellent account of W. S. FERGUSON, "Athens, an Imperial Democracy," in *Greek Imperialism* (Houghton Mifflin, 1913).

For a discussion of the Greek conception of the state see S. H. BUTCHER, "The Greek Idea of the State," in *Some Aspects of the Greek Genius* (3d ed., Macmillan, 1904), and G. LOWES DICKINSON,

The Greek View of Life (Educational Edition, Doubleday, Doran, 1932), Chap. II, "The Greek View of the State."

For the symptoms of the decline of Greek civic spirit in the fourth century see G. GLOTZ, *The Greek City*, pp. 295–351.

For the Greek idea of liberty see the chapter on "Eleutheria" in J. A. K. THOMSON, *Greeks and Barbarians* (Macmillan, 1921).

The reader may find interesting material for the study of tribal life in W. T. THOMAS, *Source Book of Social Origins* (see especially the selections from A. W. HOWITT, *Native Tribes of South-East Australia*, and SPENCER and GILLEN, *Native Tribes of Central Australia*), or in R. H. LOWIE, *The Crow Indians* (Farrar and Rinehart, 1935).

CHAPTER VI

RELIGION

Introductory

IN THE last chapter more than one passing reference was made to the identity of state and church in ancient times. It is time that we return to the subject of religion, for thus far in our discussion of the Hellenic polis we have neglected the most powerful of its constituents, its gods.

However, for a proper evaluation of the part that religion played in the historic polis, once more we must return to tribal society and tribal religion and, with this as our basis, build up the framework of Greek religion. First, then, we shall consider tribal religion, the concepts with which it operates, its object, and the place it occupies in tribal life. Next, after a brief glance at Homer's gods, we shall follow the evolution of Hellenic religion in the three successive stages of the history of the polis.

Tribal Religion

To modern man religion is an individual affair par excellence; its object he conceives as purely spiritual; and most essential in the matter of religion, he thinks, is the question of right belief. These are to him three self-evident propositions. Yet a little reflection will show that, tested by the part played by religion in early society, they are all equally invalid. For if tribal solidarity was the price paid for tribal survival, then tribal religion cannot have been anything but the concern of the group; in fact, it cannot have been a matter for individual choice, since, as we have seen,[1] the individual, in the proper sense, was as yet nonexistent.

[1] See page 5.

Ewing Galloway

Temple of Apollo at Corinth

Secondly, the chief concern of early society being the preservation of its precarious life, it follows that religion would have to serve the same purpose: it was not the saving of his soul that interested early man, but the saving of his body. What do we want of the gods? asks Cicero; and even he answers, Health and wealth. Finally, it was not right belief that interested early man, but right action. The theory justifying the cult was of small concern to him. His most pressing need was the correct performance of the ritual itself, at the right time and in the right manner, as prescribed by tribal custom; for on this depended the favor of the unseen powers, upon which, in turn, depended the life of the tribe. Therefore the loyal participation of all members of the group in the ritual was of primal importance to tribal society.[1]

These three propositions remain valid in the religious history of the polis. In Hellas religion was an affair of the community; it was part of the social order into which the Hellene was born and from which he had neither the power nor the right to disengage himself; it had for its object the survival and the prosperity of the state; and, finally, the state demanded participation of all in the prescribed ritual (with the beliefs underlying religious practice it had little concern). Greek religion, therefore, in its essentials, was a primitive religion.

Now let us turn to the concepts with which early religion operates. To early man, in his ignorance, the world surrounding him is still replete with mystery; his sense of wonder and awe is easily aroused. To be sure, neither the rising of the sun nor the rushing waters of the brook call forth any religious emotion; but a solar eclipse or the inundation of his fields by that same brook may arrest his attention, causing that fear and awe which spur him into action. It is, then, the unforeseen, the unusual phenomena of nature

[1] See W. Robertson Smith, *Religion of the Semites* (first two lectures). This book is a classic. Although it does not treat specifically of Greek religion, there is no better introduction to the subject of early religious organization.

that baffle him and make him aware of a mysterious *super*-natural power interfering in his daily humdrum existence. Thus man looks upon earthquake and pestilence, thunder-storm and drought, as so many manifestations of mysterious powers at work. In fact, he lives surrounded by a multitude of unseen forces at whose mercy he is, and against which his only defense is the tribal lore of rite and spell.

There is more than this: the religious ritual attending birth, marriage, and death, and the taboos surrounding these, mark man's awe in the presence of the mystery of life and death. The newborn babe, the woman in childbirth, and the corpse are equally taboo. What is the meaning of *taboo*? It is a Polynesian word which anthropology has borrowed to indicate that quality of sacredness with which primitive man invariably invests that which he conceives to be charged with a supernatural power. Whether this be a power for good or evil, whether it be "sacred" or "accursed," the thing is equally taboo, — it is not safe; it cannot be handled at all, or at least not without great circumspection. In a larger sense, taboo "stands for the whole mass of fear-inspired inhibitions insofar as they proceed directly from the religious emotion, as it regulates the social traditions in the relative abeyance of reasoned direction."[1]

A peculiar and again universal attribute of taboo is what has been termed its transmissibility. By this is meant that things taboo are automatically infectious: the man who has come into contact with a corpse himself becomes taboo, and if the proper ceremony for the removal of the infection be not performed he remains "unclean" and a source of danger to his fellows. Hence the important place the rite of purification plays in the history of religion. It is this belief in the infectious quality of taboo that became so important a factor in the life of early society; for it fostered the idea of social obligation, since the breaker of a taboo endangered not only

[1] Marett, in Hastings' *Encyclopedia of Religion and Ethics*, s.v. "Tabu." See also Sir J. G. Frazer, *Golden Bough* (one-volume edition), Chap. XXI.

himself but all with whom he came into contact. A second feature of the taboo infection is its purely mechanical character: mere contact suffices; even the sight of the tabooed object or person may have fatal consequences. There is no question here of moral guilt, as we understand it: the accidental shedder of the blood of a tribesman has broken a taboo equally with him who has taken a life with full intent. The only sin that primitive society knows is the transgression of a taboo. The punishment is outlawry; for he who has broken a taboo for which the tribal lore provides no remedy is thrust out of the common life and inevitably perishes.

Early society, then, is regulated by these "fear-inspired inhibitions" which "proceed directly from the religious emotion." In the worst taboo-ridden societies the whole of life is controlled by a network of taboos the greater part of which is wholly irrational.

Now the Greeks we have found to be an eminently rational people, and when we meet them in historic times they have in large measure freed themselves of the tyranny of the taboo system. But even in Hellas many irrational taboos survived. Of greater consequence is the fact that they never quite outgrew the mechanical concepts characteristic of the taboo institution, or the notions of ceremonial cleanness and uncleanness. The theme of the most powerful tragic drama of the Periclean Age remains as a witness. The Oedipus of Sophocles' play has broken two of the most awful taboos: he has slain his father and he has married his mother, both *unwittingly*. The question of moral guilt, however, does not enter into it at all. From the Greek point of view he is a *miasma*, a defiling thing, and Thebes, which harbors him, suffers the consequences: a pestilence rages among men and beasts, and a blight has fallen upon the fruits of the earth. When the unhappy man discovers himself for what he is, he blinds himself and goes into exile.

In Greek, as in Latin, the same word is used to denote a person or thing as "holy," "sacred," and "accursed." The concept of ceremonial purity was not allowed to die a natural death but was taken under the wing of the Apollo of Delphi, whose legalistically-minded priests developed an elaborate ritual of purification for which their god became the sponsor and lawgiver. Thus religious conservatism prevailed even in Hellas, — a fact which was all the more regrettable because it prevented the complete and harmonious fusion of religion and an awakened moral sense. The god at Delphi demanded not a "clean heart" but ceremonial purity; an irrational element survived which put a premium on formalism at the expense of true piety. So at the Eleusinian mysteries the mere attendance upon a ritual, with mechanical adherence to its regulations, was supposed to confer blessings in the life to come. This made the celebrated cynic Diogenes scoff at a religion which promised a better lot to Pataikion the thief than to the great patriot Epaminondas because Pataikion had been initiated and Epaminondas had not.

The irrational concepts surviving in Greek religion from early days are by no means confined to rites of purification and initiation. We have seen that primitive man feels himself surrounded by unseen powers. His first efforts are directed to establishing satisfactory relations with these spirits, that he may gain their favor or at least appease them. These spirits he locates in all manner of objects: stocks and stones, springs, caves, the entire realm of vegetation, as well as the animal kingdom, in turn are drawn upon as the dwelling place of divine power. To the entire system which makes an object of worship not, indeed, of the stone or the snake but of the mysterious spirit which dwells in these the name of *animism* has been given.[1] Of this stage abundant remains are found in the practices of Greek religion. Sacred stones have their place in Greek cults; the most famous of all was that at Delphi, the *omphalos* (navel) of the earth. It is altogether likely that Hermes himself was originally the spirit of the cairn, the sacred stone heap which guides the wandering

[1] See E. B. Tylor, *Primitive Culture.*

shepherd. From a shepherd god he became the god of the wayfaring trader as well as the guide of the dead, and to this day (we call him by his Roman name, Mercury) he has remained the symbol of travel. The Greek landscape, dotted with little chapels and shrines, furnished abundant evidence of the cult of grove and spring and sacred cave. As for the animal kingdom, although animal worship has all but disappeared from Hellas, we are familiar with the animals associated with the Hellenic gods. The owl of Athena, which through the fortuitous association with the goddess has become a wise bird, and the eagle of Zeus are among the best known. Apollo had a whole menagerie attached to his name. The explanation in nearly all these cases is that obscure animal cults survived into a more enlightened age which identified some greater god with the animal deity; and invariably a tale (*mythus*) was told to account for the association of the god with the animal.

Long before Homer's day the Greek had recognized man's superiority to the animal, and he had projected his own self into the world of powers that controlled his life. The divine agents were anthropomorphized; that is, imagination clothed them with human form and human attributes. Greek rationalism and Greek need for clarity striving to bring order into the divine chaos here encountered a task which was beyond it; it was impossible to introduce order and consistency into this welter of gods and goddesses, demigods and "heroes," with their innumerable cults and the bewildering mass of myths told of them in different centers. Nothing was accomplished before Homer but a further projection of human relationships into the society of the gods; and since monarchs ruled on earth a monarch was introduced into heaven. Then Homer came, and the Greek world fell under the spell of this poet, who was no theologian but whose genius perpetuated the chief figures of the pantheon and gave them enduring life in Greek imagination.

But the influence of Homeric poetry, important as it was

in endowing Hellas with a number of national deities whose power was acknowledged throughout the length and breadth of Hellas, did not touch the ancient local cults and rites that flourished in Greek township and countryside. It may have contributed to the fusion of cults and gods which was promoted by political and other historical developments. This *syncretism* has made of the Hellenic gods and goddesses such complicated figures that the attempts, at one time made, to explain the varying functions of such divine figures as Apollo and Artemis on the basis of a single fundamental concept were doomed to failure.

Such fusion of cults and functions was facilitated by the fluidity of Greek religion. If the Greeks had had a sacred book and a hierarchy of priests or if their religion could be traced to the work of a founder, it would be a much easier task to write a history of Greek religion. In default of these, its development was conditioned only by the Hellenic need for definiteness and beauty of form, and the Hellenic joy of life found in the religious ritual a medium of expression.

Some of the Greek gods are chiefly functional, or departmental. This is true of Aphrodite (Venus) and her mischievous son Eros (Cupid); of Ares (Mars), the god of berserker rage; of Demeter (Ceres), the corn-mother who causes the crops to grow; of Hephaestus (Vulcan), the god of fire; of Hestia (Vesta), the goddess of the hearth. But the complicated parts assigned to most of the greater gods are the result of historical developments. Thus Athena (Minerva) may have been the household goddess of the Creto-Mycenaean rulers; as such the snake was associated with her, for the snake too figures as the guardian of the home. When the Achaean princes established themselves in these palaces, and the palaces themselves were transformed into the strongholds of the war lords, Athena followed suit: she borrowed their helmet and spear, and we have the strange phenomenon of a female deity as a god of war. When the princes went, the worship of their helmeted household goddess was inherited by the city-states. She still dwelt on the same hilltop, once the site of the royal palace but now the citadel of the town, and became the patron saint of town life and of its growing needs and arts and industries. Finally, because a stirring intellectual life developed in the town which was most closely identified with her, she became par excellence the guardian goddess of mental pursuits; and to this day, at least in European countries, she is the goddess of the university.

Apollo is one of the most complex of Hellenic gods, but it is only as the god of music, poetry, and dance that he is a unique product of Greek genius. That he acquired this significance is not due to any original function he possessed; he may have been a shepherd god, not markedly different from his half brother Hermes, whose home was in Arcadia. But Apollo took possession of Delphi, a pre-Hellenic cult center which had been the home of prophecy and oracle long before his advent. This fact was to prove of momentous consequence in shaping the subsequent career of the god, whose transformation in a sense parallels the transition of his own people from early tribal life to the highest levels of civilization.[1] For prophetic utterance is exalted in spirit and therefore metrical in form; only one further step was needed to make the god of the oracle into the god of all poetry, which included dance and song. Moreover, since the spell exorcising the demon of disease was among the most powerful of incantations, we find Apollo from the earliest times associated with the art of healing.

The same rationalizing and humanizing process that we observed in the creation of the Hellenic pantheon was applied to the constantly growing myth material. We have noticed that not all myths are myths in the true sense. The Greek word means nothing but "tale," whereas we understand by "myth" a story involving divine agents and having religious signifi-

[1] There is no better illustration of Hellenic social and cultural evolution than is provided by the career of Apollo. The student will find the materials in L. R. Farnell, *The Cults of the Greek States* (Oxford, 1907), Vol. IV, Chap. IV.

cance. Now, as we have seen,[1] a great many "myths" are pure *Märchen*, or fairy tales, — stories told to amuse and entertain. Others are legends with a historical kernel, the embellished records of a dim past; such was the story of Troy.

The remainder, the true myths, are mostly of the *aetiological* variety; that is, they are told to account for something,— for natural phenomena, for geographical peculiarities, or (and this is perhaps the largest class) for particulars of ritual and social custom. Among the true myths of the first type, one of the best-known and most beautiful is the myth of Demeter and her daughter Kore (identified with Persephone).[2] The god of the nether world carries off Kore, and the grief-stricken mother searches for her in vain. Eventually the daughter is restored, but only on condition that she return to her husband for part of the year; thus the change of seasons is accounted for. Again, a conspicuous rock bearing a faint resemblance to a human face and watered by a spring is explained as Niobe, weeping for her offspring and turned into stone. And how did the rite of purification originate? The myth tells how Apollo, after slaying the Python, himself undergoes the ceremony and establishes the precedent. Why are the gods content with little more than fat and bones as their portion of the sacrifice? The answer is found in the myth which tells of the deceit practiced by Prometheus on the Father of Gods. Thus the aetiological myth professes to account for everything that needs an explanation; even the cry of the nightingale and the spider's web are thus accounted for.[3]

Such explanations must command social approval in order to survive; that is, although they are products of individual ingenuity and imagination, they are yet social products in

[1] See Chapter II, p. 25.

[2] See the beautiful Homeric hymn to Demeter in Andrew Lang's translation.

[3] See the myths of Procne and Philomela and of Arachne in H. J. Rose, *Handbook of Greek Mythology* (Dutton, 1928).

that they must fall well within the prevailing range of ideas. Belief in the truth of myths, however, was never regarded as obligatory; it cannot be repeated too often that Greek religion had neither creed nor dogma and was not concerned with belief as such: it placed the emphasis on the correct performance of the ritual. To this, then, we now turn.

Greek religion being the affair of the group, be this tribe or city-state, it follows that the most important religious rites were those in which all shared. The family in Hellas continued to have its own religious observances: there was the worship of the hearth fire and the inner gods of the house; of Zeus as the god of the home, whose altar was never missing; especially the careful tendance of the dead was a sacred duty resting upon the family.

But the more important religious ritual belonged to the community. The sacrificial feast at which men gather to eat and drink and be merry with their god belongs to tribal society,[1] and Hellas inherited its traditions. Sacrifice is the excuse for these festive gatherings. The animal itself may have been the god, and then the eating of its flesh has a sacramental character; more commonly sacrifice is conceived as a tribute to the god's power; in exceptional cases the victim is sacrificed by way of atonement.

Upon these tribal ceremonies Greek genius placed its own stamp. They took the form of (1) Panhellenic celebrations, like that in Olympia, in honor of Zeus; (2) festivals in which only a group of states united (thus the Ionians would gather in the island of Delos to worship Apollo); (3) city festivals, the most numerous and the most important in the history of the city-state. From mere merrymaking and feasting these festivals, constantly enlarging their sphere, became perhaps the most important agency for the physical and spiritual development of Hellas. To the competitions in athletic fields there were added other features, until nearly every field of human endeavor was represented; here the Greeks found an

[1] See W. Robertson Smith, *Religion of the Semites*, Lecture VII.

honorable outlet for that spirit of emulation so characteristic of them. On the occasion of these festivals the city-state would bestow its crowns [1] and honorary decrees upon the deserving citizen. That public worship of this character had an incalculable influence on contemporary civilization is apparent. The architect's noblest achievement was the temple, the dwelling place of the god; the sculptor found his chief task in the making of the cult image and in the adornment of the temple; the lyric poet composed largely for religious celebrations; performance of drama was a feature of the public worship of Dionysus. What is less readily observed is that such religious celebrations had an even greater social significance: they became a sacred bond holding men together more securely than any other; they made of political union a religious union, converting social obligation from a duty which could not be shirked into a pleasure eagerly welcomed.[2]

We are now ready to consider the chief religious developments in the three successive stages in the history of the Hellenic city-state.

The First Period

The birth of the city-state had brought new problems, — an awakening sense of civic rights and civic responsibilities and an insistent demand for social justice. In consequence of the rapid expansion of the Greek world and of accompanying economic changes the ancient crust of tradition had been broken. With the passing of the old order the Hellenic cities were in danger of being dissolved into a chaos of conflicts, external as well as internal. The new individualism had to adjust itself to the needs of group life, that is, of the self-governing polis. As yet passions were unruly. We have seen,

[1] The most famous oration of all antiquity is Demosthenes' *On the Crown*, in which the orator and patriot defended his right to receive the civic reward.

[2] See C. Delisle Burns, *Greek Ideals*, Chap. I.

however, that the tradition of social obligation survived, and regard for the common safety of the new citizens exercised a restraining influence.

It was inevitable that this social evolution should be reflected in the history of Hellenic religion, especially since the new political unit was a religious unit as well. The developments in the field of religion are associated primarily with two gods, Apollo and Dionysus. In the last analysis, Apollo fought for the cause of the group, whereas Dionysus represented the aspirations of the individual; their rivalry reflected the conflict between group solidarity and individualism. Apollo won, but found room for Dionysus in his own temple at Delphi.

The oracle of Delphi during the two centuries preceding the Persian Wars was the most steadying influence in Hellas. We have met Apollo's priests at Delphi in another role, namely, as the upholders of the rite of purification; and we have found reason to regret their activity in stressing formalism in religion. At the same time it was the institutionalizing habit of Apollo of which Hellas stood most in need, and when the god extended his influence to other fields he rendered the polis an inestimable service. In so far as he stood for the principle of order and form, he found a ready ear in a world which was instinctively aware of the need for these. Gradually the influence of Apollo's oracle spread until no important undertaking was begun without his sanction; and, indeed, his priests who daily received and conversed with envoys from all parts of Hellas were more competent to give sound advice than any other body of men.

But the greatest service Apollo rendered was in guiding and instructing the new citizens in the exercise of their new rights and responsibilities. Here again the god did not originate. The wise men of Hellas (later ages revered them as the Seven Sages) had preached the need for sanity, a sense of proportion, and self-restraint. But it was not until Apollo made their wisdom his own that it became a mighty force.

View of Delphi

"Nothing overmuch" and "Know thyself"[1] were inscribed on his temple. It was the prestige of Apollo and his sanction which established *sophrosyne* as a new social virtue in Hellas. As so often, we are dealing here with a concept which has no exact equivalent in the English language. It became the cardinal virtue in Greece because it was the one social virtue without which the polis would have perished; it stood for restraint of self, for moderation, for the recognition that, after all, man alone is but a feeble creature. Homer does not know this word; it does not belong to a poetry which sings the glories of the superman. A Roman poet has expressed it in his *est modus in rebus* — "there is a measure in things." But the idea was Greek; and when Aristotle finally made of *to metron* (the mean) the cardinal principle of all virtue, he echoed Greek sentiment. The influence of Apollo, then, was exerted in strengthening the sense of social obligation and in tempering the passions of party strife.

Now for Dionysus. Nietzsche[2] saw in Apollo and Dionysus the representatives of two antagonistic principles in life, the one standing for sobriety of mind, the other for divine intoxication. This may be fanciful, and it may easily be applied in a one-sided manner; but there is more than a grain of truth in it. Who is this Dionysus? Homer barely mentions him, and of his origin conflicting views are entertained today. Was he a Hellenic god or did he come from the wilds of Thrace? We do not know. It is certain that early in the period under consideration he made his re-entry into Greece, bringing with him a wave of religious frenzy that threatened to engulf Hellas. He was a god of vegetation and procreation, but — and in this he differed from the sober-minded Olympians — his cult was of the orgiastic type. To the accompanying beating of drums, shrieking of flutes, and tin-

[1] This "Know thyself" did not imply what Socrates later read into it; it meant, rather, "Know thyself for being only a mortal; know thine own limitations."

[2] See *The Birth of Tragedy*.

Dionysus Sailing

Interior of a drinking cup by Exekias (sixth century), in the Glyptothek, Munich

kling of cymbals his devotees celebrated their religious frenzies on the mountainsides at night, by torchlight. In their religious ecstasy, still further stimulated by whirling dances, they sought mystic union with their god, whose spirit entered into them; for he was the god of wine as well, and — like all primitive peoples — the Greeks regarded intoxication as a form of divine possession. In their Bacchic [1] ecstasy they would see visions and perform miracles; they would tear animals to pieces and devour them raw (this was perhaps a survival of an ancient sacramental rite); in short, they would surrender to the joys of divine possession until sheer exhaustion overtook them.

The towns, in their bewilderment, resorted to Apollo, and the great Master of Ceremonies did not fail them: invariably he bade them found a state cult in honor of the wild god, and prescribed the forms. Thus Dionysiac ecstasy was brought under the control of the polis, and the god entered the organized life of the civilized state. In the end he became the most beloved of all the Greek gods — the Deliverer who, for a brief spell, grants the vision of a greater glory. He made a valuable contribution to Greek life and religious experience; for without mysticism religion is deprived of its highest manifestation. And Apollo, after all, was no stranger to mysticism: his own priestess in ecstatic trance became his mouthpiece. Thus there was no incongruity to the Greek in the thought that Dionysus should dwell in Apollo's temple at Delphi during the winter months, when Apollo was supposed to be housed in Lycia; then the paean, the stately song of Apollo, gave way to the moving magnificence of the dithyramb, the song of Dionysus. And the god of intoxication, in turn, became a god of poetic inspiration and a patron of art; drama, the most splendid product of Greek poetry, was his gift to Hellas.

Finally, because his cult lent greater fervor and intensity to religious experience, it fostered the growth of belief in

[1] Bacchus is another cult name of Dionysus.

Drunken Maenads

From a drinking cup, signed by the potter Hieron, painted by Macron (early fifth century). The Neues Museum, Berlin personal immortality: the Dionysiac element in man surely could not perish! Through Dionysus the Greek hoped to escape the dreary lot of the shades in Hades; the god found his way into the Eleusinian mysteries, which promised the initiated a happier fate in the life to come.[1]

In conclusion we note that to the most pressing problem of the era, the question of social justice, religion remained strangely indifferent. Hesiod had placed "Justice" in Olympus, at the throne of Zeus. But the goddess remained an abstraction, and was of small importance in the practical affairs of the polis.

The Second Period

The Persian Wars, which opened the second period, seemed to confirm the wisdom of Apollo's teaching: sophrosyne was best. While the victory of Greece strengthened her faith in herself, the downfall of the Persian contained an object lesson not to be ignored. It looked as if an envious deity had visited condign punishment on the man who had wantonly transgressed the limits which the gods set to mortals. Nemesis, retribution, had overtaken Xerxes. Thus Herodotus, the historian of the Persian Wars, interpreted the catastrophe which had befallen Persia. The lesson of humility was echoed by his contemporary, the tragic poet Sophocles; and even Aeschylus, though he expressly repudiated the doctrine that mere human greatness provokes divine jealousy, yet saw in Xerxes' defeat a judgment pronounced by Heaven on human presumption.

The second period in Hellenic history saw also the consolidation of the city-state, and in the case of Athens, the all-but-complete integration of civic life. It is obvious that the tendency toward identification of state with church continued apace. This process which enthroned the polis as a religious power can best be traced in Athens. Ever since the unifica-

[1] See B. I. Wheeler, *Dionysos and Immortality* (Houghton Mifflin, 1899).

tion of Attica, Athens had been the religious as well as the political center of Attica. The more important local cults of Attica had been brought under Athenian supervision. The cult of Artemis at Brauron, of the corn goddesses at Eleusis, of Dionysus at Eleutherae, — to mention only the most important, — had been drawn within the Athenian periphery, and the fact was annually signalized by religious processions conducting the deity from the ancient site of its worship to Athens; such processions inaugurated the respective festivals. Pisistratus, in accord with his general policy, had increased Athenian prestige by founding the Great Dionysia. The policy of Pisistratus was carried to its consummation after the Persian Wars, and Pericles, more than any of the other Athenian leaders, had contributed to making Athens the "most religious" city in Hellas. The meaning which this phrase, as applied to Athens, conveyed to the Greek mind will throw further light on the conception of religion, so strange to us, in Hellas. It meant briefly that nowhere were the gods worshiped by more numerous festivals, in no other city were these festivals celebrated with an equal lavishness and magnificence, nowhere were the gods more splendidly housed, nowhere did public monuments and works of art show greater evidence of civic devotion. A more conclusive proof of the predominance of ritual and the externals of religion in Hellas cannot be demanded.

Now let us consider the implications of this conception of religion, coupled with the prevalent ideas concerning the state. The social ideal of life which exalted the state as the one-in-all, tolerating no other loyalty beside it, logically demanded that all religious activity serve the aims of the state. Religious cult, then, aimed not at insuring the happiness of the individual but at procuring the prosperity and well-being of the state. And not only this, but the same consideration for the common welfare demanded of every citizen that he share in the public worship, that the state might not suffer from dereliction on the part of the individual. Hence religion in Athens became synonymous with patriotism, and loyalty of citizenship with due performance of public rites.

Such devoted participation in the cult of the state gods was no unpleasant duty, — quite the reverse. As we saw above,[1] Greek ritual, mostly joyous in character, with its sensuous appeal, inviting all to share the benefits and blessings of Athenian citizenship, converted social duty into a delight; to be included was a privilege and further enhanced that sense of social solidarity which caused the Greeks to regard the emotions called forth by these social events as the most precious in all human experience.

The Anthesteria, one of the most ancient Athenian festivals, will provide us with an example of the social aspects of public worship. Celebrated in honor of Dionysus, it was combined with a much older All Souls' festival. It took place in the early spring and lasted three days. The first day was that of the "Opening of the Jars"; the second day was named after the "Cups"; the last was that of the "Pots." On the first day the taboo on the new wine was solemnly removed; then began the merrymaking, in which slaves and hirelings shared; family banquets and public feasting marked the day as one of good cheer, — such cheer as Dionysus, the giver of the wine, provides. The second day saw more ceremonial wine-drinking in the sacred precinct of the god; of course, there was a contest and a prize for him who first emptied his cup, and there was the usual badinage. The day was further solemnized by the symbolic marriage of Dionysus with the wife of the "King," the high priest of Athens. The last day was the day of the ghosts; these were now abroad, and their presence rendered the day one of the most sacred, or tabooed, days in the Athenian calendar. The temples of the gods were closed, except one of Dionysus, and special precautions were taken against the spreading of the "miasma" caused by the evocation of the dead. Each family devoted itself to the tendance of its own departed, to whom a porridge

[1] See page 157.

The Erechtheum, Athens

of *panspermia* (all-seeds) was offered in special pots, after which the day was named. Hermes, conductor of the souls, was invoked. At the close of the day the ghosts were politely but firmly bidden to depart.[1]

The most splendid festival of Athens was the Panathenaea, celebrated in honor of Athena, protectress of the city and the embodiment of the civic idea. Every fourth year it was celebrated with special magnificence and was known as the Greater Panathenaea, lasting eight days and including all manner of contests. The chief event was the great procession in which representatives of the entire citizenship took part; this procession has been immortalized in marble on the frieze of the Parthenon.

Thus in Athens a complete fusion of church and state was consummated, and with it came a promotion of the spirit of good fellowship that lay at the basis of Athenian democracy. But in a sense this same union was a check to the development of religion on Greek soil, for the prevalence of a politico-social ideal such as flourished in the Hellenic polis is incompatible with the free flowering of the religious spirit. The highest manifestations of religion are realized only through an inner harmonious relationship between the individual and his God. This could never be achieved in a world where the state stood between man and God.

The Third Period

With the outbreak of the Hellenic World War in 431 B.C. the last period in the history of the Greek city-state begins. We have seen how, under the corroding influence of that war and the innumerable futile wars which followed in its train, the Greek spirit was broken. That civic patriotism which had formed the great inspiration and sustaining faith of Hellas, culminating in Periclean Athens, began to fade. A new era is now ushered in, whose most marked characteristics are a

[1] See C. Delisle Burns, *Greek Ideals*, Chap. II.

new individualism and a new rationalism. The Greek citizen, despairing of public welfare, turned for the satisfactions of life to his own pursuits, and in the general breakdown of the world around him began to doubt the wisdom of the fathers that had created it. The Sophists made their appearance on the Greek stage. Some of these boldly challenged the traditions of the past and proceeded to apply the test of reason to all matters, sacred and profane. They operated with a new formula, which sharply distinguished between that which was valid "by nature" and that which was sanctioned "by convention" (custom). Under the last category came nearly all man-made institutions, including the polis itself and its religion. The city-state and all its institutions were thus placed on the defensive by these acute disputants, who soon gained a reputation for skill in argumentation.

Even the Sophists could not harm the cause of Greek religion very greatly. If Greek religion had had a dogma or a creed, the Greek "fundamentalists" might have taken umbrage at the rationalistic ways of the Sophists. But Greek religion had neither "fundamentalists" nor "modernists" because it was not greatly interested in right belief. Of course, when a Sophist like Protagoras declared that he did not know whether there were any gods or not, a prudent and outraged state would banish him from its territory. But when a tragic poet like Euripides denounced from the stage the belief in certain myths which represented the gods as guilty of wrongdoing, the Athenians found in his words merely another proof of the poet's idiosyncrasies and a topic for animated discussion. The Sophists and the rationalists cannot be regarded as the destroyers of Greek religion.

The fact is that the state, in appropriating religion, itself had killed it. The fervor of religion had been transformed into the fervor of civic devotion and patriotism; it had become a mighty factor in stimulating civic activities. But when this civic ardor waned, it left religion nothing but the empty husks of its ceremonial. Patriotism had transformed the rite of presentation of Athena's robe at the Panathenaea into an act of devotion arousing something akin to genuine religious emotion; that same rite after the patriotic fervor had abated became an empty mummery. The citizen was more interested in saving himself than in serving his city. Had the ground been better prepared and had circumstances been more favorable, a new religion might have sprung from the ashes of the old; for the spiritual needs of the Hellene in this era were greater than ever before. But the religious ceremonial which he knew was so indispensable a factor in the social fabric of life that it continued to function long after the spirit which had dwelt in it had departed. The Greek world remained in a state of spiritual starvation for centuries. It is true, private organizations for common worship were formed; new gods were sought and found. But on the whole — and this is characteristic of the Hellene — the educated man sought consolation rather in a new philosophy of life than in a new religion; and he left the ignorant country man to his local superstitions. But the Stoic and Epicurean belong to the Hellenistic world, the Greek world *after* Alexander.

Suggestions for Reading. On Greek religion see M. P. Nilsson, *A History of Greek Religion* (Oxford, 1925); this is the best book on the subject. See also C. Delisle Burns, *Greek Ideals* (2d ed., Bell, 1919), Chaps. I–V; F. R. Earp, *The Way of the Greeks* (Oxford, 1929), Chap. V; G. Lowes Dickinson, *The Greek View of Life*, Chap. I; A. Fairbanks, *A Handbook of Greek Religion* (American Book Company, 1910).

CHAPTER VII

MORALITY

Tribal Morality

THE sketch of Greek religion contained in the preceding pages shows it to have been, at least in origin, a tribal affair; and if in tribal society religion and morality are hardly distinguishable, both being largely dependent for their sanctions on a system of taboo, the inevitable deduction would seem to be that Greek morality too, in essence, was a tribal morality. And such in fact it was. To be sure, it was modified by the same historical and social factors that affected Hellenic religion; but in essence it remained a tribal morality down to the end.

What, then, is tribal morality? It is a body of morals which is not based upon a central principle from which its several commands are logically deducible, but which derives its authority solely from custom and tradition. It enjoins upon all members of the group obedience to the customs of the fathers, the *mos maiorum*, as the Romans called them; it stipulates behavior in accordance with the conventions and traditions which have regulated the conduct of the tribesmen from immemorial days. These include, as we saw, regulations in dealing with the gods as well as with men. But here again the peculiar gifts of the Hellenic race made of Hellenic morality something markedly different from that of other races.

The First and Second Periods

First we shall consider the effects of Greek rationalism, for it is this which has given Greek morality a certain cold and calculating character. It caused the Greeks to rest moral judgment on a strictly utilitarian basis; that is, they held that human behavior could be justified only with reference to the well-being of the agent. The word "unselfish" had no place in the Greek vocabulary. Any act, they took it, is always performed to promote the interest of the agent; intelligent self-interest, then, lies at the basis of all human conduct. The very idiom of the Greeks betrays their intellectual bias. Their word for good, *agathos*, implies reference to a purpose: good *for what*? Similarly, when a Greek had been guilty of wrongdoing, he called it a *hamartia*, which the dictionary may translate by "sin" or "fault," but which really means a "failure to hit the mark": he has aimed well, but he has missed the mark. So in Homeric phraseology a wise man is said "to *know* wise things"; a kind man, "to *know* kind things." All this reveals their peculiar rationalism. To us it seems so much nonsense: were the Greeks unaware of the fact that man often knows well enough what is right and yet does the opposite? Their reply would be that if he does, he acts irrationally and that the explanation of such foolish behavior lies elsewhere: it is because the gods have blinded him. For there is a dreaded goddess, Ate, who works havoc among men; she blinds the judgment, causing one to rush headlong to destruction. Even the noble passion which drives Antigone to act in defiance of the king's command is, at least partly, accounted for by the pious poet on this basis, even though he does not withhold his admiration for her heroism. Thus Agamemnon excuses himself for the insults he heaped upon Achilles when he deprived him of his rightful spoils: it was not he, Agamemnon, who did this; it was Ate, who had robbed him of his wits.[1] Thus the fury of passion was objectivized as a divine power which overrides reason and renders man insensible to his own interests. Human folly appeared to the Greek a thing so utterly unaccountable in its manifestations as to fall well within the limits of the supernatural: the madness of anger, the urge

[1] See Sophocles' *Antigone*, lines 582 ff., and Homer's *Iliad*, Bk. 19, lines 83 ff.

of uncontrolled desire, the daring flights of hope — all were classed, with intoxication and the epileptic fit, as cases of divine possession.

To the same intellectual temper we must ascribe the excessive regard of the Greeks for measure in all things. We have noticed that sophrosyne was their cardinal virtue — that wise self-restraint which guards against excess. The good man practices the rule of measure in all things: he is neither too parsimonious nor too generous, avoiding the "mistakes" of both the miser and the spendthrift; he condemns equally the reckless audacity of the overbold and the pusillanimous prudence of the timid. The Greek had an unpleasant habit of computing the measure of his virtue and of computing it rather carefully; here too he differed from us. As one writer observes,

> Love is accounted a good thing [among us], and we admire the man who thinks the world well lost for love. To a Greek that same man would not seem admirable, nor even amiably foolish; he would seem foolish, indeed, but he would also seem not amiable, but mad. . . . To love madly, to the Greek, is not romantic, it is pernicious; its only excuse is that the power of Aphrodite, when she comes in all her strength, is hard for man to resist.[1]

The Greek propensity toward rationalizing is revealed also in their predilection for moral generalization and platitudes. A particular act is seen as a confirmation of a general law governing human conduct; pointing a moral is the delight of poet and orator alike. Greek literature is replete with this kind of thing. No ode of Pindar is complete without the "gnomic" passage in which the author points the moral of the tale; the chorus of Greek tragedy often performs the same function; and the frequency with which Greek orators quote commonplaces and the wise saws of the fathers proves how popular this practice was with their audience.

[1] F. R. Earp, *The Way of the Greeks*, p. 43. Quoted by permission of the Oxford University Press.

But the most striking proof of the intellectual bias of the Greek is found in the traditional Hellenic attitude toward woman. She is, to his mind, a creature essentially lacking in the rational capacity which distinguishes man. Given the preponderant part which the Greek assigned to reason in his concept of virtue, it necessarily follows that he would underestimate the value of the purely womanly virtues, which are closer to instinct than to reason. That he himself vastly overestimated the part played by rational thought is clear enough to us; but it caused him to deny to woman a place in the only life that counted — public life. He regarded her as by nature man's inferior; her part is to bear children and to look after the domestic interests of the family; as for the rest, as Pericles said, hers is the greatest glory whose report, either for good or for ill, is least among men. Complete obscurity is her greatest virtue! What "the best and wisest and most just man" thought of his wife we can find out from Plato's *Phaedo* (Chap. III). The friends of Socrates are gathered in the prison house to spend that last day with their philosophical friend. The presence of Xanthippe is felt as a hindrance; she talks foolishly and tactlessly, "as women are wont to." Socrates does not deign to address her: "Let someone take her home"; and she is led off, wailing and beating her breast.[1]

The halo of sanctity with which the Christian world, beginning with the worship of the Blessed Virgin, has invested woman, the sentiment which regards woman as a being at once weaker, purer, and nobler than man — this is all utterly alien to the Hellenic world, which would have held it to be rank nonsense, something passing the Hellenic understanding. Nor had the Greek yet sublimated the passion of love. *Eros* is a plain word, and it means "desire"; to found a lasting union upon a passion so transient and so devastating

[1] For the Greek conception of domestic felicity, the reader may consult Xenophon's *Oeconomicus.* He will find it instructive and, in spots, amusing as well.

would have seemed to him pure folly. Hence the all but complete absence of romantic love from the pages of Greek literature. If we do meet it in history, as in the notable case of Pericles and Aspasia, it is an irregular union, outside of marriage. Marriage was a family affair in which considerations of expediency outweighed all others. Few poets have paid nobler tribute to womanhood than Homer, who created Andromache and Nausicaa. But of all the poets who came after him, only Euripides shows a deeper understanding of womanhood, and he was reputed to be a woman-hater!

The other distinctive trait of Greek genius is its extraordinary sensitiveness to beauty. Nothing is more illustrative of the difference between Hellenic feeling and Anglo-Saxon insensibility in this respect than the contrast between our own clumsy "beautiful" and the Greek *kalos*, one of the most powerful words in their whole vocabulary, — a word which they applied with great readiness to a beautiful person, object, or action. Whether it was a fair youth, a well-shaped vase, a generous deed, or a noble death, it was all equally *kalos* to them. In fact, their habit of identifying goodness and beauty is not a little bewildering to our minds. The phrase by which they expressed their notion of a perfect gentleman combined *kalos* and *agathos*; through it they voiced their approval of the kind of life that appealed both to their sense of form and to their moral sense. A disorderly life, on the other hand, was something disgraceful — *aischros* is the word, and it means both "shameful" and "ugly." In this way Greek rationalism and Greek aestheticism have left their impress on Greek morality.

Now when we turn to the content of Greek morality, we need not repeat what was said on the subject of the pagan ideal of life as embodied in Homeric poetry.[1] We know that this ideal was one of action, springing from a desire for glory; that the qualities most admired were those of the warrior — courage and physical prowess — and loyalty and generosity,

[1] See pages 50 ff.

all of which are precisely the virtues most admired by youth. To be a stanch friend and a redoubtable enemy, to be utterly fearless (like Achilles), and to be clever and resourceful (like Odysseus) — this purely pagan ideal of life remained valid. But it had to be modified. As we have seen, there was no room in the Hellenic polis for the reckless self-assertion of the Homeric hero. The city-state, which had come into being to ensure the survival of the group and which was first organized for defense against the outer world, soon found itself confronted with an urgent need for establishing peace and good fellowship within. The principle of justice — that is, social justice, applied without discrimination to all, under the law — was to be the bedrock on which the city-state must build. It was the duty of the state to protect the weak against the strong. *Hubris* became the great social sin. By it was meant the "wanton and contemptuous defiance of the rules that regulate a man's relations with his fellows, or with the gods"[1]; it was the challenge to justice and fair dealing on the part of the strong and powerful. The state was henceforth to stand between the *hubristes* and his intended victim. And when a new social virtue, sophrosyne, came into being, the gods themselves were enlisted in the good cause, and Apollo gave his sanction. How necessary this virtue was in the period of probation through which the city-state passed, when it might have perished through the intense bitterness of party strife, we have seen in a previous chapter. It was inevitable, therefore, that social virtues should have grown in stature in a society which could not have survived without them.

But the Homeric ideal of life which set the glory of achievement above all else was not in danger of being eclipsed. The Hellenic *arete* is but feebly translated by our "virtue." Ours is but a pale word, suggestive more of negative than of positive excellence (the virtuous person does *not* do the evil deeds of which the wicked are guilty), whereas *arete* bears a proud connotation indicating that excellence which is tested by life's

[1] See Earp, *The Way of the Greeks*, p. 211.

experiences and which proves itself in doing and daring, and a desire for recognition and reward is never far away from it. Now we have seen that while the polis approved *sophrosyne* and punished *hubris*, it nevertheless gave full scope to individual ambition and rewarded *arete* in every field. But there is this distinction: the Homeric hero labored for purely selfish ends; the citizen, though he may strive for glory, must share it with the polis, and the state will reward him, whether he be a victor at Olympia, or a writer of dithyrambs, or a plain soldier fighting in the ranks.

In the end the city-state did to Greek morality what it had done to religion: it claimed morality as its own concern. It became the chief moral teacher in the life of the citizen; it prescribed his moral behavior, its approval or disapproval serving as the strongest of all social controls; its laws defined what was right and just (according to Demosthenes, the law "wants what is *just and noble and beneficial*"). Ethics and politics became hopelessly mixed, and the good man was identified with the good citizen. The drunkard, the thief, the coward, the bully were not merely bad men: above all, they were bad citizens. The political leader was felt to be responsible not only for the material welfare but also for the moral welfare of the citizens. Solon was a statesman, but he was also a preacher. When Plato questions the services rendered to Athens by Themistocles and Pericles, he asks, Did they make the Athenians *better* men than they found them? That he could put such a question at all shows the difference between the Greek point of view and our own.

The Third Period

A few words should be added concerning the development of Hellenic morality in the last period of the history of the polis. There is no need here to repeat what was said elsewhere of the demoralization attending the Hellenic World War. It follows that a system of morals so closely interwoven with a political condition and a political framework as was Hellenic morality would be vitally affected by the disintegration of its political habitat. With the birth of a new individualism and a new rationalism, Greek morality slowly disintegrated; the period was marked by the rise of a new ethic, based not on custom and tradition but on a rational analysis of the meaning of life and a critical examination of man's nature and his needs. But so strong was the force of habit that even the new ethic was still conceived as a branch of political science. However, this attack upon the problem of life could arouse the interest of only a small minority of the Greeks; it did not affect Greek morality, and its history belongs to the chapter on philosophy.

The Sophists appealed to a larger audience; they, the purveyors of a new wisdom, a practical wisdom of life, challenged the rule of custom and tradition, and, profiting by the spirit of unrest and doubt which began to pervade Hellas, questioned the wisdom of the past. What was the inherent truth in these august commandments which the fathers had never questioned and which they had taught their sons? Could their claims to validity today be made good on the basis of their antiquity? Must not reason itself rebel at any such tyranny of the past over the present? Even the revered Marathon fighters appeared in a new light: perhaps they were, in fact, a lot of old fogies, whose shades ought to be laid to a dignified and well-deserved rest. The war had brought with it a new alignment, that of the younger generation against their elders. This, above all things, indicated the passing of the old order in Hellas; for the old order was based on tradition. It seemed as if a good case could be made against the very concept of justice as tested by the touchstone of reason. Did justice have its foundation in the natural order of things, or, on the contrary, was it a mere convention springing from a conspiracy among the weak and impotent to keep from the stronger and abler the rightful share in the world's goods to which their superior strength and cunning entitled them? In a disillusioned world, made cynical by its own failures, such questioning of the ancient ways and the old faiths found a ready hearing. Yet so firmly grounded was Greek morality in its past that, although it could be kept on the defensive, it could not be dislodged from its ancient strongholds, — not even by the adroit arguments of the Sophists. Eventually the newness of the entire movement wore off, the interest in the new problems waned, and fourth-century Hellas was content to repeat the old tunes, even though they did not fit the new tempo and rhythm of a changing world.

SUGGESTIONS FOR READING. On the subject of Greek morality see especially F. R. EARP, *The Way of the Greeks* (Oxford, 1929), and G. LOWES DICKINSON, *The Greek View of Life*, Chap. III.

CHAPTER VIII

EDUCATION

The First and Second Periods

THE factors determining the form that education will assume among any people are the same as those affecting its religion or its arts. Hence a great deal of what we have observed in dealing with Greek religion and morality will hold good for the history of Greek education as well: here too we shall note the influence of social organization and racial traits.

Now if, in historic times, the city-state claimed the individual as its own, it follows that education would be primarily education for citizenship; as such it would be a matter of grave concern to the state, and the art of education itself would be looked upon as a branch of political science. And such was actually the case. The most celebrated work of Plato is the *Republic*, a treatise dealing with political science and the ideal state but largely devoted to education. Aristotle likewise embedded his reflections upon education in the *Politics*. In this Plato and Aristotle were entirely right and expressed a point of view shared by virtually all Hellas. Nevertheless, education throughout Hellas was left, as we shall see, largely to private initiative — always with the exception of Sparta and a few other Dorian communities.

If, then, education is in the first place education for citizenship, it follows that it will be cultural; that is, it will aim at the whole man, at the development of character. The great stress laid in Hellas on physical training is not incompatible with the larger cultural aim of education. On the contrary, to attain the proper balance in educational matters, physical and mental training must complement each other; once more the Greek sense of balance and harmony prevails. For the state needs efficient citizens, and neither a flabby body nor a sluggish mind makes for good citizenship. But the aim of Hellenic education goes no farther; it does not include specialized or vocational training. If men are capable carpenters or stonecutters, they probably learned their trade from their fathers; education in the Hellenic sense knows only one profession — that of citizenship.

Let us hear Plato on the subject; and be it remembered that he is not giving his private opinion but merely stating facts on which there was universal agreement.

Education and admonition commence in the first years of childhood, and last to the very end of life. Mother and nurse and father and tutor are quarrelling about the improvement of the child as soon as ever he is able to understand them: he cannot say or do anything without their setting forth to him that this is just and this is unjust; this is honorable, that is dishonorable; this is holy, that is unholy; do this and abstain from that. And if he obeys, well and good; if not, he is straightened by threats and blows, like a piece of warped wood. At a later stage they send him to teachers and enjoin them to see to his manners even more than to his reading and music; and the teachers do as they are desired. And when the boy has learned his letters and is beginning to understand what is written, as before he understood only what was spoken, they put into his hands the works of great poets, which he reads at school; in these are contained many admonitions and many tales, and praises, and *encomia* of ancient famous men, which he is required to learn by heart, in order that he may imitate or emulate them and desire to become like them. Then, again, the teachers of the lyre take similar care that their young disciple is temperate and gets into no mischief; and when they have taught him the use of the lyre, they introduce him to the poems of other excellent poets, who are the lyric poets; and these they set to music, and make their harmonies and rhythms quite familiar to the children's souls, in order that they may learn to be more gentle, and harmonious and rhythmical, and so more fitted for speech and action; for the life of man in every part has need of harmony and rhythm. Then they send him to the master of gymnastic, in order that their bodies may better minister to the virtuous mind, and that they may not be compelled through bodily weakness to play the coward in war or on any other occasion.[1]

[1] Plato, *Protagoras* (Jowett's translation), 325 C–326 C.

If Plato correctly interprets Hellenic sentiment on the subject of education, as no doubt he does, Greek education may rightly be called cultural in its aims. But the whole system, as he describes it, with its appeal to authority rather than to reason, has also a thoroughly archaic look; the sentence about the straightening of a warped piece of wood sounds rather ominous. In fact, Greek education is not far removed from the tribal stage. For the tribe is a homogeneous group, and the training the elders give the young is such as to facilitate their complete submergence in the group; they must learn to adjust themselves to tribal life, to distinguish between what sacred tradition holds to be right and what it holds to be wrong. Education is authoritarian; it aims at conformity, and is the same for all. Now the city-state, also a fairly homogeneous group, perpetuates tribal ways in its educational methods. The citizens are to be molded in identical forms in order that they may be able readily to think and act in common; for on such common sentiment and common action depends the life of the state. In such an environment, education is naturally directed toward the whole man, the efficient citizen, rather than to the training of individual aptitude; least of all is it aimed at preparing for a gainful occupation. It is an education for life rather than for making a living.

Hellenic education, then, did not differ essentially in its aims from that of early society. It is in the methods adopted that the racial traits of the Greeks are revealed. For the Hellenic genius, pursuing its own path, sought to achieve these aims by methods that eventually led to the concept of a "liberal education," which the modern world has inherited from Hellas.

We know the racial traits of the Greeks; their instinct for order and balance, their love of beauty, their lively imagination. Through these channels they strove to educate their citizenry. They trained their youth in two subjects: the one, *gymnastic*, aiming at the proper development of the physique;

the other, *music*, aiming at the proper development of the mind. But to prepare a mere athlete or a mere savant was not on their program; in either case there would be wanting the right balance, and a warped, one-sided individual would be the result.

Their gymnastic needs no further elucidation, except that, in accordance with their peculiar genius, training in athletics was as much a training in aesthetics; mere muscular strength, if not conjoined with grace, did not greatly impress them.

Their "music," however, calls for more comment. The Greek word denotes not only music proper but also the other arts and literature. In fact, there were two types of teachers of "music": the *kitharistes*, or instructor in music proper, and the *grammatistes*, the teacher of letters and literature. The latter made Homer the basis of instruction, but other poets were by no means neglected. By an appeal to the imagination, by enkindling the boy's admiration for such a figure as Achilles, the masters tried to inculcate a love for the noble and beautiful and a hatred for the base and ugly. However, such indirect instruction was reinforced by the recitation of moral maxims that were culled principally from Hesiod's, Solon's, and Theognis' poetry, or at least from verses circulating under their names; the pupils committed to memory vast quantities of this proverbial wisdom. Thus the masters strove to improve the characters of the young entrusted to their care.

So far the educational program is perfectly intelligible. Where the Hellenes differed from us most widely was in the peculiar part they assigned to musical instruction. For they taught music not only for the adornment of man's leisure hours but also for the formation of character! They saw a parallel between the well-ordered life, the well-balanced character, and the harmony and rhythm of song and dance. In every boy there lives a savage, lawless and uncontrolled in his appetites; to bring him into the fold of a civilized and well-regulated society, Greek education employed music, including choral song and dance, as conducive to the development of a feeling for the beauty of rhythmic order and harmony. The stately rhythm of the march, the lively and yet severely controlled movement of the dance, the stirring strains of the war song — all these would attune the soul of the learner aright, until within him also would rule harmony and order and control of the mind over the body. Damon, the musician, averred that no changes can be made in musical fashions without endangering the whole fabric of society, and Plato assents.[1] The seven-stringed lyre was the popular instrument; the flute, though adopted for a time, could not find universal favor in Hellas. The reasons alleged for its rejection are both characteristic of the Hellene: in the first place, playing the flute distorts the features of the player and makes him ridiculous; in the second place, it is a wild and disorderly instrument, likely to excite player and audience beyond measure.

Hellenic education, then, aimed at the equal and harmonious development of body and mind by means of gymnastic and music. Such a simple and really beautiful educational program, for which we give the Greeks full credit, was possible only because the accumulated stores of human experience and human knowledge were as yet so scanty. These Greek boys were not plagued by the numerous factual courses with which we clutter up our programs of instruction, because as yet such information was nonexistent. We are dealing with a period which antedates the birth of the experimental and social sciences; and for the technical apparatus indispensable in this age they had only the simple equipment of the craftsman and artisan, which the son inherited from the father. But did not the young Hellene study history? Certainly. Homer and other poets were his handbook on history, and they served equally well as the storehouse of information on religion, morality, statesmanship, geography, and everything else worth knowing. Did not Hesiod set forth

[1] *The Republic*, 424 C.

the rules of farming? And where else could one find the genealogy of the gods themselves? As yet the poets ruled supreme in the council halls of education.

It goes without saying that as life became more complex, and especially as the old ideal of state solidarity declined, this educational scheme gradually gave way to a new one; but the old prevailed during our first two periods. Before taking up the story of the change which set in with the beginning of the third period and the outbreak of the Hellenic World War, we shall do well to inquire a little more closely into the workings of the traditional pedagogy.

The Spartan system was in a class by itself, and remained substantially unaltered until the end. In our account of Spartan institutions we have seen with what pitiless logic the Spartan state trained its youth to serve the civic purposes. Even here, although the intellectual side of education was sadly neglected, the aim was the production of character and conformity to the Spartan scheme of life. Nevertheless, Spartan education was narrow and had a brutalizing tendency, as was admitted even by its greatest admirers. Another equally serious drawback of the system was its overemphasis on obedience to authority and its lack of training in individual initiative and responsibility; there was too much supervision, too much control. In this respect, as in others, Sparta was the most archaic of Greek states.

For the rest of Hellas, the education as provided in Athens before the great war may serve as a fair example. Here too, although education was left to private initiative until the boy reached the age of manhood, when he took the oath of citizenship and began his military training, the general effect produced was very much the same as in Sparta. True, the boarding schools of Sparta were no feature of Athenian life, but the boy spent the entire day in school and palaestra, away from home; home influences therefore counted for very little in his life. "He learned to dissociate himself from his family and associate himself with his fellow citizens. No doubt he lost much by this system, but the solidarity of the state gained."[1] The individual edges were rubbed off until conformity to prevailing standards became a life habit. And although thc state neither provided public schools nor prescribed a curriculum, it exercised a certain supervision, as is evident from stray references in Athenian literature. It is quite characteristic of the polis that its activity in these matters betrays a greater concern for morals and deportment than for intellectual pursuits, for in tribal life the *mores* loom largest. Small wonder that we find the august Areopagus bestirring itself in the matter; and the very name of the Athenian magistrates entrusted with the care of youth, *Sophronistes* (chastener), shows the character of their duties. In Aristophanes' day the discipline relaxed. Hear his indictment: he finds a general contempt for authority, a disrespect for elders, love of ease and pleasure, bad manners, — the boys would lounge about and cross their legs; instead of observing a respectful silence in the presence of their betters, they would ask impertinent questions and argue everlastingly, — and finally, worst of all, they preferred the jazzy tunes of Timotheus to the good old classics. Aristophanes' complaint has a quaintly familiar sound.

The ordinary curriculum included as a minimum the three R's and gymnastics. Girls had no share in the educational routine, but received training for their future duties as wives and mothers at home.

Gymnastics was taught at the palaestrae, both private and public, where the boys spent a large part of the day. The *paidotribes* (trainer) supervised the exercises, beginning with the simplest and adapting them to the pupil's age until gradually there were included all the athletic sports of Hellas — running, jumping, throwing the discus and the javelin, wrestling, boxing, and the *pankration*. The state offered prizes, thus stimulating the striving for excellence in matters of great public importance, as the boys some day were to be not

[1] K. J. Freeman, *Schools of Hellas*, p. 282.

Boxing and Pankration Scenes

From a red-figured drinking cup

only defenders of their city but also its representatives at the Panhellenic festivals. We may note in passing that similar rewards were offered for excellence at "musical" contests. In addition, the state maintained gymnasia, where men of all ages gathered and where the gregarious Hellenes found an opportunity not only for physical exercise but also for enjoying the companionship of their fellows.[1]

The *grammatistes* taught the boy his letters and simple arithmetic. The latter was attended with greater difficulties than at present, not only because the Greeks used letters in place of figures (*a* standing for *1*, *b* for *2*, etc.), which made multiplication and division a cumbersome process, but also because of the dearth of material aids to such instruction. A similar difficulty attended the teaching of letters and literature. Most of the instruction was necessarily oral; and although both counting board and writing tablet had their place in Athenian schools, the scarcity of books necessitated a much greater reliance on memory than is the case with us. In compensation, the Hellenes developed far more dependable memories. Another advantage was that since all reading was done aloud, the pupils learned to enunciate correctly and to read with understanding; hasty and perfunctory reading of assigned passages was an evil they were not acquainted with. Nor was the study of literature as yet obscured by the attention paid to extraneous matters: historical setting and historical interpretation of their poets were of no concern to the Greeks. On the contrary, the attitude of teacher and pupil was completely uncritical, the poet being regarded as the mouthpiece of the Muse addressing all men and all ages.

The cost of education, which was defrayed by the parents, was comparatively trifling, for teachers were poorly paid. It does not seem likely, however, that all parents could afford the musical training given by the *kitharistes*, who taught the boy to play the lyre to accompany the singing of lyric verse. Even so, not many Athenian lads were entirely ignorant of

[1] For a description of life at the gymnasia, see Freeman, op. cit. pp. 134–142.

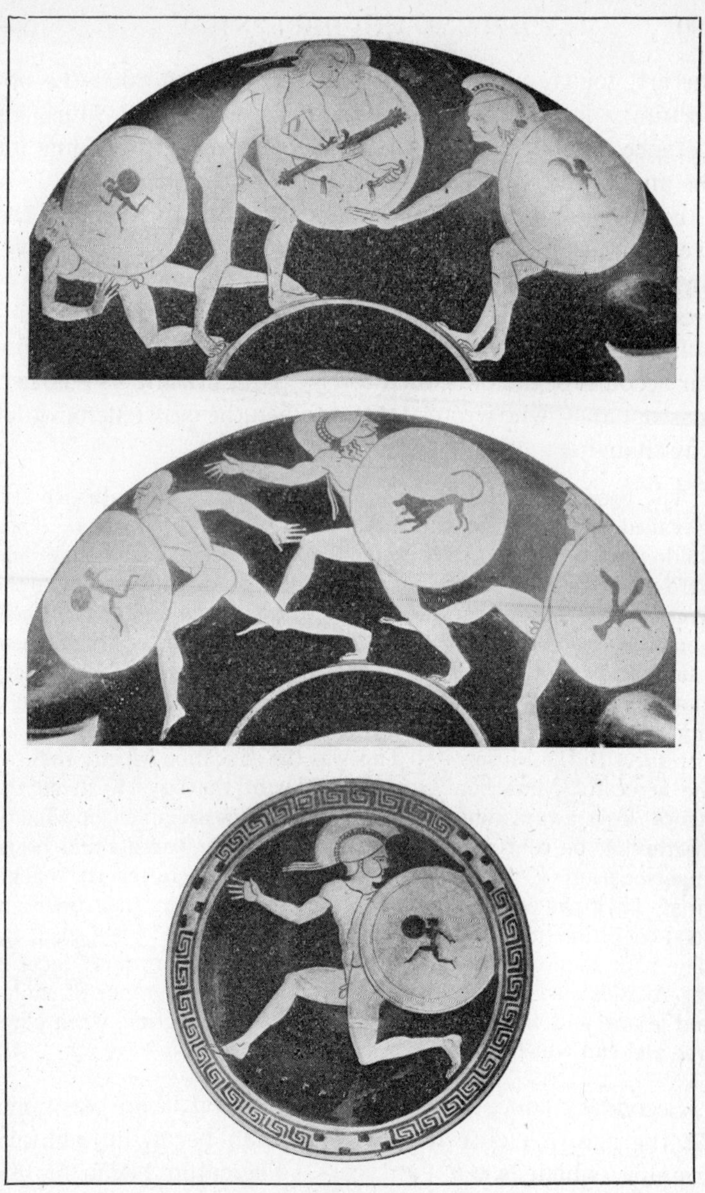

Hoplitodromoi (Runners in Armor)

From a red-figured drinking cup in the Neues Museum, Berlin

the art, for through the liturgies the state afforded the opportunity for training in choral dance and song. Thus, for instance, five choruses of fifty boys each were in training for the annual dithyrambic contest between the tribes.

From the age of six to sixteen the boys lived under the eyes of their masters, and wherever they went an old slave, the *paedagogus*, accompanied them. School was the whole of life to them, nor did they, as far as we know, require any compulsion to drive them to school and palaestra. We may close our account of the old education by paraphrasing its eulogist, Aristophanes, who wrote at a time when the old Hellenic order was changing:

> The good old style of education, in the days when Justice still prevailed over Rhetoric, and good morals were still in fashion. Then children were seen and not heard; then the boys of each hamlet and ward walked in orderly procession along the roads on their way to the lyre-school — no overcoats, though it snowed cats and dogs. Then, when they stood up square — no lounging — the master taught them a fine old patriotic song like "Pallas, city-sacker dread" or "A cry that echoes afar," set to a good old-fashioned tune. If anyone tried any vulgar trills and twiddles, he got a tremendous thrashing for disrespect to the Muses. . . . This was the education which produced the heroes of Marathon. . . . This taught the boys to avoid the Agora, keep away from the [warm] Baths, be ashamed of what is disgraceful, be courteous to elders, honour their parents and be an impersonation of Modesty — instead of running after the ballet-girls. They passed the day in the gymnasia, keeping their bodies in good condition, not mouthing quibbles in the Agora. Each spent his time with some well-mannered lad of his own age, running races in the Akademeia under the sacred olives amid a fragrance of smilax and leisure and white poplar, rejoicing in the springtide, when plane tree and elm whisper together.[1]

Secondary education, as we understand it, there was none. At the age of eighteen the young man began his military training, which lasted two years. Thereafter began his life

[1] Freeman's paraphrase (*Schools of Hellas*, p. 72) of Aristophanes' *Clouds*, lines 960 ff. Quoted by permission of The Macmillan Co.

as a citizen, and with it his higher education; for, as one of the Hellenic poets puts it, *Polis andra didaskei* ("The city teaches a man"). And if his lot were cast in a town playing an active part in Hellenic life, he would receive a many-sided upbringing indeed!

The Third Period and the New Education

With the outbreak of the Hellenic World War a new era begins, and with it a new departure in the field of education. Indeed, we may well marvel that the old education, tribal in origin and adapted to the needs of a homogeneous society, should have survived so long; it furnishes fresh evidence of the conservatism of Hellenic society and the extraordinary toughness of social customs. For the materials for a new type of education had been long accumulating in Hellas, and the tendencies of the Periclean Age had long pointed in that direction. Life in Hellas, especially at Athens, was more varied, more stirring, more interesting, than in the days of Marathon and Salamis. The economic level of life, while still comparatively low, was steadily rising. In the growing complexity of Athenian society, with its manifold and clashing interests, man was becoming more conscious of himself; more aware of the individual part he played, of his own needs and his own desires; and less and less content to sink his own personality in the organized life of the state. The war did its share in accelerating these trends. Knowledge increased, and new fields of learning sprang up in bewildering variety. The science of grammar arose; that is, man began to analyze the language he used as a tool. Etymology and synonyms were studied. Philosophers examined the physical world around them: Did Zeus cause the thunder? And if he did not, what did? They studied the heavens. Astronomy was born, and with it mathematics; the wonders of the new geometry were hailed with delight. Geography joined the group of new sciences, and maps were made. Speculation invaded the political field: What was the best form of government, — monarchy, aristocracy, or democracy? Pamphlets were written on political subjects and circulated; books made their appearance on the market. Logic of a sort came into being through the propounding of conundrums: If the dog which is yours is also a father, is he, then, your father? And, as we saw in a preceding chapter, the old tribal moralities were vigorously attacked. Above all, there was the new rhetoric, of which Gorgias of Leontini was such a brilliant exponent; and since the art of speech played so important a part in the city life of Hellas, ensuring a hearing from one's fellow citizens in the assembly, the courts of justice, and elsewhere, what would one not give to master that art, if it could be taught? Especially the younger generation was athirst for the new learning, not only because they were Hellenes and therefore intellectually curious but also because they had the ambition and energy of youth. Cleverness and the feeling of superiority that comes with increased knowledge, to be up-to-date and in touch with things — such were the objects eagerly sought in that age.

When such needs are felt in any society, they do not long remain unsatisfied. And so all over Hellas appeared a new class of men who promised to satisfy these demands. These are the *Sophists*, whom we met in a previous chapter — dealers in the wisdom of life and every kind of learning.

The word "sophist" itself needs some explanation. Originally an honorable term applied to great poets and sages alike, it denoted the man conspicuous for his intelligence and wisdom — the kind of wisdom which enabled him to cope successfully with life's problems and to enlighten others in the matter of their solution. The peculiar connotation of "sophist," and of kindred terms such as "sophistry" and "sophism," we have inherited from the Greeks themselves; for it was inevitable that in so eager a market for wisdom some of the wares offered should be spurious, and unfortunately the charlatans among the Sophists, as ever, attracted greater attention than the genuine teachers, causing the name to fall into disrepute. When, however, the Sophists made their first appearance in Hellas, the title they claimed was as yet untarnished and commanded a respectful hearing.

The varied origin of the leaders in the movement — they came from Ionia, the Peloponnesus, the Cyclades, Sicily, and elsewhere — proves that the demand for them and their wares was not confined to any single locality. Among them were not a few striking figures worthy to rank with the best in the Hellenic gallery of creative artists.

Most respected of all was Protagoras. Born (*c.* 480 B.C.) in the town of Abdera, where Leucippus had first proposed his atomic theory as a solution for the problem of the universe and had devoted his life to a grand effort to account for the *cosmos* in purely mechanistic terms,[1] Protagoras rose in protest against this theorizing as unprofitable, and majestically announced man as his theme. His most famous saying, with which he opened one of his works (now lost), runs thus: "Man is the measure of things; both of those that are, that they are, and of those that are not, that they are not." This somewhat oracular utterance has possibly called forth more discussion than any single saying of any other man. What may not be read into these simple words! Yet by them Protagoras probably meant to convey nothing more than his scorn of physical and metaphysical speculation and the avowal of his interest in man. "I do not care for your atoms, whirling through space; the thing that interests me is man; him I shall make the measure of life and of life's values. Atoms mean nothing to me, but goodness does, and beauty, and truth." Thus he became the earliest champion of Hellenic humanism in its opposition to pure naturalism; and his appeal reached an audience many times larger than the atomist could hope to interest in his doctrines.

Equally uncompromising was his attitude toward theological speculations. He professed his inability to attain

[1] See pages 378 f.

certainty concerning such matters; life is too short. He rightly held that the gods fall outside the field of human *knowledge*, thereby giving his enemies a chance to accuse him of atheism.

His interests were all in matters of a practical nature: he made the art of life itself the theme of his teaching. What is the meaning of *arete*? Wherein lies the virtue of man? That, to his mind, was the most important of all questions, for without social virtues there can be no civilization, man sinking to the level of the beast. He firmly believed that virtue admitted of being taught, logical demonstration having its place in the process of instruction. To think correctly, then, was a prerequisite to such wisdom; hence his effort to formulate a kind of logic (he wrote a treatise on "Truth").

In order to think correctly we must understand the very tools of thought, speech itself. And so he was the first to teach grammar and to lecture on "correct speech"; he inquired even into the puzzle of grammatical gender, exposing himself to the ridicule of the ignorant.

Thus Protagoras traveled all over Greece, dispensing his "good counsel" to the young and — rich, for he charged high fees for his lectures. Thereby he shocked Hellenic sensibilities; to pay for being granted the privilege of overhearing mere talk was an unheard-of thing in Hellas. Let us remember that in the total absence of institutions of higher learning the young Hellene had managed to garner life's wisdom from the lips of his elders; such was the privilege of Spartan and Athenian youth alike. And here was a man who had so much to give and would not give unless he were paid! By way of comparison, imagine the indignation with which the English would regard a popular American preacher coming over to England and charging a high admission fee for his sermons; such "profitable piety" would be open to the same type of criticism as that to which in ancient Greece Protagoras' practice gave rise.[1] Moreover, Protagoras in all his glory seemed

[1] The comparison is derived from A. W. Benn, *The Greek Philosophers*, p. 88.

bent on dazzling his audience as well as instructing it; the older and more conservative came away with an uneasy feeling that they had been not so much enlightened as bamboozled! That man's talk was altogether too clever and brilliant to be true and safe.

Thus the noblest of the Sophists, in attempting a new thing, in the long run aroused as much suspicion as admiration. If it is difficult for us today to judge him aright, this is due in no small degree to the scantiness of our materials. None of Protagoras' treatises have come down to us; our chief source of information is the incomparable Plato, who did not love the Sophists and who employed the shafts of his wit in deriding their pretensions.

Protagoras' contemporary Hippias hailed from Elis. His learning was encyclopedic, his memory extraordinarily retentive; he could discourse fluently on any subject under the sun. Astronomy as well as moral philosophy, the arts and crafts as well as political science, the ways of nature as well as the conventions of man — all were included in his curriculum. And he was even less inclined than Protagoras to hide his light under a bushel. His pompous manner and transparent vanity gave Plato's malicious pen an even better opportunity than that provided by the idiosyncrasies of Protagoras. Yet it would be difficult to discover in the reports concerning Hippias' teaching anything discreditable or deserving of blame. He seems to have preached the ordinary morality. One of his celebrated discourses pretended to report the advice which the aged Nestor gave to Achilles' youthful son; surely so respectable a figure as Nestor would not have advocated any conduct at which even the most highly conservative could have taken umbrage. Nor could any fault be found with Hippias' pride in proving that knowledge of the artisan's craft was matched in his own person by practical skill: he appeared at the Olympic games entirely accoutered in products of his own handiwork, thus proclaiming the beauty and blessedness of a simple, self-sufficient life.

But he was wont to dwell a little too insistently on the distinction between nature's ways and man's conventions, and delighted to point to the simple universality of nature as contrasted with the multiplicity of human institutions. He himself seems not to have discerned the full implication of his favorite theme; but it did not escape others. If nature ought to furnish the patterns of human conduct, what becomes of the claims of justice? In nature might is right; what, then, more *natural* than that the strong should possess what their superior prowess and hardihood enable them to seize in spite of the feeble protests of the weak? Some day a self-assertive Sophist like Thrasymachus would define justice as "the other man's advantage," as a fiction originating in a conspiracy of the weak and dispossessed — a doctrine that would seem, and deservedly so, to be wicked and anti-social.

Even more famous than "Nestor's Counsel to Neoptolemus" was the "Choice of Herakles," the product of Prodicus of Keos. Herakles stands at the parting of the ways, Pleasure beckoning him to follow her, while the stern voice of Duty bids the hero choose the nobler even though rougher path. Prodicus likewise took the art of life as his theme, teaching as conventional a morality as the great Protagoras did. He too could discourse learnedly on language, synonyms being his special subject. His learning was equally comprehensive, one of his treatises dealing with "Nature," another with the "Nature of Man."

Verily the day of the specialist had not yet dawned. Men exercised their wits on all questions that entered their heads, each feeling competent to deal with these provided he could argue with sufficient acumen. In truth, the activity of the Sophists and the eager interest of their audiences are but a mark of the intellectual ferment which Hellas experienced in the decade or so preceding the Hellenic World War and during that fatal conflict. It was indeed an age of enlightenment, soon to be followed by a profound disillusion. But, for the time being, it was very exciting; no one who cherished the old Homeric ambition to excel wished to remain outside the movement.

Of all the Sophists, Gorgias of Leontini (Sicily) was perhaps the most brilliant and was the only one to cultivate one definite subject of instruction. He is so much of a rhetorician that he deserves to be grouped rather with the rhetoricians than with the Sophists. The first to elaborate a technique of speech, he soon elevated it to the rank of the most important part of the curriculum of higher instruction. And soon the new art of speech, compared with the old, appeared as superior as a flashing rapier is to a clumsy and blunted saber.

We shall return to the subject of rhetoric in another chapter. Here we are concerned with the educational developments of the new era; and from this point of view we are bound to regard sophistic teaching as pernicious in its general effects. For even if it be granted that among the Sophists there were many able and sincere men, the importance of these was completely overshadowed in the course of time by that of the random rhetoricians. Moreover, even the best of the Sophists admittedly aimed not at knowledge as such but at *profitable* knowledge — the kind that would make for success in life. Their instruction therefore tended to substitute purely utilitarian for cultural ends in education; and instruction the object of which is appearance and form rather than substance can neither rank very high nor be productive of any permanent good. Finally sophistic teaching contributed toward the disintegration of the Greek polity, although such loosening of the old bonds was bound to come anyway. Henceforth in every Greek city there was a small minority which, because it could pay, received a higher education from whose benefits the majority remained excluded. The latter could not help looking with envy and distrust on those who thus set themselves apart from the common crowd; their suspicion and ill-will found a voice in the products of the comic poets.

When the fevers of Sophistic had passed, permanent institutions of higher education were established. The earliest of these were the rhetorical school of Isocrates and the philosophical school of Plato. But Isocrates will find a place in our chapter on prose literature, while Plato belongs to philosophy.

In closing, we note that our Hellenic heritage in the educational field is the concept of a liberal and cultural education; and the Sophists deserve at least part of the credit. In this connection it is pertinent to observe that the three foremost nations of Europe have borrowed the names of their cultural schools from these same Hellenes: the English have their *academy* (the name of Plato's school); the French, their *lycée* (after the Lyceum, where Aristotle taught); the Germans, their *Gymnasium*.

SUGGESTIONS FOR READING. For the old Greek education see KENNETH J. FREEMAN, *Schools of Hellas* (Macmillan, 1912), a book written with great sympathy and understanding; for a short and competent account of Greek educational practice and theory see JAMES DREVER, *Greek Education* (Cambridge, 1912); see also J. F. DOBSON, *Ancient Education* (Longmans, 1932). As for the Sophists, the reader may consult Grote's famous Chapter LXVII (of his *History of Greece*), the latter part of which is dedicated to a rehabilitation of the much maligned Sophists. See also Chapter III of ALFRED W. BENN'S *The Greek Philosophers* (Dutton, 1914).

CHAPTER IX

POETRY

Introductory

WHENCE springs the universal urge to poetic composition? And what, indeed, *is* poetry?

These two questions, fascinating as they are, cannot be adequately discussed within a work of the present scope. Poetry is one thing in one age and another thing in another age. Its origin is beyond historical ken; all we can say is that since it is in essence exalted speech and rhythmic in form, its first associations were probably with religion and magic. The spell casting out the evil spirit, the prayer inviting the attendance of a favoring deity, the prophetic word of the inspired seer — these were among the earliest forms of poetry the human race has known. That it was sung or chanted, and not spoken, and that it was accompanied by appropriate gesture and swaying of the body, of this too we may be reasonably certain.

This early association between religion and poetry is not without its witness in the poetry of Hellas. The Homeric epic begins with an invocation of the Muse. *She* sings the song; the poet is only her mouthpiece. The earliest Greek poets were not only priests of the Muses but prophets as well; the Greek name for the poet, *aoidos*, seems to bear that connotation, as does the old Latin name for poet, *vates*.

Who were the Muses? We know only that their ancient cult centers were in Pieria, near Mt. Olympus, in Thessaly, and at Mt. Helicon in Boeotia; hence they are surnamed "Pierian" or "Heliconian." But their original function is lost to us. If the word "Muse" (*Mousa*) means "the one who reminds," they may have been the goddesses in whose keeping was the sacred lore of the tribe, the manifold metrical formulas upon whose correct recitation, on the proper occasion, depended the tribal well-being. Later they may have become the patronesses of all metrical utterance, true goddesses of poetry. In a similar way, we suggested, Apollo, from a god of prophecy, may have grown into a god of poetry. He, in time, became the leader of the Muses (*Mousarchos*, *Mousagetes*).

But whatever the earliest history of poetry in Hellas, when we meet the Muses in Homeric poetry they are already the goddesses of poetry, inspiring the poet. Nine in number, they are associated with the three Graces (*Charites*). For rhythmic words and rhythmic movement spontaneously unite; folk dances, with an accompanying refrain chanted by all the participants, are among the oldest features of tribal life.

What was the function of poetry? As Homer and his fellow minstrels understood it, it was primarily to give pleasure. The singer is called a "sweet" singer; because his song is the delight of the guests there is always a place for him at the banquets of the kings. But, as we have seen, Hesiod took a different view of the poet's mission: not to entertain by telling beautiful lies, but to instruct by telling the truth. In fact, Hesiod harked back to what may have been the primary function of the Muses: to keep alive in the memory of the living the wisdom of the fathers. That he went much farther than this and added a great many new "truths" to the old ones is of no consequence. What counted in the history of Greek poetry was that he again placed the emphasis on the didactic function of poetry. Throughout its history it continues to play a dual role, that of giving delight *and* instruction. That poetry deliberately should have been made into a vehicle for conveying strictly useful information is surprising enough to us. But when we reflect that in the creative age of Greek poetry people lived without books and had to depend on memory (*Mnemosyne*, Memory, was the mother of the Muses), it is, after all, not so strange. The wisdom of life, as well as the practical rules of husbandry, were best set forth in verse, which could be memorized. And, as we have seen, the absence of a sacred book and of a hierarchy of priests contributed to confirm the poets in their place as teachers of the people.

This added responsibility which Greek sentiment placed upon the poet's shoulders had momentous consequences. The Greek poet was not a free lance, living a life detached from the common interests of his fellow men. The social ideal of life prevailing in Hellas would not allow even a poet to live unto himself; he too was drawn within the circle of the polis, and his function was properly socialized. The wisdom of the poet must serve the ends of the state. In the judgment in Hades, as reported by Aristophanes, Euripides is held to have been at fault because he made his fellow citizens worse than they were before, instead of better: the good poet had to be a good citizen.

Before we take up the growth and development of Hellenic poetry under the historical influences of the first and second periods, respectively, a few introductory observations will be in place.

First of all, the word "poet" is a Greek word; it means "maker." And the three types of poetry, epic, lyric, and dramatic, are all Greek in origin and name. Of these epic poetry is the heritage of the Heroic Age. The first period produced lyric poetry. The term "lyric," which means "sung to the lyre," we shall apply to elegiac, iambic, and melic poetry, although it is not strictly applicable to the first two, which gradually lost all connection with music. Melic poetry falls into two kinds: monodic (sung by a single voice) and choral. Elegiac and iambic originated in Ionia and continued to be composed in the Ionic dialect, or in what was conventionally regarded as such. Aeolian Lesbos was the home of monodic melic, and choral melic was a Dorian contribution. Of all this lyric poetry only scanty fragments have survived. Although papyrus finds have added a little to our store, it yet remains true that among the works of all these poets only those of Pindar and Bacchylides have come down to us with any degree of fullness; and Pindar is chiefly represented by his victory odes.

To the second period and the first part of the third belongs dramatic poetry. An Athenian creation, it includes tragedy, comedy, and the satyr play. The three great masters of tragedy, Aeschylus, Sophocles, and Euripides, are fairly well represented in some thirty tragedies. Comedy is known to us primarily through the eleven plays of Aristophanes.

Roughly speaking, lyric poetry belongs to the first period; dramatic poetry, to the second. The Greek world developed one type of poetry at a time and carried it to the limits of perfection that it was destined to reach; then a new age sought a new vehicle, which in turn would run its allotted course. "The history of Greek literature is not a series of chapters, but the course of a natural growth, the voice of Greek life from age to age."[1] Throughout the history of this poetry we shall take into account, first, the influence of political and social developments and, secondly, that of the Hellenic qualities of imagination, rationalism, and feeling for beauty.

The First Period — Lyric Poetry

Epic poetry, which had served for the entertainment of petty kings, had now run its course. After Homer others had taken up other episodes of the Trojan War and the return of the heroes or had given an epic version of the siege of Thebes. But Greece refused to produce another Homer. The epic stream was running dry. The best proof that the interest in the glories of the past was giving way to a greater concern for the present is found in the appearance of parodies in the epic style; one such, the *Battle between the Frogs and the Mice,* has come down to us. In addition, a number of

[1] R. C. Jebb, *Essays and Addresses,* p. 103.

so-called "hymns" have survived under Homer's name. The largest of these, those to Apollo, Hermes, and Demeter, composed in the conventional epic diction, are narrative poems of considerable and contrasting merits. The hymn to Delian Apollo furnishes us with the prototype of the contest in poetry; the hymn to Hermes tells in a sportive vein of the adventures of the one-day-old god who stole Apollo's cattle; the hymn to Demeter has been justly admired for the beauty of its pathos. All are products of an age much later than Homer's.[1]

Between 700 and 500 B.C. interest shifted. It was inevitable that these centuries, which saw the awakening of man, should seek and find a new mode of poetic expression; for with the Greeks a change in subject means a change in form. The stately hexameter was well suited to bear the weight of Homeric narrative. New measures would have to be found for the expression of new interests. The first departure from the Homeric verse was timid enough; to the hexameter was added an alternating pentameter, to form the so-called elegiac couplet. This was the vehicle chiefly employed by the poets of the new civic patriotism, who call upon the new citizens to fight bravely in the ranks and to accept the responsibilities of citizenship along with its rights. Such patriotic songs Callinus wrote for the Ephesians (about 700 B.C.), Tyrtaeus for the Spartans (about 650 B.C.), and Solon for the Athenians (600 B.C.).

Soon the sphere of elegiac verse was extended to cover other phases of the new civic life. We hear in it the echoes of the discord that filled the cities. Solon defends his policy in elegiac verse, and Theognis, the Megarian aristocrat (late sixth century B.C.), bitterly assails the insolence of the commoners; for in Megara democracy has gained the upper hand, driven the aristocrats into exile, and distributed their large land holdings among the poor. Evidently there was no "reconciler" like Solon in Megara. There is no better commentary

[1] See the interesting introduction to Andrew Lang's *Homeric Hymns*.

on the fierceness of partisan strife in the little city-states of Hellas than the verse of Theognis. But political wisdom means the wisdom of life in the Greek atmosphere. Thus Solon dons the garments of the preacher and warns his people that wealth and insolence lead to folly and disaster; that Zeus watches over the conduct of man and visits punishment, — if not upon the wrongdoer, then upon his offspring, even to the generations yet unborn. The moralizing bent of the Greeks found delight in this "gnomic" poetry, a considerable quantity of which has come down to us under the name of Theognis.

The elegiac couplet lent itself equally well to commemorative epigram and inscription, and the polis utilized it to record praise to gods and men. Most admirable among these are the epitaphs which have come to us under the name of Simonides (fl. about 500 B.C.). And the melancholy Mimnermus (late seventh century B.C.) reflects in elegiac verse on the brevity of human life. This new poetic form, indeed, proved the most enduring and most adaptable of all Greek verse. In Hellenistic times it received a new lease of life, and it was, in turn, taken over by the Romans as the verse of sentimental love and epigram.

The true individualist note is struck in iambic verse, which makes its appearance in the early seventh century B.C. It signalizes a complete break with the past. The rhythm of iambic meter, close to the cadence of ordinary speech, is better adapted to express individual mood and sentiment. The chief representative of this poetry is Archilochus (fl. about 650 B.C.), in whom we have the first Greek poet who has revealed himself in verse. A masterful character, he carried his fortune on the point of his lance. War, love, and wine are the subjects of his song. He led a stormy life and illustrated in his own person the combative spirit of the new Hellas, — the unruly passions so characteristic of his age and so incompatible with the new ideals of orderly city life. He was a great poet, of marked originality; and while his fame rests upon his iambics, he essayed other metrical forms as well. It is a great pity that so little of his poetry has come down to us; but his verse could serve no social purpose, and the sentiment of the polis looked with increasing disfavor upon a natural freebooter like Archilochus.[1]

Melic poetry, as we have seen, is divided into solo and choral song. The Greek melic includes words, music, and dance; but the words are always supreme. The accompanying music was of the simplest character; though "harmony" is a Greek word, of our musical harmonies they had no idea. The instruments were the lyre, perfected by Terpander (first part of the seventh century B.C.), and the flute, or rather the clarinet, an Asiatic importation somewhat suspect, as we have seen, to Greek puritans as an instrument too stirring and exciting for those who practice sophrosyne.

Aside from the chief representatives of monodic melic, Sappho, Alcaeus, and Anacreon, we shall have some difficulty in appraising Greek melic at its true value. In the first place, the range of Greek lyric poetry, even in Sappho or Pindar, is much more limited than that of modern lyric. We have developed an inner life of greater depth and a wider range and subtlety of emotion than can be found in this people of extroverts (if we may borrow from the jargon of contemporary psychology). Moreover, historical developments which threw all the emphasis on the social side of life were not likely to promote the cult of a mystical and romantic poetry. It is a significant fact that monody itself, after a brilliant beginning, in the sixth century B.C., practically died with the aristocratic society which had produced it, and that choral melic, the direct heir of tribal song, which voices the sentiments of the community, vastly overshadows it in importance. But even if social conditions had been more favorable, it is not likely that Hellas would ever have produced a Keats or a Shelley. Perhaps we can clarify the inherent difference between Greek and modern lyric by a com-

[1] See G. Murray, *History of Ancient Greek Literature*, pp. 86 ff.

parison. Both Alcman, the Greek, and Goethe, the German poet, have given in lyric verse a wonderful description of the stillness of the night, when there is peace over the mountain tops, the forest, and (the Greek adds) the deep. The German poem ends: *Warte nur, balde ruhest du auch* ("Wait only and thou too shalt rest"). That is, Goethe reads into the stillness of the night a message to his own weary heart. Now this last line, which to us contains the very essence of the lyric, is lacking in Alcman, and we shall look for it in vain in all Hellenic poetry. The Greek describes the natural scene in telling lines; but he lets it go at that. He does not feel nature communing with him; in fact, such a line as the last verse of Goethe's poem would have struck him as rather absurd. For it is not only the lack of development of an inner life that stands in the way but also Greek rationalism. The wistfulness of romantic poetry had no place in a youthful Hellas which was desperately trying to see the truth in the cold light of reason. We must be content to take Greek poetry for what it is and not complain when we cannot find in the cold, hard glitter of its clear-cut gems the softer lights and subtler nuances of modern poetry.

Secondly, Greek melic is marked by regard for form, by perfection of technique, in short, by scrupulous attention to what we regard as the externals of poetry. Indeed, we suspect that a preoccupation with the niceties of composition is fatal to spontaneity of expression and obstructs the generous flow of genuine inspiration, although the example of the great Bach might remind us that a highly elaborated technique, when completely mastered, is — in the field of music at least — not incompatible with truly inspired composition. That the Greek attitude toward form would be at variance with our own was to be expected. We are the heirs of the ages; there is so great an abundance of rules and canons, of forms and styles, that in our quest for the new we abjure rules and canons altogether and finally try to achieve originality by formlessness itself. But the Greeks inherited a miscellaneous mass of ritual, regulated by tradition, and crude folk songs and folk dances. Their instinct for beauty and their passion for order bade them create definite form, clarity of outline, a balancing of parts in a well-constructed whole. In short, as in politics their lawgivers "work like architects, with ruler and compass," so the great masters of poetic architecture labored with mathematical precision and perfected a technique of poetic composition such as the world had never seen before and will never see again. Pindar speaks of poets as "skilled builders, fitting together the sounding words."[1] Thus for the monodic melic Alcaeus (600 B.C.) created, among others, the stanza called after his name, — a metrical invention of surpassing charm. This four-lined stanza, with its perfect artistry, its varied rhythms, and its nice balance, proved one of the most fitting vehicles for the singers of the joys of war and peace, of the hardships and delights of life. Both Alcaeus and Sappho belonged to the Lesbian aristocracy; they sprang from a fiery race, sensuous and beauty-loving. Alcaeus' stormy life again mirrored the political woes of his age. Sappho's range was narrower but deeper; she sang of love, and no other Greek poet equaled her in depth of feeling. The Ionian Anacreon followed them (530 B.C.); his fame rests chiefly on his drinking songs.

It was, however, in the choral melic, tribal in origin, that the Greek passion for beauty, and for beauty through order (*kosmos*), found its fullest expression. The marriage song, the dirge, the processional and the lively dance, the solemn hymn and the joyous song of thanksgiving, the maidens' song and the encomium in honor of the victorious athlete — these and many more, the heritage of their tribal past, were now cast in elaborately constructed molds, the most characteristic feature of which is the stately *strophe*, balanced syllable for syllable by an *antistrophe* and finished with an *epode*. Out of such *triads* did these joiners of song construct their metrical framework. Though the names of the originators of

[1] *Pythian Odes*, iii, line 113.

these types (for different meters and combinations belonged to different classes of melic) have come down to us, it would be of little use to enumerate types and names which must remain shadowy for lack of illustrative material. Even where, as in the case of Pindar and Bacchylides, our material is relatively abundant, this type of poetry, depending so much on the music of language and rhythm, loses more in translation than any other.

There is yet another barrier preventing our full enjoyment of Greek melic. We have nothing but the bare text. But the Greek did not *read* this poetry; he *heard* it sung, and further insisted on *seeing* it in the figures of the dancing chorus. Moreover, every melic poem had its setting, either at the religious festival or on some other public occasion at which the crowd gathered to hear the poet voice their collective sentiment. All this we can recapture in imagination, but only with difficulty and never adequately. In short, this most Hellenic of all poetry, part of the very tissue of Hellenic life, all but refuses to yield its secret to us.

PINDAR

Of all the writers of choral melic, antiquity unanimously proclaimed Pindar the greatest, and of all types of choral melic the *epinikion*, the victory ode, as the most splendid. We are fortunate, then, to be in possession of the victory odes of the greatest of Hellenic melic poets.

Pindar's period of activity covers the first half of the fifth century B.C. and falls, therefore, in our second period. We place him among the poets of the first period because his poetic output is the consummation of a development in the history of Greek poetry which in essence belongs to the first period. Pindar was a Theban by birth, the scion of a noble family, an aristocrat in feeling and outlook. In his poetry we catch a glimpse of that pride of race which, especially among the Dorian aristocracies, became the guiding principle of a life dedicated to the strenuous practice of *arete*, manly virtue. With these it was *noblesse oblige*. Pindar lived through those stirring years that ended in the triumph of Hellas over Persia; but he was a Theban, and the Theban oligarchy had chosen to Medize rather than join in the defense of the common cause. That was one of Pindar's handicaps; for, being a good Greek, he was first of all a Theban. But Pindar was Panhellenic as well; and when he had become the acknowledged master of all melic poets, his services were bespoken by men from all parts of Greece. He traveled a great deal in pursuit of his profession, even to far-off Sicily, where he spent two years (476–474 B.C.) at the brilliant court of Hiero, tyrant of Syracuse. His training in the technique of melic, including musical composition, he received at the hands of Athenian masters during a sojourn in Athens.

His fame rests chiefly upon the victory odes. These were composed in honor of a victor at one of the four national festivals: the Olympian, in honor of Zeus, celebrated at Olympia, in Elis, once every four years; the Pythian, in honor of Apollo, at Delphi, once every four years; the Isthmian, in honor of Poseidon, on the isthmus of Corinth, once every two years; and the Nemean, in honor of Zeus, near Phlios, once every two years. The earliest mention of athletic contests in Greece dates from Homer: the twenty-third book of the Iliad contains an account of the contests given by Achilles in honor of his slain comrade Patroclus. These games, participated in by the Achaean chieftains, present in essence the type of contests which remained the basis of all Greek athletic festivals. These were the foot race, the chariot race, throwing of the discus and javelin, boxing, and wrestling.

So far the story of Greek athletics is perfectly understandable. Now we come to a point that needs further elucidation. We find these contests dedicated to the gods. This association of religion with athletics is perplexing to us. To be sure, we can evade the difficulty by saying that with the

Greeks, church and state being one, and secular and religious functions of the state being constantly fused, it follows that the celebration of athletic contests under the aegis of the polis makes them also religious celebrations. But we should completely fail to gauge the nature of Greek sentiment in these matters if we should be content with a purely mechanical explanation such as this. There is a deeper, more intimate bond uniting the two. We know the Greeks worshiped not a spiritual and moral power, exalted above and outside the natural world, but gods who dwell in the very heart of nature, and who are of the earth earthy. They worshiped the divine *in* nature and *in* man. The perfect human body, well proportioned and finely developed, called forth in them an aesthetic emotion which they felt as religious because in this physical perfection they saw a revelation of the divine. When Odysseus confronts Nausicaa, he expresses his admiration for the beauty and grace of the maiden in these words: "Awe holds me looking upon thee"; that word *sebas*, "awe," which is the term by which the Greek denotes the awe of man in the presence of the handiwork of God, gives the secret away. Greek art made Apollo himself into the prototype of manly vigor and beauty. And the Greeks never worshiped brute strength as such; only the union of strength and grace met their approval. It is, then, only natural that this pagan people, which had not yet degraded the body to the status of an instrument for the wiles of Satan, should glorify bodily excellence as a manifestation of the divine. And therefore it was altogether fitting that athletic contests should be celebrated in honor of the gods.

Over and above the contests within the polis stood the four great Panhellenic festivals. They were all connected with some ancient center of worship. Of these the oldest as well as the most august was the Olympic festival. It was commonly believed to have been founded by Herakles; but the first historic Olympiad dates from 776 B.C. No other festival was of equal importance in Hellas. A sacred truce was proclaimed which protected not only the land but all those traveling to and from Olympia. Participation, at first confined to the neighboring states in the Peloponnesus, gradually extended to all Greece, including the Greater Greece of the west. These periodic meetings did much to promote the feeling of unity in Hellas; for only freeborn Greeks were allowed to compete. States and individuals vied here to gain that prestige which a victory at Olympia bestowed; it is not too much to say that to a Greek youth the acme of bliss was to be proclaimed an *Olympionikes*, a victor at Olympia. The prize was a crown of wild olive; but city-states wishing to stimulate their youth to the greatest efforts frequently added a more substantial reward.

This absorbing interest in athletics as a feature of the life of the city-state reached its height during and after the Persian Wars. "The victory of the Greeks was the victory of a handful of trained athletes over hordes of effeminate barbarians."[1] With the outbreak of the Hellenic World War, and the decline of the social factor in Greek life, the fine civic idealism that inspired Greek athletics gradually waned, and professionalism made its appearance. But Pindar's activity fell entirely within the period when Greek athletics was at its best.

The splendor of Olympia in its heyday, with its sacred enclosure where stood the great temple of Zeus and in it the most celebrated work of art Hellas possessed, the Zeus of Phidias, and where the combined skill of architect and artist had contributed to make this shrine worthy of the great god and the hallowed traditions of the place — that Olympia to which sacred embassies from all states wended their way to take part in the solemn procession and the sacrifice at the ancient altar — all this splendor may help us to understand why the greatest lyric poet of the age should be called upon to celebrate the victors at Olympia, as well as at the other Panhellenic festivals.

[1] E. Norman Gardiner, *Athletics of the Ancient World*, p. 42.

We may now inquire what form this victory song took in the hands of Pindar. The Pindaric ode is made up of a greater or less number of triads, each consisting of a strophe and antistrophe sung and danced by a chorus of men and followed by an epode sung by the chorus standing, the whole forming a massive framework to bear the burden of the song. That the proper performance of such an ode required no little outlay of money and effort goes without saying; and Pindar's price was high. No wonder we find so many kings and tyrants among his patrons; in fact, his poems do not celebrate the commoner. The Pindaric ode is marked by a lofty tone, by splendor of imagery, and by grandeur of language. Perhaps no other poet has been so intoxicated with the vision of the sublime as Pindar: the victory he celebrates is transfigured into the triumph of the ever true and noble over the false and base. He speaks with the accents of a priest and prophet; his tone is oracular. The details of the victory do not concern him, and the individual whose distinction occasions the song is celebrated only as one more in the heroic pageantry of Hellas; his glory adds only to the greater glory of the past; the new victory only attests afresh the triumphant procession of Hellas through the ages. Herein we may find an expression of the social ideals of Hellas, which sees the individual only as a member of a group. But Pindar goes beyond this: his song of victory becomes in truth a tribute to man, the greatness of his daring, his fearless challenge of life. In the end he joins the company of those Hellenes who have glorified man as the arbiter of his own destiny. Herein he is at one with the other prophets of that great age: Aeschylus, the dramatist; Polygnotus, the painter; and Phidias, the sculptor. And yet he would not be Greek if he did not add his word of warning: power and opulence lead to satiety; this, in turn, leads to *hubris* (insolence), *Ate* (blindness of heart), and heaven-sent woes. Thus he shows that he has learned from Apollo the lesson of *sophrosyne*. But not this is the keynote of his song, but rather that *arete* which bids men bravely to face danger and, by overcoming the obstacles in their path, to gain everlasting fame. Such is the message of Pindar, and in spite of the handicaps the passing of time has placed upon our full appreciation of his song, we can, if we make the effort, still catch a faint echo of that message.

SUGGESTIONS FOR READING. Consult R. C. JEBB, *The Growth and Influence of Classical Greek Poetry* (Houghton Mifflin, n.d.), Lecture V. Jebb is at his best here. See also R. W. LIVINGSTONE, *The Pageant of Greece*, pp. 87–93, which contains an excellent translation of the eighth Isthmian ode, with equally excellent comments. Selections from all the poets discussed in this section may be found in HOWE and HARRAR, *Greek Literature in Translation* (Harper, 1924), pp. 101–131, or G. SHOWERMAN, *Century Readings in Ancient Classical Literature* (1925), pp. 45–59.

The Second Period — Dramatic Poetry

The first period, which in great measure had liberated the Hellene from the bondage of tribal tradition and had bestowed upon him the rights and responsibility of citizenship, had also fashioned a new literary tool. However, we have seen that, of all "lyric" poetry, that type prevailed which voiced the sentiments of the group rather than of the individual. Pindar's choral song marks the culmination of the movement.

Among the varied types of tribal song which the Hellenic instinct for order and beauty transformed into finished products of art, there was one which, by certain essential qualities, stood apart from all the others. This was the dithyramb, sacred to Dionysus; and just as the cult of this god, orgiastic and ecstatic, contained an element not present in that of the other gods, so the song in his honor was imbued with a more impassioned spirit. The dithyramb had been given artistic form by Arion (fl. 625 B.C.). The celebrants of Dionysus, obeying his mystic call, were wont to disguise themselves in order to enter into closer communion with their god. Among the mythical beings which Greek imagination saw following in his train, *satyrs*, goat-like beings personifying the obscure instincts of nature, were the most prominent. What more natural than that the celebrants should disguise themselves as satyrs? Mimetic dancing, then, became a feature of the Dionysiac song, and Arion's dithyramb was sung by a chorus of satyrs. Such a chorus was called "tragic," from *tragos*, "goat"; "tragedy" itself is the "song of the goats."

But the dithyramb of Arion was not yet a tragedy in our sense. He may have broken the succession of strophe and antistrophe with a few verses recited by the single voice of the man who answered the questions of the chorus (he was called the *hypocrites*, or "answerer"); but it was Thespis (535 B.C.) to whom occurred the idea of making the "answerer" into a real "hypocrite," — a pretender, who, dressed to represent one of the characters in the myth of Dionysus, became a real actor. This man would retire into the booth (the *skene*, "scene") at the back of the circular dancing place (*orchestra*), where the chorus of satyrs performed its dance and song, and there attire himself in the appropriate costume.

Such were the dithyrambs and "dramas" (acted songs) when Pisistratus made them into a feature of the Greater Dionysia, thus ensuring the future of the dramatic contests, the first of which, according to tradition, dates from 536 B.C.

The next step in the development of the drama was taken when the poets went outside of the Dionysiac mythology for the subject of their song. That meant a change in the conventional costume of the goat chorus. In the course of time the satyr was in danger of disappearing altogether from the Athenian orchestra. But the people would not tolerate the abolition of so indispensable a feature of a Dionysiac celebration, and eventually there was reached a compromise, which involved the emergence of a new art form. While it restored to the Athenians their beloved satyrs, the satyr play was per-

Aeschylus (?)

Capitoline Museum, Rome

Euripides

National Museum, Naples

formed at the Greater Dionysia as an afterpiece; it preserved the sportive element for the Dionysiac festival. The invention of satyric drama was attributed to Pratinas (500 B.C.).

And now there appears upon the scene a man of surpassing genius, to whom we owe real drama as an art form and who is justly called its father. Aeschylus (525–456 B.C.) did what may seem a small thing, and obvious at that: he added a second actor. Nevertheless, it was this second actor that transformed drama from a potentiality into a reality. From now on, the stage becomes the scene of a conflict between clashing wills, without which drama is unthinkable. Sophocles (496–406 B.C.) added a third actor, which greatly increased the dramatic appeal of the stage. Beyond this number the Greeks did not go. Not that the number of dramatis personae was confined to three (the same actor might take several parts in succession), but there were never more than three actors on the stage in the same scene.[1] The choice the Greeks made was deliberate and is due to their love of clarity: more actors would have confused the issue.

Now the history of the Greek tragedy is mainly the story of the gradual encroachment of the spoken dialogue upon the choral song and dance. In the oldest play we possess (the *Suppliants* of Aeschylus) the chorus, representing the fifty daughters of Danaüs, still form the center of interest, and the songs into which they pour the anguish of their struggles and sufferings make up more than half the play; it is still a predominantly lyric performance. But as the dramatic possibilities of the two and the three actors gradually dawned upon the playwrights the chorus lost in number (from fifty it was reduced to fifteen) and importance. And yet the best Greek drama could not dispense with it.

It can expound the past, comment on the present, forebode the future. It provides the poet with a mouthpiece and the spectator with a counterpart of himself. It forms a living background of common humanity above which the heroes tower; a living background

[1] The real or apparent exceptions to this only confirm the rule.

of pure poetry, which turns lamentation into music and horror into peace; . . . for [the] creation of atmosphere, of contrast, of escape and relief the Greek chorus in the hands of its masters is consummately used.[1]

Dramatic performances remained a feature of the state worship of Dionysus, and, above all, the Greater Dionysia, in the early spring, furnished the occasion for the production of tragedy.

The theater (the word is Greek and means a "place for seeing") was an unpretentious affair in the creative period of Greek drama. The most essential part was the circular dancing place of the chorus (the orchestra). In the center stood the altar of Dionysus. The stage building — as we have seen, originally a booth (*skene*) and dressing room for the actors — came to represent a building, usually a temple or palace; and from the days of Sophocles it was covered with a painted canvas and pierced by three doors. The audience found accommodation upon wooden tiers of seats erected upon the southern slope of the Acropolis; we hear of thirty thousand spectators as being present. In later days a permanent auditorium was built, and the stage building gained in architectural magnificence; but these elaborations date from an age when the creative work of the Greek dramatist was over.

The playwrights submitted their work to the king-archon, the magistrate in charge of religious matters; he "assigned a chorus" to three poets. In addition to the poet, the choregus and protagonist had important duties to fulfill. The poet supervised the production, although in later times a great deal of the actual training of the chorus was in the hands of a professional trainer. The choregus saw to the mounting of the tragedies and defrayed the expenses; it was one of the "liturgies" the state exacted from its wealthy citizens, and provided one of the most eagerly sought opportunities for individual distinction. Finally, there was the protagonist, in

[1] F. L. Lucas, *Tragedy*, p. 66. Quoted by permission of Harcourt, Brace and Company.

the days when poets themselves ceased to perform the main part in their dramas; he was the chief actor and provided the subordinate actors. From about 450 B.C. one protagonist was assigned by the archon to each poet.

Each of the three poets who had been fortunate enough to receive a chorus competed with a tetralogy; it consisted of three tragedies and a satyr play (with Aeschylus the tragedies usually form three successive chapters in the same story, — a practice abandoned by his successors, who preferred to mount three independent plays). The three tetralogies were performed on three successive days, the performances beginning early in the morning. At the end the prizes were awarded by ten representatives of the tribes, picked by lot from a number of names submitted to the archon. Of the votes of these representatives only five decided the award. Both poet and choregus were honored by the crown of ivy, sacred to Dionysus, which was the token of victory. The mounting of the tragedy was a comparatively simple matter in those days of an open-air theater, where changes of scenery were limited to the absolutely indispensable. There was no curtain, and a great deal was left to the imagination of the audience. Greater care was bestowed upon the dress of the actors and the proper training of the chorus. The actors wore masks, surmounted by the *onkos*, and the celebrated *cothurnus*, a thick-soled shoe, — both to increase their height; and magnificent long flowing robes further enhanced the importance of the actor as compared with the chorus. Such accouterments precluded acting in the modern sense. Greek tragedy, conditioned by the exigencies of place and tradition and ruled by convention, was a more statuesque and dignified affair than are modern plays; hence we shall never be able to detect in Greek plays more than an approach to that realism which we prize so highly today.

In the matter of dramatic structure we observe again that same predilection for clarity of line, that same passion for well-balanced construction, which mark the efforts of the

Hellenes in other fields. Nothing is more lucid than a Greek play, unless it be a Greek temple; the same instinct is at work in the making of both. The drama usually opens with a prologue, which, in the best cases, without disturbing the illusion, informs the spectators of such things as they need to know in order to be able to follow the unfolding of the plot, and which arouses their curiosity as to the manner in which the author has chosen to present the well-known story. Next comes the *parodos*: the chorus enters singing to the accompaniment of the flute players' music, in marching rhythm. Then follows the first *epeisodion* (episode, literally "entrance"), a spoken dialogue between actors or between an actor and the leader of the chorus. This is succeeded by a choral song, a *stasimon*; then episode and stasimon alternate in regular succession; sometimes, marking the crisis of the play, an interchange of lyric song between chorus and actor — a *kommos* — interrupts this succession. Finally, the *exodos*, as Aristotle says, is that part of the play which comes after the last stasimon. Such, in brief, is the usual structure of a Greek play, which is marked by a greater simplicity of outline and of plot than that to which we are accustomed in contemporary drama. Once these conventions concerning structure had been established, they were rigidly observed.

Greek tragedy, then, differs from modern tragedy in many respects. In the first place, it is conventional in form. Its form betrays its origin: here were united the iambics of the Ionians (the dialogue is usually written in iambic verse) and the Dorian choral melic, with its wealth of rhythm. And the tyranny of tradition was so strong that this Attic drama shows in its iambics an Ionic tinge, in its choral songs a Doric coloring. But most of the differences between ancient and modern drama can be traced to the tribal origin of Greek tragedy. Sprung from the matrix of the tribal festival, (1) it is choral; (2) it deals not with the marital career of Mr. and Mrs. X but with the heroic figures of tribal song; (3) it united all the members of the group in a common ritual, by which the city-state, successor of the tribe, did homage to a god whose power for good or evil was so great. But from the fact that Greek drama is choral spring further differences. The presence of the chorus naturally entails those famous "three unities" which have so greatly vexed the history of later drama. For with a stationary chorus no change in scene was possible (unity of place). The most vitally important action often took place off stage and was reported by a messenger; hence the messenger's speech is a characteristic feature of Greek tragedy. The presence of the chorus had a similar limiting effect on the time supposed to elapse during the action of a Greek play: it begins with sunrise and ends before sunset (unity of time). Finally, when the conventions governing the number of actors allowed on the stage were once fixed, a complicated plot was out of the question (unity of subject). But the Greek playwrights, who knew nothing of the "three unities," have dealt in a sovereign way with these obvious limitations imposed by convention. Changes of scene occur more than once in the extant Greek tragedies; time often does hurry while the chorus sings its songs (Aeschylus' *Prometheus* seems to cover not a day but centuries); and even unity of subject is not always observed by the Greek playwright. Nevertheless, it remains true that Greek tragedy is more conventional in spirit, more simple in plot and structure, than its modern offspring. But the reasons for this are purely historical. It is absurd to extend the tyranny of Hellenic tradition into other eras and exalt it into a principle of art, valid at all times.

AESCHYLUS

Aeschylus was born in the township of Eleusis, in Attica, in 525 B.C. His literary activity covered the first half of the fifth century. He lived through that great crisis in Hellenic history, the Persian Wars; what is more, he fought at the battle of Marathon (490), and ten years later, in company with his fellow Athenians, was forced to abandon his country to the invading hordes of Xerxes. No doubt he fought at Salamis as well. These were tremendous experiences, which left a lasting impression on his mind; and when, shortly before his death, he composed his own epitaph, he had not a word to say about his dramas, but wrote that "the famed grove of Marathon and the long-haired Mede will bear witness to his valor." These simple words bear eloquent testimony to that conviction, so firmly implanted in the Greek mind, that the greatest glory belongs not to the poet or artist but to the citizen fighting bravely for the preservation of the state and the ancestral institutions. The needs of Athens may have sent him to other parts of Hellas; we know that he was in Sicily on more than one occasion and that he died there in 456 B.C. He is said to have written ninety plays. Of these only seven have come down to us; but we are fortunate in the choice posterity made. In the first place, these seven plays illustrate the development of his art. The earliest, the *Suppliants*, may date from 492 B.C. and shows the first tentative employment of that second actor which he introduced; the latest, the *Oresteia*, belonging to 458 B.C., reveals him in the full maturity of his powers. Secondly, these seven plays include the one example of a historic drama which we possess, the *Persians*. Finally, in the *Oresteia* we have a complete Aeschylean trilogy, three plays presenting three successive phases of the legend.

The *Suppliants*, with its archaic features, proves itself the oldest of the Aeschylean dramas, and for that reason alone repays the reader's attention. There is no prologue; the chorus still has the main part, its songs occupying more than half of the play; the second actor is still an experiment and could be eliminated altogether; there is no background, the entire play centering around the altar in the orchestra; and of a dramatic plot in the strict sense of the word there is hardly a trace. But the drama has great beauty and charm. The situation is this: The fifty daughters of Danaüs, descendants of that Argive Io who was beloved of Zeus, flee from Egypt in order to escape marriage with their fifty cousins — an incestuous marriage according to the ancient ideas of exogamous society — and with their father seek sanctuary in ancestral Argos. The king of Argos — he is a constitutional monarch and bears no resemblance to the imperious Agamemnon of Homer — grants their request, after he has duly consulted with his people. And when the blustering herald of Egypt appears on the scene, demanding the maidens' return, he is refused. The situation is exciting from the beginning, the orchestra swarming with the tearful Danaïds in exotic costumes, and reaches a moment of superb dramatic tenseness when the terror-stricken maidens descry the coming of the Egyptian ship and are left alone to face the anger of the Egyptian envoy and his minions. Like a spider "he has caught them and carries them seaward step by step, — a nightmare, a black nightmare!" But the king of Argos arrives in time to rescue them.

The second play of the trilogy continued the story of the Danaïds. Forced after all to acquiesce in the abhorred union with their cousins, they slew them in the bridal night, — all but one, Hypermnestra, who spared her husband. Her fortunes formed the subject of the closing play.

The *Persians*, performed in 472 B.C., may be separated by twenty years from the *Suppliants*. This play too lacks a prologue, but the second actor is more freely used; the actors, however, do not yet embody the conflict of wills in the drama. The plot is slight. The scene is laid in Persia, and the play depicts the impression made at the Persian court by the victory of Salamis. The poet has interpreted the Greek victory as Heaven's judgment upon the presumption of man. The might of the Persian is a challenge to the power of the gods, and throughout the play the sinful pride of the Persian forms the main motif. Herein Aeschylus does not greatly deviate from the prevailing view of the Persian defeat, which is echoed in Herodotus. There is a chorus of Persian elders, who first give voice to the foreboding of evil; the poet, with refreshing naïveté, makes them utter that perfectly sound Hellenic doctrine of the heaven-sent "Delusion, which lureth man astray into her snares." Atossa, the queen-mother, confirms their fears by relating a disquieting dream, a vision of the night before. Presently a messenger arrives who gives a dramatic account of the battle of Salamis. This forms the heart of the play, and we note that, while many of the Persian grandees are singled out for special mention, not one individual Greek — not even Themistocles himself — is thus honored. The next scene brings our first ghost on the stage of Europe: Darius is evoked from his tomb. The great king himself condemns the mad enterprise of Xerxes, which he too interprets as being due to the baneful influence of an offended god. "When man hasteneth to his own undoing, God too taketh part with him." Xerxes, who bridged the Hellespont and defied the god of the sea, — was he not suffering from some "distemper of the soul"? Indeed "Zeus is a chastiser of overweening pride." Let it be a lesson to Xerxes and to all of Persia. The drama closes with the return of the hapless Xerxes, amid the lamentations of the chorus of elders.

The *Seven against Thebes*, produced in 467 B.C., is the last unit of a trilogy dealing with the house of Laius, king of Thebes. Laius has been forewarned by the oracle of Delphi that if a son is born to him, this son will slay his father and marry his mother. Laius, upon the birth of his son Oedipus, has him exposed in the mountain wilds of Cithaeron; but a shepherd takes the child to the court of Corinth, where he grows up to manhood. Eventually the oracle is fulfilled; and when Oedipus discovers himself the murderer of his father and the husband of his mother, he blinds himself in despair. But the curse pursues even the third generation; for now Eteocles and Polynices quarrel over the succession. This is the subject of our play, which begins with a prologue: Eteocles calls upon the citizens to defend their city against Polynices, who is leading an army of allied chieftains against the seven gates of Thebes. A scout confirms the tidings of the arrival of the seven hostile chieftains. The chorus of Theban maidens enter; they are panic-stricken at the approach of the enemy and are duly rebuked by Eteocles, who in his tone and words voices the orthodox Greek view of womankind: "You, I ask, insufferable creatures that ye are! is this the best course to save the town, . . . to shout and shriek and make decent folk detest you?" Let them bide within; matters abroad are man's care. But Eteocles finds it very difficult to restrain the emotional outbursts of the women: "O Zeus! what a breed thou hast given us in womankind!" The main part of the play concerns the pairs of heroes about to fight at the seven gates. Eteocles himself undertakes to meet his brother's assault upon the seventh and last gate. Nearly all the attacking foes are conspicuous for their *hubris*, the insolence with which they defy god and man. But if ever additional proof were needed of the Greek's love of battle, as shown in the delight he takes in details of armor and in heroic demeanor, the reader will find it in this celebrated passage, which verily is "full of the war god," as Aeschylus himself is made to say in the play of Aristophanes.[1] Of the actual repulse of the grand assault we see nothing, but in due time are informed of the deliverance of Thebes, even though both Eteocles and Polynices have fallen, slain by each other's hand. Presently the bodies of the two brothers are borne upon the stage, and there follows a magnificent dirge in which their sisters, Antigone and Ismene, take part in antiphonal song. When the herald announces that Polynices, who has fallen in an assault upon his own city, is denied burial, Antigone refuses obedience to the decree and sets out at the head of one procession with the body of Polynices, Ismene joining the other half of the chorus in the funeral rites for Eteocles. As in the *Persians*, narrative and lyric parts of the play rather than dramatic action proper engage the interest of the audience.

[1] *Frogs*, line 1021.

Even less action characterizes the *Prometheus Bound.* It seems as if with the nailing of Prometheus to the rock on which he is to expiate his sin the drama itself must remain static. Yet there is a certain progress, if only in the degree of Prometheus' defiance, until the final catastrophe, when the divine sufferer is hurled into Tartarus. Prometheus, the discoverer of fire, is one of those heroes of civilization who throng the myths of many lands. It is interesting to see what a great poet like Aeschylus could make out of slight and unpromising material. Hesiod knew Prometheus as the god who abstracted fire from Olympus, but could envisage him only as a cunning trickster who delights in deceiving Zeus. Out of this character of the popular saga Aeschylus has created a heroic figure — the champion of humanity, who will not suffer man to perish but teaches him the ways of life. Helpless in the power of Zeus, this god, in the possession of a secret known to him alone, has yet the means to force Zeus to come to terms. Now there was a story, invented to glorify Achilles, to the effect that an oracle had foretold that Thetis, the goddess of the sea, would give birth to a son who would be greater than his father. This story is utilized by Aeschylus. Prometheus, in the possession of this secret, knows that there are many suitors for the hand of Thetis, including Zeus, and that if his suit is successful he will be overthrown by the offspring of this union. This is the weapon Prometheus is made to wield in the unequal combat with Zeus.

The date of the *Prometheus* is uncertain, but the apparent employment of a third actor would place it between the *Seven against Thebes* and the *Oresteia.* The play opens upon a desolate scene at the very end of the world; there Prometheus is being riveted to the rock by Hephaestus, the kindly god of fire, and his heartless helpers, "Power" and "Force." The chorus consists of the daughters of Oceanus, tenderhearted goddesses full of compassion for the sufferings of the spirited antagonist of Zeus. Their father, ancient Oceanus, himself comes to counsel moderation, but in vain. The other actors are Io and Hermes — Io changed by Zeus into a heifer to escape the jealousy of Hera, and driven by the gadfly to wander restlessly over land and sea. Prometheus proceeds to describe her past and future course. The world is still a marvelous place, and the poet takes delight in describing the wonders of distant lands and peoples. Io too is a victim of Zeus. When finally the defiance of Prometheus reaches the limit of endurance, Hermes appears, the messenger of Zeus, demanding that Prometheus declare the meaning of his enigmatic speech. Upon his refusal, the hero is hurled into Tartarus. The great beauty of the play lies in the portrayal of Prometheus, to which we shall return later.

Finally there is the *Oresteia* (produced in 458 B.C.), the trilogy dealing with the legend of the return of Agamemnon from Troy. It tells how he was treacherously slain by his faithless wife, Clytemnestra; how Orestes, his son, avenged the murder of his father at the command of Apollo; and how the matricide, pursued by the Furies, was acquitted by the Athenian court presided over by Athena. Aeschylus has availed himself of the third actor, introduced by Sophocles; but the plot is still simple and lacking in complications, the action marching straight to the goal. We can only briefly summarize the salient points of this most impressive of all Aeschylean works.[1] The scene is laid in Argos, before the palace of Agamemnon. The watchman stationed on the roof of the palace, weary with a year's watching and waiting, hails the beacon light which announces the fall of Troy. The chorus enter, a company of old men. They sing of that war, a visitation from heaven on Greeks and Trojans alike, which has now lasted ten years. Clytemnestra enters; the chorus asks her why she has summoned them into her presence. But she heeds them not. The song of the chorus continues, and slowly the clouds gather: insensibly the audience, listening to the woeful chant, is brought into the right mood to wit-

[1] For an excellent account of the trilogy see J. T. Sheppard, *Aeschylus and Sophocles* (Longmans, 1927), pp. 16–39.

ness the horror that is to come. The chorus tell at length of the great king's dreadful sacrifice, — the slaying of his own daughter Iphigenia at Aulis, where the Greek fleet had assembled and lay becalmed. The chorus find its solace only in the thought of Zeus, who leads men through suffering to understanding. Thus the poet skillfully creates the proper atmosphere for the ensuing scenes. And now Clytemnestra, masterful from the start, explains why the altars of the gods are smoking with incense and sacrifice: Troy has fallen, and she sets forth the marvel of the beacon lights that leaped from peak to peak. But the tale is not of the joy of victory alone. What of the vanquished? And did the conquerors keep themselves clean of guilt with respect to the gods? She closes on an ominous note.

The chorus sing of the fall of Troy; but there is no exultation in their song: it is, rather, an expression of awe at the doom of Troy, at the stern justice meted out by Zeus to the town which shielded Paris, the great sinner. Helen brought "to Troy destruction in place of dower." And the old men shudder at the price paid for the Greek victory; they do not envy the conquerors. A herald now enters; he confirms the tidings, told by the beacon lights, of the fall of Troy. But Clytemnestra does not suffer him to dilate on his theme. Let him bid her husband come quickly, to find her loyal and devoted.

The herald, questioned by the chorus concerning Menelaus, is loath to mar a day of joy with a tale of woe; for Menelaus' ship, swept from sight by the storm that broke upon the Achaeans, has not returned.

With the herald's departure the old men bethink themselves of Helen, — her beauty the marvel of men, "love's flower, that stingeth the heart," a beauty which turned into a curse.

And now Agamemnon enters; in his train follows Cassandra, the daughter of Priam, the unhappy maiden whom Apollo has endowed with the gift of prophecy because he loved her, and whom he has condemned never to have her prophetic words believed because she spurned him. She has been awarded to Agamemnon as his prize.

The king addresses Argos and the gods of Argos; both pompous and self-righteous, he yet shows himself slow-witted and vacillating in the ensuing scene with Clytemnestra. The speech (lines 855–913) with which she welcomes him remains one of the greatest in the dramatic literature of the world. She lies magnificently, and the audience, we need not doubt, caught the scornful irony hidden in her lowly words. Agamemnon treads the purple tapestries with which she has strewn his path ("that Justice may usher him to a home he ne'er hoped to see"), but not without misgiving, and enters the palace where death awaits him.

In the following scene, the most powerful of the entire drama, Cassandra, god-possessed, breaks forth into prophecy. The veil is lifted from her eyes and she sees the palace for what it is, — a charnel house, the scene of horror in the past (when the flesh of his own children was served up to Thyestes by his brother Atreus), and the scene of bloodshed which is to come; her own miserable death is to form part of the tragedy. Then she enters the house, and soon the death cry of Agamemnon is heard. The old men are in tumult, when the doors of the palace are flung open and Clytemnestra stands there exultant over the bodies of Agamemnon and Cassandra. She boldly proclaims her deed and defends its justice. Was he not the slayer of her child? But she admits the fiend of the race had his part in her action. Finally Aegisthus, her paramour, appears, and a threatened outbreak of revolt on the part of the chorus, provoked by the smirking mien of the cowardly bully, is stilled by the master hand of Clytemnestra. But they have recalled that in Orestes, Agamemnon's son, there yet lives an avenger. Thus we are prepared for the second act of the great drama.

The *Choephoroi* ("Libation-bearers"), which brings us the story of the vengeance taken by a son upon his mother, falls into two parts. The first part centers about the grave of

Agamemnon, where Electra, the loyal daughter of Agamemnon, and Orestes, who has returned to Argos at the behest of Apollo, meet and invoke the ghost of their father to speed Orestes and his friend Pylades on their mission of vengeance. The second part deals with the reception of these two by Clytemnestra, who, believing their tale of Orestes' death, sends for Aegisthus. Aegisthus, summoned by the old nurse of Orestes (the woman is a pathetic figure in this gruesome setting), walks into the trap. His death brings Clytemnestra upon the scene; after a vain appeal for mercy, she is driven into the house, where she meets her doom. The last scene discloses Orestes standing by the bodies of the slain, the branch of the suppliant in his hand. Then, in what is undoubtedly the finest scene of the play, he tells what he has done and why he did it, and he displays the robe, "the net," in which his father was caught. Even as he is speaking, his reason becomes darkened, and the Furies, these "wrathful sleuth-hounds that avenge my mother," come upon him. The chorus closes on a note of sorrow and despair: "When will the fury of Ate, the madness that now vexes the third generation, be lulled to rest and find an end?"

The same subject, the vengeance of Orestes, has been treated by both Sophocles and Euripides; a comparison of these three plays throws much light on the progress of dramatic art in the fifth century and on the differing aims and methods of the three playwrights. Remembering the similar problem of Hamlet, we are apt to think that Aeschylus has failed to exploit the psychological possibilities of the situation: the conflict of duties does not rage within the breast of Orestes but, in a thoroughly Greek fashion, is made objective and is fought out between Apollo, who stands for the rights of the father, and the Furies, who represent the older claim of the mother upon her children.

The story of that conflict is told in the last play of the trilogy the *Eumenides* (literally, the "Kindly Ones," a euphemistic name of the Furies). Orestes has been purified by

Apollo at Delphi, where the opening scene of the play is laid. Despite this ceremonial cleansing, the Furies, urged on by the shade of Clytemnestra, continue the pursuit and track him to Athens. Here Athena hears the conflicting claims. With her appearance it is as if we enter into a cleaner atmosphere: the old blind forces of passion demanding a life for a life, the savage cry of the Furies, the ancient mystical rites of purification, — all the warring elements of a dark and primitive world, — are brought before the tribunal which the wise goddess of city life and a new, enlightened society establishes for all time to come. The trial opens. After both sides have presented their case, and the jurors are equally divided between acquittal and condemnation, Athena herself casts her vote for acquittal. When the Furies are not minded to abide by the verdict, she persuades them by the promise of a new honor they will receive in the city, where they shall guard the ordered institutions of a new society — the Hellenic polis. Thus the poet has contrived to tell the legend of the past and to find the solution for the mighty issues involved in the historic institutions of his own city, Athens, where the venerable tribunal of the Areopagus judged the murderer, and where the Furies, invoked as the "Kindly Ones," received the worship of the people in the cave beneath the hill of Ares, which was the seat of the tribunal itself. But Aeschylus' master stroke as a dramatist was the introduction of the Furies. To bring these dreaded goddesses of the Nether World upon the stage, in their weird garb, snakes entwined in their hair, blood dripping from their eyes, — this was in itself a thing of unparalleled audacity. We hear of a panic seizing the audience when the opening of the temple doors of Delphi revealed their hideous forms huddled in the inner sanctuary. Henceforth Orestes is almost forgotten, a mere pawn in the battle between the warring gods; the savage Furies hold the stage, and the haunting terror of their great song (lines 307–396), the spell they weave over their victim, has never been surpassed in the dramatic literature of the world.

Judging by these plays, we acknowledge the justice of Aeschylus' claim to be the creator of drama as a new art form. The epic and lyric elements are still present. Indeed, owing to the limitations of the Greek stage, the narrative element, the messenger speech relating what had taken place off stage, could hardly ever be eliminated. And the choral song had proved itself a useful instrument for many purposes, — to create atmosphere, to offer comment, to voice the emotions called forth by the action; as a lyric interlude between the spoken portions of the drama the choral song remained. But the purely dramatic element gained more and more on the older parts, and Aeschylus himself pointed the way. Consider the *Agamemnon*: the watchman dancing for joy on the palace roof; Clytemnestra kindling the altar fires; the splendor of Agamemnon's entrance, the purple coverlets under his feet; the raving Cassandra; blood-bespattered Clytemnestra by the side of her victims; the distracted elders; Aegisthus defying them and drawing his sword, — all this is real drama.

This new art Aeschylus ennobled by lending it a pomp and splendor which left nothing further to be done by his successors; if drama was to develop, its future growth was to be along different lines. For he is the poet of sublimity and grandeur. His language reflects it; the lyrical portions of his plays, in particular, are fairly overwhelming in their wealth of imagery and the bold, soaring quality of the thought. In fact, these songs, developed from the ecstatic dithyramb, do not lend themselves to a precise analysis; rather, with rhythmic dance they enthrall and exalt the spectator. The dialogue itself has a dignity and a pomp of language wholly in keeping with the high function of tragedy as conceived by its maker. For Aeschylus is one of those rare artists who live habitually in a world of the imagination wherein life assumes titanic proportions. It is not the ordinary characters that interest him, nor the paltry emotions of commonplace humanity and its humdrum ways, but, rather, the weird, the vast, the terrible,

Witness the setting of the *Prometheus,* — the desolation, the solitary rock, and the mighty Titan chained to it; witness the other actors of the drama — the daughters of the sea in their winged chariot; the ancient god himself on his flying griffin; Io, the horned maiden; Hermes, the swift god with the winged sandals and the magic wand; and then the final catastrophe — thunder and lightning, earthquake and whirlwind, and the rock sinking into the depths of Tartarus. Truly, Aeschylus, the first of Greek dramatists, was also the most sensational.

To a man thus minded, the meaning of life is not exhausted by noting its surface movements; behind and over it he descries mighty powers, mysterious forces, at work. A curse is on the house of Laius, and a heaven-sent madness drives Eteocles and Polynices to their death; a demon dwells in the palace of Argos, and three generations in turn are tormented by its baneful presence; even Xerxes himself suffers under a delusion and is blinded by the gods because of his pride of power. Does Aeschylus, then, deny the freedom of the will? Are these heroic characters mere puppets in the hands of the gods? No, Aeschylus would answer. They willed, indeed, what they did, and they willed it because such was their nature. But it is all a mysterious business, for in what they willed and did they carried out the purposes of a Higher Power. And of one thing he felt sure: that this Higher Power is a Moral Power, who punishes the evildoer and teaches wisdom through suffering. This Marathon fighter was a man of great moral earnestness, who shared the common view that power and pride lead to *hubris,* which in turn brings madness and disaster. But he emphatically rejected the equally popular view of divine jealousy: it is not human greatness which provokes God's envy, but human wickedness which provokes his wrath. In groping his way toward some conception of a moral order of the world, Aeschylus hit upon Zeus as its upholder. However, he is a poor theologian, or, rather, a better poet than theologian; for the marvels of the myths were the very breath of his nostrils, and his imagination fed on the wonders of the sacred history of Hellas. Had he been more of a theologian, he would have perceived that the multitude of Greek divinities is incompatible with a moral order of the universe, which postulates a single will — in fact, monotheism.

But while enthralled by his vision of Zeus's majesty, he is yet essentially the singer of the majesty of man. His world is one of heroic proportions. There is as little subtlety in his portrayals as complication in his plots; the figures are drawn with a few bold strokes. How grand a vision of man do they reveal — a humanity which includes such towering figures as the dauntless Eteocles, the masterful Clytemnestra, and, above all, the defiant Prometheus! Aeschylus belonged to an age which as yet had no such misgivings concerning man's place and his mission in the universe as vex our days. A comparison between Aeschylus' *Oresteia* and a recent treatment of the same theme will bring out the heroic quality of the Aeschylean version and the immense gulf that separates us from him. O'Neill's *Mourning Becomes Electra* is a far subtler play, more realistic and truer in its psychology; but it leaves us with a bitter taste in the mouth, for it brings a poignant revelation of the sordidness, futility, and insignificance of life. But the blow of the ax with which Clytemnestra dispatches her husband we hear reverberating through the universe; even the gods are shaken out of their Olympian calm. We are here confronted with the strange paradox that the horrors of an Aeschylean drama actually have an exhilarating and exalting effect. We are reminded of the Shakespearean horrors and their strangely heartening effects. Well, a common faith breathes in both Aeschylus and Shakespeare; and as the age of Marathon and Salamis produced the one, so the strenuous age of Elizabeth produced the other.

Finally, what of Prometheus, whom we have included in the heroic gallery of Aeschylus? To be sure, Aeschylus says he is a god, a Titan, who defied Zeus. But let us look a little closer. We are familiar with the peculiar Greek way of objectivizing the inner processes of the mind. Love leads Helen to seek Paris: Homer says that Aphrodite took her by the hand. Sober sense causes Achilles to thrust back the sword he is drawing against Agamemnon: Homer says that Athena seized him by his yellow hair. Bitter remorse drives Orestes from the ancestral palace: the Greek poet asserts that the Furies pursued him. The pride and reckless self-assertion of the Pelopid princes becomes Ate, a malignant spirit dwelling in the royal house. Now Prometheus is a "culture hero"; he has invented the ways of civilized life. Aeschylus makes him say that he found men witless and gave them sense. They had eyes but saw not, and ears but heard not, and he taught them to use their wits. From him they learned the use of numbers and the art of writing, to build houses, to watch the seasons, to tame the brute beast, to roam the sea, to cure the sick. In short, "every art possessed by man comes from Prometheus."

Prometheus did this in the face of a hostile power who controlled the world — Zeus himself; and *this* Zeus, be it noted, cares nothing for justice or morality but relies on force, and force alone. At bottom, who is Prometheus but the indomitable spirit of man, striving onward and upward in the face of a Zeus, that is, a universe indifferent to his aims, alien to his aspirations, nay, actually hostile to their realization? To be sure, Aeschylus does not say it this way — he speaks the mythological language of his age and his race; but in the adventure of Prometheus he has summed up the total achievement of the human race in its laborious climb from savagery to civilized life. Surely we cannot be wrong if we interpret this splendid tribute which the poet pays to the indomitable will of the Titan as the proclamation of his faith in man — that faith which was the priceless possession of his own age.[1]

[1] The translations are taken or adapted from H. W. Smyth's prose version (Loeb Library).

SOPHOCLES

The life of Sophocles (496–406 B.C.) covers almost the entire fifth century. In his youth he took part in the celebration of the victory of Salamis (480 B.C.); he died shortly before the battle of Aegospotami (405 B.C.) ended the Athenian dream of empire. Yet he is identified especially with the Periclean Age, whose spirit he reflects most faithfully in his dramas. He was of good birth, handsome in person, of genial temperament, and enjoyed unvaried good fortune. He exhibited his first plays in 468 and, if we may believe tradition, won the prize in competition with Aeschylus. From that time until death ended his career he remained the most honored of the tragic poets, gaining the first prize no less than eighteen times. Moreover, he fully participated in the civic life of his time, on one occasion even holding the office of *strategos* as the colleague of Pericles, and he served on the board which administered the finances of the empire.

Of his dramatic output, which comprised more than a hundred plays, only seven remain. Of late years a considerable portion of one of his satyr dramas and fragments of other plays have been recovered; but these additions do not materially affect our estimate of his place in the history of Greek drama. The seven extant plays belong to his maturer years; even the earliest, the *Ajax* and the *Antigone*, he wrote when past fifty; and the last two, the *Philoctetes* and the *Oedipus at Colonus*, which show no impairment of his genius, date from the last decade of his long life.

To the innovations he introduced belong, as we have seen, the third actor and painted scenery. We find that the spoken parts in his plays have gained at the expense of the choral parts.[1] He abandoned the Aeschylean practice of presenting in his trilogies three successive stages of one story; the plays

[1] Whereas in the *Agamemnon* of Aeschylus the lyrical and spoken parts divide the play almost equally between them, the proportion in Sophocles' *Oedipus Rex* is about one for the lyrical to four for the spoken parts.

of Sophocles forming a trilogy are on independent themes and are somewhat longer than the average Aeschylean plays. His skillful use of the third actor led to greater complication in the structure of his plots, which, in marked contrast to the archaic simplicity of Aeschylus, do not admit of a brief analysis. We shall be content to indicate the themes of the surviving tragedies.

The *Ajax* tells how, after the death of Achilles, the Achaean hero is defrauded, as he thinks, of the award of Achilles' arms, which the chieftains gave to Odysseus. He plans vengeance, but, blinded by Athena, falls upon the cattle and sheep instead. On discovering the nature of his folly, he commits suicide. The second part of the play deals with the disposal of his body. The dishonor which Agamemnon and Menelaus had planned to inflict upon Ajax, even after his death, is averted through the interference of Odysseus, who represents the cause of wisdom and warns against excess. The captive Tecmessa, the mistress of Ajax, is, next to the hero, the most appealing figure of the play in her womanly devotion to her captor, who is singularly indifferent to her fate.

The *Antigone* elaborates the theme introduced at the close of the *Seven against Thebes*. Antigone, the daughter of Oedipus, resolves to bury her brother Polynices in spite of the edict of Thebes's new king, Creon. She suffers the penalty of her transgression; but Creon too is punished for his offense against the gods of the Nether World through the suicide of his son, to whom Antigone was betrothed, and that of his wife when she learns the fate of her son.

The *Electra* treats the same theme as the *Choephoroi* of Aeschylus, — the vengeance taken by Orestes upon the murderers of his father.

The *Oedipus Rex* is Sophocles' masterpiece. A skillfully constructed plot unfolds the story of how Oedipus discovers that he has slain his father, Laius, and that he has been living in incestuous union with his mother, Jocasta. The drama is the most effective the Greek stage has to show.

Sophocles

Lateran Museum, Rome

In the *Trachiniae* we learn how Deianira, the wife of Herakles, attempting to retain the love of her husband, sends him a robe anointed with what she believes to be a love charm, which is, in reality, a violent poison. Upon learning the consequences of her tragic error she takes her own life. Herakles bids his son deliver him from the torments of the poison and place him upon a pyre.

The *Philoctetes* recounts how the Achaeans, finding that Troy cannot be taken without the bow and arrows of Herakles, send an embassy to Philoctetes, in whose possession they are. In the first year of the Trojan War they had abandoned him, as he was suffering from a noisome disease, upon the uninhabited island of Lemnos; and after nine years of solitude and pain Philoctetes is in no mind to aid the Greek cause. But Neoptolemus, the son of Achilles, duly instructed in his part by the wily Odysseus, gets possession of the arms by a ruse, only to repent of his treachery! The play would end in a deadlock but for the timely appearance of the deified Herakles, who orders Philoctetes to renounce his just anger and tells him of the glory he shall gain in the capture of Troy. The interest of the play lies largely in its character studies.

The *Oedipus at Colonus* relates the marvelous ending of the tragic career of Oedipus. Driven from Thebes, accompanied by his loyal daughter Antigone, he has wandered until an inner urge now sends him to Athens; here he finds shelter, and is protected against the selfish schemes of Polynices and Creon by Theseus, king of Athens. An old man now, Oedipus is still the same — masterful, headstrong, quick to anger, and terrible in his wrath. But a miraculous translation into a larger life is awaiting him; and at the end of the play, he, the blind, leads the way to his eternal resting place. Only Theseus may know the spot whence he, a beneficent spirit, will watch forever over the fortunes of Athens. No one wishing to understand Greek mysticism at its best can afford to leave the exodus of this play unread.

Nothing will better illustrate the advance in dramatic composition made since Aeschylus' day than a comparison between the *Choephoroi* and the *Electra.* As we saw above, the action of the *Choephoroi,* slight as it is, does not deviate from its straight course. After Orestes has revealed himself to Electra, and brother and sister have invoked the aid of the gods, there are no complications until the murder of Agamemnon is avenged. Neither Orestes nor Electra stands clearly revealed to us by a poet whose chief interest is, rather, in the mighty issues involved in the story of the matricide.

Now let us look at the Sophoclean play. The scene is laid before the palace of Agamemnon at Mycenae. Orestes enters, accompanied by Pylades and a faithful retainer of Agamemnon. They make their plan: first the old man is to go to the palace and announce that Orestes has been killed in a chariot race; later Orestes and Pylades will arrive, bearing an urn containing the supposed ashes of Orestes. We note the departure from Aeschylus' naïve handling of the death report. There are two separate messages: the first is to give an elaborately detailed account of the mishap that ended Orestes' life; the second, in the shape of the funeral urn, will bring ocular demonstration of the truth of the first message.

Furthermore, Orestes and Pylades plan to visit Agamemnon's tomb. Upon hearing a voice from the palace the three withdraw. The voice they have heard is Electra's, who now appears upon the scene and pours forth her lament at the wrong to her father, still unavenged; from the beginning she is the loyal daughter of Agamemnon. There follows the parodos. The chorus of women come to grieve with her and yet to counsel moderation. But Electra protests her inability to forget while the pair of evildoers glory in their wickedness. Oh, where is Orestes? How long will she have to wait? And now the poet introduces Chrysothemis, Electra's sister, a more pliant character, whom he cleverly uses as a foil to the heroine. Electra is harsh in her judgment of her sister's more prudent conduct, displaying that intolerance of weakness and compromise which is characteristic of the heroic temper. But the amiable Chrysothemis well knows her sister's vehemence, and she proceeds on her errand. What is her errand? asks Electra; and finds that Clytemnestra is sending offerings to the grave of Agamemnon, as she has been alarmed by a dream (here Sophocles borrows from Aeschylus). A sudden light shines in the eyes of Electra: O gods of the house, can it be that at last deliverance is at hand? A new note of tenderness in her voice, as she addresses Chrysothemis, marks the change in her mood. "Dear sister, cast away these wicked offerings; rather let us make our own gifts and pray that our father may give his aid and Orestes may live to set his foot upon his foes." Wonderful to say, Chrysothemis enters into Electra's hopeful mood; and the two sisters are united.

The chorus echo their hopes in a song prophetic of the vengeance to come (first stasimon). The second episode brings Clytemnestra upon the scene. Mother and daughter engage in bitter reproaches; Electra is defiant, for she has seen a ray of hope. Clytemnestra turns for comfort to Apollo, the very god who has sent Orestes upon his dreadful mission; the irony of the situation does not escape the audience. And now, in pursuance of the plan agreed upon in the prologue, the old man enters and in a dramatic speech gives a circumstantial account of the death of Orestes. Clytemnestra listens with mingled emotions: he was her child, and yet this message brings her the final relief for which she has prayed. But Electra is plunged into despair; the last faint glimmering of hope has vanished. The scene has gained immeasurably in dramatic power from the presence of these *two* listeners to the old man's tale. When Clytemnestra and the messenger enter the house, Electra releases the stream of emotion struggling for expression, and the anguish of her grief is echoed by the chorus; this kommos, an interchange of lyric song between the protagonist and the chorus, takes the place of the second stasimon.

Chrysothemis returns from her mission to her father's tomb. She has found fresh offerings (made by Orestes) and joyfully exclaims that these can be from no other but Orestes himself! Of course she is right, and the audience knows it; but Electra, deceived by the false message, acquaints her sister with the supposed fact of Orestes' death, and makes her appeal to Chrysothemis: will she join her in slaying Aegisthus? Let her think of the glory of such a deed! But Chrysothemis stands aghast at this proposal; her counsel of prudence is harshly rejected by Electra.

The choral song which follows comments on the scene that has just ended. And now Orestes enters, bearing the funeral urn. Electra stands in the presence of that brother whose coming she has so eagerly awaited; but she sees in him only the bearer of the ashes of her beloved Orestes, and he, on his part, does not know her. This is a supreme moment of dramatic suspense, and the audience, in breathless silence, wonders how the poet will contrive their mutual recognition. She asks for the urn and over it utters a most touching lament: this is the end of her hopes; now she only prays to rejoin him in death. In the following dialogue Orestes, who now knows whom he confronts, gradually reveals the truth; the sudden reversal is nowhere in Greek drama managed with greater skill. Electra forgets everything in the transports of joy that possess her. Orestes fears that the radiance of her face will betray her secret. They are interrupted by the old man, who warns them, quaintly observing that unless they act with greater caution "their plans will enter the house before they do themselves." He announces that everything is in readiness, and all go into the palace. After a very brief choral ode Electra rushes out. Orestes and Pylades are ready to strike; she will stand guard against the coming of Aegisthus. And then the terrible cry of Clytemnestra rings out. Orestes, emerging from the house, announces that all is well "if Apollo's oracle spake well." This is the only hint of the inevitable coming of the Furies which the poet allows himself; for they can have no part in the drama of Electra's heroism. Upon the approach of Aegisthus, the slayers hastily withdraw into the house. Aegisthus, who has been informed of the message the men from Phocis have brought, does not try to hide his satisfaction. The ensuing dialogue between him and Electra is a masterpiece of tragic irony. "Can he see the corpse with his own eyes?" He can; the doors open and disclose a shrouded corpse. "Call me Clytemnestra," he says. Orestes, who is standing near him, says, "Lo, she is near thee." The harrowing discovery follows. He is driven into the palace to meet his doom, and the play closes on a note of joy: the house of Atreus has found peace. But the audience knows that Apollo spake *not* well, and that Electra and Orestes rejoice on the brink of an abyss. But that is another story, which Aeschylus has told so well that the spectators do not think Sophocles will care to tell it again.

Even a cursory examination of Sophocles' *Electra* reveals the immense strides that had been made in dramatic art since the day when Aeschylus, by the introduction of his second actor, had made drama possible. Compared with the *Choephoroi*, the drama of Sophocles has a complicated plot; the resources placed at the disposal of the dramatic writer by the introduction of the third actor have been utilized in a way of which Aeschylus did not dream. Not less striking is the complete shift in interest and emphasis which distinguishes the *Electra* from the *Choephoroi*. Sophocles ignores the momentous issues involved in the story of the matricide Orestes, — issues which formed the very core of the Aeschylean play and which demanded a sequel in the *Eumenides*. Instead Sophocles centers the interest in the characters of the participants and, above all, in the character of the protagonist, Electra. The unfolding of the story serves one main purpose, the revelation of the character of the heroine; she is the mirror in whom the entire action of the drama is reflected. First we see her sorrowing and indignant; then her heroism is revealed in its full harshness when she rejects the council of the chorus and upbraids the weakness of her sister; but her mood changes when the report of Clytemnestra's dream awakens hope in her heart, and, confronting Clytemnestra, she boldly challenges her. Then comes the blow dealt by the false messenger. Orestes' supposed death arouses in her the courage of despair: she will do the deed herself. Yet when she holds the funeral urn in her hands, the depth of her anguish leaves no room for other thoughts; she is crushed and prays for death. And at last, upon the discovery of the truth, completely overwhelmed she surrenders; and the heroic Electra now stands revealed as a tender-hearted woman, a loving sister, eager to seek shelter in the strong, protecting arms of her brother and rescuer. Thus Sophocles, with admirable skill, has manipulated the incidents of his plot in such a way as to draw forth every variety of emotion from his chief character, and to this day the *Electra* continues to provide a splendid part for the emotional actress.

The drama of Sophocles, then, marks a distinct advance over that of his predecessor both in structure of plot and in delineation of character. And if the sole function of poetry is to delight and entertain the audience (and in passing we remember that Greek poetry always implies an audience), then we might rest content with having proved Sophocles' right to be counted among the great poets of Hellas. But, as we saw above, the Greeks had a strange notion that poetry must *instruct* as well as give pleasure; and a growing social ideal imposed upon the poet a social responsibility of which modern poets take no cognizance. From what source was the Greek poet supposed to draw the wisdom he teaches? The Greeks have a twofold reply: either, they say, he has gained this insight through superior intellectual endowment and experience of life or he is a madman, a person possessed, who in some mysterious manner apprehends the truth revealed to him by a god. If we may believe Socrates, most Greek poets were of the latter variety: they say beautiful and striking things, but they seem to be unable to give a rational account of their own words.

Now if these Greek notions concerning poetry and poets are stripped of their peculiarly Hellenic garb, we shall discover that, after all, our conception of the function and meaning of poetry does not differ so greatly from that of the Greeks. For to us too the meaning of poetry is not exhausted by the pleasure it provides. In all great poetry we look for a stimulus beyond mere delight; we anticipate not only the thrill of pleasure but that of discovery as well. We look for the common facts of life arranged in a beautiful pattern, but the beauty of the setting must also impart a new significance to these same common facts. Verily there are more things in heaven and earth than our philosophy has dreamed of! And we too, like Socrates, hold that the poet accomplishes this greater mission not by an appeal to the reason but by an appeal to the imagination; he does not demonstrate, he only communicates his vision; he is a madman, if you will, a man divinely inspired. In other words, intuition, the immediate apprehension of truth, is the mark of poetry. We seek, then, in our poets a new reading of the facts of observation, an enlargement of our own experience: "The poet expresses his intuition of life and the audience recognizes the 'likeness,' the semblance of reality, . . . we have been sharers in a presentation of life not otherwise revealed to our normal existence."[1] This, after all, is the highest function of all art. We may have gazed indifferent and uncomprehending upon the face of a grizzled veteran, who has grown old in service; but when we look upon him as painted by Rembrandt, we are strangely moved, for the artist has put into that face all the woes of man and his stern endurance. We listen to those first four notes of Beethoven's fifth symphony and we respond immediately to their prophetic ring.

Now how does the dramatic poetry of Hellas appear when judged by these standards? We are ready with our reply so

[1] E. E. Sikes, *The Greek View of Poetry* (Methuen), p. 126.

far as Aeschylus is concerned. For he had an authentic vision and left the audience no room for doubt as to the nature of his message: he interpreted the ancient legends as fragments of life which alike form part of a great moral order in which Zeus and Destiny and Justice join hands. A journalist might feature the slaying of Agamemnon as "Unsuspecting Husband Slain by Vengeful Wife"; Aeschylus saw in it the finger of God and the fulfillment of the dark destiny of a self-willed race. But with Sophocles the answer is not so easy. We shall have to examine his plays afresh. When we do so, we may at once discount the moral platitudes with which he, like all Greek poets, has interlarded his plays; they are all of the copybook variety and contain such orthodox doctrine as the socially-minded poet was expected to parade. We must look not for the explicit but for the implicit teaching of his plays. We may take the *Antigone* first.

Here is Creon, a just king, newly called to the throne by the deaths of Eteocles and Polynices; Creon, in his joy at the deliverance of Thebes, is going to make an auspicious start: henceforth all shall know that the good citizens will have their reward and the traitors will be punished. He will set an example. Eteocles, who fell in defending his city, shall be honored by a public funeral; but the traitor Polynices, who led a hostile army against the walls of his city, bent upon its destruction — his body shall remain cast out, a prey to birds and dogs. He suspects that such treatment of even an enemy's corpse will be shocking to prevailing sentiment; but with the deadly peril of his city fresh in mind, he burns with the zeal of the reformer to set things right — there must never be another Polynices. He discourses at length on the wisdom of his course. Here is Antigone, loyal daughter of Oedipus, loving sister of Polynices and Eteocles, a proud princess who has seen the last survivors of her race perish at the gates of Thebes; and now comes this fresh insult to her race, the decree of Creon, who treats her brother's body as carrion, to be mangled by a passing dog. Ah, she feels sure that decree was meant for *her* (in point of fact, Creon had not even thought of her); but she will challenge that upstart king even at the price of her own life. And now the battle begins. She is caught in the act and, brought before Creon, defies him to his face. Did she dare to disobey his law? he asks; and in reply she scornfully compares his one-day-old law with the everlasting decrees of heaven, which enjoin upon the living the care of the dead. As for punishment, let him do as he pleases; for death is welcome to her. Her attitude leaves Creon no choice; she is led away to be immured and to perish in her living tomb. But, anticipating the death awaiting her, she takes her own life, while Creon in turn pays the penalty for his preposterous wisdom. What is the ultimate meaning of this tragic conflict? Given the characters of the two antagonists, we see that the clash was inevitable, and the tragic ending a foregone conclusion. For they do not understand each other: the wrongheaded Creon knows only the wisdom of the statesman; Antigone obeys the prompting of her heart. He, being a man, reasons and continues to reason; but she, being a woman, knows only this: "it is her nature to join in love and not in hatred." Poor Creon! He who was to be so wise a ruler, the city's savior, accomplished the destruction of his own happiness. And Antigone goes to death because she was so loyal and so brave. Is that just? "No," says Sophocles, "there is no justice in it, but something even greater than justice, truth; and in what I have shown you, I have revealed the mystery of human suffering and the irony of life."

We turn to the *Oedipus Rex*. The god at Delphi tells Oedipus he is destined to kill his father; Oedipus turns his back on Corinth, where his supposed father lives, and on his road to Thebes unwittingly kills his real father. Upon arrival at Thebes, he solves the riddle of the Sphinx and as a reward receives the hand of the queen; and she, though they know it not, is his mother. He is now a thing of defilement, a source of pollution; and presently a pestilence rages in Thebes. The oracle says, Find the murderer of Laius. All turn to their king, Oedipus, who delivered Thebes from the Sphinx, and Oedipus solemnly calls down the curse of heaven on the head of the murderer. The seer Tiresias denounces him as the murderer; he takes the accusation as an insidious attack upon his power. His wife, Jocasta, in seeking to relieve his mind from further anxiety, rouses his first suspicion as to the identity of Laius' slayer. A messenger from Corinth comes and tries to set his mind at rest with regard to that prophecy of Apollo which predicted his marriage to his mother, and in so doing the Corinthian brings about the discovery of the awful truth.

Deianira, the most conspicuous example of gentle womanhood on the Greek stage, unwittingly inflicts most cruel torments upon the man she loves. Troy cannot be taken without the aid of him whom the Greeks kept at a distance for many years; and the very honesty of the youth (whom the wily Odysseus took with him, the better to prevail with resentful Philoctetes) proves the nemesis of the undertaking. Orestes comes in response to Electra's prayer, but his arrival as the disguised messenger almost proves her undoing. Deluded Ajax sits in the midst of the slaughtered sheep and thanks the goddess for the aid she graciously gave him. And so it goes; for Sophocles seems to say, we are like that Homeric Ajax, battling in the darkness and praying vehemently for the light. It is the tragic irony of life which the poet reveals in his plays; his figures move in the clear daylight, but they are encompassed by an invisible power which makes mock of their brave strivings. The Sophoclean tragedy deepens the sense of the mystery of life and reveals an aspect that lies hidden beyond the realm of reason. It is a significant fact that in no less than four of the seven extant plays (*Ajax*, *Antigone*, *Oedipus Rex*, *Trachiniae*), the catastrophe is immediately preceded by a song of hope or victory, and that two of his plays end in a situation of tragic irony, of which the audience, but not the characters, are aware. The *Trachiniae* ends with the agony of Herakles, who bids his son place his body on the pyre and end his anguish; in his last words he rails at the harshness of the gods and the callousness of that reputed divine father of his. But the audience knows that not his death is at hand but his deification, and the very god whom he denounces will be his savior. The *Electra* ends with a scene whose irony, not less poignant, would not escape the Athenian audience. And in the final scene of the *Oedipus at Colonus* we come to grips with actual miracle and religious mysticism.

Is man, then, nothing but the plaything of a malicious god? That would be a strange message to come from the lips of a poet who lived in the Periclean Age and who was acclaimed by that age its greatest poet. No, he would say, life is great only because it is tragic. Antigone is greater than Ismene; Electra greater than Chrysothemis; and even Ajax, taking his own life, greater than the worldly-wise Odysseus. It is just this darkness, enshrouding the fate of man, which calls forth the heroic quality in him, and it is the mystery of suffering which ennobles him. Such, we imagine, would be the reply of Sophocles. It is an answer which would be understood in the Age of Pericles.

The Third Period

EURIPIDES

Pindar, Aeschylus, Sophocles — all were apostles of the heroic life; their vision saw man built on the grand scale. For theirs was an age of a great and living faith.

In 431 B.C. the Hellenic World War broke out. Its fearful spiritual ravages, of which we have spoken elsewhere, were enhanced by the pestilence. The spirit of disillusion and skepticism engendered by the war found allies in the disruptive teachings of the Sophists; under the combined onslaught of these agents the splendid edifice which Hellas had reared began to totter. There opens a new era, which we might well call the Age of Doubt; for its essential quality lies just in this, that the unquestioning faith in life begins to give way to a growing uncertainty, and the civic patriotism which had been the inspiration of the Periclean Age begins to lose its hold on the minds of men.

The disillusion of the new era is mirrored in the plays of Euripides, the last of the three tragic poets. His message came too soon for the crowds gathering in the theater in his day; for they were loath to surrender the ancient traditions. It was better understood in the cosmopolitan Greece of the Hellenistic Age, when his popularity eclipsed that of his predecessors. Hence the surprising fact that Euripides, who as a dramatist is inferior both to Aeschylus and to Sophocles, has survived in nineteen dramas, a number surpassing the combined total of his predecessors' extant plays.

He was born in 484 or 480 B.C. (the evidence is conflicting) and died shortly before Sophocles, in 406 B.C., at the court of Archelaus, king of Macedon. Tradition tells of unhappiness in his domestic life; but in point of fact little is known of his private life. He seems to have shunned the bustle of the agora and was prone to retire to the privacy of his estate on Salamis; even many centuries later, visitors were shown the cave where he was reputed to have composed his masterpieces and where he may have indulged his love for meditation. More important is the fact that he is known to have been one of the earliest collectors of a library.

The nineteen surviving plays (he wrote over ninety) comprise one satyr play, the *Cyclops*; one of doubtful authenticity, the *Rhesus*, which, if it is his, may be an early effort; and the *Alcestis*, which was performed in 438 B.C. as the fourth of a tetralogy, and thus took the place of a satyr drama. The remaining sixteen tragedies all date from the Hellenic World War. Nevertheless, it is surprising that the poet who was a younger contemporary of Sophocles and who spent the best years of his life under the Periclean regime should yet so strikingly reflect the spirit of the succeeding era.

To illustrate the gulf that separates him from Sophocles

we can do no better than examine a few of his tragedies. We shall take three of his plays treating of the Trojan cycle; this will give us the advantage of dealing with material with which we have become familiar, and it may afford us an opportunity for comparison with previous treatment of the same themes by Euripides' predecessors. We shall take in order the *Iphigenia at Aulis*, the *Troades* (the *Women of Troy*) and the *Electra*; all these plays belong to the last ten years of his life.

The scene of the *Iphigenia* is laid before Agamemnon's tent at Aulis. The Greek host assembled at the king's bidding is waiting for favorable winds to sail for Troy. But the seer Calchas has declared that the anger of Artemis will not suffer the Greeks to depart; the price of her favor is the sacrifice of the eldest daughter of Agamemnon, Iphigenia. Reluctantly the king has consented to send for her; but his message to Clytemnestra deceives her into believing that her daughter is being summoned to Aulis in order to marry Achilles. When the play opens we see Agamemnon in an agony of remorse; with the aid of an old servant whom he takes into his confidence he attempts to send a second letter, recalling the first. A chorus of women from neighboring Chalcis now enters. Curiosity has led them to Aulis to view the Achaean array; they recount what they saw of the Greek chieftains and the assembled fleet.

The old servant re-enters, accompanied by Menelaus; for the king's brother suspects the nature of the old man's errand, and presently he wrests the fateful letter from the hands of the loyal slave. The commotion brings Agamemnon out of his tent; he is promptly and bitterly reproached by his brother for his disloyalty to the Achaean cause. He had promised of his own free will to surrender his daughter, and now he has basely retracted; is such a man fit to captain the Achaean host? Agamemnon defends his conduct: shall he sacrifice his innocent daughter that Menelaus may regain his wanton wife? Their quarrel is interrupted by a messenger announcing the imminent arrival of Clytemnestra and Iphigenia. The unhappy father is overwhelmed with grief at this unexpected news, for now that his daughter has come, he foresees that escape will be impossible; he gives way to tears. Then it is Menelaus' turn to relent: let them disband the army; he will not be the cause of grief to his brother. Agamemnon brokenly thanks him for his change of heart. But, alas, it is too late. Well he knows the temper of the army. If they should be informed that the expedition is to be abandoned because he will not give up his daughter, even if the lips of the seer could be sealed, some ambitious rogue, like Odysseus, is sure to let the cat out of the bag, and the whole army will turn against their princes and slay not only Iphigenia but Agamemnon and Menelaus as well. No, it is too late; but Clytemnestra must have no inkling of the truth.

The song of the chorus ignores the present crisis; they sing of the power of love and of Paris' judgment. And now, riding in the royal carriage with her children, Clytemnestra and attendants enter. The scene is alive with the bustle and excitement of her arrival. Clytemnestra, elated, like any mother, by the prospect of her daughter's marriage to a man of rank, is in command of the situation. First the dower is to be taken from the carriage. Then let them assist Iphigenia in descending; the women of Chalcis are to look after her. Now she will descend herself, with their help; "but watch the horses!" In the midst of the commotion she does not forget the babe Orestes, and lo! he is asleep; but he must wake, for it is his sister's wedding day! Presently the anxious father joins his family. Iphigenia runs to meet him and with a cry of joy throws herself into his arms. But what ails him? Well, he answers, a king has many cares. But not now, she says; now he belongs to her. There follows a dialogue of exquisite beauty between the unhappy Agamemnon and his artless daughter; he tries to excuse his sudden tears by the prospect of her marriage: these partings are so heartbreaking. At last Iphigenia releases him; and after she has entered the tent, Clytemnestra, like a careful mother, inquires into the lineage and the antecedents of the prospective husband of her daughter. Agamemnon satisfies her curiosity, but when he tries to persuade her to return to Argos, he meets with unexpected resistance; she stoutly refuses, and vows she will not leave her daughter now.

The choral ode which follows again offers no comment on the tragic situation; its subject is the impending doom of Troy.

Achilles now enters, seeking Agamemnon; for he and his men are impatient at the delay. When will the expedition start on its way to Troy? Clytemnestra has overheard his cry and joyfully runs out of the tent to meet her future son-in-law. The scene between these two borders on the comic; and when Achilles, not a little amazed at hearing of his supposed betrothal to Iphigenia, vows that Agamemnon never spoke of marriage to him, Clytemnestra, confused and bewildered, is ashamed to look him in the face. The true state of affairs is now revealed to Clytemnestra and Achilles by Agamemnon's old slave, the same confidant of his master whom we have met earlier in the play. Clytemnestra, horror-struck by the disclosure, appeals to Achilles to save Iphigenia; and he, in his anger that his name has been used to lure Iphigenia into the camp, swears that Agamemnon shall not touch her. But first let Clytemnestra try to persuade her husband to desist from his fatal purpose.

The choral ode once more functions purely as a lyric interlude; its subject, the marriage of Peleus and Thetis, has no conceivable bearing upon the situation. It closes with a remarkable epilogue: "What has become of modesty and virtue? when godlessness prevails, virtue is neglected and lawlessness rules; the jealous wrath of god is no longer feared."

And now Clytemnestra pleads with her husband, and a clever, well-reasoned appeal she makes; even more powerful are the pitiful entreaties of his daughter. But it is all of no avail. There is no escape for Agamemnon; all Greece looks to him, and he must not fail. There follows a lyric lament by Iphigenia. Achilles returns and in excited tones reveals to Clytemnestra the dangerous state of affairs prevailing in the camp: the men, almost in open rebellion, are clamoring for the life of Iphigenia; they are in an ugly mood, and have found a leader in the villainous Odysseus. Achilles admits he is helpless; his own men are completely out of hand. But, even so, he plans to don his armor and defy the mob. Iphigenia, who has listened in speechless wonder to the tale he unfolds, now breaks her silence; a new light shines on the face of the young girl. Nay, let not Achilles rush to his own doom; she has made up her mind. Yes, she will die, if that be the will of heaven, and offer up her paltry life for the good of Hellas. Achilles is amazed at the revelation of such nobility of character in one so young; now he truly loves her. He shall go to the altar where she is to die, ready to rescue her if at the last moment she will permit him. Iphigenia then bids farewell to her tearful mother and tries to console her: let her not weep, for her death is glory. A kommos and choral song speed Iphigenia on her way.

The final scene brings a wondrous tale and an unexpected ending; a messenger brings the report to Clytemnestra. The sacrifice had been made, — the blow had been struck by Agamemnon's own hand, — but at his feet lay the body of a deer; Iphigenia had vanished. More we cannot affirm of the ending of the play, the text of which has suffered. The play was produced after the death of Euripides, who may have left it unfinished.

But the uncertainty concerning the exact form of the exodos does not prevent a just estimate of the character and spirit of Euripides' art as revealed in this, one of the last of his works. The revolutionary change he has brought about in the dramatic art of Hellas is unmistakable. Who are these men and women appearing on his stage? To be sure, the names are the same familiar names: Agamemnon, Menelaus, Clytemnestra, Achilles, Iphigenia. We know them all as familiar figures in the heroic saga of Hellas. But they are changed beyond recognition. What has come over Agamemnon, the masterful leader of the host? Is this the mighty Achilles, whom his faithful Myrmidons used to follow unto death? As Euripides portrays them we look in vain for their counterparts in that heroic world of the past, which had lived in the imagination of Hellas, hallowed by time; we shall find their counterparts in the market place, the assembly, and the homes of Euripides' own world, a world torn by war and demoralized by its ravages. Agamemnon, Menelaus, and Achilles are the distracted leaders of a disorderly democracy, — leaders of a mob whose evil instincts they cannot control. The rabble howling for the life of Iphigenia has its parallel in the Athenian mob clamoring for the lives of the generals who had commanded at Arginusae.

This was the transformation of a familiar world effected by the revolutionary art of Euripides: he has brought the heroic saga and the heroes themselves down from the nebulous heights in which they dwelt — down to earth; no longer above the human level, they are seen in a new guise, in their likeness to a contemporary humanity. And how pitifully human they are! Clytemnestra is an ordinary mother of middle-class society as she arrives in state and fussily looks after the important details of the wedding. Iphigenia is a lovely girl with all the shamefaced charm of the maiden about to meet her future husband. On discovering the truth, she naturally recoils from the ordeal and, just as naturally, with the generous ardor of youth, surrenders her life, since only thus can she save those dear to her. Agamemnon faithfully reflects the weaknesses of ordinary man; political ambition, a genuine love for his little daughter, shame, and fear drive him hither and thither. Thus Euripides interpreted the heroic legend. There is no vision here of an ideal grandeur, no exaltation of the spirit as he unfolds his canvas; instead there are the pity and the tears of a sensitive poet and thinker, who was deeply and sincerely moved by the spectacle of the erring humanity of his own day.

We now turn to the *Troades*. As a specimen of Euripides' dramatic art it does not rank high. Its structure is archaic in that, like some of the Aeschylean plays, it lacks a plot, portraying a situation in a series of tableaux. The scene is laid before the walls of Troy; in the background there is a tent. Troy has fallen, and the woes of the Trojan women form the subject of the drama.

The prologue is spoken by Poseidon and Athena, who take their departure from the ruined city; their words bear evil omen for the victors. In the succeeding scenes the wretched lot of the Trojan captives is portrayed. There are four such episodes, bound together by the continuous presence of Hecuba, the erstwhile queen of Troy; upon her old head break the billows of disaster. First she is informed of the fate of her daughter Cassandra, who is to follow Agamemnon; of the death of her daughter Polyxena, who has been slain at the tomb of Achilles, she remains in ignorance (the herald vaguely says, "All is well with her"). Andromache has been allotted to the son of Achilles; Hecuba herself is to go with Odysseus. Cassandra, in prophetic frenzy, sees the approaching doom that will overtake her captors as well as herself. The second scene brings Andromache, who reveals to Hecuba the grievous truth concerning Polyxena. Her little boy, Hector's son, is taken from her; the Greeks, acting upon the advice of the rascally Odysseus, will fling him from the battlements of Troy. The third scene confronts Helen, the prime cause of all the woes of Greeks and Trojans alike, with Menelaus; she pleads her cause very skillfully, but Hecuba refutes her plea. In the final scene of the play the herald returns with the body of Astyanax, the innocent victim of the Greek fury of revenge; Hecuba makes moan over her grandchild. Now the torch is applied to Troy, and the drama ends amid the wailing of the women.

The *Troades* was performed in 415 B.C. The preceding

year had shown Athens in her ugliest mood; for it was the year when she committed the wanton act of aggression on the little island of Melos.[1] The spectacle of a small Hellenic state attacked without provocation and blotted out by a vastly superior Hellenic power had profoundly shocked Greek sentiment; it was an act of *hubris* inviting divine punishment. What impression the destruction of Melos and the brutal treatment of its inhabitants made upon the sensitive mind of Euripides we can guess from the *Troades*. For it seems as if the poet, utterly saddened by the sight of his beloved city disgraced by an act of barbarism, in this play lifts his voice in impassioned protest against the folly of the world about him. There was the Trojan War; it had always been looked upon as a most glorious chapter in the sacred annals of Hellas. "But," says Euripides in effect, "there is yet another side to this story"; and in a succession of harrowing scenes he confronts his audience with that other aspect of the war: the unmerited suffering inflicted on the innocent Cassandra, the noble Andromache, and that figure of utter pathos, the aged Hecuba herself. What of the noble conquerors themselves? They stand revealed not as heroes, whose glorious exploits were a fitting theme for the bards of a later age, but as cowardly bullies, princes brutalized by war, of whose inhumanity even their own herald is ashamed. And when Andromache bitterly accuses the Greeks of adopting the ways of barbarians, were there not thousands in the audience who, the fate of Melos still fresh in their memory, could not help seeing that the shafts of the poet were aimed at themselves? We wonder at the audacity of Euripides; for he lived in a world which still looked upon war as the test of manhood and as conferring the true badge of honor. Small wonder that this audience did not like Euripides!

Before leaving the play we note that the chorus here once more fills its ancient part. The captive women of Troy share the sufferings and feelings of their nobler sisters.

[1] See page 115.

Not less novel is Euripides' treatment of the legend of Electra; indeed, in no other play has he made so elaborate an effort to wrench the ancient tale from its grand setting. It was probably produced in 413 B.C., just before the second Athenian armament left on its ill-fated mission to Sicily. On the whole, Euripides has not been very happy in his efforts to secure a new setting for the story. The means employed are the marriage of Electra to a poor farmer, who, out of respect for Electra's royal lineage, has elected to be her husband in name only, thus affording the poet an opportunity to moralize on the noble traits so often found in the poor and humble. But it must be admitted that the farmer becomes somewhat tiresome, and we do not regret his total disappearance after the second act of the play.

The stage, then, is set for the terrible vengeance to be exacted by Orestes. It is not a Homeric palace, however, all shining with gold, but the miserable hovel of Electra's husband. Electra herself, in mean attire, her locks shorn, is found engaged in menial duties: she is carrying a jug to fetch water from the well. Sympathizing women of the neighborhood, forming the chorus, try to inveigle her to join in Hera's festival; but, she protests, not only is her mind on other things but she cannot show herself in the festive procession in such rags as she wears. We are not spared the comic touch; for commonplace things become comic because of their incongruity with the tragic milieu. Orestes and Pylades appear; since they are armed, Electra and the chorus, like any peasant women, flee in dismay. Orestes intercepts Electra as she runs to the hut, and tries to soothe her fears; she prays to Apollo to save her from death! At last Orestes persuades her that he has come with the best of intentions; he brings tidings of her brother. In turn she informs the stranger (for such he is to her) of her plight, that he may report her misfortune to her brother. At this juncture the peasant husband returns to find his wife engaged in earnest conversation with a total stranger! But when he hears of the welcome tidings the youths bring, he forthwith invites them into his humble home. For this display of hospitality, as soon as the guests are out of hearing, he is promptly chided by Electra, who reminds him of the poor store she has with which to regale any visitors. At her bidding the peasant goes off to fetch an old retainer of Agamemnon who, after the king's death, carried off Orestes to a place of safety in distant Phocis. When the old man comes (and his garments too are tattered), he brings meat and drink for the entertainment of the guests. (Again we are spared none of the details: we hear of a suckling lamb, cheeses, and a little wine.) It is this servant who recognizes Orestes, but only after Electra, by implication, has vigorously criticized the outmoded devices employed by Aeschylus in his recognition scene. And now they lay their plans for the successful execution of the vengeance. The old man makes a happy suggestion: Aegisthus is in the country near by, about to sacrifice to the local nymphs; he is unattended and off his guard. This fortunate coincidence gives Orestes his opportunity, and he and Pylades go off on their mission. Later a messenger relates how the unsuspecting Aegisthus, hailing the strangers, invited them to a share in the sacrifice, and how Orestes slew him and was acclaimed by the thralls of Agamemnon as the long-looked-for deliverer. In the meantime Electra plots to lure Clytemnestra to the peasant's hut. The same old man, after guiding Orestes to Aegisthus, is to summon Clytemnestra on the plea that her daughter Electra has given birth to a son. (Electra is sure not only that she will come but that she will weep over the babe's lowly parentage!) Clytemnestra arrives in due time, but not before Electra has gloated over the body of the hated Aegisthus. After a lengthy altercation between mother and daughter, Clytemnestra enters the hut; but "let her have a care that the smoke-begrimed walls do not besmirch her regal attire." Orestes waits within. He is torn by doubt. Was Apollo right? Can even a god justify matricide? At the crisis his courage fails, and it is the hand of Electra which guides the death-dealing sword. When brother and sister reappear on the stage, they are overwhelmed with remorse, Electra taking the blame for the dreadful deed. The epilogue is provided by the appearance on high of Pollux and Castor, the divine brothers of the slain queen; they place the blame on the folly of Apollo, and predict the coming acquittal of Orestes before the Athenian court.

This is Euripides' way of telling the story which had been invested with tragic grandeur by Aeschylus, and which in the hands of Sophocles had become a character study of a loyal daughter of a regal house. Not that Euripides means to be frivolous; on the contrary, he is in dead earnest. But to him it was a sordid tale of sordid passions, of cruel vengefulness and a barbarous lust for blood; that a god should have commanded the act of matricide is plainly repellent to his mind. Therefore he strips the legend of all the glamour and glory that the past had lent it; and in the process the chief characters of the heroic legend lose their halo. Electra herself is not a loyal daughter but a woman whom years of wrong have made into a morbid creature obsessed with the thirst for revenge; the deed accomplished, her mind is freed, and she looks with loathing upon her part in the crime. Nor is there anything heroic about Orestes: first the poet makes him slay the man who has invited him to be his guest, and that at a religious rite; then, when confronted with the dreadful duty Apollo has laid upon him, he is only pitifully human and pitifully weak. As for Clytemnestra, she is no figure of tragedy at all, as a discerning critic has observed.[1] In spite of her royalty and her remarkable past, she has the ordinary instincts of a middle-class woman; she would rather have peace than anything else, and she would be kind to her rebellious daughter if only Electra would let her.

Even a cursory examination of these plays, then, reveals the great gulf that separates the Euripidean drama from that of his predecessors. It is true, not all his plays show the

[1] G. Norwood, *Greek Tragedy*, p. 254.

poet in the same mood of disillusion. Sometimes his touch is lighter, as in the *Helen*, which is a fantasy. (Helen had never run off with Paris, but only her phantom; the real Helen is awaiting her husband in Egypt!) Another example is the *Iphigenia in Tauris*, which is pure romance. It tells how Orestes, in far-off Tauris, is recognized by his sister Iphigenia when, as priestess of Artemis, she is about to slay him, and how they escape from the land of the king. The *Alcestis*, in turn, tells how the heroine died in order to save her husband from his appointed doom, and how the timely intervention of Herakles rescued her from the grasp of Death. Of his other plays we may mention the *Medea* (431 B.C.), justly regarded as one of his best because of its truthful portrayal of a woman who, cast off by the man she has loved and has saved, in murderous rage destroys his intended bride and slays her own children; the *Hippolytus* (428 B.C.), perhaps his finest play, which tells of the guilty love of a stepmother for her stepson and of the tragic death of both (Racine treated the same subject in his *Phèdre*); the *Ion*, a remarkable play, with a most skillfully constructed plot, but marred by the poet's insistence upon making of it a theological treatise; the *Orestes* (408 B.C.), the most melodramatic of his plays, which contains at least one unforgettable scene, in which a sorrowing Electra attends upon a distraught Orestes; and, finally, the *Bacchae*, in which Euripides, at the end of his career, does homage to the mysterious life force worshiped under the name of Dionysus.

In all these dramas it is, after all, "Euripides the human" who speaks to us, and his message is that of the new age which was fast learning to question the old and seek the new; for Euripides was a thinker, or, rather, he was given to brooding over the riddle of life as he saw it. We hear of his friendship with the philosopher Anaxagoras, whose philosophy, however, he did not adopt any more than that of the others who professed to have discovered the truth. He remained in doubt, though to the end of his life he was devoted to that search for the truth without which he could not live. A strangely modern figure, he has made a profound appeal to men in all ages who have heard in his plays the echoes of their own questionings.

In another sense also he belonged to his age, which was the age of the Sophists. Their new mode of speech, their skill in argumentation, often degenerating into mere sophistry and subtlety, seems to have pleased Euripides inordinately. The love of argumentation, probably popular enough with his keen-witted audience, has invaded almost every one of his dramas; and the moment for displaying the new rhetorical art is not always happily chosen. There is hardly a Euripidean drama unmarred by one of these untimely debates in which each contestant defends his or her action with a lengthy array of arguments which are usually more arresting by their novelty than by their intrinsic truth. These debates (in the plays discussed above there is one in the *Troades*, between Helen and Hecuba, and another in the *Electra*, between Clytemnestra and Electra) strike us as particularly frigid. But we must not blame Euripides alone for this. There is no question that the Greeks, with their intellectual bias, were fond of explaining on rational grounds acts committed in a momentary outburst of rage and passion; and such afterthoughts delighted them the more, the more fantastic they were.[1]

Even more disturbing to the dramatic illusion are the monologues with which Euripides interrupts his dramas. On occasion he uses these as a means to convey to the spectator an idea of the struggle going on in the heart of the speaker. A celebrated example is the speech of Medea, who is torn between the desire for revenge on Jason and her love for her children; here the use of the monologue is entirely legitimate, and succeeds admirably in revealing her anguish. But more often the poet's rationalizing and moralizing habits get the better of him, and the monologue degenerates into rhetorical ranting and platitudinous generalizations. Frequently these

[1] There is a good example in Sophocles' *Antigone*, lines 904 ff.

rhetorical displays are ill-timed in that they come at a moment when moral indignation or some other overmastering emotion possesses the speaker. A good example is the outburst of Hippolytus when he is informed of Phaedra's guilty passion, — a particularly frigid speech by which the poet has contrived to spoil a splendidly dramatic moment. Similarly ill-timed is the speech of Electra over the body of Aegisthus.

Equally nondramatic are many of his prologues and epilogues. Both are due to his intellectual bent, to the need for lucidity which is a characteristic of Greek mentality. The legends he dramatizes are mostly well known to his audience, but there were several versions current. Now Euripides felt bound at the outset of the action to give the audience exact information concerning the antecedents of the play. He could have done this, as Sophocles did, by a dialogue in which one actor informs the other, and incidentally the audience, of the events leading up to the play. Thus, Ismene had not heard of Creon's decree; Antigone informs her and announces her own intention to disobey. But Euripides prefers another method which will leave no room for misunderstanding: one of the characters, in a monologue often entirely unmotivated, rehearses the chief events of the past and unfolds the salient features of the present situation. These prologues are not always lacking in dramatic significance; but more often than not they are matter-of-fact in tone and destroy the dramatic illusion. Thus the *Electra* opens with a monologue in which the peasant rehearses the story of Agamemnon: how he destroyed Troy and came home laden with the spoils of war and was slain "by his wife's guile and by the hand of Aegisthus." (Euripides wishes to inform the audience that he goes back to an older version of the legend which made Aegisthus and not Clytemnestra the actual slayer.) The farmer then enlarges upon Aegisthus' motives and his present rule of Argos; next he refers to Orestes' sojourn in Phocis; and finally he explains at some length (for this is a feature of the story which comes as a complete surprise to the audience) how it happened that Electra is living at his house. He ends with a wordy explanation of his relations to Electra. A more efficient way of acquainting the audience with the facts necessary for understanding the drama could not have been chosen; at the same time a more disconcerting affair than this typical Euripidean prologue is hardly imaginable. Why should the hardworking peasant begin his day's labors with a recital of these facts, addressed to no one in particular and completely lacking in dramatic justification?

A similar desire for clarity causes Euripides to introduce at the end of his play a supernatural character, usually a god appearing on high, the famous *deus ex machina*, who frequently, in an equally matter-of-fact tone and often without a suggestion of divine majesty, performs the useful office of untying the knot, or of informing the audience of the more distant events which are to follow, thus giving the story its proper finish. These epilogues betray Euripides' mentality: not satisfied until he has neatly rounded off the story, he sacrifices the dramatic unity of the play to his love of logic. These epilogues are a mechanical device, which break the dramatic continuity and form an external appendage to the dramatic organism. Such, for instance, is the epilogue of Apollo in the *Orestes*; he unties the knot and predicts the future: the audience may rest assured that matters will be set to rights. Occasionally Euripides is more successful in welding the god's appearance into closer union with the body of the play, as in the *Hippolytus*. Finally, we may add that the *deus ex machina* is not to be interpreted as evidence of Euripides' inability to bring the story to its natural conclusion; he seems deliberately to have preferred this type of ending for his drama.

The extant plays bear abundant testimony to his skill in the construction of dramatic plots. In this respect his practice marks an advance over Sophocles' art, for he sometimes introduces the element of surprise or suspense in his plays —

there are sudden turns of events taking the spectators unawares. Melodrama may look upon Euripides as its sponsor. The *Ion* and the *Orestes* provide the best examples of the novel complications he introduced into his plots. In the *Ion* a mother, ignorant of her true relationship to her son, attempts to poison him; the crime is forestalled, but the enraged youth demands the life of the woman who plotted against his life; an unexpected recognition scene between mother and son ends the suspense. In the *Orestes* a frenzied Orestes is seen on the roof of the palace on the point of plunging his sword into the body of the daughter of Menelaus; the sudden appearance of Apollo saves the girl, who, as is revealed by the god, is eventually to marry the very man now bent upon taking her life!

Of Euripides' treatment of the chorus we have seen two contrasting examples in the *Iphigenia at Aulis* and the *Troades*. On the whole, the tendency toward detaching the choral odes from the body of the drama continues; they are more and more apt to be treated as lyrical interludes to the dramatic action, although it would be wrong to assert that such was the consistent practice of this last of the great dramatists.

What, then, is the part Euripides has played in the history of drama? To put it briefly, he paved the way for secular drama. The Greek world knew only religious drama, whose theme was the heroic past of the race. It was performed at a religious festival, attended by all the people, whom it united in a common emotion. But religion in Hellas, and especially in Athens, had been transmuted into an exalted patriotism; religious ardor had been identified with civic devotion. With the decay of the social ideals of Hellas, the city festivals themselves were robbed of their true significance and inspiration. For the survival of dramatic art a severance of religion and art would have been necessary. But for such a revolutionary step Athens was not prepared. The City Dionysia, after the Greater Panathenaea the most magnificent religious festival of Athens, were so firmly established in the traditions of city life, and the performance of drama was so indispensable a feature of its traditional form, that it would not have occurred to any Athenian that a change in the established custom was possible, even if it were desirable. And so it happened that year after year following the passing of Euripides and Sophocles the Dionysia continued to be celebrated with the performance of works of dramatic art that were stillborn. The art which had discharged a grand and noble function in the days of its creators degenerated in the fourth century B.C. into a lifeless and meaningless mimicry of the ancient forms. A great social art — and such was Greek tragedy — can flourish only when its roots strike deep into the life of the society which gave it birth; when these wellsprings begin to fail, the art itself withers. Such was the fate of Greek tragedy. The countless imitators of Euripides who perpetuated the ancient forms, and who attempted to improve on their master by decking the old materials with newer and gaudier dress, were not his successors; the real successor of the Euripidean drama was the New Comedy of the late fourth century B.C. — the comedy of manners, as Menander created it. Let anyone who doubts this kinship read the *Ion* of Euripides and compare it with such poor remains of Menander's art as we have. It was Euripides who put on the stage the ordinary man, with his amiable intentions, his foolish ambitions, his moral weakness; he introduced the humble slave, the helpless child, and woman in her varying moods. Menander took them over from Euripides and borrowed his bag of stage tricks as well. But he dropped the pretentious names of legendary fame under which Euripides' characters had paraded; they are no longer Agamemnon and Menelaus but plain Mr. Smith and Mr. Brown. This art form, however, could flourish only in a society in which cosmopolitanism had taken the place of the civic idealism of the fifth century B.C.

COMEDY

In the course of our discussion of Hellenic poetry we have seen that there are two propositions which may be affirmed of all Greek choral poetry. First, the ultimate origin of all these types can be traced to tribal song and dance. Second, after their conversion into definite art forms the subsequent history of this poetry is inextricably interwoven with the fortunes of the city-state; indeed, we may go one step farther and affirm that the polis claimed these art forms as its own and converted them to its own uses. Thus, choral melic had been incorporated into civic life; and, above all, one species of choral melic, the dithyramb and its offspring tragic drama, having found favor in Athens, had been utilized to foster the civic ideals of that city.

Now of Greek comedy these two propositions hold good as well; in fact, the history of comedy furnishes the best illustration of the inner bond which unites the products of Greek genius to the political organization of Greek life.

Comedy, the song of the *komos*, — that is, the band of revelers, — originated in the rustic celebrations in honor of Dionysus, the god of wine. At certain seasons the countryside would ring with the merry shouts of the celebrants moving in joyous procession, carrying aloft the emblem of fertility, and giving unrestrained vent to their animal spirits. Mimicry and buffoonery were the invariable concomitants of these Dionysiac revels. In such time-honored customs the germ of comedy lay hidden. As with that other manifestation of Dionysiac frenzy, the dithyramb, here also the Dorians took the lead in giving it artistic form. In Megara, in the sixth century B.C., a crude form of comedy was staged in which the Dorian instinct for drollery and farce found expression. In far-away Sicily another Dorian, Epicharmus (first half of the fifth century B.C.), had improved on the crudities of the Megarian farce and had provided his comedy with a plot.

But it was only natural that Athenian comedy should borrow from its sister, tragedy, rather than be guided by alien products. Athens did not recognize the new art until some fifty years after it had taken tragic drama under its protection. Not until about 485 B.C. (during the decade which separates the battles of Marathon and Salamis) was comedy admitted to the Dionysiac festivals and a comic *agon* added to the tragic contests; such contests in comedy became a feature of the Lenaean festival, held in midwinter, as well as of the Great Dionysia.

From tragedy comedy borrowed plot, prologue, and alternative succession of *epeisodion* and *stasimon*. Peculiar to comedy was the *parabasis*: at a convenient point in the play the chorus lay aside their theatrical garb, and the poet addresses his fellow citizens on almost any subject under the sun. This parabasis, in its complete form a thing of complicated structure, undoubtedly conceals an important ingredient in the history of comedy. It is evident that originally it came at the end of the play, for in the plays of Aristophanes it is introduced at a point where the structure of the plot is virtually complete; the scenes which follow it elaborate the final situation and are loosely strung together.

The chorus of comedy consists of twenty-four members, whereas tragedy had only fifteen *choreutae*. Did the chorus traditionally divide into two sides, and was a contest between two rivals, each encouraged by his own followers, another inheritance from the rustic merrymaking? We dare not affirm either of these theories, tempting as they are, in the absence of definite historical data. In fact, the plays of Aristophanes constitute our main source for the historical forms of comedy. He is admittedly the greatest of all writers of comedy; but he belongs to the era of the Hellenic World War. His predecessors who fill the fifty-year period between Salamis and the outbreak of that war had paved the way for Aristophanes and had made of comedy an important factor in the political life of Athens; but not a single one of their products has reached us. With Aristophanes the Old Comedy perished; civic in spirit and political in its outlook, it decayed with the polis. The shift in interest on the part of the audience brought a complete change in the form and contents of comedy. The New Comedy seeks its subject matter in the *private* life of the Athenian citizen: in spendthrift sons and parsimonious fathers, in rascally slaves and intriguing females, in boastful soldiers and clever parasites. Euripides had shown the way by reducing the grandeur of the heroic past to the puny status of contemporary humanity, and even in the matter of plots the New Comedy borrowed from the tragic poet rather than from Aristophanes.

We get then, in outline, something like this for the history of Attic comedy:

I. 485–400 B.C., the Old Comedy, social and political in spirit.

II. 400–320 B.C., a period of transition; the decay and downfall of the city-state.

III. 320–250 B.C., the New Comedy, of Hellenistic and cosmopolitan Greece.

This last falls outside the scope of the present work. And since next to nothing is left of the period of transition apart from two Aristophanic plays, it follows that our task will be confined to an examination of the comedy of Aristophanes.

Of Aristophanes' life there is little to be told. He was born after 450 B.C. and made his debut as a writer of comedy in 427 B.C. Throughout the Hellenic World War and for fifteen years after it he entered his plays for competition at the Lenaea and the Great Dionysia and was recognized as Athens' foremost writer of comedy. Of his literary output we possess eleven plays, nine of which fall between 425 B.C. (the *Acharnians*) and 405 B.C. (the *Frogs*); the two remaining plays, composed in 392 B.C. and 388 B.C., differ utterly in spirit and form from the great plays on which his fame rests. It is important, therefore, to remember that the really significant part of his career as a playwright falls entirely within the period of the Hellenic World War.

Now the comedy of Aristophanes differs so widely from the literary comedy of the modern world that a present-day reader into whose hands a correct version of an Aristophanic play might fall would be not a little surprised at this product of the Greek workshop; he will find very few points of comparison, and he will be at a loss to classify the newly discovered genus. In truth, there are certain preliminaries to be attended to before the unwary reader is to be trusted with a sample of Aristophanes' art. These preliminaries pertain, first, to the historical origins of Attic comedy and, secondly, to the society for which it was composed.

First, then, as to its history. There are two facts of prime importance which will help to clarify the problem of proper evaluation. Foremost of these is the fact already referred to, that Attic comedy, the song of the revelers, had its origin in the rustic celebrations in honor of Dionysus. Attic comedy was therefore bound to be *choral.* But the Dionysus who was the object of worship was not only the god of fertility and vegetation but especially the god of wine — the god who, by his gift, sets man free from all the ordinary restraints and inhibitions of life. In plain language, the realm of Dionysus is that of intoxication, of drunkenness. As long, therefore, as comedy remained in essence a song of Dionysiac revelers, divinely possessed, it would move not in the world of sober realities but in one of exuberant fancy, a fantastic world, the product of a disordered imagination in which anything and everything was possible. Hence it follows that the plots and characters of the Old Comedy do not correspond to anything in the matter-of-fact world of reality but, rather, reflect the fancies of a mind possessed by the mighty god of wine. We shall, then, no longer be surprised to find that the chorus of an Aristophanic comedy consists of Clouds, or Wasps, or Frogs; that we are transported into Hades, where Dionysus is looking for a tragic poet; that a disgusted farmer mounts a gigantic beetle to soar to Heaven in order to free the imprisoned goddess of Peace; that the philosophic Socrates is suspended in a basket that he may get the benefit of the rarefied air of the upper strata; that the weary citizens Plausible and Gullible decide to build themselves a city, Cloudcuckootown, in a strategic position midway between the worlds of gods and men; or, crowning absurdity (to the Hellenic mind), that the women have seized the management of affairs because men seem incompetent to rescue the world from ruin.

But there is more. Intoxication may raise man to the level of the gods; it equally may reduce him to the level of the beast. Although Attic refinement of taste never allowed comedy to descend to the depths of pure bestiality, yet a certain frank indecency is a cardinal feature of Old Comedy. It is not that Aristophanes is "immoral," but the action and especially the speech of his characters are marked by a frankness and a robust outspokenness that prove rather too much even for the hardihood of those moderns who affect to eschew "Victorian" standards in these matters. In all this we may see further evidence of the exuberant vitality of a robust age, heightened, to be sure, by the Dionysiac influence.

The first fact of prime importance for the proper understanding of Aristophanes is, then, that his comedy had its origin in intoxication. The second fact to which we had reference is that at these same rustic festivities there prevailed a spirit of raillery, of banter, that invariably took the form of personal abuse; that is, on these occasions even friends and neighbors would cheerfully exchange insults and ribald jests, and the grosser the epithets and the more extravagant the abuse, the greater would be the delight of the bystanders and the louder would be their acclaim. There is no question that these outbursts had originally a religious significance: they were held to have a cathartic effect and may roughly be classed with other rites of purification. Dionysus, the Deliverer, loosens man's tongue and allows him to unburden himself of all the meanness and envy that lies festering in his mind, and he at whom the abuse is aimed escapes with a verbal drubbing; after it is over, all is serene. Hence it is that Attic comedy is so terrifyingly personal; the malicious gossip always rife in a city like Athens, where everybody knew everybody else, found most audacious public expression on the comic stage. The jibes launched at private individuals, often of obscure status, are so numerous in Aristophanes' plays that they are robbed of a great deal of their effectiveness today.

We now come to the social setting of the Old Comedy. What was the audience which sat in judgment on Aristophanes' plays? The Old Comedy, like every species of Hellenic poetry, addresses itself not to a clique, a select group of connoisseurs or dilettanti, but, having its roots in tribal custom, continues to serve a social purpose. In order to succeed, it must be understood by the majority of those thousands of citizens who crowded the theater on festival days; it must seek to please them. And, being comedy, it must please them by arousing their mirth.

Now what would be the subjects most likely to affect the risibilities of the Athenian democracy? We may take it that the majority of even the Athenian democracy was conservative at heart and distrustful of innovations; also that, like any democracy, it was jealous of its own sovereignty, and therefore critical of its leaders and intolerant of the assumption of superiority on the part of any man or any group of men. Moreover, the material of the Old Comedy must have social significance: it must concern the common interest and be of public import. And so it became the business of comedy to attack whatever the herd instinct disapproved, whatever it shied from because of strangeness, such as a new fashion in music, in dramatic art, in education, in political leadership. For the crowd condemns whatever is unfamiliar, whatever it fails to understand; and it delights in seeing it ridiculed. Thus, a poet like Euripides, who dressed his heroes in rags and caused the daughter of Agamemnon to worry about the contents of her larder; the Sophists, with their ridiculous pretensions to a new learning; the new political leaders, loud-mouthed demagogues and upstarts who had never led an army in the field — all these, and others like them, provided the material for the comic stage of Aristophanes. If he assailed them with a zest and persistence that must have made them wince, it was not because he necessarily shared the prejudices of the crowd but because he had a genius for writing comedy and instinctively knew how to raise a laugh. And he lived in a town where freedom of speech was claimed as the citizen's proudest birthright — a freedom which was ever in danger of degenerating into license, and had to be curbed more than once by the state.

Aristophanes became the spokesman of that largest and most conservative portion of the Athenian citizens, the small farmers. They loved the sacred traditions of their country, the old ways and the old songs, and they found themselves in a world which was rapidly passing into a new order. And it cannot be said that from their point of view they were altogether unjustified in their distrust of the new; in a way they were right in regarding Euripides and Socrates and all such other pretentious wits as dangerous revolutionaries. They saw that Athens had been great through the patriotism and simple loyalty of such as themselves. The Marathon fighters had had no need of finely spun theories to sustain their courage in the hour of danger; their leaders had been men like Miltiades, Aristides, and Cimon — honest gentlemen of respectable families. Now it was some uncouth tanner or lamp-maker who was presumptuous enough to aspire to leadership. What they, of course, failed to perceive was that war and pestilence had accelerated tendencies which had long been dormant in the bosom of their society. The mental horizon was widening. The new gains would not fit into the old forms. Tradition was challenged by reason, and the irresistible course of events was sweeping away the very foundations of the old familiar world. All this brought with it enlightenment, to be sure, but in its train followed many evils of which former generations had been ignorant. Thus Aristophanes staged in comic form the vigorous but ineffectual protests of the old Hellas against the new.

The plays of Aristophanes fall into three clear-cut divisions. The first group consists of those produced between 425 and 421 B.C. and reflects Athenian conditions in the first ten years of the war. The *Acharnians* (425 B.C.) contains a protest against the war. The good farmer Dicaeopolis, disgusted at the conduct of affairs, concludes a private peace with the enemy; if his fellow citizens will not return to sanity, at least he and his family can enjoy the blessings of peace. The next play, the *Knights* (424 B.C.) is the vehicle for a savage attack on the most powerful political leader of the day, the "tanner" Cleon, the uncompromising advocate of war to the finish; his downfall is brought about by a sausage-seller who finds favor with old man Demos (the people) because of a combination of vulgarity, low cunning, and even greater vituperative power than his rival possessed. The following year saw the production of the *Clouds* (423 B.C.), in which Socrates is most unfairly held up to ridicule as the representative of the new learning. The old ways and the new ways are contrasted in an effective passage in which these two face each other. In Strepsiades, an old farmer overwhelmed with debts, eager for the new learning and for the new art of argumentation, in order that he may confound his creditors, Aristophanes has created a character of great comic force. Next in order is the *Wasps* (422 B.C.), in which the poet once more turns his guns on the demagogues; the mania of the older generation for serving on the jury also comes in for its share of ridicule. In the *Peace* (421 B.C.), as the name implies, Aristophanes once more gives voice to the longing for peace that prevailed among the small landowners of Attica. One of their number flies up to Heaven on a monstrous beetle, like a new Bellerophon on his Pegasus. He finds Heaven deserted by the gods, who are disgusted with the affairs of men; only the god of War is in possession. He is about to pound the Hellenic cities in a huge mortar, but the pestles (the war leaders) are missing. While he is gone to look for them, the farmer, with the help of his fellows, rescues Peace from the pit in which she lies buried. She is greeted with shouts of joy: "For thirteen long years we have been pining for you."

> When our fightings are stayed
> And our tumults allayed
> We will hail thee a Lady for ever:
> And, oh, put an end to the whispers of doubt,
> The wonderful clever
> Ingenious suspicions we bandy about;
> And solder and glue the Hellenes anew
> With the old fashioned, true
> Elixir of love and attemper our minds
> With thoughts of each other more genial and kind.[1]

Well, a peace was patched up that year; but, as we know, it proved to be delusive.

It is not until seven years later that the second group of plays opens. To it belong the *Birds* (414 B.C.), the *Lysistrata* and *Thesmophoriazusae* (411 B.C.), and the *Frogs* (405 B.C.). There is a marked change in tone. Until 421 B.C. Aristophanes seems to have believed that all the ills of Greece sprang from wrong leadership and the pernicious teaching of the Sophists and others of their kind. In the seven years that separate the *Birds* from the *Peace* the Athenian democracy began to show itself in an ugly mood. The affair at Melos revealed the temper of the people (416 B.C.). The expedition to Sicily sailed the following year — a bold bid for power and a reckless challenge to the rest of Hellas. After the disastrous failure of the Sicilian expedition the smoldering fires of civic discord broke forth in full force, and in 411 B.C. the democracy was overthrown. Even after its restoration the old rancors and mutual suspicions remained. The democracy crowned its willful career by putting to death the generals who had led

[1] *Peace* (tr. by Rogers, Loeb Library), lines 990–998.

it to victory at Arginusae (406 B.C.). It was during these trying years that Aristophanes wrote the four plays of the second group. He now sees that he has been attacking only the symptoms of the disease and that the malady, growing ever more fearful in its ravages, is beyond his power to mend. Accordingly his plays deliberately turn from the realities of the political situation; they belong to the "literature of escape."

The *Birds*, performed when there was not a person in the audience who did not have a relative or dear friend with that armada which had sailed the previous year, provided that relief from the strain of war which the people craved. Cloud-cuckootown, with its brisk and enterprising founder, its feathered inhabitants, its ridiculous gods, and with its charming lyrics celebrating the gathering of the birds, furnished a welcome interlude amid the anxieties of the situation at home. The *Lysistrata* and the *Thesmophoriazusae*, performed in the dark days of the oligarchic coup, serve no other purpose. In the *Lysistrata* the poet solves the troubles of man by handing the management of affairs over to the women. The trial of Euripides, the subject of the other comedy, for sheer drollery and rollicking fun takes the prize among all Aristophanic plays. The women, angry at Euripides for his persistent slander of the sex, are plotting to destroy him. The poet's elderly uncle, disguised as a woman, ventures to plead his nephew's cause; he is discovered, and ultimately rescued by Euripides. It is impossible within the limits of this section to do justice to the wit, the inexhaustible fancy and inventive power, that Aristophanes displays in this farce. Finally, in the last year of the war, Aristophanes, in the *Frogs*, took the audience with Dionysus on a journey to Hades, whither the god goes in quest of Euripides. The play falls into two parts. The first deals with the adventures of Dionysus, who is portrayed as an arrant coward and who, on his romantic mission, is provided with a regular Sancho Panza as companion in the person of Xanthias, the slave. The doings of this ill-assorted pair amid the perils, real and imaginary, of Hades form a succession of riotously funny scenes. The second part consists of a contest between Euripides and Aeschylus, with Dionysus acting as umpire. Euripides is severely criticized for having failed to do his duty as a poet; his scandalous plays do not make men better but worse; moreover, his prologues are mechanical in construction, and his music is debased. But Aeschylus does not go scot-free either. As an essay in dramatic criticism the play does equal credit to the acumen of Aristophanes and to the discernment of the audience. The two parts of the play are separated by a remarkable parabasis, justly renowned in antiquity; it contains an earnest plea to the citizens to unite and, forgetting all past differences, to join in a last effort to rescue the state.

The last two plays, the *Ecclesiazusae* and the *Plutus*, forming the third group, were performed, respectively, in 392 and 388 B.C. They proclaim the passing of the old order, and neither of them adds to the fame of the author. In the first the Women in Parliament have turned Athens into a communistic society; in the second the blind god of wealth, restored to sight, brings about a more equitable distribution of wealth. In both plays the chorus has a negligible part; and both are conspicuously lacking in that verve and gusto which was Aristophanes' greatest asset. They belong no longer to the Old Comedy but to a new, a tamer, type of play. They are addressed to an audience more interested in theoretical discussion than in practical application, more inclined to political speculation than to political action. In fact, with the passing of the fifth century the creative genius of Hellas abandoned poetry as a means of expression and sought and found new channels. Poetry continued to be produced, if for no other purpose than to serve at the state festivals; but it had ceased to be an important social factor or to express the common aspirations of the people. The mood of exaltation which marks the grand century, at least in Athens, gave way to a spirit of doubt which began to examine the premises on which another age had built. In short, the age of poetry was over, and the age of prose had begun.

SUGGESTIONS FOR READING. For a good introduction to the history of Greek tragedy see J. T. SHEPPARD, *Greek Tragedy* (Cambridge, 1920).

A fuller and more systematic account is found in A. E. HAIGH, *The Tragic Drama of the Greeks* (Oxford, 1896).

ROY C. FLICKINGER'S *The Greek Theater and its Drama* (University of Chicago Press, n. d.) combines a full discussion of the Greek theater with an analysis of the factors that have influenced Greek drama.

See also JAMES T. ALLEN, *Stage Antiquities of the Greeks and Romans* (Longmans, 1927).

For the general reader the most interesting discussion of Greek tragedy will prove to be GILBERT NORWOOD, *Greek Tragedy* (Methuen, 1920). The same author has contributed a volume on *Greek Comedy* (Methuen, 1931).

On Euripides see GILBERT MURRAY, *Euripides and his Age* (Holt, 1913), and F. L. LUCAS, *Euripides and his Influence* (Marshall Jones, 1923).

For Aristophanes consult M. CROISET, *Aristophanes and the Political Parties at Athens* (tr. by J. Loeb) (Macmillan, 1909). GILBERT MURRAY, *Aristophanes* (Oxford, 1933).

CHAPTER X

PROSE

The Second Period — Historiography

POETRY addresses itself primarily to the imagination and to the emotions. Prose speaks a more sober language and lends itself to reflection and criticism. In the history of human culture, therefore, poetry has always preceded prose; indeed, it is not until a people is well advanced in the arts of civilization and long after poetry has found a home among them that they conceive of prose as a possible literary and artistic vehicle. Like M. Jourdain in Molière's *Bourgeois Gentilhomme*, they discover late in life that they have always been speaking prose without being aware of that important fact! Poetry, moreover, easily survives by word of mouth; verse and song are memorized, and live immortal on the lips of man. But literary prose must depend on writing material for its survival; hence the art of prose writing will not be cultivated until such material is readily at hand in abundant quantity. This did not happen in Greece until the Egyptian papyrus reached the Greek city-states in sufficient quantities; even so, books continued to be scarce until well into the fifth century B.C.

The beginnings of prose writing date from the sixth century B.C.; and naturally it was Ionia which led the way. The stirring life of the Ionian cities — Miletus foremost among them — provided the stimulus. Here the intellectual curiosity characteristic of the Hellene was first prompted to seek answers to the manifold questions which a widening experience was ready to ask. The world was full of marvels. Although the expansionist movement of Hellas had carried the intrepid colonizers far into the western Mediterranean, into the vastness of the Black Sea and into Egypt (land of mystery), yet the farther they went the more tantalizing loomed the unknown, and their appetite for information was constantly whetted by stray bits of foreign news brought by contact with the "barbarians." Over and beyond this they were confronted by the great enigma of the universe itself. What was its meaning? Whence had it sprung? Once a demand for such information is voiced, response is not long in forthcoming. Treatises on philosophical and religious subjects appeared; the first maps were made.

Yet it was in one especial field that these first attempts at prose writing were destined to come to full fruition and lead to the creation of a new literary species. Among the many objects engaging the interest of the Ionians the past was not neglected. Who had founded their cities? And under what circumstances? What past achievement had lent distinction to the great families in their midst? Such were the questions asked, and the "story-makers" (*logopoioi*), taking up the task where the writers of epic (*epopoioi*) had left off, supplied the information in accounts of foundings (*Ktiseis*) and in genealogies. The desire to please was uppermost in the minds of these writers, and, with the glorious example of the epic before them, they composed glowing accounts of the wonderful deeds of past generations. Concern for the truth was naturally not a marked trait of these early writers, and of rational criticism of the sources at their command they were completely innocent, until one day, in the first quarter of the fifth century, one of their number, a certain Hecataeus of Miletus, vented his indignation in a remarkable book which he opened with a great blast. "Hecataeus of Miletus thus speaks: I write as I deem *true*, for the traditions of the Greeks seem to me manifold and laughable."[1] Thus *historia*, or inquiry into the truth, was born, and to Hecataeus belongs the glory of having discovered the important fact that an account of the past needs to be *true* as well as entertaining. It marked a revolution in the ways of thinking in Hellas.

[1] On Hecataeus see Gilbert Murray, *Greek Literature*, pp. 125 ff.

The "storytellers," successors of the writers of epic, had based their right to be heard on their power of pleasing their audience, even as Homer himself had done; the added demand for truth and the necessity of careful inquiry led to the birth of history in Hellas.

But it is a curious fact that the pioneer in the field (480 B.C.) should have been severely criticized by his successor, Herodotus (who came about a generation after him, 450 B.C.), for his failure to ascertain the truth, while Herodotus, in turn, is held in utter contempt by Thucydides, the historian of the Hellenic World War. Thus the concept of historic truth changed in a few generations, and it has changed still further in the many centuries that have passed since Thucydides. Indeed, the whole meaning of history has undergone a complete transformation. For many centuries historians were content to take their cue from the politically-minded Hellenes and to confine history to the political and military aspects of the past. Today history is all-embracing. It includes the entire past, and all its "data must be viewed as part of the process of social development, not as isolated facts"[1]; they must therefore be interpreted as interrelated, as constituting an intelligible whole. That is, the history of any nation at any period includes all aspects of its civilization; the historian may not neglect its religion, its literature, its art, any more than its political institutions or its economic development. Indeed, of late years perhaps too great an emphasis has been placed on the economic phase, and we seem to be desperately attempting to account for all historical phenomena on this narrow basis; in an up-to-date history of ancient Hellas we are apt to read as much of exports and imports, dried fish, pitch, and hides as about Sophocles and Socrates. An army of historians today is at work gathering economic data, and there is no question that these same lowly data have shed a certain measure of light

[1] J. T. Shotwell, *An Introduction to the History of History* (Columbia University Press), p. 5.

Herodotus

Thucydides

National Museum, Naples

on other, noneconomic phases of past history. We perceive, then, that the historian of today does not neglect any fact of social significance and that he attempts to co-ordinate all his data and make them mutually intelligible. In this way history becomes more and more a study of tendencies and impersonal forces; the stature of the individual agent in history diminishes correspondingly. Instead of being entertained by the exploits of generals, kings, and patriots, we hear of a struggle for markets, for outlets of surplus population; we read of economic pressure, of imperialism, of nationalism. The modern historian, in fine, overwhelms us with an avalanche of formidable abstract terms under which the feeble individual of the period described lies completely buried.

Now the Hellenic historian on whom had fallen the mantle of the writer of epic song had naturally a totally different conception of his task. Homer had stressed the great heroic figures of the past; in what they did and said and suffered lay the interest of his account. It is not different with Herodotus. Let us compare, for instance, the explanation he offers for the origin of the Persian Wars with the efforts of modern historians to account for the World War. The problem of the origin of that last war presents such baffling complications to the historians of today that we may for the present despair of unanimity on so highly controversial a matter. Perhaps future generations of historians will offer us at last the solution on which all can agree; yet even now they are at one in blaming certain *historic tendencies* for the catastrophe. Now let us listen to Herodotus. He has told us of the Ionian rebellion: how the Athenians took part in it; how Sardis was burned; how Darius, king of the Persians, heard of it and asked, "Who are these Athenians?" and how, being told, the proud king called for his bow, laid an arrow on it, and with a prayer for vengeance shot into the sky, charging his slave to remind him thrice, whenever he set dinner before him, "Master, remember the Athenians."

Verily, Herodotus observes, these twenty ships the Athenians sent to Ionia were the beginning of evils for Greeks and barbarians alike. What could be simpler?

But here it is time to note a curious fact. While it is true that historians differ on the question of the origin of the World War, there were — and are — millions of people with no such doubts; they knew the villain of the piece, and "Hang the Kaiser!" was their way of explanation and cure for the world's misery. The historian does not write for such as these; he cannot reach them; he addresses only a small fraction of his fellow men, the "historically-minded," whose number is infinitesimal. But the "Father of History" wrote for the people at large, and, bearing the unique distinction of being himself the only historian, could not even appeal to the judgment of his fellow historians. In other words, history in Hellas was as much a social product as its mythology and its poetry.

We have found, then, that to Herodotus the personal factor is supreme in history; the anger and the desire for vengeance on the part of Darius causes the Persian War even as the anger of Menelaus and Agamemnon caused the Trojan War. Was it, then, the example of Homer that prompted Herodotus to choose a war as the theme of his work? Let us begin by recognizing that the historian of ancient Hellas found a task fraught with as great difficulties as does the modern historian dealing with the same subject. The political history of the Oriental monarchies presents no such problems: the successive dynasties form the framework, and within these outlines the picture can be completed as well as the materials allow. But Hellas formed no political union; it was impossible to write a national history, because there was no nation, at least not politically. It did not occur to the average Greek that the past of his own town would be of interest to anyone but his townsmen, and the local "story-writers" worked on this basis. Not only was a connected account of the fortunes of the numerous city-states making up Hellas a task beyond the historian's resources, but the product, when completed, would have been totally lacking in appeal to the ordinary Greek. That is, Greek particularism was so intense, the political horizon of each polis so narrow, that a history of Hellas as a nation was out of the question. The "story-writers" knew their market and produced accordingly. It was not until the Persian Wars, which drew first Ionia and then the rest of Hellas into some semblance of unity, that the historian of Hellas found a *national* theme, one sure to appeal beyond the confines of a particular polis. Hellenic historiography therefore begins with the story of the national struggle against Persia, and the next historian took for his theme the Hellenic World War; these two form the two major crises in Hellas at large.

So much, then, for historiography and for its beginnings in Hellas. And now, who was this Herodotus who wrote the story of the Persian Wars? What were his qualifications for the task he set himself?

HERODOTUS

Of the private life of Herodotus we know very little. He was a native of Halicarnassus, a Dorian settlement on the Anatolian coast just below Ionia. Before Herodotus' day the Halicarnassians had adopted the dialect of their Ionian neighbors; so Herodotus composed his work in Ionic. He became involved in the political disturbances which followed the liberation of Ionia from Persian control, and left his native town for Athens. Later (*c.* 443 B.C.) he joined the new colony, Thurii, which was founded under Athenian leadership on the ancient site of Sybaris, in southern Italy. He eventually returned to Athens; but whether he died there or at Thurii remains uncertain. Equally uncertain is the date of his death, though we know he did not live to see the end of the Hellenic World War. He was a great traveler, and may have toured Hellas as a professional reciter of his *logoi* ("stories"); Athens, at least, seems to have rewarded him munificently. But he went beyond the Greek world. We know that he visited Phoenician Tyre, Egypt, and Cyrene. He extended his travels into the Greek towns on the Black Sea and probably reached its northern shores. How far he penetrated eastward into the Persian Empire we do not know, but many hold that he describes Babylon and Persian Susa and Ecbatana as an eyewitness. The most traveled man of the age, he carried with him everywhere his inexhaustible freshness of mind, his keen power of observation, his ready sympathy with all things human and — his notebook! Besides, he was extraordinarily fair-minded, expressing his admiration for the good qualities of the Persian, the national enemy, with surprising candor. Above all, he had the gift of story telling; there is not a dull page in his book. These were his chief qualifications for his task as a historian.

But how much may we believe of what he chose to tell us? "For myself," he says, "though it be my business to set down that which is told me, to believe it is none of my business, and let that saying hold good for the whole of my history."[1] We may take him at his word, he reports faithfully what he sees and what he is told, but it is for the reader to exercise his own judgment as to what to believe or to reject as false. Of his good faith there is no question, but his critical ability to separate the chaff from the wheat we well may doubt; and of course he had never heard of the modern historian's stern demand for documentation and the critical examination of original sources. Today historians and archaeologists are busily reconstructing the past of Egypt from the monuments themselves. Herodotus saw these, but was content to take the word of his guides as to the story they told. The result, as may be imagined, is rather fantastic; for instance, he placed the pyramid-builders several centuries after the Twelfth Dynasty, which as a matter of fact they preceded by more than five hundred years! Besides,

[1] Bk. VII, Chap. 152.

being Greek, he saw everything through Hellenic spectacles and made his outlandish characters think and speak as if they were good Greeks themselves; herein he is markedly naïve. Moreover, neither of constitutional history nor of military matters does he show clear understanding; and his chronology, always a troublesome matter to ancient historians, is shaky.

But, with all these reservations, his work remains one of the greatest treasures Hellas has bequeathed to us; better still, it represents a vivid picture of the world as the intelligent Greek saw and knew it. In his knowledge we may see mirrored the knowledge of Hellas; in his mind, the mind of Hellas. For he was no "superior" person; he was a Greek of the Greeks and shared their outlook to the full. It was his good fortune to live in an age which had no need of a new interpretation of life but was busily engaged upon the immediate tasks at hand. Herodotus reflects the zest of life, the insatiable curiosity, and the infinite variety of interests that mark the Periclean Age. In religious matters as well he was in perfect sympathy with his time. His attitude toward "things divine" is the attitude common to his day — an attitude which we may discover also in Sophocles, who is reputed to have been his friend. It is better expressed by the word *eulabeia*, a cautious regard for all that is considered supernatural, than by *eusebeia*, reverence. Herodotus was everlastingly on the lookout for indications of divine interference with human affairs, and his book abounds in oracles, divinations, and miracles. At the same time, he shared the outlook of a generation which felt competent to deal with its own problems and rather feared divine interference than prayed for divine assistance. Yet he knew that the gods are powerful and that there is one sin above all others which exposes man to divine anger and envy, namely, arrogance; "for it is heaven's way to bring low all things of surpassing bigness" (thus speaks Artabanus, Xerxes' uncle;[1] but it is

[1] Herodotus, Bk. VII, Chap. 10.

good Greek dogma). And so he interpreted the Persian conflict as a tale of moral significance, containing an object lesson: thus the gods deal with man when he is swollen with pride, when arrogance invites to *hubris*, and when the wise restraint that prudence enjoins is forgotten. In fine, the traditional religion and morality of Hellas have found in Herodotus their best exponent. And so, with the Croisets, we may find in him "a droll mixture of scientific alertness, romantic imagination, good humor, acute discernment, and candid piety."[1]

His work has been divided into nine books by the Alexandrian scholars of a much later age. While his proper theme is the Persian Wars, he planned his work on an epic scale and, like Homer, gave more space to the preliminaries and to the setting than to the central theme itself. He did this not in order to explore the ramifications of the conflict but in order to make the combatants more interesting to his audience, even as Homer shows us Hector with Andromache. It makes him the most discursive of all historians; it is plain that many an episode is enlarged upon and many a tale inserted in the body of his work because of the author's delight in its telling. Moreover, he knew that his audience was keenly interested in geographical and ethnological matters; so he regales us with descriptions of distant lands and reports strange customs, like those of the Thracian tribe which receives the newborn babe with lamentations, recounting all the sorrows in store for it, and buries the dead with jollifications because they are now quit of all the ills of life! Especially for nature's marvels he had a keen eye, and the farther we get from the Greek homeland the greater the marvels. He tells of ants bigger than foxes; spice-bearing trees guarded by winged snakes; sheep with tails three cubits long which are carried on little carts; one-eyed men who steal gold from griffins ("but I don't believe it," he

[1] A. and M. Croiset, *An Abridged History of Greek Literature* (English translation), p. 274.

adds); snub-nosed men who are bald from birth and have long white beards; oxen that go backwards as they graze, and troglodytes who live on snakes and lizards. He is full of digressions, interrupting his story to tell of the fortunes of a family or to relate past historical events. Above all, he delights in anecdotes. While they may be spurious, they are of invaluable assistance to us in appraising the temper and spirit of the Hellas of his day — more so than any amount of statistical information, even if such had been at his disposal. And he loved to add the moral to his stories.

Of the nine books the first recounts the story of Lydia and the overthrow of the Lydian Croesus by the Persian Cyrus. The story of Cyrus is continued with that of his successor Cambyses, who added Egypt to the Persian Empire. The second book contains the wonderful digression on Egypt. The third book continues with the career of Cambyses, relates the dynastic troubles following his death, and tells of the succession of Darius. Now comes another episode, the famous story of Polycrates, tyrant of Samos. We return to Darius and to a description of the vast resources of the Persian Empire. The fourth book is taken up with Darius' Scythian expedition, which leads to an excursus on Scythia and the countries bordering upon it. And now Herodotus is anxious to tell us what he has learned of the countries of Northern Africa and declares that Darius meditated an attack upon Cyrene; we do not quite believe him, but we welcome the opportunity he thus found for inserting his interesting account of the founding of Cyrene. Darius meanwhile has gained a footing in Europe, for southern Thrace is permanently occupied by the Persians. The fifth book brings us a description of Thrace, and now that the stage is set the story proper begins. With the fifth and sixth books we reach the Ionian rebellion and the expeditions of 492 and 490 B.C., including the battle of Marathon; but there are numerous digressions interrupting the narrative. The last three books are occupied with the great conflict between Xerxes and the Greek city-states; here are the accounts of the battles of Thermopylae, Salamis, Plataea, and Mycale. The work ends rather abruptly with the capture of Sestos.[1]

Whereon, then, rests Herodotus' claim to be regarded as the "Father of History"? As Homer had eclipsed the singers of the shorter lays and ballads, so Herodotus, building upon the works of his predecessors, the storytellers, and following the example of the traveler and geographer Hecataeus, chose the story of a great national crisis for the subject of his tale, which he interpreted consistently both as a conflict between two contrasting cultures and as a judgment of Heaven upon the presumption of man. In this way he contrived to create a work of artistic unity, the first work of art in prose which we possess. We will, then, not blame him for his shortcomings but, rather, bestow on him the praise he deserves as the pioneer in his field.

The Third Period — Historiography

THUCYDIDES

With Thucydides, the historian of the Hellenic World War, the age of prose begins; for Herodotus was only a precursor, having greater affinity with the epic and the heroic drama of Sophocles than with the soberer mood of the prose writers coming after him.

Thucydides was between thirty and forty years old when the war broke out. His father's name has an outlandish sound. He was related to Miltiades, the victor at Marathon, who had married a Thracian princess; and the fact that the historian had a family interest in the gold mines of Thrace

[1] The reader who wishes to gain an insight into the methods of Herodotus should not rest content with the excerpts found in the anthologies. If he must forgo the pleasure of reading this most fascinating and charming of all Hellenic prose works, he should read at least one entire book; the first or the seventh are perhaps best suited for that purpose.

points in the same direction, namely, to a Thracian strain in the ancestry of Thucydides. He was born in Athens, however, and was well enough thought of by his fellow citizens to be elected to the office of strategus, in 424 B.C. His failure to prevent Brasidas, the energetic Spartan general, from seizing Amphipolis, and the consequent loss of that important city to the Athenian Empire, brought disgrace upon him: he was deprived of his command and spent some twenty years in exile. But the world has been the gainer; for thus he found leisure to write his account of the war, and the opportunity to visit that part of Hellas which was open to the allies of Sparta. After the war he was recalled, but did not live many years beyond its termination, leaving his great work unfinished.

Thucydides was a most extraordinary person; he would have been so in any age. He stands out among his contemporaries even in that city which was so productive of men of marked originality. For this discredited general, calmly brushing aside his own resentments and wounded self-respect, instead of devoting himself to the rehabilitation of his own person in the eyes of the world, set himself to record the events of a war which he foresaw would be of momentous consequences to his world. Again, here was an Athenian, an ardent patriot, who, in writing the history of the life-and-death struggle in which his city engaged against the allied powers of Greece, did so with such detachment that, had he not himself confessed being an Athenian, it would be impossible to infer from his work with which side he sympathized.

In the performance of his task he took his cue not from the "storytellers" of a bygone age nor yet from the genial historian of the Persian Wars but from the Ionian physicists and students of medicine! With these men, who possessed in a rare degree that rationalist temper which distinguishes the Hellenic race, he felt a natural kinship. They were bent upon banishing the irrational element from their universe.

Their medical schools made incessant war on the deep-rooted notion that the ills afflicting the human body are due to the action of evil demons and other mysterious agents. With them the need to understand was imperative, and they knew that no progress was possible in that direction until the human mind had freed itself from the superstitions which darkened its vision. Above all, they saw that the necessary preliminary to such understanding was the observation and the recording of the facts of experience; and had they possessed our tools, the progress of science might have been hastened a full two thousand years. Yet, even with such handicaps as were inevitably theirs, they entered upon their labors with a zest and a devotion that knew no limits, and their efforts brought substantial results. We shall return to them in our chapter on philosophy and science. Here it is enough to note that the birth of the scientific spirit antedated Thucydides; and it has been demonstrated that he was well acquainted with the work and the methods of these pioneers.[1]

It was in the spirit of Ionian science that Thucydides approached his task. Like his fellow scientists, he intended to observe accurately and to record the facts observed for the future benefit of mankind.

As to the facts of the occurrences of the war, I have thought it my duty to give them, not as ascertained from any chance informant nor as seemed to me probable, but only after investigating with the greatest possible accuracy each detail, in the case both of the events in which I myself participated and of those regarding which I got my information from others. And the endeavour to ascertain these facts was a laborious task, because those who were eye-witnesses of the several events did not give the same reports about the same things, but reports varying according to their championship of one side or the other, or according to their recollection. And it may well be that the absence of the fabulous from my narrative will seem less pleasing to the ear; but whoever shall wish to have a clear view both of the events which have happened and of those which will some day,

[1] See C. N. Cochrane, *Thucydides and the Science of History* (Oxford, 1929).

in all human probability, happen again in the same or a similar way — for these to adjudge this record profitable will be enough for me. And, indeed, it has been composed not as a prize-essay to be heard for the moment, but as a possession for all time.[1]

Such, then, were his aims: the ascertaining of the facts and the elimination of all irrational elements in order to promote a clear view and to furnish a record that would be of permanent value. In this spirit might a devoted scientist undertake the study of a devastating plague and record his observations for the benefit of posterity. Indeed, it is in Thucydides' description of the pestilence which ravaged Athens during the war that he shows most clearly his affinity with scientific workers. He begins with an introduction (II, 47–48) which tells of the origin of the plague in Egypt and the East, whence it was carried into the Piraeus and Athens:

> Now any one, whether physician or layman, may, each according to his personal opinion, speak about its probable origin and state the causes which, in his view, were sufficient to have produced so great a departure from normal conditions; but I shall describe its actual course, explaining the symptoms, from the study of which a person should be best able . . . to recognize it, if it ever should break out again. For I had the disease myself and saw others sick of it.[2]

He then sets forth the symptoms and the course of the disease, describing these with a cool detachment and analytical power worthy of a great scientist. He continues with a vivid account of the fearful demoralization which attended the epidemic. But the reader must turn to these well-known chapters himself (II, 47–53); for they will furnish him with the best — in fact, an indispensable — illustration of the manner and method of this historian. Thucydides seems to have looked upon the war very much as if it too were some species of plague or major epidemic, and felt that if this kind of malady

[1] Thucydides (translation of C. Forster Smith; Loeb Library), Bk. I, Chap. 22.

[2] Ibid. Bk. II, Chap. 48.

were ever to be brought under control, the whole process had to be described in all its minutiae, the symptoms to be tabulated, and these somehow to be shown as causally interrelated. And so he prepared his scientific record, which he fondly hoped would be a "possession for all time." He has been much blamed for that supposedly presumptuous phrase; but he spoke only as might any modest scientist who expresses the hope that his truthful record may be of permanent value. And when he spoke of the "events which have happened and . . . will some day, in all human probability, happen again in the same or a similar way," he spoke but too truly. It was not until after the World War that the real significance of the Thucydidean record could be duly appreciated. For a second time in the world's history the great civilizing center of the world was drawn into a useless conflict. We have learned that modern nationalism is fraught with even greater dangers than Greek "politism"; that it is easier to start a war than to stop it; that it cannot be ended with the simple process of signing a treaty of peace. War, if indulged in on a large enough scale, ends in unbalancing the minds of the combatants; such seems to have been the verdict of the Hellenic historian. He never says so directly, and only once does he plainly hint at such a conclusion.[1] For he conceives it to be his duty as a scientific historian to state the facts, not to pronounce judgment upon them; to describe symptoms, not to prescribe the cure.

That this new type of history should have found little favor is no cause for wonder. It was not his aim to please but to enlighten; and he knew that, in contrast to Herodotus, he was writing for only a small section of his contemporaries. Neither should we, perhaps, complain that he has been so often misunderstood, even by professional historians. Professor Shotwell[2] rebels, "with the modern reader," against

[1] See Book III, Chapters 82–83, a passage referred to in an earlier chapter.

[2] In his *Introduction to the History of History*; see the chapter on Thucydides.

the "scrupulous care with which the historian takes us through years of desultory fighting, raids, skirmishes, expeditions by land and sea, debates in council, strategy in battle," and, he might have added, political intrigue, treachery, and exhibitions of brutal callousness, "until our memories are fairly benumbed by the variety of incident and the changes in policies, leadership and fortune." How blind was Thucydides, thinks Professor Shotwell, to what ought to have been his theme: the splendors of the Periclean Age! "The tale he tells is not what we most wish to hear." Well, we might as well find fault with Pasteur and his whole-souled devotion to his microbes when he might have lavished his power of observation on the beauty of a healthy body!

A man obsessed as Thucydides was with the passion for facts and their rational interpretation would naturally have little patience with the supposed intervention of gods and other supernatural agencies in the course of human events. The oracles and miracles with which Herodotus so plentifully besprinkled his account of the Persian Wars are never admitted in lieu of rational explanations in the pages of Thucydides. He knew that such fabulous matters influence the minds of ignorant men and that statesmen have to take account of them. But for him they only obscured the real issues. A scientific observer who would account for an event by the introduction of extraneous matter, the supernatural, and the like, which does not yield to rational analysis, has, in fact, abdicated his office. Thucydides allows the presence of an incalculable element in the affairs of men; a chance event will upset the most careful computations. Such an event was the plague itself — even a Pericles could not have foreseen it. But to put it down as a manifestation of the divine wrath does not help our understanding of it. Equally averse is he to evaluating the course of events by reference to allegedly eternal and divine standards of right and wrong. Herodotus had explained the fall of the Persian as the doom pronounced on human presumption by a jealous and vengeful deity. Thucydides was totally indifferent to such considerations. The reason is plain: a scientific historian is not concerned with alleged absolute truths; like any scientist, he can deal only with relative truths; everything beyond that lies outside the range of his observation and is unverifiable. Whether or not the gods were pleased at the conduct of the Athenians may be an important consideration, but the historian is not competent to pass judgment. Hence Thucydides washed his hands of the matter.

Yet he was well aware that with the mere chronicling of events his task as a historian was not finished. He had to penetrate below the surface and detect the wellsprings of the actions he described. The facts must be correlated and in the process the significant be segregated from the unimportant. In short, the account had to assume the form of an intelligible whole, capable of being apprehended in its true significance by the mind of the reader. The historian, then, must be an interpreter as well as a scribe. Now Thucydides knew very well that with the assumption of the interpreter's role the pretense of strict objectivity could no longer be maintained; the subjective element, the very thing his scientific zeal abhorred, was now bound to enter. Had he been a modern historian he would have taken refuge in statistical data, especially from the economic field; from these he might have extracted the proof of certain trends and currents which, in turn, might of themselves reveal the underlying forces at work. But Thucydides had no such data at his command. Moreover, in the events of the war which he described he saw, rightly or wrongly, the effects not of economic trends but of psychological causes at work either in the mass mind or in the minds of individuals. In passing we may note that even modern historians have failed to prove the existence of economic causes powerful enough to account for the outbreak of that war. It was a state of mind, jealousy and fear on the part of Athens' enemies, that precipitated the Greek war, as Thucydides saw it. In order, then, to construct an intelligible account of that war, he found it necessary to analyze the motives of the leaders and those confusedly present in the mass mind. Now in a desperate attempt to maintain the scientific character of his record he had recourse to a curious device: he quotes what purports to be the speech or speeches made on certain momentous occasions — the debates which preceded action, the appeal of the orator and statesman which won the day. For instance, he allows us to hear what the Corinthians had to say to the Spartans the year preceding the outbreak of the war, and what the Athenians said in reply. Thus he reveals what was going on in the minds of the chief actors of the drama while he himself continues the part of the impartial reporter. But he foresaw that his records would be challenged: how could he truthfully give a verbatim report of proceedings at which he could not have been present? This is what he says in forestalling his critics:

> As to the speeches that were made by different men, either when they were about to begin the war or when they were already engaged therein, it has been difficult to recall with strict accuracy the words actually spoken, both for me as regards that which I myself heard and for those who from various other sources have brought me reports. Therefore the speeches are given in the language in which, as it seemed to me, the several speakers would express on the subjects under consideration the sentiments most befitting the occasion, though at the same time I have adhered as closely as possible to the general sense of what was actually said.[1]

In this way he has contrived to reveal the mental currents that determined the course of action. It is true, these are not verbatim reports: they are far better; for the superb analytical mind of the historian and his philosophic grasp of the essentials of the situation permitted him to reveal the real significance of the issues more clearly and more concisely than the actual speakers could have done on the actual occasion. They are all made to speak the same language,

[1] Bk. I, Chap. 22.

the language of Thucydides; and yet the personality of the speaker stands revealed in every important case. The modern historian, with his scrupulous regard for exactitude of record, may well shake his head at such flagrant disregard of the principles of documentation. In truth, it was a somewhat naïve device that Thucydides chose to employ. But, from Homer down, the Greeks expected to hear the very words of their leaders; epic practice and its continuation by Herodotus had thus paved the way for the adoption of a device which Thucydides, in his anxiety for the preservation of apparent objectivity, eagerly grasped.

One more observation, and we have finished. It so happens that this same Thucydides, pioneer of scientific historiography, was also a literary artist of the first order; of the artist's intrusion into the laboratory of the scientist we shall have to take due account. He was well aware of the tragic character of the story he unfolded, and "a greater master of stern pathos than Thucydides never lived."[1] History in his hands remained a branch of literature. Moreover, he had come under the spell of the new rhetoric. He had probably heard Gorgias, on his visit to Athens in 427 B.C., displaying his new art, which caused such a sensation at the time; at any rate the influence of the new teaching is unmistakable, especially in the composition of the speeches. However, it is in such portions as the material allows that his literary gifts and his sense of the dramatic show themselves to the greatest advantage. It would be difficult to find in the entire body of historical literature a more masterly and at the same time a more moving account than the tragic story of the Sicilian expedition as set down in his seventh book. He maintains the austere attitude of the impartial observer, his diction is as restrained and sober as ever; and yet he awakens in the reader a realization of the profound pathos of the situation. No one who has read the story will ever forget the pathetic figure of the ailing Nicias, the graphic account of the defeat

[1] R. C. Jebb, *Primer of Greek Literature*, Part II, Chap. II.

in the harbor, of the despondency and despair of the men when they feared they were trapped, and of the last desperate attempt of the doomed army to escape. This was the end of the dream of Pericles and his patriots. Doubtless with a heavy heart the faithful historian recorded the events which meant the passing of that vision, but the sober narrative does not betray the emotion of the writer. Such was Thucydides, and many generations were to pass before he found a successor.

XENOPHON

Of the major crises in the history of Hellas the first, the Persian Wars, had furnished Herodotus with a theme for his prose epic; the second, the Hellenic World War, had found, for the greater part at least, an impartial and scientific witness in Thucydides. But the history of postwar Hellas was hardly such as to invite the attention of the best Greek intellect. Torn by feuds, the city-states persisted in a course of action that was equally devoid of reason and of intelligent purpose. The best minds in Greece turned rather to speculate on possible solutions of the ills of the day than to record the miserable facts of the story they saw enacted before their eyes.

Moreover, after Thucydides we are well into our third period, and the symptoms of the decay of civic spirit and the disintegration of social solidarity become increasingly evident. To these also we may justly attribute the decadence of historiography. For history deals with social themes, and the spirit of the age turned men to other interests: the individual began to look for the satisfactions of life in his private concerns. In the pages of Thucydides the individual remains submerged in the flow of social events; in the works of his successors he looms larger and larger. Xenophon, who finished the account of the Hellenic World War (but without the genius of his predecessor), and continued the story of postwar Greece down to the battle of Mantinea (362 B.C.), gave greater prominence to his hero, the Spartan king Agesilaus, than any Greek had enjoyed in the works of Herodotus or Thucydides. Theopompus (350 B.C.) named his chief work *Philippica*; the title itself is significant. Ephorus, his contemporary, wrote a sort of universal history of Greece from the beginning down to 340 B.C. This work, like the *Philippica*, is lost, but of its character we may find an indication in his account of the origin of the Hellenic World War: he relates that Pericles, fearful of being unable to account satisfactorily for the eight thousand talents transferred from the treasury at Delos to Athens, acted upon a hint of his precocious nephew Alcibiades and stirred up the war in order that in the midst of the general disorders he might escape any personal danger! Yet it was Theopompus rather than Ephorus who was called a *maledicentissimus auctor*, "a most slanderous writer," by a later Roman historian. Indeed, in the preoccupation these writers show with individual psychology, and in the malicious delight they take in revealing the sordid motives behind the patriotic protestations of their leaders in public life, we may find not only an indication of the increasing interest in the individual but also a symptom of the fatal malady that afflicted fourth-century Hellas. Euripides, who had dragged the heroic figures of the legendary past from their lofty pedestals, found imitators in those writers who dealt with the recent past; and if the *Philippica* of Theopompus had come down to us, we should find in its pages plentiful evidence of that general disillusion of which Euripides was the first herald. The utter disgust which the noblest minds of postwar Hellas felt at the sorry spectacle of contemporary political life has found expression in a celebrated passage in Plato's *Republic* wherein he speaks of the man who, grieving at the madness of the world about him, "like one who has fallen among wild beasts, holds his peace and does his own business," "he is like one who retires under the shelter of a wall in the storm of dust and sleet which the driving wind hurries along; and when he sees the rest of mankind full of wickedness, he is content if only he can live his own life and be pure from evil or unrighteousness and depart in peace and good-will with bright hopes."[1] If such were the feelings evoked among the best of the Hellenes by the contemplation of the political maelstrom of their day, it is not to be wondered at that of the three most gifted writers of that age none undertook the historian's task. The first, Plato, put forth his greatest effort in describing an imaginary polis in which reason ruled; the second, Isocrates, the foremost teacher of the age, issued a number of political pamphlets — which all remained equally unheeded — advocating more than one scheme which should deliver Hellas from its evils; the last was the great orator and patriot Demosthenes, who dedicated his life to the hopeless task of reviving the social ideals of a bygone age, which once had made Athens the foremost city of the world.

But if the chaos and anarchy prevailing in Hellas was unlikely to stimulate interest in historical writing, the individualism which is so pronounced a feature of that same age led to the creation of two new literary types, the personal memoir and biography.

Among the writers who tried their hand at these there is one who, for a variety of reasons, deserves a place in any cultural history of Greece. He is that Xenophon mentioned above as the historian bold enough to continue the history of Thucydides. He was at one time better known to many generations of schoolboys as the author of that *Anabasis* in which they had toiled in imagination with him and his Ten Thousand through the desert of Mesopotamia, over the Carduchian mountains and the Armenian snows, until at last they came again within sight of their beloved sea.

Xenophon was born in Attica, sometime near the outbreak of the Hellenic World War. His family apparently belonged to the country gentry of Attica, and love of country life remained one of his conspicuous traits. Early in life he

[1] Bk. VI, p. 496.

conceived a warm admiration for Socrates, attracted by the essential goodness of the man, without, however, penetrating to the real significance of the teaching of that most original of all Athenians. Some years after the close of the war his friend Proxenus of Thebes took service with a band of mercenaries under Cyrus, brother of the king of Persia. Now this was the young Cyrus whose friendship with Lysander, the Spartan general, had contributed so greatly to the downfall of Athens, and it was a nice question whether an Athenian could remain a loyal patriot and yet serve under the former foe of Athens. But since Xenophon was a young man of high spirits and great ambition, the prospect of adventure and a distinguished career even in foreign lands lured him away from postwar Athens, where the outlook may have been dreary enough. So, at the invitation of Proxenus, he joined the expedition. Neither of the two friends knew for what purpose Cyrus had gathered the expeditionary force (he had, in all, some thirteen thousand Greek mercenaries, to bolster up a larger force of native troops). But by degrees it became clear that he intended to march into the heart of his brother's kingdom, with the object of wresting the royal power from him. Cyrus then proceeded to within fifty miles of Babylon before his brother disputed his further advance; and there, at Cunaxa, a battle was fought in which the Greeks once more were victorious over the barbarians, but in which Cyrus himself perished. Not long afterward the Greek generals and a number of their captains were treacherously done away with by the Persians, and the gallant little band found themselves leaderless, hundreds of miles away from home, without knowledge of the country in which they were trapped, and almost destitute of resources (for one thing, they lacked horses, and cavalry was the strongest of the Persian arms). It was then that Xenophon, gentleman from Athens, took the lead; and owing to his intelligent leadership, as well as to the loyalty and intrepidity of the rough adventurers whom he led, they managed to extricate themselves from the surrounding perils and fought their way back to the Greek coast of Asia Minor. Xenophon has given us an account of this, his great adventure in life, in the first personal memoir we possess, the *Anabasis*; and though it makes rather tame reading when compared with such a work as Lawrence's *Revolt in the Desert*, we must give him credit for having written one of the most engaging books bequeathed to us by Hellas.

In 399 B.C. Socrates was put to death in Athens by the restored democracy; and this served to estrange Xenophon, who loved his master with a deep and sincere devotion, still farther from his homeland. Return to Athens was out of the question. He took service under Spartan command, and eventually met Agesilaus, then campaigning in Asia Minor; when the outbreak of the Corinthian War recalled him to Greece, Xenophon followed in his train. In the battle of Coronea (394 B.C.) Xenophon fought on the side of Agesilaus, for whom he had conceived an inordinate admiration, against the allied Thebans and Athenians. From now on he was an exile from his country; but the Spartans presented him with a beautiful estate in Elis, where he lived for some twenty years, dividing his time between the management of his estate, hunting, riding, and the duties of authorship. His sons received a Spartan education. When the battle of Leuctra (371 B.C.) made an end of Spartan supremacy, Xenophon shared the changed fortunes of his adopted country and lost the security and leisure which Spartan bounty had bestowed upon him; but when his son Gryllus atoned for his father's defection by gallantly sacrificing his life on the Athenian side in the battle of Mantinea (362 B.C.), Xenophon was recalled to Athens, where he ended his days.

We have under his name, in addition to the *Anabasis*, a large number of works, some of them, however, undoubtedly spurious. His *Hellenica*, the first two books of which form the continuation of Thucydides' work while the last five contain a political history of the Greek states down to 362 B.C., is altogether an inferior work. Xenophon lacks the impartiality of Thucydides (he is violently pro-Spartan); he lacks his grasp of affairs and his powers of analysis; and, finally, by ascribing the downfall of Sparta to the displeasure of the gods, he introduced again these elements which Thucydides had so rigorously excluded.

In his *Memorabilia* he set himself to vindicate his master, Socrates, against his detractors and accusers. We shall return to it in due time.

The *Cyropaedia* (the "Education of Cyrus") is one of the most curious works of antiquity. Pretending to be an account of the education and the life and character of the founder of the Persian Empire, it is in reality a romance in which the author sets forth his ideas of the ideal ruler and the ideal government. The ideal ruler turns out to be a mixed product of Socratic wisdom (as understood by the good Xenophon) and Spartan discipline as he admired it in Agesilaus. With the publication of this book Xenophon joined the ranks of the political reformers who dreamed of reclaiming Hellas by the proper training of its youth and the right kind of government.

Among the other political essays that have come down under his name there is one *On the Lacedaemonian Polity*, in which he once more avows his faith in Spartan institutions. But the essay *On the Athenian Polity* is certainly not from his pen but dates from about 420 B.C. and is the earliest surviving political pamphlet. The author, aptly dubbed "the Old Oligarch" by Zimmern, pays grudging tribute to the Athenian democracy, without, however, succeeding in concealing his oligarchic leaning.

The *Oeconomicus* is another of the self-revealing works of our author. We see him here as the ruler of his household and the model husband of a meek wife; we hear him gently rebuking her fondness for cosmetics; we behold him arranging the household utensils in order and showing that there is beauty even in well-placed pots and pans. We cannot refrain from smiling at the smug self-satisfaction of the husband, nor can we withhold our sympathy for the long-suffering wife who, withal, is so deeply impressed with the superior wisdom of her lord and master.

If we have accorded Xenophon an amount of space altogether out of proportion to his real worth, — for he is admittedly a person of mediocre gifts, — it is because we know him better than any of our classical Hellenes. And if we ask what, then, is the personality that emerges from the pages of his voluminous works, the answer is not difficult; for there is no subtlety about him. If one were in search for a caption to head this section devoted to him, one might pertinently call him, as C. Delisle Burns has done, the Gentleman of the Old School. This writer, born in postwar Attica, follower and friend of Socrates, and not unacquainted with the thought of his day, a witness to the changing world about him, remained steadfast to the traditions of the past. He loved the old, simple country life, with its ancient pieties, which was to him the only normal and wholesome life. The city, with its chattering populace and its wicked demagogues, he abominated. An aristocrat at heart, he was attracted to the steady, conservative ways of Spartan society. Moreover, he was a great believer in health, in keeping the body fit; and here again the Spartan ideal made a strong appeal to him. He believed in order and efficiency. He liked to take command and see to it that his orders were properly executed; whether the sphere of his activity were the farm or the battlefield made little difference to him. Besides, he was an inveterate moralist, who enjoyed hearing himself discourse on weighty themes and impart these moral precepts without which life, he thought, is a disorderly affair. Life presented no great complications, no insoluble problems, to this man who was so sure of himself. In the age in which it was his lot to live he was an anachronism, a curious survival and at the same time a witness to the extraordinary hold which the old traditions still had upon his people. He has been compared to the conventional retired colonel; and to be sure there is a surface likeness. Yet he was a Hellene and therefore, in spite of his dogmatism and his dictatorial ways, a remarkably human person; and if he resembles the country squire in his love for animals, he adds something which that estimable person usually lacks. For he knows that a healthy body is apt to be a fair one; he admits that he might well be "lost in astonishment at the beauty of the hare" he hunts; and he declares that "a prancing horse is a thing of beauty, a wonder and a marvel, riveting the gaze of all who see him, young alike and grey beards; they will never turn their backs or weary of gazing so long as he continues to display his splendid action." "Comment is superfluous," says C. Delisle Burns, on quoting this passage from Xenophon's *Horsemanship*, and adds, "We see here the feeling which made the frieze of the Parthenon possible." [1]

SUGGESTIONS FOR READING. On the Greek historians the best book is J. B. BURY, *The Ancient Greek Historians* (Macmillan, 1909).

On Herodotus see T. R. GLOVER, *Herodotus* (University of California Press, 1924), and on Xenophon the same author's *From Pericles to Philip* (Methuen, 1917), Chaps. VI, VIII, and IX.

On Thucydides see G. F. ABBOTT, *Thucydides, A Study in Historical Reality* (Routledge, 1925), and the book of C. N. COCHRANE referred to above.

Rhetoric and Oratory

Of the many causes contributing to the decline of historiography the most potent has not yet been mentioned, the rise of rhetoric. The extraordinary favor that it found in fourth-century Hellas caused a shifting of the emphasis from content to form. Thucydides had attempted to convert history into a science. His successors turned in a different direction: they made it into a branch of literature, a department of belles-lettres, a tradition which henceforth prevailed in

[1] *Greek Ideals* (Bell, 1917), p. 146.

the ancient world. Theopompus and Ephorus, historians of the fourth century, were both pupils of Isocrates the rhetorician. Livy, the historian of Rome, was of the same lineage. We turn, therefore, to the study of rhetoric and oratory, which, in the field of prose literature, form the chief contribution of the third period.

It has been well remarked that oratory was instinctive with the Greeks. Even in Homer we find the ideal man to be "both a speaker of words and a doer of deeds." But for the free development of oratorical skill a constitutional form of government, guaranteeing equality and liberty of speech to all, provides the best soil. Such a favorable setting was provided especially by the democratic city-states of Hellas. The ambitious citizen wished to take part in the debates at the town meeting; he had to hold his own when called upon to justify his conduct as a magistrate; even in his appearance before the juries of his fellow citizens his skill in presenting his case, either as a plaintiff or as a defendant, would be a large factor in determining the issue. Indeed, the marvel is that among a people with so pronounced a sense of form and so prone to the formulation of theory, the birth of rhetoric was so long delayed.

Its actual beginnings date from about 465 B.C., when, after the expulsion of the tyrants from Syracuse, a multitude of lawsuits arose in consequence of the attempts of those whose estates had been confiscated during the rule of the tyrants to re-establish their claims to the properties in question. It was then that a certain Corax instructed his clients in the art of defending their claims and taught the kind of argumentation which would prove most effective with a jury. His success was so great that he wrote a book on the subject and took pupils, some of whom became his rivals.

However, the whole Sicilian school, precursor of the Sophistic movement, cannot be dignified with a higher title than that of a training school initiating the hopeful pupils into the tricks of the trade. The real impulse to the study of rhetoric came from the Sophists. But since an account of the Sophistic movement has been given in the chapter on education, we may confine ourselves here to a brief mention of the services rendered to the cause of rhetoric by that greatest of the Sophists, who had a larger share in the creation of artistic prose writing than any of his rivals, Gorgias of Leontini. Of his appearance in Athens in 427 B.C. and of the electrifying effect of his address on his hearers we have spoken on another occasion. What was the secret of Gorgias' success? He was the first speaker the Athenians had ever heard who made of prose an *artistic* vehicle of persuasive speech, the first to show them that the spoken word, by proper choice and arrangement, could be made into a thing of beauty and that the composition of an oration, no less than that of a poem, admitted of being reduced to an observance of definite rules. Gorgias was a showy orator: archaic and poetic words, formidable compounds, sonorous phrases, striking assonances, and gorgeous metaphors rolled from his lips in amazing profusion, cunningly arranged in rhythmic order and with meticulous balancing of sound and meaning; the like of it had never been heard in the Athenian assembly, and loud acclaim followed the brilliant speaker. Yet, if the truth be told, this first artist in prose produced an artificial effect rather than an artistic one. He had made a great discovery, but he had not yet learned to curb his exuberance and to avoid excess. It was all very impressive, but also somewhat stiff and pompous and pedantic. However, Gorgias was a teacher of a novel art; exaggeration in the application of his newly discovered principles was necessary and, under the circumstances, unavoidable. If he wished to create a sensation, he evidently did not fail of his mark. From his appearance in Athens (427 B.C.) we may date the evolution of the art of speech in that city. It was left to his successors to build upon the foundations he had laid. These later developments led to the creation of three distinct types of oratory.

First comes forensic oratory, the speech of the law courts. Derived equally from the Sicilian school and from the Sophists, it led to the rise of a new profession, that of the *logographos*, speech-writer (carefully to be distinguished from the *logographos*, or storyteller, who had been the precursor of Herodotus). Since the law demanded that plaintiff and defendant make their plea in person, a skilled speech-writer could render a valuable service to the diffident novice by writing for him his address to the jury; he had only to learn the speech by heart and deliver it in court in accordance with the instructions. But it was also evident that in order to be successful these speech-writers would have to adapt their words to the character of the man who was to deliver the product of their art. No great display of rhetorical skill would have been in place — not even ingenious argumentation. Rather was it their task to make their client tell his story with a disarming candor and seeming simplicity; he must make the impression of placing his reliance on the unadorned recital of the facts themselves. This was the skill in which Lysias excelled, who wrote hundreds of these speeches which he later published as literary works! His activity as a *logographos* covers the first two decades of the fourth century. It was the loss of his considerable property during the rule of the Thirty Tyrants which drove him to join the profession when he was already well advanced in middle life.

Second comes epideictic oratory, the oratory of display. The occasion for this was provided by a great public gathering, such as a religious festival or a public funeral. Thus, the well-known funeral oration of Pericles belonged to this class, although in point of time it comes before the rise of formal rhetoric. Gorgias is the creator of the artistic type, but it was Isocrates who perfected it.

The last type is deliberative oratory, the oratory of political debate. The scene is the public assembly, and the speaker is avowedly making a bid for political leadership. It is the oratory of the statesman under a republican form of government. This, the most important form of eloquence, could not survive the death of political liberty. Of the many authors of deliberative speeches known to antiquity, Demosthenes, by the unanimous testimony of the ancient world, stands first.

The Alexandrian scholars canonized *ten* Attic orators; we shall content ourselves with a brief account of the two most prominent figures among these, Isocrates and Demosthenes.

ISOCRATES

Isocrates was born in Athens in 436 B.C. and died in 338 B.C., soon after the battle of Chaeronea, which sealed the doom of the city-state and political liberty in Hellas. His life covered nearly a century — and how eventful a century! Born in the days when Athens, under Pericles, was at the height of her glory, he was a young man when the failure of the Sicilian expedition dealt a fatal blow to the imperial aspirations of Athens; he was in his early thirties when Athens surrendered to the Spartan Lysander; he lived through the terror of the thirty tyrants and, like many others, found himself after the restoration of the democracy a ruined man; his friend and teacher Socrates was executed in 399 B.C.; he lived through those decades when Sparta played the tyrant over Hellas; he witnessed the overthrow of Spartan power and Thebes' short span of leadership; he saw his own Athens regain a semblance of her naval power and again surrender her pretensions; he lived through the bitter years of chaos and confusion preceding the rise to power of Philip of Macedon; and finally, in his ninety-eighth year, he watched the last struggle that Athens, allied with Thebes, made against the Macedonian menace.

By nature a man unfit for action, he might, like Plato, have retired into the ivory tower of philosophy. But, caring more for practical wisdom, he became the foremost teacher of Hellas, its most accomplished writer of prose, and its most eloquent political pamphleteer. As a teacher Isocrates aimed high. He scorned the Sophists, who at best trained their pupils to engage in profitless disputations on conduct or to participate in verbal battles on paltry subjects; he denounced them for the extravagant promises they made to prospective students, as if the success of the pupil did not depend primarily on his own natural aptitude. Equally pronounced was his aversion to all forms of abstract learning, be it mathematics or philosophy, because it did not concern itself with the actualities of life. His aim was the whole, harmonious development of man as he understood it. He wished to fit men for the duties of life by furnishing them with what we should call a cultural education; a broad and comprehensive training in practical thought and speech was to be the royal road which should lead to the creation of the *kalos kagathos*, the Greek equivalent of the gentleman. Hear his conception of the educated man:

Whom, then, do I call educated? First, those who manage well the circumstances which they encounter day by day, and who possess a judgment which is accurate in meeting occasions as they arise and rarely misses the expedient course of action; next, those who are decent and honourable in their intercourse with all with whom they associate, tolerating easily and good-naturedly what is unpleasant or offensive in others and being themselves as agreeable and reasonable to their associates as it is possible to be; furthermore, those who hold their pleasures always under control and are not unduly overcome by their misfortunes, bearing up under them bravely and in a manner worthy of our common nature; finally, and most important of all, those who are not spoiled by successes and do not desert their true selves and become arrogant, but hold their ground steadfastly as intelligent men, not rejoicing in the good things which have come to them through chance rather than in those which through their own nature and intelligence are theirs from their birth. Those who have a character which is in accord not with one of these things, but with all of them — these, I contend, are wise and complete men, possessed of all the virtues.[1]

[1] *Panathenaicus* (translation of G. Norlin; Loeb Library), Sects. 30–32. Isocrates composed this "oration" in his ninety-fourth year!

Note the phrase "wise and complete." No technical proficiency, no one-sided and lopsided development, is the aim, but the old Hellenic *arete*, the ideal of the amateur capable and good at anything; and combined with it is the Hellenic ideal of becoming conduct, of self-control and freedom from all forms of *hubris*. Isocrates became the teacher of many generations of ambitious and able youths who flocked to him from all parts of Greece. He was the first "gentleman and scholar" of whom we have any record.

But he rendered greater and more lasting service in another field. It was left for him to turn the promise of Gorgias into accomplished fact. He utilized the discoveries of Gorgias to the full, but pruned away the excesses. Gaining complete mastery over the tools which his predecessor and teacher had fashioned, he taught the world that came after him to write fluent and beautiful prose; the style of Isocrates became a tradition and a standard. Like a true Hellenic artist, he took infinite pains in perfecting the work in hand. Euphony and rhythm as subtle as they are unobtrusive, a well and clearly designed structure of sentence, an invariable smoothness of execution — these mark him a very virtuoso in language. But the very perfection of his composition, the continuous flow of his long, well-rounded, and well-balanced periods, in the end threatens to become a weariness and a defect. We become aware that in him the artist has killed the man; the force of conviction of the man is submerged in the anxious striving of the artist to clothe his thoughts in the most beautiful form; form has triumphed over content.[1] His Hellenic admirers, with their greater sensitiveness to beauty of form, would condone this to us obvious defect in the master more readily than we can.

There remains to consider what he himself thought his chief task, his role as the political counselor of Greece. For his most ambitious efforts were embodied in a series of political pamphlets which, although never actually delivered

[1] See A. and M. Croiset, *An Abridged History of Greek Literature*, pp. 365 ff.

by him to any audience, were published in the form of orations. As models of artistic prose they rank high; as practical advice to a distracted world they are negligible, and do more honor to the innate nobility of their author and to his guileless character than to his insight into the realities of the situation. For throughout his long life he adhered to this thesis, that the remedy for the ills afflicting contemporary Hellas lay in a union of all Greek states for common warfare against the ancient enemy, Persia. It was not a new idea; Gorgias had made it the subject of a great oration in 408 B.C., and Lysias had echoed him some twenty years later. Of Isocrates' political pamphlets the two most important are the *Panegyricus* (380 B.C.)[1] and the *Address to Philip* (346 B.C.).

In the first he advises the Greeks to unite under their ancient leaders, Athens and Sparta, although he would give first place to Athens, justifying his choice by a long recital of the honorable part Athens has played in the past and rebuking Sparta for the wrongs she has committed against the Greek states in the last twenty years. Now if we recall the condition of postwar Greece about 380 B.C., — when the mutual hatreds and suspicions of the city-states would not allow the establishment of a lasting peace among them, when racial divisions and historical factors seemed destined forever to range polis against polis, a time when the clearest-sighted among the Greeks might well despair of this nation divided against itself, — the advice of this well-meaning professor of rhetoric and things-in-general seems rather futile. Thus might an idealist today urge the nations of postwar Europe to unite because it can be shown that unless they do their ultimate ruin is certain. If men were creatures of reason, the advice, sound enough in both cases, might be heeded. But as long as passion and prejudice rule the minds of men, it is folly to look for sanity of action simply because it can be shown to be sane.

[1] It was said that it took him ten years to compose this "oration." The anecdote is spurious, but illuminating.

As an illustration of the naïveté of Isocrates' arguments we may turn to a passage in the *Panegyricus* (Sects. 173–174) in which he expresses his conviction that, once the united Greeks have conquered Persia, an enduring peace will follow; for he ascribes their everlasting strife to their poverty. Rid of this and in possession of the wealth of the East, they will live in a genuine spirit of concord and mutual good will! Comment is superfluous.

In the *Address to Philip* he has abandoned the idea of uniting the Greeks under the hegemony of some Hellenic state, and calls on Philip to assume the leadership in the common war on Persia. The advice is as excellent as it is fantastic. Isocrates refuses to believe the "slanderers" of Philip who accuse him of having designs against the liberties of Hellas; far from entertaining such base suspicions against the king of Macedon, he sees in him the gallant and capable leader of a union of free Hellenic states — a pleasing vision and one which Adolph Holm, the historian of Greece, shares with Isocrates. But Philip was too much of a realist to hope for voluntary concord among the city-states; he knew they would tolerate only a union forcibly imposed upon them. The idea of war on Persia appealed to Philip, and after Chaeronea he planned a campaign of conquest of the East, but the happiness of Hellas was certainly no part of this plan.

Isocrates, in addition to being a gifted writer, was also an honorable and a most reasonable person. It is a pity that his lot was cast in an age in which these two qualities were so conspicuously lacking in most of the men entrusted with the public affairs of Hellas. Now we turn to one of the "slanderers" of Philip.

DEMOSTHENES

Demosthenes was born about 384 B.C. When he was seven years old his father, who had been conducting a prosperous business, died; and when the boy had grown to manhood he found that his faithless guardians had wasted the substance of his patrimony. He was an unusual boy, of delicate health, shy and perhaps somewhat morose; but from his earliest years he showed his passion for justice and his inability to suffer wrong passively. He undertook the battle with his shifty guardians, and after a long struggle, which covered some three or four years, he finally brought them to justice. That the recovery of the moneys was not a primary consideration with him, but rather the principle involved, is proved by the fact that he donated the recovered sum to the state in the form of a *liturgy*. There is no question, however, that this prolonged struggle had embittered the best years of his life. Poverty drove him into the career of a speech-writer, and the practice thus gained paved the way for his political career. His active participation in the political life of Athens began when he was about thirty years old, and in 351 B.C. he delivered the first *Philippic*. For eleven years he continued a figure of growing importance in the ranks of the "Opposition" and delivered the series of harangues that have made him the greatest political orator of all time. Not until 340 B.C., when he was finally entrusted with the direction of affairs, did his impassioned appeals prevail. Two years of feverish activity followed. But it was too late. There were some slight successes, and Thebes was won over as an ally; then the battle of Chaeronea (338 B.C.) was fought, which made Hellas a political appendage to Macedon. The death of Philip, in 336 B.C., led to a new revolt against Macedonian overlordship; it was quickly and masterfully suppressed by Alexander. Another rebellion, in 323 B.C., upon the death of Alexander, ended no less disastrously. This time Athens lost more than half its citizens, the poorer classes, who were transported into Thrace and elsewhere. Athens was provided with a new constitution harking back to the days of Solon, and abolishing all the democratic foolishness. She had to pay an indemnity, and a Macedonian garrison was lodged in Munychia, overlooking Piraeus. Demosthenes, now sixty-two years old, fled from his country

Demosthenes

After Polyeuctus; the Vatican. (The hands and scroll are a false restoration)

with some other anti-Macedonian leaders, and when overtaken at Calauria, at the temple of Poseidon, where he had sought asylum, took his own life.

We may consider Demosthenes' career under a twofold aspect, as that of orator and patriot. But it will be found that the two are inextricably intermingled; in his case it is impossible to appraise the orator apart from the man and the man apart from the patriot.

We have a number of speeches, no doubt partly spurious, which he composed as a *logographos*; for necessity compelled him to continue his professional work until 345 B.C. and perhaps even later. His fame rests not on these. Perhaps they are as good as the work of Lysias or as that of his reputed teacher Isaeus; but in these speeches we cannot find the explanation of his unquestioned pre-eminence among the orators of antiquity. His fame rests on his political harangues delivered in the eleven critical years referred to above (351–340 B.C.) and on the oration *On the Crown* which is the *apologia pro vita sua*.

Now wherein lies the secret of his spell? To the casual reader of today, who has his own ideas of "oratory" and who has no knowledge of the man and the times, Demosthenes' works will hardly appear to be oratory at all; he notes with disappointment the almost complete absence of the features he associates with oratory — the grandiloquence, the oratorical fireworks, the flourishes, and perhaps the bombast, he looks for. Was the judgment of antiquity, then, at fault?

Let us hear the man himself. It is in the year 341 B.C. Demosthenes faces the Athenian assembly; he has briefly reviewed the recent activities of Philip, his acts of aggression in all directions:

> What is wanting to make his insolence complete? . . . Yet the Greeks endure to see all this; they seem to view it as they would a hailstorm, each praying that it may not fall on himself, none trying to prevent it. And not only are the outrages he does to Greece submitted to, but even the private wrongs which each suffers privately;

nothing can go beyond this! Has he not wronged the Corinthians, by attacking Ambracia and Leucas? the Achaeans by swearing to give Naupactus to the Aetolians? the Thebans by robbing them of Echinus? From us — I omit the rest — but does he not keep Cardia, the greatest city of the Chersonese? Still, under these indignities we are all slack and disheartened and watch our neighbors, distrusting one another, instead of the common enemy. And how think ye a man who behaves so insolently to all — how will he act when he gets each separately under his control?

But what is the cause of all this? There must be some cause, some good reason, why the Greeks were so eager for liberty then and today are so eager for slavery. There was something, men of Athens, something in the hearts of the multitude then, which there is not now, — something which overcame the wealth of Persia and maintained the freedom of Greece and quailed not under any battle by land or sea; the loss of which has ruined all and thrown our affairs into the present chaos. What was this? Nothing so very hard to discover: simply that whoever took money from those who wished to enslave Hellas or corrupt her were universally detested: it was dreadful then to be convicted of bribery; the severest punishment was inflicted on the guilty and there was no intercession or pardon. The favorable moments for enterprise which fortune frequently offers to the careless against the vigilant, to them that will do nothing against those that discharge all their duty, could not be bought from our politicians or generals; no more could mutual concord nor distrust of tyrants and barbarians, nor anything of the kind. But now all these things have been sold as in open market and those matters imported in exchange by which Greece has been afflicted as with a mortal disease. What are they? Envy, when a man gets a bribe; laughter, if he admits it; mercy, if he is convicted; hatred of those that denounce the crime and all the usual attendants upon corruption. For as to ships and men and revenues and abundance of all other materials, all that may be reckoned as constituting national strength — assuredly the Greeks of our day are more fully and perfectly supplied with these than the Greeks of the olden time. But they are all rendered useless, worthless, profitless by the work of those traffickers.[1]

It is impossible to miss the tragic note in this impassioned appeal. What is it that has come over the men of his time?

[1] *Third Philippic* (translation of C. R. Kennedy, with some slight changes), Sects. 32–40.

he asks. Why are they so indifferent to the common weal? Why are they so disloyal to their glorious past? What is this strange malady that has afflicted Hellas? He is both sick at heart and plainly bewildered. His diagnosis was not quite correct. He lived too close to the evil itself; and the activities of Philip among the less scrupulous of the Greeks being well known, he saw bribery and treason everywhere, even where probably there was none. But of the intensity of his indignation, of the fervor of his devotion to the national cause, there can be no doubt. For he was an idealist as well as a realist. To him Athens was a living reality but also an idea; this city lived in his imagination as a Higher Being, endowed with a definite character and personality. Fearless and honorable, magnanimous and disinterested, generous and compassionate, she had, in his view, played a noble part in the history of Hellas. Therefore she was entitled to the loyalty and devoted service of her citizens, such as they had given her in the best days of the Periclean Age, when that great leader had named her citizens "lovers" of their city. In the quality of his patriotism, Demosthenes harked back to that glorious age, and in his conception of the role of the statesman and leader he agreed with those who believed that a political leader was a moral leader as well and was responsible not only for the material welfare of the city but even more for her honor; an Athenian statesman ought, in particular, to see to it that his city should never stoop so low as to prefer the safer and easier, but more disgraceful, course to the dangerous and honorable one. For Athens could not afford to dishonor her past, and Philip knew it, so Demosthenes affirmed.

He did not live, however, in the Periclean Age, but at a time when apathy and indifference to public concerns confronted him on all sides. There were those who, while regretfully dwelling on the glories of the past, were yet sincere in their belief that, especially after the fiasco of the second Athenian league, Athens lacked the resources to play the preponderant part in Hellenic affairs that once had been hers. There were honest patriots — men like Eubulus, the able manager of the Athenian treasury — who, realizing that the poorer citizens looked to the city for their support, were averse to involving Athens in the adventure of war. They knew that public spirit was at a low ebb, and that the Athenians, who in the days of Pericles — according to the saying of their enemies — looked upon their bodies as not their own, were now reluctant to risk their lives in military service and would rather vote to send mercenaries in their stead. Others, again, were indifferent, or pretended to be so, and paraded their cynicism as a mark of their superiority. Finally, there were those demagogues who flattered the crowd by catering to its love of ease and its cupidity — men whose conduct was explicable to Demosthenes' mind only on the supposition that they had sold themselves to the arch-enemy Philip. Moreover, Demosthenes had made many personal enemies, foremost among whom was Aeschines, the orator, whose hatred of his great rival became the inspiration of his career, — a man totally lacking in political principle or vision, but whose commanding presence and splendid voice gave him an advantage over Demosthenes which the latter's superior eloquence could not always offset. It is no wonder, then, that in such a society the voice of Demosthenes was for years as one crying in the wilderness.

Yet it must not be supposed that he confined himself to moral and political preaching in the abstract. Nothing is farther from the truth. There is no other orator who comes so well fortified with facts. A close student of history, he was an ardent admirer of Thucydides, whose entire work he is said to have transcribed eight times; and while he tried to awaken his fellow citizens to a sense of their duty to Athens by many an appeal to their imagination, his greatest reliance was on their capacity to reason and think. "For God's sake, consider!" he will say and repeat again and again; hence it is argumentation that fills the bulk of his speeches. When, having finally proved his point, he proposed definite measures to fit the emergency, these measures were never extravagant in their demands but nicely calculated with a view to practical possibilities and present expediency.

Nor was he a saint. Especially when addressing not the assembly but the Athenian juries he would abuse his opponents with the full latitude permitted by the manners of his day. The jurymen took great delight in these verbal combats, and Demosthenes could be as scurrilous as the best or the worst of them. The foulness of abuse to which he descended in attacking Aeschines in the speech *On the Crown* is to our minds a serious blot on the character of the speaker. But his own world judged otherwise. Nor was he always as scrupulous in his political career as we might like him to have been; in the vehemence of his striving to obtain the end desired he would not be overcareful of the means employed. This too must be condoned in view of the character of political life in his age, and perhaps in every age.

As an orator he is the despair of the schoolman; as one of his finest critics has observed, "The only rule he followed was that of following none." While in Isocrates, as we saw, the artist killed the man, in Demosthenes the patriotic fervor of the man is the very soul of his eloquence. So true is it that with him it is impossible to separate the man from his art.

His greatest oratorical effort was reserved for a time when his active career as a statesman was practically over. In 336 B.C., after the cause to which he had dedicated his life had gone down to defeat, a certain Ctesiphon proposed that the great orator should be crowned with a golden wreath in the theater of Dionysus as a reward for his services to Athens. Aeschines raised legal objections, and the case was not tried until six years later. At the trial Aeschines spoke first. He did not confine his speech to the purely legal aspects of the case but endeavored to show that Demosthenes, far from having rendered any service to the state, had by his advice and his leadership largely contributed to the ruin of Athens.

That gave Demosthenes his opportunity: the speech *On the Crown* became the justification not only of his own career but of the course of action Athens followed in these last short years when she obeyed his voice. In ringing tones he declared that, even if they had possessed foreknowledge of the event, the Athenians could not have acted otherwise than they did; for it is better to die fighting for a noble cause than to live in disgrace and servitude:

> It is not possible, men of Athens, it is not possible that you were wrong when you risked the perils of war for the common redemption and the liberties of man. I swear it by our forefathers who died at Marathon, at Plataea, at Salamis and by all the brave men who rest in our public sepulchres, buried there by a country that accounted them all to be alike worthy of the same honor . . . Athenians did not ask to live, if they could not live as free men.

Aeschines lost his case and, failing to obtain one fifth of the votes of the jurymen, went into exile. Thus Demosthenes' defense became the funeral oration over the liberties of Hellas; and indeed all his political orations remain as the literary monuments of the last and final crisis in the history of Hellas — the last witness to a vanishing ideal of life, the Hellenic concept of the city-state and of the meaning of citizenship.

Forty years after his death Athens dedicated a statue of the great patriot. A good copy of this has come down to us. The sculptor, Polyeuctus, was a man of genius, for he has succeeded in revealing the soul of the man in his features and in his very form and figure. There he stands, his clasped hands betraying the intensity of his feeling, his thin, almost ascetic features facing us with an unspoken plea, his attitude not that of the statesman in the hour of his triumph, but of a prophet rejected by his people.

SUGGESTIONS FOR READING. On the history of Greek oratory see A. and M. CROISET, *An Abridged History of Greek Literature*, Chap. XX, or J. F. DOBSON, *The Greek Orators* (Methuen, 1919).

For Demosthenes consult S. H. BUTCHER, *Demosthenes* (Appleton, 1882), or A. W. PICKARD-CAMBRIDGE, *Demosthenes* (Putnam, 1914).

CHAPTER XI

ART AND ARCHITECTURE

Introductory

OUR knowledge of Hellenic art and architecture rests chiefly on a study of the actual remains, supplemented by such information as has been gleaned from Greek and Roman writings on the subject.

The remains themselves consist of the following: (1) Objects of stone (marble, limestone, etc.), such as buildings, sculptures in the round or in relief, and sepulchral monuments. (2) Objects made of durable metals (like bronze), such as statues and vessels. These, however, being easily convertible and having commercial value, have rarely survived, and then only by the merest chance. (3) Objects made of baked clay. These are practically indestructible and have survived in the largest number; hence, of the minor arts of Hellas, none is so well represented today as the work of potter and vase-painter. (4) Gems and other works of the jeweler and goldsmith, including engraved coins. The products of the painter have all but entirely perished, as was inevitable; and of the minor arts the greatest loss we have suffered is the complete disappearance of Hellenic textiles.

Every one of these relics of the Hellenic past bears unmistakably the imprint of the genius of Hellas; furthermore the same geographical and social factors, whose influence we have found of paramount importance in other fields, have also deeply affected the development of Hellenic art and architecture.

Geographical and climatic conditions are by no means negligible quantities in the evolution of art. It is no accident that Greece, with its pitiless sunlight and boldly outlined mountain scenery, was the home of sculpture, whereas

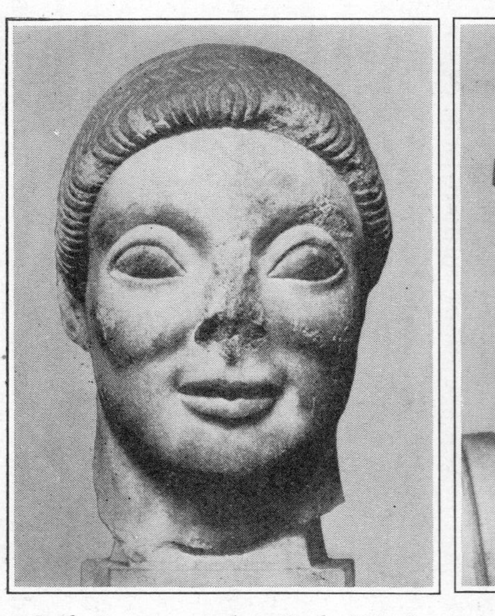

Sixth Century. Archaic Head of Youth
Copenhagen

Fifth Century. Apollo
West pediment of temple of Zeus, Olympia

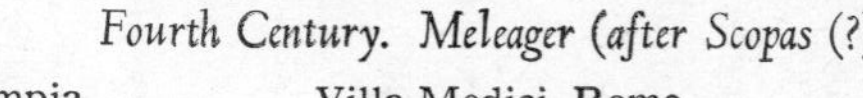

Fourth Century. Meleager (after Scopas (?))
Villa Medici, Rome

Holland, with its perpetual rains and watery atmosphere, produced a race of painters. The Dutch countryside, with its tremulous light and fleeting shadows, presents itself to the eye of the beholder as the product of a landscape painter, while the stark outlines of the Greek scenery have the appearance of being the work of a master sculptor.

Again, marble temples can be built only in a country where marble is relatively abundant; the Parthenon was built within sight of the quarries whence its blocks were drawn. The abundance of building stone in Greece made possible that evolution in architecture which here again made Hellas the pioneer and the teacher of later ages.

Finally, the very climate of Greece, inviting an outdoor life, would lead to a type of architecture which would stress rather the outlining of space, the picture presented to the eye by temple walls surrounded by colonnades, than the enclosed space itself. A building like a cathedral, with its rich and impressive interior, would have been an anomaly in Greece, where public gatherings took place in the open and where even the theater was open to the sky. But the outlines of a Greek temple were a delight to the eye of the spectator who saw it from the outside. Hence, as an acute critic has observed, Hellenic architecture, from an aesthetic point of view at least, is of two dimensions only; it lacks depth.

The influence of geographical factors, however, must not be overstressed in the domain of art and architecture. Other lands have not lacked building stone and yet have failed to produce a distinctive architecture. For that matter, Hellenic architecture itself, in its most characteristic product, the Doric temple, consists of a translation into stone of what began as timber construction.

Of far greater consequence in the evolution of Hellenic art were the racial factors. The Hellenic race was a blend in which an original Aegean or Mediterranean stock was fused with later northern elements. In the genius of the race we have found the evidence of this blend: the instinctive thirst of the Aegean for beauty is tempered by the sober rationalism of the Northerner. This makes Hellenic art the unique phenomenon which it is; for here, as in the field of literature, we discover an identical striving to achieve beauty through the rigid logic of form and design. In this respect a Greek temple and a Greek play are wholly akin.

Rationalism, then, which gave its characteristic quality alike to Greek political thinking and to Greek religion and poetry, put its stamp on Greek art as well. This intellectual bias betrays itself first and foremost in the emphasis laid on design and form. Compare any two Greek temples and any two Gothic cathedrals. The Greek temples will be found to resemble each other very closely; the Gothic cathedrals, most likely, will present striking divergences. The Greek architect produced a type from which he did not greatly deviate. And why not? Religious conservatism may have been a contributing cause, though not the primary cause. The truth is that to the logical Hellenic mind the building of a temple resolved itself into the question of finding the proper means to achieve a definite end. Now the function of the temple was to house the image of a god or goddess. There seemed to be only one logical solution of this problem: a rectangular cella, roofed over and provided with a suitable entrance. From this fundamental design the Greek architect did not depart; the size of the cella, the number of the columns employed, the details of ornamentation, might vary, but, as the French saying has it, "the more it changes, the more it is the same thing." It is as if some prehistoric Plato had gathered the early temple-builders into his prehistoric Academy and had explained to them that there was one ideal temple, one perfect pattern, which it was their duty to convert into stone, and as if all the successive generations of temple-builders had striven to realize the Platonic idea of a temple.

But the Hellenic concept of design passed beyond mere outline and envisaged an organic whole in which, through the proper co-ordination of component parts, there was achieved that harmony and balance which both delights the eye and satisfies the reason. While architecture will furnish us with the best illustrations of the Greek feeling for beauty of design (the Parthenon remains as its most perfect embodiment), even in the minor industrial arts, such as that of the potter, we find the same principles applied, the same search for form adapted to purpose. The wine cup, the oil flask, the mixing bowl, the water jar — these and all the others in the course of time assumed a typical form in the potter's assiduous striving after the perfect union of beauty and usefulness. Hence it is that the concepts of the beautiful and the useful, which to our minds are apt to stand for contrasting principles and even mutually exclusive ideas, were not so considered by the Greeks. Quite the reverse: they could hardly conceive of beauty apart from practical utility; if we may believe Xenophon, Socrates was wont to maintain the identity of the two. Art for art's sake, then, had no place in their society, nor could they divorce grace of form from the purpose the object was to serve.

Now it will be objected that this may be all very well in the case of architecture or pottery, where man does not copy nature but may fashion as he pleases; but where art is constrained to use the models furnished by nature, as, for instance, in sculpture or painting, what becomes of the striving for balance and harmony of proportion? The Greek artist had his answer ready. He would retort that order and balance were not of his invention but the very principles on which the world of nature itself rests; he would point with reason to the structure of the human body, and to animal and plant life itself. He would admit that in nature's works this mathematical equilibrium is never fully attained. There are always blemishes, always certain vagaries and irregularities, in the products of nature's laboratory; but these he thought it his duty to eliminate or amend. Thus in the earliest images of man which the Hellenic sculptor fashioned, we notice his

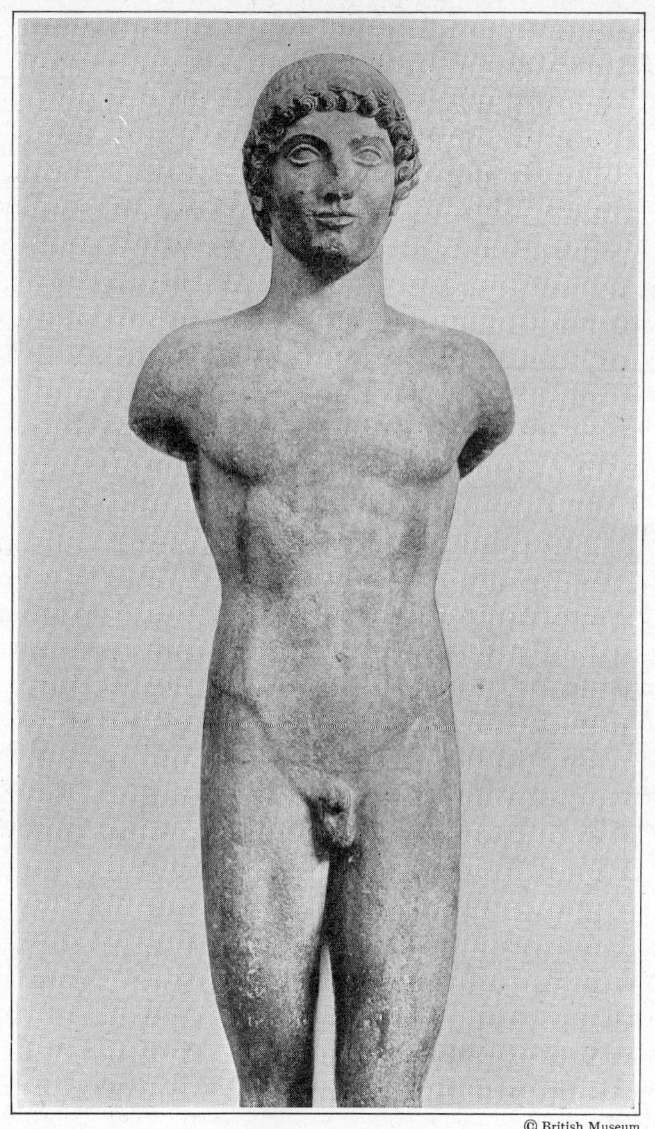

"The Strangford Apollo"

strong preoccupation with plan and design; it is this which makes these archaic heads and bodies more successful from a decorative than from a naturalistic point of view. True, these early artists were a little clumsy; they did not know as yet how to handle their tools. A great deal of their schematizing of the human head must be attributed to this. But when, with the coming of the Periclean Age, the sculptor attains a perfect mastery of technique, what do we find? No slavish copying of nature, no realistic portraits, but the "classic profile"! Forehead and nose form an almost straight line; the face itself is a perfect oval; the small mouth with the finely chiseled lips, the strong chin, the small, well-modeled ear, the eyes placed high — such flawless beauty does not belong to any living human being. The effect produced by these ideal heads, which seem to reflect through the outward harmony of their features the inner concord of the soul, is one of lofty serenity and detachment. This sculpture ignores the blemishes of the actual for the portrayal of the ideal; it passes beyond the accidents of time to the creation of the eternal.[1]

And not only in the rendering of the human head or body do we observe this striving for beauty through order and harmony of design. The same thing is true of the treatment of drapery. The Charioteer at Delphi provides an excellent illustration. One may see this at its best in the so-called "Three Fates" from the eastern pediment group of the Parthenon. Nothing could be more pleasing to the eye than the arrangement of the draperies of these divine women; if one should try to duplicate this effect on living bodies, it would immediately be apparent what element the Greek artist has introduced that is only imperfectly present in the actual.[2] Now it is, of course, not maintained that idealism in art is a product of

[1] For a typical example see the so-called "Bologna head," Fig. 614, in Gisela M. A. Richter's *Sculpture and Sculptors of the Greeks,* and remember that this is only a copy of an original, probably from the hand of Phidias.

[2] Cf. the instructive remarks of G. M. A. Richter, p. 89, and cf. illustrations 249 and 250.

Bronze Statue of Charioteer, Delphi

rationalism; for idealism springs from the sheer love of beauty, and this holds true in the domain of Greek art as well. But there is a certain abstract quality in the Hellenic sculptor's rendering of beauty which unmistakably betrays his intellectual bias.

To this same trait we may attribute that love of clarity, of the definite, that directness of observation and simplicity of execution, which characterize Greek art. It always moves in clear daylight; there is nothing mystic, dreamy, or indefinite about it. Therefore, just as we found that Greek poetry had only a limited field, we shall discover Greek art sharing these limitations. To see clearly, to move out of the twilight of ignorance and superstition into the light of day — that was the destiny and the mission of Hellas, and her art confirms it. That is why it is so simple, so sincere, and so straightforward. The Greek temple stands squat upon the ground, and its clear-cut lines present us with a definite and easily understood concept. Contrast the Gothic cathedral: its soaring mass moves us deeply, but the mind, unable to grasp what it sees, loses itself in mystic adoration.

The Greeks were not only intellectual; they were also true lovers of beauty. This is proved not only by the idealizing bent of their art but, even more, by their patient persistence in perfecting its traditional themes. The Greek artist moved in a comparatively narrow field, but within that field he never ceased in his search for perfection; no other people has spent so much unremitting effort on the elaboration of detail as did the Hellenes. Here again the Doric temple furnishes a good illustration. A less artistic people would have turned away from the tyranny of its design and the conventions of its construction long before the Greeks did and would have tried its hand at something else; again, a more practically-minded people would have attempted a new solution for the engineering problems involved. The Greeks paid slight heed to either consideration; instead they lavished their efforts on the perfection of the work at hand.

Discobolus

After Myron

Even the comparative simplicity of the Doric column and capital presented to these fastidious artists a number of problems which exercised their skill for generations. There was the question of the relative height and width of the column and its mathematical relationship to the superstructure it supported. The capital consisted of a square block (the *abacus*), resting upon the *echinus*, the curving line of which assisted the eye in the transition from the vertical line of the column to the horizontal lines of the entablature above; here the problem was the perfection of that curve. Now anyone looking, for instance, at the remaining columns of the ancient temple of Apollo at Corinth will note the widely flaring line of the echinus; if he follows the history of the echinus he will come upon many and varying solutions of the problem before he reaches the refinement of the echinus of the Parthenon columns, which begins as a straight line and ends in a subtle curve inward to the abacus.

Indeed, the Parthenon as a whole may serve as a striking example of that "will to perfection" which characterizes the Greek artist. Its columns taper in an apparently straight line toward the top; but if the spectator will look closely he will discover, to his surprise, that there is a slight swelling in the line of the column (*entasis*).[1] Furthermore, the outside columns lean decidedly inward. If we continue our measurements and explorations, it will appear that such "refinements" form a feature of the entire building, which is constructed not with mathematical rigidity but with subtly curving lines; the horizontal lines of the building conform no more than the vertical ones to mathematical precision. The curvature of the base line (the stylobate) amounts to about four inches on a length of two hundred and twenty-five feet; the two fronts, base and entablature, are convex; the side walls slope inward; the abacus and crowning molding slope outward. What was the object of all this? It changes

[1] This is plainly visible in a good photograph. See, for instance, Walter Hege, *Die Akropolis* (Berlin, 1930), illustration No. 15.

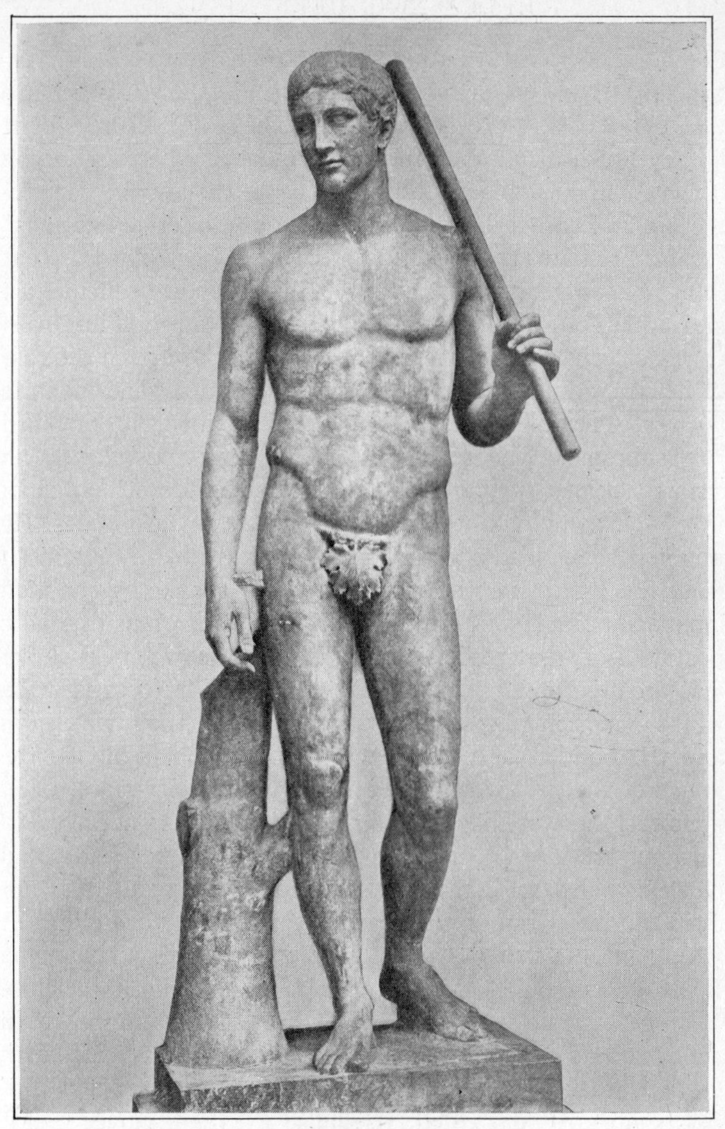

Doryphorus

After Polycletus

the building from a mathematical formula into a living organism. Even in its ruined state the Parthenon proclaims the secret of the excellence of Hellenic architecture; for it is the exquisite character of the workmanship bestowed upon it which makes this building unique in the annals of architecture and an everlasting object lesson to later generations.

There remains the social factor in the history of art. What influence did social environment have upon Hellenic art and architecture? This question, usually one bristling with complications and difficulties in the history of art, in the case of Hellas admits of a comparatively simple and definite answer. Once more, the city-state and the ideals it embodied rule supreme. The socially-minded Greeks postulating an organic society, it follows that the artist could not hold aloof from the common interests any more than the poet. He might perhaps lead the way, but he could not sever himself from the group life; he would have to speak the common language and express the common ideals. Even as dramatic poetry discharged a social function, so it was with Greek art and architecture. The temple was not built to satisfy the whim of a rich patron of art but to house the civic deity; and the builder, as well as the sculptor who fashioned the image of the god, worked in the pay of the city-state. Hellenic art, therefore, is in the service of the polis; hence it is a religious art as well, since the polis represents both state and church. With art remaining wedded to the state (and not even the industrial arts escaped the effects of this union), it was inevitable that the vicissitudes of the state and changing social ideals should prove a determining factor in the development of Hellenic art. So we find it essentially conservative in spirit and fairly continuous in its evolution; it works with certain patterns which have found common favor and cannot be abruptly discarded. Hellenic art, then, moves — if it moves at all — within the framework of tradition. Accordingly, we meet here with none of that bewildering variety, none of those bizarre experiments, so common in modern art.

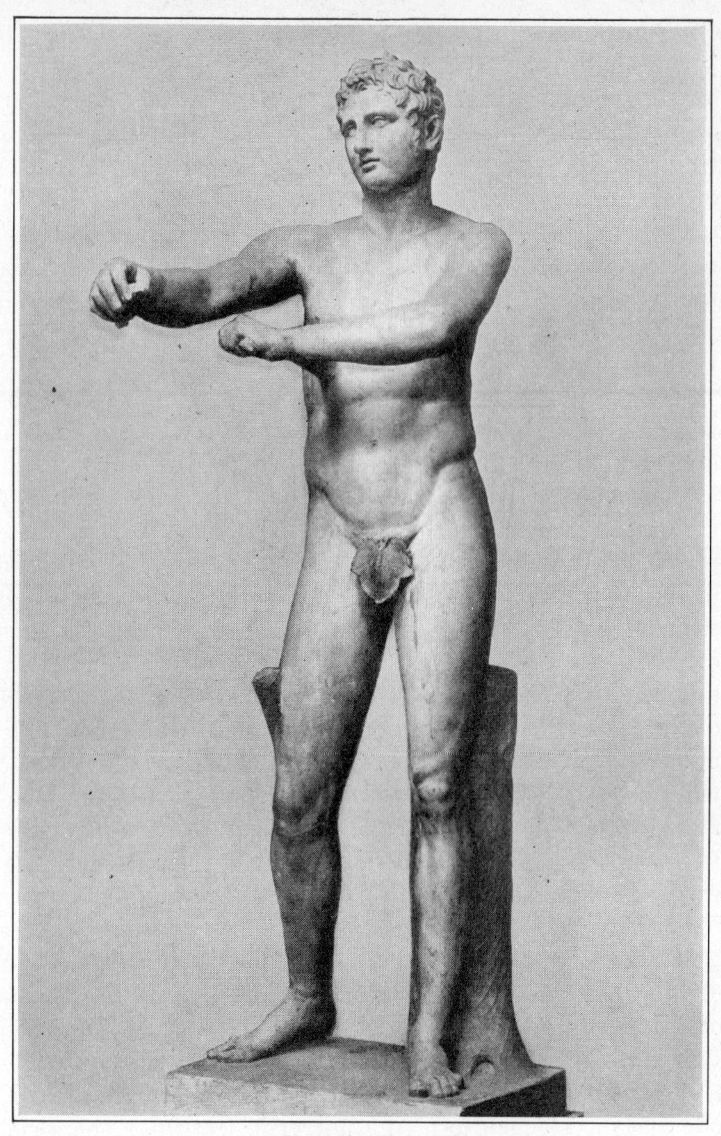

Apoxyomenus

After Lysippus

Greek art served, after all, a fairly homogeneous society. It is true that in the first period the impulse came as often from an enlightened "tyrant" as from the citizen body itself; but even the tyrant was not minded to disregard the force of tradition and the common preferences, which, as a matter of fact, he no doubt shared. It is equally true that art frequently lagged behind and continued to express the ideal of one period in the opening years of the following era. Thus the art produced in Hellas during the Hellenic World War as yet failed to reflect the gradual change that was coming over Hellenic society.

The interdependence of state and art accounts also for the fact that Hellenic art and architecture eschewed the colossal and magnificent; the slender resources of these city-states, even though the art treasures of many of them proportionally far exceeded those of the average modern city, kept these public works within a modest scale. Here were no powerful monarchs who sought to impress the world by the splendor of their palaces or their tombs. Greece has nothing to offer comparable to the architectural wealth of Luxor and Karnak, in Egypt. On the other hand, the social environment typical of the Hellenic city-states could not fail to react powerfully upon the evolution of their arts. Foremost among these features of city life were the palaestrae and, later, the gymnasia, which gave the Greek sculptor an unrivaled opportunity to observe the athletic youths of their day at their exercises. Among the earliest efforts of the sculptor are his renderings of these nude youths, and these *kouroi* (whether they are meant to represent divine or human beings does not greatly matter) continue in unbroken line from the beginnings of the art until, at the end of the fourth century, we reach Lysippus. Hardly less important were the religious traditions which ruled these city-states — the games, processions, choral dances which formed a universal feature of the social life of the polis. This too is reflected in their art. The most august of all Greek temples, that of Zeus at Olympia, was adorned with pediment sculptures celebrating the legendary horse race by which Pelops won his bride; the frieze of the Parthenon celebrates the procession of the Panathenaic festival. We observe the same tendency to render homage to the present by the idealization of the past. The legends of the heroic age which furnished the material for melic and dramatic poetry supplied also the plastic arts with their themes, some of which, such as the labors of Herakles or the battle of centaurs and Lapiths, they never tire of repeating. When this trend toward the idealization of the heroic past ceases to operate, we shall know that the old social order is passing and that a new era in art is ushered in.

To sum up, we have found that geographical and climatic conditions, racial characteristics, and social environment are faithfully mirrored in the art and architecture of Hellas and have made of these also typically Hellenic products. We are now ready to trace the part which art and architecture have played in the cultural history of Greece during the three historic periods.

The First Period

The first period, which roughly includes the preceding one hundred and fifty years as well (for the so-called geometric style makes its appearance as early as 900 B.C.), is known in the history of Hellenic art as the *archaic period*. It was the age of the pioneers, when the Greek discovered a new world and dotted the Mediterranean shores with settlements. The spirit of adventure led him to attempt things never tried before. It is no cause for surprise that in the plastic arts as well he broke the bonds of tradition and in his very borrowing from alien sources created something entirely new. The exuberant vitality which marks the age is reflected in its artifacts. Of these we have abundant remains, especially of the products of the potter, the sculptor, and the architect. Moreover, they are originals. For our knowledge of Greek sculpture at its zenith we have to rely mostly on copies; but the works of the earlier artists, in large measure discarded by later generations, have been brought to light again by the labors of the indefatigable archaeologist.

The Greeks of Anatolia once more take the lead. They seem to have had a stronger Aegean strain in them than the Dorians of the mainland. This may account for their delight in grace and sensuous beauty, in the elegance of curving line; it may explain the emphasis they placed on the purely decorative; it may have caused their occasional lapses from the canons which rule Hellenic taste. But it is a gracious and smiling art, delicate and somewhat feminine.

Opposed to it is the austere Dorian art. The Dorians of the Peloponnese and of the west show the peculiarly Hellenic tendency to create beauty through neatness of design and chastity of form, through symmetry and balance. This is their chief contribution in the domain of art. With it goes a preference for strength and solidity, which gives Dorian art its male character, as contrasted with the feminine traits of Ionian art. The Dorians may not have been the creators of the art forms they employed: the column was probably borrowed from Egypt; the same country furnished the prototype for the large statue of stone; even the plan of the Doric temple may have been derived from the ground plans of the Achaean palaces which they found in the Peloponnese and elsewhere. Nevertheless, they infused into these old forms a new element which made them their own.

Of the first period the most conspicuous achievements are the gradual mastery of technique and the progressive humanization (which means Hellenization) of the arts.

The most abundant evidence is within the field of ceramics. Here we can trace the gradual evolution of an industrial art which, however, remains in close contact with the major arts. The earliest is the geometric style; it belongs to a rude age. The decoration consists of straight lines, forming a pattern; there may be several bands of these linear combinations. Later there is a greater variety of decorative patterns,

Black-Figured Vases

Upper row: drinking cups. Middle row: two jugs, large stamnus (jar), flanked by an alabastrum (for ointments) and an oil flask. Lower row: a stamnus, flanked by an amphora and a crater (mixing bowl). (Metropolitan Museum of Art, New York)

including curved lines; the enlarged field now holds human figures as well as animals, though they are severely schematized into angular caricatures of the living forms. The shape of the vase itself is still stiff.

Presently we observe the influence of contact with the East. Sphinxes and griffins and other fabulous animals tempt the artist. He gains in skill, and half-forgotten memories of Aegean days are revived: plant and flower motifs make their reappearance; mythological and legendary themes engage the attention of the artist, and delightful subjects such as Satyrs and Maenads make their first appearance. The West originates the "black-figured" technique which gradually spreads over all Hellas: the figures stand out in black varnish upon the reddish clay of the vase. Shapes are improved, and harden into types. And now pottery becomes one of the staple products of Greek industry, furnishing the Hellenic cities, along with their wines and olive oil, an article for exchange in a world which is slowly emancipating itself from complete dependence upon agriculture. Corinth becomes one of the chief centers of the manufacture of pottery.

In the second half of the sixth century a new technique originates in the Athens of Pisistratus: the "red-figured" vase leaves the figures in the color of the clay but covers the background with a black slip; details in the figures are added in brown lines. The East and its fabulous monsters are left behind by the new interest in man, his pursuits, and his environment. The sphere of the artist is constantly widening; he depicts the life about him with all its animation and variety — banquets and revelry, women at the well, boys in the palaestra, the interior of the women's quarters, the very workshop of the potter himself. In short, there is hardly any aspect of Hellenic life which has not been preserved to us by the brush of the vase-painter; but myth and legend maintained their hold upon his imagination as well. Proud of his skill, he signs his product with his name.

In sculpture we observe the same gradual mastery of technique; progress is slow but steady. At first (that is, from the seventh century on) the influence of Egypt is manifest and dominant in the series of standing male figures in the nude that have come down to us, — the same broad shoulders and narrow waist, the same stiff frontal pose, — symmetrical figures which testify to the decorative sense of the early Greek artist. Gradually we observe an approach to a closer imitation of nature until, at the end of the period, such a work as the "Strangford Apollo" brings certain promise of that emancipation which is to follow with such bewildering rapidity in the following period.

Ionia led the way in discovering the added beauty offered by the employment of drapery. The draped female statue originated there. We can study in the Attic imitations not only the Ionian sensitiveness to grace and delicacy of detail but also its lack of artistic balance in its overemphasis on such matters as the niceties of embroidery. These Attic maidens rescued from the ruins left by the Persian and now housed in the Acropolis Museum illustrate one phase of Hellenic sculpture and that a passing one. The ideal treatment of drapery, in which the artist has struck the right balance between the decorative effect aimed at and truth to nature, was not effected until the fifth century.

In addition, seated figures were attempted by the sculptors of the sixth century. The earliest, such as the Branchidae, members of a priestly family in charge of the temple and oracle of Apollo near Miletus, are clumsy attempts; but the archaic seated goddess, now in Berlin,[1] reveals the progress that here too was made.

Another contribution made by Ionia was the introduction of the technique of hollow casting of bronze. This considerably enlarged the opportunities of the artist, which had been improved already by the introduction of marble to replace the softer stone used before.

What purposes did these sculptors serve? First of all, there

[1] See G. M. A. Richter, *Sculpture and Sculptors of the Greeks*, illustration 65.

were the gods of the city-state whose images were housed in the temple. But these civic shrines themselves needed adornment with sculpture in relief; and later the pediments found room for sculpture in the round. Other civic architecture was not lacking and, in turn, provided the sculptor with further opportunities. Then there were statues of victorious athletes, monuments of civic pride dedicated by the polis. Furthermore, there were funerary monuments, usually in relief, and votive offerings, both public and private. With the increasing prosperity of the Hellenic city-states, these demands grew and, in turn, stimulated the development of the artist's skill.

It will be with surprise that the modern reader hears that Greek sculpture did not disdain the use of color. But we should keep in mind that primitive art delights in vivid coloring; tradition, therefore, demanded it, and the example of Egyptian art confirmed the Greeks in their habit. Here too we find the same gradual development from the traditional and decorative use of color to a more naturalistic one. There can be no doubt that the vivid coloring of some of the earlier limestone sculptures (as an example we may cite the ancient pediment sculptures at Athens) would strike us as barbaric and grotesque rather than as beautiful. In the course of time, however, the artist learned to restrain his exuberance and to confine the use of color to its legitimate function.

Finally, it was during this period that both the Doric and the Ionic order of architecture originated. The plan of the Doric temple is simple. It developed from a single rectangular chamber, the cella, with an entrance porch formed by a prolongation of the side walls, terminating in pilasters (*antae*); such a temple is called *in antis*. The next stage does away with the *antae* and provides columns in front, the *prostyle*. When the motif is repeated in the rear we get such a building as the little Ionic temple of Athena Victory on the Acropolis of Athens; it is called *amphiprostyle*. Later, if a building of sufficient size and importance, the temple was surrounded entirely by a colonnade; such is the *peripteral*, or *peristyle*, temple. The Parthenon is both amphiprostyle and peripteral.

The Doric order indicates an architectural unit consisting of foundation, column, and entablature. The foundation is stepped; on the upper step (*stylobate*) the shaft rests. The Doric column, then, stands directly on the stylobate; it has no base. The column itself is no monolith (except in the case of a very small building) but is built up of drums; it is fluted and has the swelling (*entasis*) of which we spoke above; it terminates in the capital consisting of the *abacus* and *echinus*, carved out of one block. The flutings of the Doric column meet in sharp *arrises*. The entablature embraces the *architrave*, solid blocks of plain and unadorned surface, resting on the sturdy columns; the *frieze*, consisting of an alternate succession of *triglyph* and *metope*, and the cornice. The Doric genius asserts itself in the sturdy proportions of the order, its rhythm, that is, in the repetition of the same motif (such as the alternation of triglyph and metope), and its mathematical spirit. It diverges little from its early appearance, and this chiefly in the direction of a lightening of the weight of the entablature; with the lessening of the burden there follows logically a lengthening of the column, which becomes more slender, without, however, abating its Dorian strength.

The Ionic order differs in that the column itself is more slender and graceful; it has a rather elaborate base; the flutings are more numerous, deeper, and separated by flat bands. The capital, much more ornate than the sober Doric one, is marked by its scrolls, or *volutes*. Finally, the entablature consists of an architrave divided into three horizontal bands; the frieze above forms a plain surface which lends itself admirably to the adornment of a continuous relief; upon it rests the cornice, with its dentils (a succession of blocks) and a continuous upper block, projecting far beyond the dentils. Such is the more ornate and graceful Ionic order. Its occasional tendency to introduce ornament where its use is questionable is seen, for instance, in the columns of the old temple of Artemis at Ephesus, where the lowest drums were decorated with sculptured relief — a device which was employed again when the temple was rebuilt in the fourth century.[1]

The essential features of these two orders remained unchanged, side by side, though not without mutually influencing one another. What progress was made was in the gradual refinement of proportions, decorations, and contours, especially of base and capital.

And now the pioneer age draws to a close. The artisan and artist have learned the use of their tools. The movement has been from a straining after purely decorative effects to a greater fidelity to the facts of nature, from a scattering of interests to a concentration upon what were destined to become pre-eminently Hellenic themes of art; a number of art forms and patterns have been created. The stage is set for the splendor which the fifth century was to bring.

The Second Period

The Persian Wars furnished the greatest stimulus to the creative energy of fifth-century Hellas. The signal victory gained over the mighty Asiatic power heightened the self-confidence of the Hellenes; it was a further proof that theirs was a superior way of life, as contrasted with the "barbarism" of the world around them. Athens in particular was to benefit from that conflict. We have seen how she first led the Aegean Greeks in their relentless warfare on the Persian, and then united them under her command in the Athenian Empire. She herself gained in power and prestige

[1] For details and illustrations the reader may consult F. B. Tarbell, *A History of Greek Art*, Chap. III, or H. N. Fowler and J. R. Wheeler, *A Handbook of Greek Archaeology*, Chap. II.

day by day until, under the enlightened leadership of Pericles (461–430 B.C.), she stood first and foremost among Hellenic cities. The inevitable consequence was that she became the center of art as well. Pericles had also succeeded, in large measure at least, in converting into fact the social ideals and trends of Hellenic city life — the integration of all the varied activities of the citizens for the pursuit of a common end; the socialization of the arts and architecture followed as a matter of course. It is in the union of these two, the heroic temper and the civic spirit, that we must seek the characteristic qualities of the art of Periclean Athens; this lent it both its monumental character and its ideal grandeur. In this respect the art of Polygnotus and Phidias did not differ from that of Aeschylus and Sophocles.

It was only natural that the art of the vase-painter, after reaching its full maturity in the first half of this period, should gradually decline; for it could not play its part in this movement and lacked the means for expressing contemporary ideals. True, in the more ambitious specimens of the vase-painter's work we detect occasionally a reflex of the achievements of the major arts — of the painting of Polygnotus, of contemporary sculpture and drama; it is equally true that the Athenian potter's work reveals the same scrupulous attention to detail, the same persistent will to perfection, that mark the art and architecture of the era. But eventually the vase-painter resigned himself to the humbler part which the transformation of the other arts left him. Signatures become rare; a florid style begins to prevail; and with this the art entered upon a steady decline hastened by the disastrous course of the Hellenic World War, which deprived Athens of the greater part of its export market.

Polygnotus is the chief representative of the age in the field of painting. Not an Athenian by birth, he yet seems to have spent the greater part of his life in Athens, where he may have gained citizenship. Concerning the technical character of his work we may say that, consisting chiefly of great mural paintings adorning the walls of porticoes and temples, it should be classified rather as colored drawing than as painting in our sense. He was sparing in the use of colors (in fact, he used only four basic colors) and applied these in flat tone. It was a very sober, somewhat severe art, which cared little for perspective and nothing for gradation of color in the rendering of light and shade. In true Hellenic fashion the emphasis was laid on clarity of outline rather than on depth of view. Polygnotus struck a popular note; of this there can be no doubt, for commissions came to him from all parts of Hellas. The secret of his power, according to the unanimous testimony of antiquity, lay in his ability to render *ethos*, as the Greeks called it: his life-sized figures had a noble dignity and grandeur, both in face and demeanor, which no previous painter had been able to convey. Nothing has survived of the art of Polygnotus, — not even a copy in mural painting or mosaic. But there is no possibility of mistaking his significance: he did in painting what his contemporary Aeschylus, poet of the sublime, did in dramatic poetry; he paid his tribute to the glory of his own era by idealizing the legendary heroic age.

We have fuller material for the history of sculpture, although originals of this period are mostly confined to temple sculptures. The works of the three great masters of the fifth century, Myron, Polycletus, and Phidias, have survived only in copies.

From the beginning of the period we note the disappearance of the archaic symmetry in the statues representing youthful athletes. The weight now rests principally on one leg, which affects both hips and shoulders; the head is turned; and the spine loses its rigidity. Finally, in the "Polycletan stance," we reach perfection of ease and grace of attitude. Polycletus, whose activity falls between 460 and 420 B.C., belonged to Argos and the Peloponnesus, and represents the Dorian tradition rather than the Attic school. By nature and inclination an academician rather than a pioneer, he created in his "Doryphorus" what became to later ages almost a norm. His "Diadumenus," a youth binding a fillet around his head, has greater animation, and in his "Amazon" he even allowed the wounded warrior maiden to lean on a pillar. He worked chiefly in bronze, but there has been no great difficulty in identifying these three masterpieces of his in the numerous Roman copies that have come down to us.

In strong contrast to Polycletus stands Myron. His career lies approximately between 480 and 445 B.C.; chronologically, therefore, he precedes Polycletus. His chief title to fame rests on the audacity of his work and his technical skill. Two of his masterpieces have been identified with certainty: the celebrated "Discobolus" and the "Marsyas."[1] Both illustrate the artist's predilection for seizing the dramatic moment: the violent and strained action of the discus-thrower and the sudden backward movement of the startled satyr are admirably rendered. In these two works we may find the complete emancipation of sculpture from the shackles of tradition.

But neither Polycletus the traditionalist nor Myron the innovator had struck the true note. Myron had caught the momentary, the passing, but the age demanded the monumental, the abiding; both sculptors had stressed the body and all but ignored the mind. The spiritual message of the "grand century" had as yet found no echo in the art of the sculptor. It was reserved for Phidias to translate the idealism of the era into stone.

Phidias was an Athenian by birth. We hear that he was commissioned to make the colossal bronze Athena on the Acropolis, which became one of the landmarks of the country, the cost to be defrayed "from the spoils of the Persians who landed at Marathon." This seems to show that even about

[1] The Marsyas was grouped with a youthful Athena. The goddess, having invented the flutes, has cast them away in disgust; the satyr, eager to recover the treasure, starts back at sight of the goddess.

470 B.C. he was a well-known artist. His career covered more than forty years; for it was not until 438 B.C. that the temple statue of Athena in the Parthenon was finished, and not until 432 B.C. that the temple was completed.

His great opportunity came through Pericles. This enlightened statesman saw that the proper restoration of the Acropolis as the civic and religious center of Athens was indispensable to the maintenance of the city's prestige. The Persians had left it a ruin and a desolation, and unwittingly had done their share in offering Pericles an opportunity he was not slow to seize. He used it in a manner which proves him to have been a man of extraordinary vision. A lesser man might have been content to endow Athens with a temple of such dimensions and such wealth of adornment as to impress the vulgar with the power and resources of his city. Pericles' aim was altogether different. He meant to erect a building which should be an abiding monument of the devotion of her citizens, a testimony to their loyalty and love, a source of inspiration to their patriotism. He acted when the time was ripe, and never in the history of the world has there been a like combination of circumstances making possible the creation of monumental and significant works of art. First, there was the leader in the enterprise, Pericles himself; there was a united people, vigorous and self-confident and intelligent enough to follow his leadership; there was the civic spirit necessary for the undertaking; money was not lacking, contributed by the "allies" (not for this purpose, indeed, but it was for Athens to dispose of as she saw fit); the arts of sculpture and architecture had reached the stage which made them competent to undertake the charge laid upon them; the marble quarries of Mt. Pentelicus furnished abundant material; and, finally, the greatest artist of all time was there, to preside over the execution of the plans. Under the joint leadership of Pericles and Phidias there arose in an incredibly short time a succession of monumental works of art which have put posterity forever in the debt of Periclean Athens.

Let us hear what Plutarch, the biographer of Pericles, has to say upon the subject some five centuries afterwards:

So then the works arose, no less towering in their grandeur than inimitable in the grace of their outlines, since the workmen eagerly strove to surpass themselves in the beauty of their handicraft, and the most wonderful thing about them was the speed with which they rose. Each one of them, men thought, would require many successive generations to complete it, but all of them were fully completed in the heyday of a single administration. . . . And it is true that deftness and speed in working do not impart to the work an abiding weight of influence nor an exactness of beauty; whereas the time which is put out to loan in laboriously creating, pays a large and generous interest in the preservation of the creation. For this reason are the works of Pericles all the more to be wondered at; they were created in a short time for all time. Each of them, in its beauty, was even then and at once antique; but in the freshness of its vigor it is, even to the present day, recent and newly wrought. Such is the bloom of perpetual newness, as it were, upon these works of his, which makes them ever to look untouched by time, as though the unfaltering breath of an ageless spirit had been built into them.[1]

Of the buildings erected we mention the Odeum (Odeion), a hall built on the southern slope of the Acropolis for the performance of musical contests introduced by Pericles into the Panathenaic festival; and the Propylaea, a magnificent structure which served as the formal entrance to the Acropolis. Mnesicles was the builder, and its symmetrical plan, though never completely carried out, with its central portal, its porticoes, and its skillful combination of Doric and Ionic columns, shows that a Greek dared to deviate from the ordinary norms when occasion demanded. In its preliminary state it was completed in five years (437–432 B.C.). The considerable remains still excite the admiration of the visitor.[2]

But it was in the Parthenon and its sculptural decorations that Phidias found his great opportunity. The building itself

[1] Plutarch, *Pericles* (translation by Bernadotte Perrin; New York, 1910), Chap. 13, Sects. 1–3. Quoted by permission of Charles Scribner's Sons,

[2] Excellent photographs in W. Hege's *Die Akropolis*.

is ascribed to Ictinus and Callicrates as the joint architects. It is of the peripteral type; that is, it has a surrounding colonnade, with eight columns at each end and seventeen on each side (counting the corner columns twice). The shafts are about thirty-four feet high, with a lower diameter of six and one-fourth feet. The six columns of the front and rear porticoes are somewhat smaller than the outer columns. The measurements of the temple on the upper step of the stylobate are approximately one hundred by two hundred and twenty-five feet. The temple proper was divided into a larger chamber, the cella, which housed the statue of Athena, and a smaller rear chamber, which probably served as a treasury.

The sculptural decorations of the Parthenon, apart from the image of the goddess, consisted of the groups filling the two pediments; "the frieze," a sculptured band (some five hundred and twenty-five feet long), in low relief, which, beginning over the architrave resting on the columns of the front (eastern) portico, continued at the same level on both side walls of the building and ended in the same position over the architrave of the rear (western) portico; and, finally, the carving, in high relief, which adorned the ninety-two metopes. This wealth of decoration, surpassing that of any previous Doric temple, was without doubt planned and executed under the supervision of Phidias.

The colossal statue of Athena, rising (with its base) to a height of some forty feet, was acclaimed by antiquity as rivaling, in beauty of execution and grandeur of conception, the celebrated image of Zeus at Olympia, a work by the same master hand. Made over a wooden core, it was plated with gold and ivory, the ivory representing the flesh, the gold the remainder of the surface. Athena was represented as standing, her garment reaching to her feet but leaving the arms bare; her head was covered by a helmet, sumptuously adorned; on her right hand rested a Victory; her left hand held a spear; shield and traditional serpent were not lacking; and on her breast she wore the aegis, with the Medusa head.

But the real excellence of this statue, of which the very inadequate extant imitations can give us only a faint impression, was not in its precious materials, nor in the wealth of its detail, but in the ineffable majesty, serenity, and grandeur of the whole. To other Greeks it may have been an embodiment of the mind of Hellas itself, unruffled and at peace within; to the Athenian it was the image of his own city, wise, noble, and gracious.

The sculptural adornment of the pediments confronted the artists of Hellas with its own problems. Here was a triangular space to be filled in such a way that the position and grouping of the figures might seem natural, — not constrained by the inherent limitations of the enclosing frame. In what ways successive generations of sculptors attempted to solve this problem would make a long story. Leaving out of account the efforts dating from the archaic period, actual remains of three pediment compositions dedicated during the second period have enabled us to trace the progress that was made. The three temples in question are that of Aphaia at Aegina (about 500–480 B.C.), of Zeus at Olympia (about 460 B.C.), and the Parthenon. A composition had to be devised with a central figure or group, the remaining figures gradually diminishing in height to fill the sloping space on both sides. This is not the place to make comparisons; but it is universally acknowledged that in the composition which filled the eastern pediment of the Parthenon the genius of Phidias has completely triumphed over the inherent difficulties. The subject is the birth of Athena; the moment is the break of day. The central group, now entirely lost, contained the enthroned figure of Zeus, from whose head Athena had sprung full-armed; Athena, crowned by Victory; and Hermes. The momentous event is announced to the world by joyful messengers whose rushing garments add to the life and movement of the scene. Some of the divine beings to whom the message is addressed are represented as awakening to the summons; others are still reclining in profound slumber. This treatment of the theme furnished Phidias with an opportunity for filling the sloping sides of the pediment in a most natural manner, and the transition from the sleeping figures to those stirred into response has the added charm of being psychical as well as physical. The extreme ends are filled, at the left, by the spirited horses of the sun rising from the sea; at the right, by the soberer horses of the setting moon. Of this entire magnificent composition we have only the figures which Lord Elgin saved from destruction and transported to England. They are now housed in the British Museum, whose chief treasure they are. The most important central figures are irretrievably lost; but in the remains, even in their mutilated condition, we recognize the grandeur and sublimity of the art of Phidias.

The western pediment group portrayed the contest between Athena and Poseidon for Attica, and in dignity of conception and skill of execution was a worthy companion piece to the eastern group.

The continuous band of sculpture in low relief, now generally known as "the frieze of the Parthenon," was an unusual feature in a Doric temple; we may see in it an approach to the Ionic style. The subject of the frieze was the most impressive ceremony of the great civic festival of Athens, the Panathenaea, in which the whole people, represented by its fairest members, old and young alike, in stately procession rendered homage to the city goddess and dedicated an embroidered robe to their divine protectress. The whole contained some five hundred figures, including youths on horseback, graceful maidens, magistrates and priests, musicians and marshals of the procession; even the cattle and sheep led for sacrifice are not wanting; in the center, over the eastern entrance, the gods were assembled as spectators of the event. Never has an artist paid finer tribute to his people than Phidias has done in this noble work; for that it was his planning and his idea cannot be doubted. It was an idealized picture of a society devoted to individual freedom and yet aware of a common purpose. Thus it may serve as a commentary on the funeral oration of Pericles as well as on Plato's ideal commonwealth — a symbol of the civic spirit of Periclean Athens. The incredible skill of the artists who wrought it may be illustrated by the fact that on a relief which seldom exceeds two inches in depth as many as five horsemen riding abreast are represented in most lifelike fashion, with a total absence of confusion. However, it is rather the nobility and the unruffled serenity of the whole which gives it its unique place in the annals of art; all the more amazing is the fact that it is never so much as mentioned in extant classical literature.

Of the sculptured metopes it is not necessary to speak in detail. The subjects, so far as we can tell, were of the traditional kind, — combats of centaurs and Lapiths, and the like.

We have given much space to the Parthenon in our rapid survey of Hellenic art and architecture of the second period. The reader may get the totally erroneous impression that this is the only surviving monument deserving of his attention. The best-preserved of all Greek temples, the so-called Theseum at Athens, has not been so much as mentioned; nor has any reference been made to the numerous civic shrines, precursors and rivals of the Parthenon, erected elsewhere in Hellas. Indeed, the development of Doric architecture can best be traced in the impressive remains in Sicily and southern Italy. Yet it may justly be affirmed that in the Parthenon alone may we find the very epitome of Hellenism and that more can be learned from a thorough examination of this single building concerning the ideals governing Greek society at its best than from a hasty survey of all the remaining monuments of Greece. It has been called the noblest embodiment of reason itself; it bears abundant testimony to that will to perfection so characteristic of Hellenic art; but it is also an eloquent witness to the social ideals of the Hellenic polis, for it is a civic monument, in name dedicated to a goddess, in reality to the city and to the men who made it.

In the last analysis the Parthenon, like the *Prometheus* of Aeschylus, is the tribute of a great artist to the genius of man. And if Phidias had been in search of a proper motto for the building he might have found it in that immortal line of Sophocles' *Antigone*, a play which was performed for the first time while the Parthenon was being built:

POLLA TA DEINA, KOUDEN ANTHROPOU DEINOTERON PELEI.

Many are the wonderful things, and nothing is more wonderful than man.

The Third Period

The Parthenon had hardly been finished when the Hellenic World War broke out. There is no need to list anew the spiritual aftereffects of this war. We are prepared to look for a corresponding change in the field of art; but here the transformation proceeded at a slower rate and was more gradual than in the domain of letters, where it appeared with startling suddenness in the works of Euripides, Thucydides, and Aristophanes. Both architecture and sculpture were carried along for a time by the tremendous impetus imparted by the Periclean Age. The remaining decades of the fifth century saw the completion of two further additions of enduring value which the Athenians built on the Acropolis: the, Erechtheum and the little temple of Athena Victory (known also as Wingless Victory).[1] Both are in the Ionic style; indeed, the Erechtheum is the most perfect specimen of the order that has survived. Its irregular plan, due to traditional factors, and its caryatid porch put it in a class by itself. Of the other temple, it is perhaps the celebrated figure of Victory adjusting her sandal — part of the sculptured balustrade — which calls for special mention, not only for its intrinsic loveliness but also because of the treatment of the drapery, which now becomes transparent. This strikes a new note in the history of sculp-

[1] For photographs see W. Hege, *Die Akropolis*.

ture; the contemporary Victory of Paeonius (at Olympia) exhibits the same feature in her wind-swept garments.

Not until the fourth century were the full effects of the suicidal conflicts between the city-states reflected in art and architecture. The decay in civic spirit is best illustrated by the almost complete cessation in temple-building. The Doric temple had been the chief monument of the political and social ideals of what now was definitely the past. Its majestic grandeur manifestly could not express the restless spirit of that distracted age; and the resources of the city-states, although they were assuredly no less than in the preceding century, were now used to meet new demands. It is a most significant fact that the outstanding architectural achievement of this era was the sepulchral monument erected by Queen Artemisia to her husband Mausolus in Caria (Asia Minor). The greatest artists of Hellas lavished their efforts on the magnificent tomb of a half-Hellenized Asiatic prince! It was accounted one of the Seven Wonders of the World.

In the absence of all actual evidence there is not much to say of the art of painting. But even such meager information as we possess reveals the change which the art has undergone. We are told that the painters of the fourth century excelled in rendering *pathos* rather than *ethos*, which means that the idealization of character gave way to the portrayal of emotion and sentiment. This was directly in line with the prevailing trend in contemporary sculpture. As for the rest, it may be regarded as certain that the painters of this age finally succeeded in crossing the boundary line which divides colored drawings from true painting.

Sculpture, however, supplies us with the best evidence of the changing times. Here two great masters illustrate the predominant moods of the age and admirably complement one another. They are Praxiteles and Scopas. Both reflect the individualism of the era, its greater depth and range of feeling; but Praxiteles illustrates its indolence, love of pleasure, and gentle cynicism, whereas Scopas reveals its darker aspects, its distraction and despair. Both are genuinely Hellenic; their art remains ideal; it still obeys the Hellenic law of sobriety and restraint. But the idealism is no longer informed by the ethos of the fifth century; it is sheer straining after beauty. This new art found no delight in heroic grandeur but descended to a purely human level and to human interests. Man is still the center of interest, but it is not man in the likeness of God; the reverse obtains: gods now assume the likeness of men. We have observed a similar transformation in the drama of Euripides.

A list of the works of Praxiteles and his followers will prove an illuminating commentary on the character of this art. We mention only these: a youthful Hermes, playing with the infant Dionysus; a slender Apollo, spearing a lizard; a lovely Eros; a nude Aphrodite; an indolent Satyr; a girlish Artemis, fastening her dress. This was the kind of statuary with which in a later day the Roman noble filled his villa and his park; of no other ancient work have so many copies come down to us as of the Praxitelean Satyr (the "Marble Faun"). And yet no other artist's work was so difficult to copy as that of Praxiteles. We have an original from his hand. The recovery of the Hermes, one of his minor works, from the ruins of Olympia, has brought a veritable revelation: it has shown how far even the best of Roman copies are removed from the perfection of the original; the bloom on the marble body of the god, the subtlety of the modeling, the dreamy expression of the face, may give us an inkling of what Praxiteles achieved in his masterpieces, such as the Eros and the Satyr.

In the all but complete disappearance of the remains of Scopas' art we have suffered a grievous loss. But there is monumental and literary evidence to show that the anguish of the age found its interpreter in him. Scopas was the sculptor of pathos par excellence; with him the last vestiges of the godlike calm of another era disappear; violent emotion is rendered in agitated pose and anguished features.

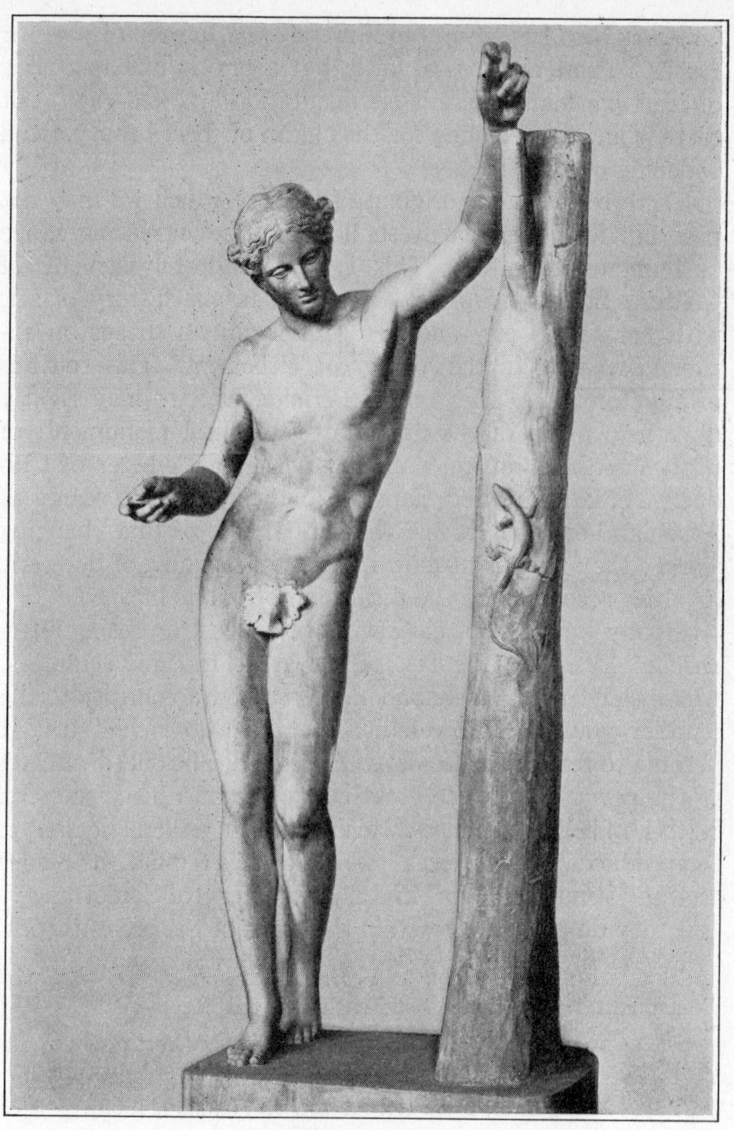

Apollo Sauroctonus

After Praxiteles

Thus these two sculptors illustrate the temper of postwar Hellas. There is a loss of faith, but a gain in understanding of man *qua* man; there is less exaltation and less vigor, but there is an added feeling for the charm of sheer beauty and a widening of its appeal.

There is one other original of the age which we may not pass by, for it throws fresh light on the increasing range of human sympathies. This is the wonderful Demeter of Cnidus. She, the first *mater dolorosa* in the history of art, with her gentle pity and her gentle sadness strikes an entirely new note in the history of Hellenism. This spirit is totally foreign to the Age of Pericles, but we may rightly discern in many of the numerous sepulchral monuments of postwar Athens an inner affinity with the Demeter of Cnidus. These sculptured slabs, with their affecting scenes of Athenian home life, reveal the gentler side of that changing world; they may even show us that a deepening of domestic loyalties accompanied the disillusion of public life.

Finally we may not close without at least a passing reference to Lysippus, the last of the great Hellenic sculptors, whose slender athletes stand in so marked a contrast to the sturdier youths of Polycletus. But he whose chief task it became to render the features of Alexander belonged already to the new world of the great conqueror and his successors. With him began the chaos which we term Hellenistic art. It too produced masterpieces; we need only remind the reader of the "Venus of Milo" and the "Victory of Samothrace." But they do not belong within the scope of the present work.

SUGGESTIONS FOR READING. F. B. TARBELL, *History of Greek Art* (Macmillan, 1927). A small and useful handbook.

GISELA M. A. RICHTER, *The Sculpture and Sculptors of the Greeks* (Yale, 1930). The best account in English; very finely illustrated.

ALLAN MARQUAND, *Greek Architecture* (Macmillan, 1909).

Consult also ALFRED M. BROOKS, *Architecture* (in series Our Debt to Greece and Rome, Marshall Jones Co., 1924), Chap. I. Unfortunately the book has no illustrations.

Demeter, from Cnidus

For a brief introductory essay on Greek architecture, that of SIR REGINALD BLOOMFIELD in *The Legacy of Greece* (ed. R. W. Livingstone, Oxford, 1922) is unsurpassed.

A. DERIDDER and W. DEONNA, *Art in Greece* (Knopf, n.d.). A very illuminating book.

CHARLES DUGAS, *Greek Pottery* (Black, 1926). The best introduction to the subject for the lay reader.

On Athens see E. A. GARDNER, *Ancient Athens* (Macmillan, 1902), and CHARLES H. WELLER, *Athens and its Monuments* (Macmillan, 1913).

On Olympia, E. N. GARDINER, *Olympia* (Oxford, 1925).

On Delphi, F. POULSEN, *Delphi* (Gyldendal, 1920).

CHAPTER XII

SCIENCE AND PHILOSOPHY

Introductory

THE inclusion of two such different things as science and philosophy in the same chapter may well surprise the reader of today; for he is accustomed to think of science as dealing with a well-defined subject matter, — as specialized knowledge, admitting of practical application to the actual problems of life, — whereas philosophy appears to him as something nebulous and remote and, worse still, of very little use. In an age like ours, when the application of scientific discovery to practical ends has had such tremendous consequences in transforming the material conditions of life, it may seem little short of blasphemy to mention science and philosophy in the same breath!

And yet the two are not so far apart in aim and method as may appear at first sight. Both aim at the ascertainment of truth; both begin with the careful observation of pertinent facts and strive to draw the correct inference from the facts observed; both rely on the uniformity of nature, taking it for granted that the relation between cause and effect is constant and invariable. The only difference between them lies in the scope of their inquiries, science reserving for itself only well-defined fields of investigation, while philosophy claims the whole as its domain. The aims of science, then, are more modest: it deals only with proximate causes; it is satisfied with the immediate explanation, with relative truth. Philosophy is in search of an ultimate explanation, the absolute truth. Now it may be that the attempt to wrest a final explanation from the multiplicity of phenomena the universe presents is doomed to failure. But should we, then, not make the attempt at all? If there be no other result, we may, at least, have clarified the problem to ourselves and, in seeking a solution for the "riddle of the universe," have learned the limits set to human understanding.

Furthermore, with regard to this association of science and philosophy, we are dealing here with Hellenic philosophy and Hellenic science; and the Hellenes, the pioneers in the field, made no distinction between them. They had only one word which covered both, *philosophia.* Their earliest philosophers were also their earliest scientists. Thales, usually regarded as the first of their philosophers, was one of the great mathematicians and astronomers of his time; his pupil Anaximander made maps and constructed a sundial. If the Greeks had been called upon to make any distinction, there is no question what their judgment would have been concerning the mutual relationship between the two: they would have subordinated the lesser task to the greater and reduced science to the rank of the servant of philosophy. For with their well-known desire for clarity of understanding, they would have asked how we should expect to understand the part without comprehending the whole; and once we granted them that the sciences serve only as means to an ulterior end, they would have insisted that the study of the end ought to take precedence over the preoccupation with the means. Herein their attitude was the reverse of ours; for if we have failed to hold the true balance, it is due to our preoccupation with the particular to the neglect of the general. With the Greeks, born theorizers that they were, the theory accounting for the facts interested and delighted them more than the facts themselves; their natural propensity for abstract thought led them to force the phenomena they observed into an all-embracing scheme which should satisfy their reason. It is the old story over again — the old striving for form and design, for that rational order in which they discovered beauty as well.

Once more Ionia took the lead. Miletus, which saw the birth of philosophy, was the wealthiest and most enterprising of the Ionian towns. Here dwelt the spirit of adventure which had sent out group after group of citizens to found new homes on the Hellespont and on the shores of the Black Sea; and after a century of bold advance to the fringes of their terrestrial world they set forth no less boldly to explore the unplumbed depths of the universe. In their search after the unknown they were hampered neither by a hierarchy of priests nor by sacred book or religious dogma.

It is a significant fact that the greatest achievements of Greek philosophy belong to the Hellenic period, while the greatest advance in the sciences belongs to the Hellenistic world. The first era is marked by the joy of discovery and creation; the second by the systematic garnering of the fruits and the laborious cultivation of the fields of knowledge. Plato marks the end of the Hellenic period; Aristotle opens the Hellenistic Age. Even so, Greek genius has played a greater part in the history of philosophy than in the history of science. The reason is not far to seek: the phenomenal advance of the modern world in science has been made possible by the more refined tools which human ingenuity has placed at its disposal. What progress in biology was possible without the microscope; in astronomy, without the telescope? However, this does not tell the whole story. There is no question that the Greek preoccupation with man, — and was he not the discoverer of man? — just as it limited his scope in art, also restricted his activity in the field of science. Nature per se left him indifferent; hence we find that of the entire field of science, at least in the Hellenic era, his interest was confined to mathematics (and the related astronomy) and medicine, — the first because of its abstract mode of reasoning, the second because of its manifest importance in the life of man. We shall begin with an inquiry into the history of Greek mathematics and medicine.

Mathematics and Medicine

In mathematics the Greeks began as borrowers. Egypt taught them their first lessons in the science of "land-measuring" (for that is what geometry means). But the science which in Egypt had sprung from practical needs was emancipated in Hellas, and cultivated for its own sake. As we saw above, Thales of Miletus (*c.* 600 B.C.), the first of the philosophers, was also a good mathematician; and from Thales on, the interest in geometry never waned. The works of Plato betray no little acquaintance with that branch of mathematics, which he never grows weary of praising as an indispensable element in mental training. The extant works on mathematics, however, date from after Alexander's conquest of the East, and belong, accordingly, to the history of the Hellenistic world. It is sufficient to mention Euclid, whose *Elements* remained the textbook on geometry for two millenniums.

It is the same with astronomy. The Greeks profited from the observations and records made by Egyptians and Babylonians, but the emancipation of the science is once more the achievement of Hellas. They severed it from astrology, even though they did not succeed in entirely destroying this pernicious delusion, which continues to vex the minds of the ignorant to this day. Again, Thales is reported to have been deeply interested in astronomy and to have predicted the eclipse of 585 B.C. After him many of the Greek philosophers made valuable contributions to the solution of astronomical problems. But the really great achievements in the field were made by the scholars of Alexandria, the city which the illustrious conqueror had founded in Egypt and where his successors, the Ptolemies, established a new center for research in the famed Museum.

Concerning medicine a different story will have to be told. In this field the Hellenic genius scored one of its greatest triumphs. Recognition for the science had to be won against

Hippocrates

almost insuperable odds. The new school of medicine was called upon to introduce the rule of reason in a field which from time immemorial had been the domain of spell and magic. We recall the account of the plague with which Homer opens the Iliad. Who is called upon to deliver the Achaean armament from its visitation? Calchas, the prophet and seer, who reveals that Apollo's anger has caused the affliction. When Apollo has been appeased and the army has been ceremonially cleansed, a cure is effected. Even though Homer was not unacquainted with the skill of the physician, the call made upon Calchas is typical of the attitude of early man toward bodily ills. Either a deity has been offended, or an evil demon vexes him, or perchance he is under a spell cast upon him by his enemy; and the cure corresponds to his conception of the cause. A sacrifice, a pilgrimage to a sacred shrine, a magical ceremony, the wearing of an amulet — such were the common means with which Egyptian, Babylonian (his demonology was the most elaborate of all), and Greek alike fought the ravages of disease. Among the Hellenic gods it was Apollo to whom fell the chief role as healer; eventually he was eclipsed by Asclepius (Aesculapius). Homer knows of Asclepius only as a Thracian prince skilled in the art of healing. Greek legend tells how, upon the entreaty of Artemis, he restored Hippolytus to life and was slain by Zeus for his interference with the order of nature. How and where his apotheosis came about we can no longer trace; but in historic times he was worshiped as a god, and to him, as the great physician, numerous shrines arose all over Hellas, the most famous of which was at Epidaurus, in the northeastern Peloponnesus. These cult centers in many cases were transformed into regular health resorts, where the patient could find the kind of mental relief and diversion associated with similar centers in the modern world. There may have been a medicinal spring, as at present-day Wiesbaden; or it may have been the healthful and beautiful location of the place that contributed to the cure. In addition to these natural and legitimate means for combating disease, magic and religion were called upon to do their share. One of the commonest practices was that of "incubation": the patient laid himself to sleep within the sacred enclosure, praying for a nocturnal dream or vision in which the deity should reveal to him the manner of his cure. Needless to say, the desired revelation seldom failed to come, and many miraculous cures effected by the god are attested by the inscriptions and votive objects that have come down to us.

It was, then, in direct and open challenge to tradition that the founders of the science of medicine opened their campaign for a more rational view of the matter. It goes without saying that their victory was at best but partial; the old ways continued to exist beside the new. But this cannot detract from the debt which humanity owes to these pioneers. The movement had its beginning in certain medical centers, of which that in Cos enjoyed perhaps the greatest fame. We can trace the Coan school back into the sixth century. But it was not until the following century that there appeared a man of such marked originality of mind and such commanding genius that afterages have identified his name with the science itself.

Hippocrates of Cos was born *c.* 460 B.C. Some sixty works, all dating from the fifth and fourth centuries B.C. and attributed to his authorship, are extant. Only a few of these bear the imprint of the master himself; the rest were composed under the influence of his teaching. He seems to have been the first to grasp and formulate the fundamental principles of medicine. They are essentially the same as those of modern science, and may be summarized as follows: All disease is due to natural causes (even the "sacred" disease, epilepsy, was not to be explained as a demoniac seizure and was not to be held more sacred than any other disease). Nature is uniform, the same causes producing the same effects. If, therefore, the problem of disease is to be attacked with any hope of success, a careful observation of the symptoms and the gradual accumulation of such records is a first and indispensable condition. On the basis of these records classification under certain types may begin. Thus we may hope to arrive at a correct diagnosis at an early stage of the disease, and we may venture upon a prognosis, a forecast as to its probable course. However, in trying to effect a cure we cannot do more than assist nature. Hippocrates called himself a "servant of nature." He maintained a remarkably high ethical standard for the new profession; the "Hippocratic oath" is still sworn to by the graduates of many modern medical schools.

Hippocrates and his followers used both surgery and drugs in their attendance upon the sick. In addition to the study of pathological cases, they brought normal phenomena as well under their observation, and in consequence came to rely on such simple prescriptions as suitable diet, fresh air, and exercise for curing as well as preventing disease; "hygiene" also is a Greek word. It was inevitable that in their ignorance of anatomy and physiology (even the circulation of the blood was not guessed at before Alexandrian times) they should have made innumerable mistakes. But in formulating for medicine a program to emancipate it from religion and magic, they rendered an invaluable service to humanity.

The new science, however, soon found itself compelled to fight not only its natural foes but even its avowed friends. The new philosophy threatened for a time to make havoc of the simple, straightforward program; for the philosophers also were scientists. Empedocles, for instance, was philosopher, prophet, and physician all rolled into one. These philosophers, in whose fertile brains theories, and plausible arguments to defend them, would arise with alarming readiness, were prone to invade the field of medicine, and preferred the short cut of logical demonstration upon *a priori* assumption to the laborious methods of observation and deduction employed by the physicians. It was by way of warning against this very real danger to his profession that one of these physicians wrote:

> One must have regard to reasoned experience rather than to plausible argument. . . . I approve of reasoning if it takes observed fact as its point of departure and methodically draws its conclusions from the phenomena; . . . if it [reasoning] does not start with what is certain, but with specious and fictitious theory, it often leads to a grievous and painful situation . . . I think the entire art [of medicine] has been perfected by observing the outcome of every condition and bringing the observation of it into a system.[1]

This protest may serve as an indication of the truly scientific ideals of Hellenic and, specifically, of Hippocratic medicine. The founder of that school justly deserves to be ranked with the primary geniuses of Hellas.[2]

Philosophy

In turning to the realm of philosophy we cannot help observing a notable difference in atmosphere. Gathering data for the explanation of all the facts of existence was a staggering task. Yet the very nature and character of the universe as revealed to the senses seems to proclaim its amenability to reason. Concealed below the surface of the phenomena of sense the Greek divined a rational order; any other supposition was repugnant to his mind. Why should the problem not be made to yield to the power of sheer thought without the preliminaries of detailed investigations? And so the Ionian thinkers put on their seven-league boots and, marching majestically through the unexplored territories of the experimental sciences, arrived at their stupendous conclusions. We may blame them for attempting metaphysics before they had laid even the foundation for physics, and for excogitating the rationale of a universe of which they *knew* so little; but the fact remains that their brilliant guesses at truth have partly anticipated the results later gained at the

[1] Quoted from the Hippocratic *Precepts* by W. A. Heidel, in *The Heroic Age of Science* (the Carnegie Institution of Washington, 1933).

[2] On Greek science see *The Legacy of Greece* (ed. by R. W. Livingstone; Oxford, 1922), pp. 97–248.

cost of much hard work. Even their mistakes (and they are legion) have helped to clarify the problem. In fact, they have largely furnished us with the ideas and concepts with which we still operate. Finally, they led the way in awakening the world to a consciousness of the problem that has faced and ever will face man.

The attention of the reader has been called to certain conditions obtaining in sixth-century Hellas and, above all, in Ionia which favored the growth of speculative thought. But it must not be imagined that the path of these pioneers was entirely smooth and free from obstructions. True, Greek religion was burdened with neither sacred dogma nor priestly tyranny. But Greek religion itself was the product of a mode of thinking, a habit of mind, so characteristically Hellenic that we cannot but marvel that these early thinkers on the whole succeeded so well in freeing themselves from this bias. As we saw in another chapter, this mental habit, usually called "mythological," had led the Greeks to project human personality and human attributes into the world of nature. The raging sea was an angered Poseidon, the calm that followed it a placid god, the sun a heavenly charioteer, the sky above them a watchful Zeus, the winter a desolate Demeter mourning for her daughter, the spring the return of Persephone; and so on. This was the world of their imagination, in which they dwelt with wonder and awe and yet at ease; for it was not an indifferent universe nor a senseless mechanism but a world of human gods who could be prevailed upon by prayer and gift. Accordingly, if the philosophers of Hellas hoped to lure the Greeks away from the beauty and glory of this vision into their philosophical universe of abstract reality, their expectations were foredoomed to disappointment. Indeed, Hellenic religion went very much its own way and, as we have seen, was more deeply affected by its political entanglements than by the onslaughts of philosophy. But it was, on the part of these thinkers themselves, no small achievement to have shaken off the mental inertia so natural to man, to have freed their minds from that inveterate mythological mode of thinking and to have grappled resolutely with the problem of life and nature.

Here we might do well, for the sake of clarity, to outline briefly the history of Greek philosophy. It has been divided into three periods. The first of these extends from 600 B.C. until 430 B.C., when the activity of Socrates opens a new era. This stage of Greek thought is therefore called that of the Pre-Socratics. The whole era coincides with the last century of our first period and with the whole of our second period. The second stage comprises the careers of Socrates, Plato, and Aristotle, and closes with the death of the latter in 322 B.C. It corresponds to our third period. The Post-Aristotelians form the last group of Greek philosophers; belonging to the Hellenistic Age and the Graeco-Roman era, they are outside the limits of this book. The great creative work of Hellenic philosophy belongs to the first two chapters of its history; indeed, the Hellenic period may be regarded as having stopped with Plato. Aristotle, in this view, opens the Hellenistic Age; he, the tutor of Alexander, led the way in the systematic consolidation of the gains made so far, and in mapping out the fields of science and philosophy to be explored by his pupils and those who came after him. In the present survey we shall, accordingly, confine ourselves to the Pre-Socratics, Socrates, and Plato, without in any way belittling the genius of Aristotle, whose thought was destined to dominate the Western world for many centuries.

The pre-Socratic era, then, covers all the sixth century B.C., and the fifth down to the beginning of the Hellenic World War. For the first fifty years Ionia proper was its home; after Cyrus' conquest of Ionia, half a century later to be followed by the destruction of Miletus, the philosophical speculations of the Ionians were carried on chiefly in other parts of the Greek world, where Hellenic enterprise had founded new homes. Thus Croton, an Achaean colony, became the home of Pythagoras and his followers; Elea, in southern Italy, sheltered the refugees from Phocaea, among whom Parmenides was to carry speculative philosophy to new heights; the Teans founded Abdera, where in the course of time Democritus was to propound the atomic doctrine. Xenophanes hailed from Colophon and found a home in the same southern Italy; and Anaxagoras, who migrated to Athens upon the invitation of Pericles and Aspasia, was a native of Clazomenae. The credit of having broached the subject of philosophy therefore belongs to the Ionian branch of the Hellenic race.

But it is not only racial kinship that unites these first philosophers; there is, in spite of individual differences, a decided similarity in aim and outlook. They all tried to solve the problem of being, of existence; and the various solutions were all of the mechanistic type, that is, they thought of nature as a process complete in itself, independent of any outside control or interference, and without design or end. Were they, then, materialists? We have no right to call them thus because — and this is another characteristic they all share — they made no distinction between "mind" and "matter"; their primeval stuff was as much mental as material. The Pre-Socratics, then, unite in giving a purely mechanistic explanation of the universe which excludes the theory of design. Pressed for an answer to the question Why? they would reply, in one form or another, *Ananke* (necessity). Not *why* things are but *how* was their main concern. Even Anaxagoras, who did make a distinction between mind and matter, expressly denied purpose to his primeval mind-stuff and gave it credit only as the prime mover of the universal machine.

Meanwhile we are wondering why Athens figures, thus far, so little in the story of philosophy. During the fifth century that city was the center of Hellenic culture, — the school of Hellas, as Pericles had called it. Indeed, it is at first not a little puzzling to find Athens remaining so indifferent to the philosophical ferment prevailing elsewhere. Yet upon re-

by which the apeiron had passed into the finite was the conflict between opposites, as hot and cold, dry and moist. So far as we know (for none of the works of the Pre-Socratics have come down to us; we possess only mere scraps of that great literature), the details of the stupendous scheme he developed are somewhat fantastic. But the essence of the theory resolves itself into the belief that the visible world has its roots in an indestructible, everlasting Something, which, remaining the same, combines into the definite but perishable forms of the world perceived by the senses. In one leap Anaximander had arrived at the conception of nature as a complete, self-sufficient process. He tried to trace also the history of man, and, anticipating the verdict of a more scientific age, pointed out that man, with his prolonged period of helpless infancy, could not have survived the conditions surrounding him in a primeval world. Hence he asserted man's descent from another animal species; he was "like a fish in the beginning." One more title Anaximander has to immortality: he wrote a book *On Nature*, in which he set forth his doctrine; it was the first work in Greek prose of which we have knowledge.

Anaximander had raised a tremendous problem. If, as he had affirmed, the universe remains the same in substance, how can we maintain the reality of the forms which it assumes? If this variety of form is real, how can we hold to the belief that Being remains unchanged? We may regard the universe in two aspects, either as static or as dynamic; we may view it as substance or as a process, as matter or as energy, or again, as the Greeks would say, as Being or as Becoming. Heraclitus of Ephesus (born *c.* 535 B.C.) shared the view of Anaximander that nature is one and everlasting, but he found its essence in change, in Becoming rather than in Being. But his philosophic vocabulary was limited; he had at his disposal neither "dynamic" nor "energy," words which *we* have borrowed from later Greek philosophy. And so he fixed on Fire as expressing the essence of nature as a process and made Fire the world substance as well. He pointed out that nothing *is*, — that everything changes, and changes constantly. Transition seems the dominant characteristic of the world: "You cannot step into the same river twice." On this unceasing flux of things he bids us fix our attention: *Panta rhei* (All things are flowing). Even opposites fade into one another; for the universe consists of action and reaction, day waning into night, and night waxing into day. "All things have their birth in strife"; "out of discord comes the fairest harmony"; and "war is the father of all." But this everlasting warfare is, after all, an order. The process of transformation is itself the Logos (word-thought) of the universe; that is, it is the law of its being; it is the principle which makes it intelligible to the reason of man. That he called it the Logos rather than the law of nature was because, to the Hellenic mind, law implies a lawgiver, an authority over and above that upon which it exercises its dominion. He calls this Logos divine; logically, therefore, his system is pantheistic, implying, as it does, that God is all and in all. There is no evidence, however, that he himself drew this conclusion from his doctrine. This Logos he further identified with Justice, — not with the justice obtaining in human relationships, which is, after all, relative, but with the absolute justice inherent in the natural order itself. Nature then is one, in virtue of its Logos. Nevertheless, its essence is Becoming rather than Being; its dynamic aspect is its dominant characteristic.

Heraclitus of Ephesus had challenged the world to point to anything that really *is*. Parmenides, of far-away Elea, countered by defying him to find anything that *is not*. "Do not trust your senses," he said in effect, "for they are notoriously misleading. Trust rather your reason. The senses leave us with the impression of an ever-changing world; but if only you will think it out to the bitter end you will discover your world of sense perceptions to be one of illusion rather than one of reality." And then he returned to the charge. Can we conceive of *nothing* as *being*? Can that which is not, be said to have existence? But if nonbeing is unthinkable and nonexistent, the only admissible corollary is that Being, and Being alone, *is*. This looks like a harmless enough proposition; but now see what amazing conclusions Parmenides drew from it. Holding on to his fundamental *Being* which *is*, he abolishes motion, time, and change, and banishes the whole kaleidoscopic drama of the universe to the limbo of Illusion. For, he said, how could Being move? What would it move into — into a vacuum? But that would be nonbeing, which does not exist. It could only move into itself, but that is not motion. Could Being change? What conceivable thing could it change into? Could it cease to be, for any time, and reappear as something else? But there is nothing outside of Being. Could it perish? It would be nonbeing then, which we admitted has no standing in our court. Is it divisible? But if we divide Being, what could hold it apart except that same nonexistent nonbeing? Could Being exist at one time and not at another? The question answers itself. Hence the inescapable conclusion to which we are driven, said Parmenides, is that motion and change, death and decay, time itself, are not real in so far as they can affect Being; and Being itself he conceived of as a perfect sphere, timeless, unchanging, complete in itself and final. Thus at one stroke he sundered the world into two halves, the world of Real Being and the world of Illusion; and, harking back to Hesiod's way, he wrote a poem in which he set forth the "Way of Truth," dealing with Being itself, and another poem, "The Way of Opinion," of which the illusory world of our senses was the theme.

The great paradox of Parmenides was not meant as a mere *jeu d'esprit*, and his influence remains to this day; for he raised the question how the world of observed facts is to be reconciled with the postulates of reason. He is the father of rationalism, the attempt to explain reality by relying not on the evidence of our senses but on the process of rigorous thought; and if reason flies in the face of facts, so much the worse for the latter!

Is it to be wondered at that Gorgias, accepting the tenets of Parmenides, maintained that "nothing is," by which he meant that nothing comes within the range of human observation which can be said to have any more than *relative* existence? What, indeed, can man hope to discover concerning *objective* reality? For had not Parmenides effectively closed the door upon all who were seeking a solution of the problem of reality?

But the door would not stay shut. The restless Hellenic search for the truth, beating in vain against the inexorable logic of Parmenides, would not be denied in the end. Common sense protested against so monstrous a verdict. To be sure, the senses are often misleading and may bear watching; but can they be altogether so deceptive as the logic of Parmenides held? The first object of attack was that terrific incubus of Absolute Being which the great rationalist had fashioned, — that solid yet transparent Sphere. It was broken up into the "Four Elements" of earth, water, air, and fire — probably a revival of a popular concept — or into small particles, all partaking of the nature of the whole, but each with one quality predominating over another — the *homoiomere* of Anaxagoras (as we saw above, the same philosopher introduced mind as the prime mover of the particles). But it was reserved for Leucippus and Democritus to shatter Parmenides' Sphere into infinitesimal bits.

Of Leucippus we know next to nothing; but Democritus of Abdera (on the coast of Thrace) is a real figure of flesh and blood. Born probably some time between 470 and 460 B.C., he seems to have enjoyed independent means enabling him to lead the life of a student, traveler, and writer. He was a voluminous author, and a good one at that; there is no greater loss in the history of Greek philosophy than the all but complete disappearance of his works. He lived to be at least ninety years old, a genial person on whom the after-world bestowed the title of the "Laughing Philosopher," in contrast to the haughty and scornful Heraclitus, who was called the "Weeping Philosopher."

Leucippus and Democritus agreed with Parmenides that the phenomenal world is not Real Being; but they would not simply dismiss it as so much false show. Again, they agreed with him that Being is indestructible and unchangeable; but their common sense demanded that this imperishable world-stuff should somehow account for the actual phenomena of the senses. So they broke up Being into atoms, indivisible particles of Being; and to give them room to move in they posited a void, in defiance of the logic of Parmenides. The universe, then, is an immense vacuum in which the atoms move and, jostling one another, clustering, and falling apart again, give rise to the variety of phenomena presented to our senses. For these atoms are not all of one size; they vary in shape and weight, and the variations cause them to combine in different forms. But variations which we perceive in quality must be reducible to quantitative terms; for the atoms are absolutely homogeneous, — they are the very stuff and substance behind the colorful and variegated appearance of the world as revealed to the senses. What causes these atoms to spin about in the great void? Democritus will not allow an outside agent to enter the mechanism of his universe: atoms are caused to fall by their own weight, and their own inequalities must account for their mutual clashing and rebounding. Yet it is not chaos but Necessity which rules their course; whatever occurs is ordained by Necessity. Once more it is a unifying principle which holds the world together and renders it intelligible; for by Necessity Democritus meant the mechanical and unvarying sequence of cause and effect. Thus the superb imagination and the penetrating mind of Democritus conjures up before our eyes the vision of a universe forever changing and yet forever remaining the same; of restless atoms combining into patterns innumerable and breaking up again; of new forms of life arising from the universal welter and whirl, only to perish again in the course of time. In all this, Democritus perceived the rule of law. "Nothing happens at random." Herein lay the hope he held out to man that by patient inquiry he might reach a fuller understanding of nature's processes. "Fall to, then," he says in effect to the scientist; "track the atoms to their lairs, chart their courses, and presently we shall lift a corner of the veil that hides the face of nature."

It is a pity that the implications of this philosophy were not acted upon for a long time. Hellenic speculations were turned into another direction; and while Plato's pre-eminence in the field of thought is undisputed, his philosophy proved a blight upon purely scientific endeavor. It may be argued, however, that the hour of science had not yet struck; many of the problems which the pioneers had tackled were beyond their competence. There was the question of knowledge itself. Democritus, who denied existence to anything but atoms, held that the mind also was made up of those indivisible particles of eternal matter, and he propounded a fanciful theory to account for the possibility of knowledge at all: somehow the mental atoms are allowed to come into direct contact with the atoms abroad, beyond the disturbing interference of the senses! How, indeed, could he be aware of the true character of the problem involved, living, as he did, in an age which had not yet learned to distinguish between conscious life and the purely material?

Nevertheless, these early philosophers had not labored in vain. In pressing for an answer they had made the world aware of the question; their brilliant suggestions furnished their own contemporaries with a wealth of ideas on which we still may draw.

Finally, before leaving the Pre-Socratics, let it be understood that we have only placed a few signposts along the highways of a vast expanse of territory. We have not explored the byways. Had we done so, we should have come upon many an arresting personality and many an uncharted field. There is, for instance, Pythagoras, who attempted to find in numerical and geometric relationships the key for apprehending the nature of Being, and who strangely combined this truly Hellenic idea with a mystical view of life not without its counterpart in Hellenic religion (which harbored more than one heterodoxy), but more akin to Eastern mysticism than to the clear-eyed vision of Hellas. And if we have passed by such names as Xenophanes and Empedocles, it is not because they do not belong to an account of Hellenic culture but because considerations of space forbid.

SUGGESTIONS FOR READING. The beginner will find a brief and clear account of the Pre-Socratics in A. K. ROGERS, *A Student's History of Philosophy* (Macmillan, 1928).

For a further venture into the field he can do no better than read the chapter on Heraclitus in B. A. G. FULLER'S *History of Greek Philosophy* (Holt, 1923), Vol. I, or consult J. M. WARBEKE'S *The Searching Mind of Greece* (Crofts, 1930).

The Third Period

SOCRATES

The quest for an abiding reality behind the changing world of phenomena had led to no definite results; the disagreements of the philosophers themselves seemed to prove the bankruptcy of the entire enterprise. There appeared a new class of men who also aimed at enlightenment, but at enlightenment of a totally different character, — one that suited the tastes of their contemporaries more than the profitless speculations of the nature philosophers. We have spoken of the Sophists in a different context; they belong rather to the history of Greek education and Greek rhetoric than to any account of Greek philosophy. For the wisdom of these itinerant teachers was of a practical kind; and in so far as they denied any interest in truth for its own sake, their activities fall outside our present field. Yet if we ignored them, our version of Socrates' work would be incomplete; for in a way they were his fellow workers, and the thoughtless multitude could see in Socrates only another Sophist. Let us therefore briefly recall their aims and methods. They strove to furnish instruction in the many new departments of knowledge which the enlarged horizon of the age had opened up; but it was a learning applicable and useful to life itself. Naturally they found a more ready hearing than the philosophers. If we may trust our amusing friend Strepsiades, the hero of Aristophanes' *Clouds*, the general impression seems to have been that a course of instruction under these professors of the new wisdom would place in the hands of the disciple a tremendous weapon with which he could tackle all the problems of life, including that of confuting his creditors.

Their one great merit, however, was that they raised a new problem: can the art of life itself be taught? They answered with an emphatic affirmative. But in the same breath they denied that there existed any discoverable objective standards for measuring moral relationships, just as no objective Being could be apprehended behind the phenomenal world. All knowledge, therefore, they held to be relative. They were the first to point out that human society is ruled by convention or tradition, which they sharply contrasted with "nature." On this basis they might have attacked all the cherished traditions of Hellenic life. That they did not do so but, on the whole, stuck pretty closely to the accepted conventions was due to the practical nature of their task, which was not to make people think but to provide them with the tools for the successful mastery of their environment.

Herein Socrates differed from the Sophists: his aim was exactly this, to make people think.

He was born in Athens, in 469 B.C. His father, a sculptor, in accordance with good Athenian usage trained his son in his own craft; but Socrates eventually gave up his pro-

Socrates

fessional career to dedicate his life to poverty and the pursuit of wisdom. Disclaiming to have anything to teach, he did not exact any fees, wherein again he differed from the Sophists. The best years of his life were passed under the Periclean regime; but the chief period of his activity as a teacher and missionary belongs to the Hellenic World War and the dark days following it. Throughout his life he recognized the validity of the claims the city had on him. He served probably on the armament that Athens sent against Samos in 440 B.C.; if so, he may have been under the command of Sophocles, the poet, on the occasion when the Samians, led by Melippus the philosopher, defeated that portion of the Athenian fleet. He saw service as a hoplite at the siege of Potidaea (432–429 B.C.), and again at Delium (424 B.C.) and Amphipolis (422 B.C.), always displaying the same unflinching courage, whether in victory or in defeat. As for the rest, the duties of citizenship sat rather lightly on him; for he was content to remain outside the turbulent political arena, where his unswerving devotion to truth and justice would speedily have led to his undoing, as he came very near finding out on the one occasion when the lot placed him on the council.[1] The greater part of the day he spent in the gymnasia, the market place, and wherever the Athenians gathered, in endless discussion with whoever would join him. He had no use for the country; for trees and birds could not talk with him. Athens offered greater attraction to this inveterate talker than any other place on earth; and there he was content to remain. Of his domestic life we know little. He seems to have married when well advanced in years, and later gossip has delighted in making his wife, Xanthippe, the perfect shrew. She was probably as uninteresting a person as most Greek wives; and if she was a bit more shrewish than the average, she probably had some justification, for we suspect that Socrates was not as good a provider as Athenian husbands were expected to be. In 399 B.C., when he was

[1] In 406 B.C. Cf. Plato's *Apology*, Chap. XX (32).

seventy years old, the ill will that many of his fellow citizens bore him found vent in an indictment laid before the Athenian courts by some of his personal enemies. On the day of the trial he maintained the same fearless and imperturbable attitude which he had revealed during his whole life when facing any crisis. His accusers obtained a verdict of death against him, and on the appointed day he drank the fatal hemlock.

So much for his life. We have now to examine the historical significance of that life. Here the first question pressing for an answer concerns the sources of our information; for he himself has not left a line to enlighten us. There are three primary sources at our disposal; all three offer contemporary evidence, and all three present us with different versions.

The first is Aristophanes, who in the *Clouds* has, indeed, given us not a portrait of Socrates but a willful caricature; for it was his business to raise a laugh. He represents the comic press, and from his play we may safely conclude that even as early as 423 B.C. Socrates was vaguely identified in the popular mind with that objectionable new wisdom at which the conservative majority in Athens took umbrage.

Xenophon, who wrote his memoirs of Socrates as a tribute to his master and friend, belongs to a different category. This "gentleman of the old school" was a genuine admirer of the sage, and the condemnation of so excellent a man had aroused in him both amazement and indignation. He set himself, therefore, to show the injustice of that verdict and succeeds admirably in proving the essential goodness of his master. But the mystery of Socrates' tremendous influence and of the violent antagonism he aroused Xenophon fails to clear up. In fact, in spite of his generosity and his devotion, the author of the memoirs, a man of mediocre talents, completely failed to apprehend the greatness of him whose memory he tried to vindicate.

Finally there is Plato. He had assiduously cultivated the company of Socrates during the last eight years of that philosopher's activity. By far the most gifted of his followers and friends, he has left us the portrait of Socrates which has lived ever since in the imagination of the world. For not only was Plato a thinker who could do ample justice to the originality of his master, but he was also a great literary artist and the foremost writer of Attic prose, not excepting Isocrates. His portrait is without doubt somewhat idealized; therein the art of Plato conforms to Greek canons. But just as we may see in Polyeuctus' statue of Demosthenes a true revelation of the personality of the orator, so may we in the *Apology* discover the true lineaments of the immortal Socrates. Are the Platonic reports equally reliable for the contents of the master's teaching? The works of Plato are cast in the form of dialogues; the *Apology* (Socrates' reputed speech of defense at the trial) is only an apparent exception. In most of these dialogues Socrates is the chief interlocutor. Thus Plato has seen fit to present the whole of his own philosophy as issuing from the mouth of his teacher. So we must carefully distinguish between the original tenets of the master and the amplifications and the additions which belong to the disciple. This is not always easy. Fortunately, scholars are fairly well in agreement on the essentials.[1] There are certain dialogues that are classified as "Socratic," and from these, with such confirmatory evidence as we may glean from Xenophon, there emerge a personality and a body of teaching which we may provisionally regard as truthful and consistent.

Now it is abundantly plain from the pages of Plato that the true explanation of the power which Socrates wielded over the minds of his time must be sought in his remarkable personality. What sort of man, then, do we find Socrates to be?

His outward self indicated the uncommon quality of the inner man. He was an odd person, who would immediately attract the attention of the crowd by his singular appear-

[1] The reader ought to be warned that this agreement is by no means complete. For a different interpretation of Socrates, consult A. E. Taylor, *Socrates* (Appleton, 1933).

ance: his bald head, his snub nose, his protuberant eyes, his prominent stomach, his waddling gait, his feet unshod in winter and summer, his shabby cloak, his idiosyncrasies, such as his occasional fits of abstraction, when he would stand stock-still for hours at a stretch — all this would make him a marked man in any age. Within this unpromising exterior there was hidden a sterling character, upright, honest, and fearless. But the qualities that invariably attracted youth to him were his tremendous zest for life, his truly Hellenic vitality, his unwavering optimism, and his willingness to share their enthusiasm. Youth is eager to question, keen for adventure, and ready to follow a leader who assures them that their quest is not in vain. They found in Socrates a man ready to discuss any topic, but preferably those which had a bearing on the practical interests of man. Here is an ambitious youth who, in the Homeric phrase, wishes "ever to be the best and to excel among the others." He has heard of the arrival in Athens of Protagoras, and he knows no rest until he has met the great man face to face; he gets up before daybreak — and rushes off to Socrates! For here was the friend whom you count on to understand your zeal, — one who would not frown upon it as your elders were apt to do.[1] How these young and eager Athenians loved Socrates, even if he looked more like a satyr than a man. How good-humored he was, how patient, how kind! And how clever was he, how unanswerable his arguments, and at the same time how playful his manner, how witty his speech!

And so Socrates, who claimed he had nothing to teach, became the most successful of all teachers of the young in Athens, — their corruptor, his accusers said. Was he entirely candid in this persistent assertion of his own ignorance? He was unquestionably sincere in that, unlike the Sophists, he did not pretend to be in possession of any special knowledge concerning the art of life. He was, like many persons of great vitality, a born optimist; he firmly believed that "no

[1] Cf. the opening chapters of the *Protagoras*.

evil can happen to a good man, either in life or death." But the basis of this conviction was religious rather than intellectual, for he was somewhat of a mystic and a man of marked religiosity. There was that inner voice, which always checked him when he was about to commit an act that would cause him harm,— the mysterious *daimonion* to which he refers in the *Apology*. Moreover, he never doubted that Apollo had laid on him the task of searching himself and others for that wisdom which the god said he possessed; that was his mission, and he did not intend to desert the post Apollo had assigned to him, even if death were the penalty.

But while he believed in the communion of man and god as a fact of experience, he repudiated any claim to esoteric knowledge such as was not open to anyone. If he differed from others it was in this, that *he regarded moral insight as the one indispensable condition to human happiness*. In the *Apology* he is made to say that "the unexamined life is not worth living." This he might well have made the motto of his whole career. He professed to obey the command of Apollo, "Know thyself." This search of self and others he carried on along traditional Hellenic lines. In fact, in the conclusions Socrates arrived at he did no more than bring into clear light the inherent trends of Hellenic morality. In another chapter we drew the reader's attention to two characteristic features of the moral physiognomy of Hellas: its intellectual bias and frank utilitarianism. Intelligent self-interest based on careful calculation of means and end — such was fundamentally the Hellenic concept of right conduct. It tends to stress reason at the expense of will and feeling; moreover, on such a view, wickedness will be identified with mistaken judgment rather than felt as moral transgression. Now Socrates' formula crystallizes these obscure trends in Hellenic thought and bluntly states that virtue *is* knowledge. The virtuous man is brave because he *knows* how to distinguish between what he ought to fear and what he ought not to fear; he is just because he *knows* what is due to others and what he owes to himself; he is temperate because he *knows* the right measure in things. And, possessing the right knowledge, he cannot fail to act upon it; for that anyone knowing his true objective should deliberately or willingly deviate from the right course and miss the mark was unthinkable to Socrates. Even the cardinal sin of *hubris*, the willful and violent disregard of the rights of others, is now seen to have its origin not in moral turpitude but in sheer ignorance.

This is the so-called Socratic paradox, — not, however, so startling a paradox to his own people and in his own country as it is to us, who are the heirs of the ages. Since Socrates' day, Christianity, philosophy, and finally the rise of science and the scientific spirit have had their share in complicating the central problem. If Socrates is guilty of an intellectual bias, the modern mind is likely to be cluttered with a surprising variety of prejudices, often mutually incompatible. In the most common view — which is part of our Christian heritage — the individual soul is divided into two halves, a natural sinful self and a supramundane principle; and the two are at war. The Christian reply to Socrates is that we often know well enough what is right, but do what is wrong; we "yield to temptation," for "the spirit is willing but the flesh is weak." This kind of dualism is alien to Hellenic thought: natural man, in their view, is a rational creature, guided in his conduct by his reason; that seemed to them a self-evident proposition. The doctrine of Socrates in the last analysis, therefore, amounts to no more than an earnest exhortation to achieve that inward unity of which he himself was so conspicuous an example.

But if virtue be knowledge, such knowledge, in order to be effective, must be precise and accurate; there must be nothing hazy or confused about it. Here again Socrates is only obeying that Hellenic urge toward clarity. Therefore he went about asking for definitions. Now there is nothing so notoriously difficult as framing a definition, and the unhappy victims of Socrates' questioning, when called upon to state in so many words their objects in life and their understanding of happiness, soon found themselves involved in a maze of contradictions. Many a one, especially if he thought rather well of himself, henceforth hated the inconvenient questioner, instead, as Socrates naïvely remarks, of hating his own ignorance. The method of Socrates' procedure was from particulars to generals. The form of his inductive reasoning does not, however, start from objective facts; he begins with what are commonly agreed to be facts and then draws a general conclusion covering these. Aristotle credits him with the introduction of definitions and the inductive method. Familiar as they are to us, their consistent employment made a new era in the history of human thinking; for it was precisely their being unaware of this need for exact definition which had played havoc with the speculations of the Ionians.

If Socrates differed from his fellow Athenians, it was in his interpretation of the term "knowledge," which he would apply only to the kind of understanding that excludes all obscurity and ambiguity. "Apollo maintains," he said in effect, "that I am wiser than the others; what he means is that I at least am aware of my lack of true wisdom, while they are not." He also held that this true wisdom was possible of attainment; certainty could be found in the agreement of the human mind with itself when the last possibility of contradiction had been removed. To reach the coveted goal, self-examination was not sufficient; rather in the contact of mind with mind did he see the way leading to valid conclusions. Hence his endless disputations with whomever he could find. This attitude of the seeker after truth, again, contributed to making him the matchless teacher he was. Far from assuming a superior mien, he affects to be in doubt and humbly asks for enlightenment. That is the famous "Socratic irony." Behind this assumption of humility is the firm conviction that neither he nor anyone else can ever impart the truth to his fellow man: it must be elicited by skillful questioning, which will bring the disciple step by step to a clear understanding of the problem raised. He used to liken his task to that of his mother, at one time a midwife; for he too assisted the disciple in giving birth to the idea with which he was laboring. But he never forced his own views on the minds of his hearers. They must be made to agree; their objections must be met, their mistaken notions shown to be untenable. He never failed to wait for their answer before putting the next question and always framed his queries in brief form so that they might be easily grasped. In short, the essential part of his whole method is that both teacher and learner share in the task of discovery. Thus he became the greatest teacher the world has ever known. The proof of it is that all manner of philosophical schools, in spite of the wide divergence of their tenets, claimed him as their ultimate founder. He himself had no tenets except that there is no happiness without virtue and no virtue without knowledge — such knowledge as is within the reach of all who will take the trouble to seek it. In this respect he is at one with all the great spiritual leaders of the past, offering a simple message, and that a message of hope, enforced by a life which was a consistent lesson in itself.

It was fortunate for him and for the cause he had so valiantly defended that his career ended the way it did, for his trial and condemnation offered him the opportunity for a last and crucial test. He passed it triumphantly. The terms of the indictment lodged against him may be found in the *Apology*. They do not greatly matter; for his accusers found but a clumsy form in which to clothe their objections to the man. They said that he did not worship the gods of the city — which was not true; that he introduced new and strange deities — which had never been a misdemeanor in a city always eager to welcome a new divinity; that he corrupted the youth of Athens — which was a foolish as well as a wicked accusation. The real truth was that he would force men to think; that was the cardinal sin he committed, and it was one which even the Athenians could not condone. In his speech of defense he calls himself, with just pride, the greatest blessing which a kindly Providence has ever bestowed on Athens; at another time he likens his activity to that of a "gadfly which the god has attached to the state, and all day long and in all places I am always fastening upon you, arousing and persuading and reproaching you."[1] But neither the Athens of the fifth century B.C. nor any city of men in any century has ever willingly submitted to such interference with its habits of life and thought. The marvel is not that the Athenians put Socrates to death but that they allowed him to live for seventy years. Consider for a moment the full implications of his teaching. The society in which he lived relied for its social controls on tribal custom, on the force of a tradition hallowed by time, on the wisdom of the fathers, on the accumulated sacred lore of the past — all of which Socrates now proposed to examine in the light of reason, inviting his fellow Athenians to exchange the traditional basis of life for a rational one. Moreover, he was the first to assert the freedom of the human conscience; for while allowing, like a good Greek, the claims of the state, he maintained at the same time that his first duty was to himself and to the god who had laid this mission on him. All this made him into a revolutionary and a rebel, causing him to incur the ill will and hatred of the "pillars of society." Should this man be allowed to unsettle the minds of their sons, on so many of whom he seemed to have cast an unholy spell? That, some time or other, he would be brought to book for this challenge to society was a foregone conclusion. Nevertheless, had he chosen, he might have escaped death by going into exile; for the only objective of his accusers was to rid their beloved city of this meddlesome busybody. Socrates rightly saw that this would have been an act of base betrayal on his part which would give the lie to all his brave assertions in the past; and so he wisely chose to die.

Plato has given us in the *Phaedo* an account of the last day of his master. We find him in earnest discourse with his loyal

[1] *Apology*, Chap. XVIII (30).

friends, the subject of their conversation being the immortality of the soul. We may not credit Socrates with all the ingenious arguments Plato has put in his mouth. However, of the essential truth of the picture as a whole there can be no doubt: the philosopher on the day of his death, his mind still keen and fresh in its interest in intellectual matters, calmly and cheerfully discussing with his companions the everlasting mystery of life and death. Many centuries later a French philosopher, Pascal, overwhelmed by the sense of loneliness that besets the thinker of the modern world, said, "I shall die alone." What a contrast! The Greek, surrounded by his friends and keenly enjoying their conversation, retains his unruffled calm to the end, confident that "no evil can happen to a good man, either in life or in death." His last words were a jest.

SUGGESTIONS FOR READING. The reader wishing first-hand information concerning Socrates can do no better than begin by reading Aristophanes' *Clouds* (it comes first in point of time); then he should consult the first two chapters of the first book of Xenophon's *Memorabilia* and continue his acquaintance at random with that honest but commonplace author. Next he should read carefully Plato's *Apology*, the most illuminating and the most authentic document we have concerning Socrates, and the *Crito*, its companion piece. For an example of the Socratic method he should go to such a dialogue as the *Lysis*; or he will find a grander specimen in the *Gorgias*; the first chapters of the *Protagoras* make delightful reading, and aid in the understanding of Socrates' personality; and, finally, the closing pages of the *Phaedo* contain a sober yet moving account of his death.

PLATO

Plato was born in 427 B.C., of aristocratic lineage. After having dabbled in poetry in his early years, he soon fell under the spell of Socrates, and during the last eight years of Socrates' life was one of his most devoted followers. In 399 B.C. he was driven from Athens by the condemnation and death of his master, not to return until time had healed the wound. He went far afield; he may have visited Egypt and certainly stayed for years in the Hellenic west. There, in southern Italy, he came into contact with the Pythagoreans and may have found some solace in the esoteric doctrines of that school; at any rate, he studied their mathematics, and the interest in that subject remained with him during the rest of his life. He returned to Athens after an absence of more than ten years and founded the Academy, where he continued to teach until his death, in 347 B.C. His career as a teacher was twice interrupted by visits to Sicily, where he thought he saw an opportunity to convert his theories into practice, only to meet with disappointment.

His works (we seem to possess all that he ever published) consist of a number of dialogues, — imaginary conversations, of varying length, in which Socrates usually performs the part of chief interlocutor. So lasting was the influence exercised on him by these early conversations with his master, that he could not think of the search after truth except in the Socratic manner. In the earlier dialogues both the setting and the personalities of the speakers are drawn with a skillful hand; they are masterpieces of dramatic art as well as philosophical inquisitions. But as he grew older the interest in the dramatic side of his compositions waned, and in the case of the last, the *Laws*, we are inclined to think that he would have done better to abandon the fiction of a conversation altogether.

It must be understood, then, that nowhere in Plato's works do we have a systematic account of his philosophy. Instead, he takes us into the philosophic laboratory, allowing us to watch philosophy in the making. This constitutes one of the difficulties besetting the path of the student of Plato. However, it is by no means the greatest. For as we read him we begin to doubt whether Plato himself would have been able to pour all his thought into one mold. In fact, the most baffling question concerns not his doctrines but the Protean character of the man himself. Hence there are as many interpretations of Plato and Platonism as there are interpreters, each one responding to the rich and fertilizing thought of Plato in accordance with his own nature and predilections. The mystic discovers in him the arch mystagogue; the aesthete hails the eternal artist in the man; the dialectician, brushing the mystic and aesthete aside as mere triflers, concentrates on his metaphysics, but fails to convince the moralist, who, in turn, accuses him of misreading the evidence. In truth, in the case of the Platonic philosophy, as in all creative work, a final interpretation is neither attainable nor even desirable. For Plato was not only a philosopher but a poet and artist as well (and incidentally the greatest master of Greek prose). Like Socrates, he approaches his problems with a keen, analytic mind; but, unlike Socrates, also with the imagination of the poet. He shares with the philosopher the love of truth, but with the artist the thirst for beauty; if reason will no longer serve he takes his refuge in the intuition of the artist, abandoning the patient search after truth for the recital of one of his incomparable myths. Moreover, the Hellenic passion for justice burns in him as fiercely as in any Greek, all the more since the death of Socrates remained with him as an unforgettable instance of man's inhumanity to man.

In truth, there is no other Hellene who so completely unites in his own person the dominating traits of Hellenism as does Plato; no other is so fully representative of all its phases. His extraordinary flair for abstract thought, his soaring imagination, his quick response to the charm of beauty, his absorbing interest in man and all that pertains to man — these are the qualities that make him the Hellene par excellence. As such we propose, therefore, to consider him in the following pages; thus the section devoted to him may form a fitting conclusion to our efforts to penetrate into the meaning of Hellas and Hellenism.

The easiest approach to Plato is through Socrates. He was

Socrates' disciple, and in a sense remained so to the end. Now his master had made philosophy a practical concern in the life of man, and such it was with Plato. When he founded the Academy, it was not as a school of research, remote from the world and its concerns, where scholars might devote their lives to the disinterested quest after truth. Nothing was further from Plato's mind. He lived in postwar Hellas; his activity as a teacher fell in that era when both within the city-states and in their mutual relationships affairs were in a progressive stage of chaos — a world tottering on its ancient foundations. Plato did not live to see it fall, but he was a witness to the disintegrative process and did not mean to stand aloof. To enter the political arena at Athens in person was farthest from his mind; he thought, like Socrates, that he could promote the common good more effectively in another way. The crying need of the times, as he saw it, was the union of wisdom and political power, and he founded the Academy to further that end. Thus he became the rival of that other teacher at Athens, Isocrates; but while the latter continued in modified form the traditions of the Sophistic school, Plato was the legitimate heir of Socrates. The great rhetorician cast his scorn on the profitless theorizing of the Platonic circle, and Plato, for his part, denounced the superficiality of Isocrates' teaching; but both alike strove to find a remedy for the cancerous malady afflicting postwar Hellas.

Such, then, was the conception of the philosopher's task which Plato inherited from Socrates. Now Socrates had sought to save his fellow men by forcing them to think; he had tried to sweep from their minds the cobwebs, the vague words and phrases they habitually used without having probed their meaning; he had been satisfied that if men could be made to see the truth, the insight gained would prevent them from going astray. Plato agreed with his master that happiness is the natural concomitant of a rational life and that no rational life is possible without a searching examination of the self. But he did not quite concur in the Socratic view that knowledge of the truth would automatically result in right conduct. Plato's psychology was a little more complicated. He held the soul to be one, but it is an organism like the body; and as the health of the body depends upon the proper functioning of all its parts, so the health of the soul is conditioned by a like functioning of all *its* parts. Now in Plato's view, the nature of the soul is tripartite. First, there is the appetitive, or acquisitive, element. By nature insatiable, it will ever cry for more — more pleasure, more wealth, more of all things it hankers after; if allowed full sway it will gradually enslave the better elements of the soul and degrade man to the level of a preying beast. The virtue pertaining to this part of the soul is temperance, moderation, self-control, or however we may translate the untranslatable *sophrosyne*. Next comes the *thumos*, the spirited part of the soul, which makes one desirous of gaining distinction in the eyes of men; it bids us not to quail in the face of danger, and stirs us to indignation and angry protest when we see the just cause trampled under foot by the unjust. The virtue pertaining to this part of the soul is courage; if not properly controlled it may easily lead to reckless audacity and self-assertion. Finally, there is the rational part of the soul, the most precious and lordly of the three, which enables us not only to arrange our lives rationally, with clear preception of end and means, but also to catch a glimpse of the eternal verities behind the fleeting appearance of the phenomenal world. The virtue of this, the reasonable element in the soul, is wisdom. Each part has its proper function, each has its own delights and pains and penalties; but it goes without saying that the rational part must exercise control over the two others. Plato likened it to a charioteer guiding a pair of winged horses. One of these is of noble breed, the other ignoble; both are unruly and need a strong hand to guide them as they go, plunging and struggling to reach the goal. The charioteer must strain to the utmost to remain in control; for if he fails, the chariot will be overturned and the race lost. In the *just* soul, reason exercises its proper function, forever on guard that spirit and appetite remain within their own spheres and do not usurp rights not belonging to them. Therein consists the justice of the soul, — in the maintenance of the right balance between the three component parts. Such a soul has achieved harmony, and by it order and well-being and beauty.

We have watched Plato neatly and deftly putting together the human soul and assigning to the four cardinal virtues — temperance, courage, wisdom, and justice — their respective spheres of action. We cannot help observing the natural affinity between the philosopher and the other builders of Hellas, be they architects, poets, or lawgivers. There is a strong family likeness among them: all are striving to create order by a just co-ordination of the parts composing the whole, a nice balancing of relationships, a clear grasp of means to end. There is, indeed, more than a passing resemblance between the Parthenon and the Platonic concept of the human soul, both typical products of Hellenic genius. And if Plato ever entered that great shrine and stood enraptured before the image of the goddess fashioned by the hand of Phidias, did he discover that his vision of spiritual bliss, of harmony achieved through the control of reason, had long ago been anticipated by the great artist? There the goddess stood; the light of intelligence dwelt on her brow, the dignity and nobility of her mien proclaiming the supremacy of Reason. Thus Phidias had rendered in plastic form what Plato was to put into words.

This, then, is Plato's counsel to the anxious questioning of his age: there is only one road to happiness, namely, by achieving that inner harmony which will ensure a completely integrated life; thus the soul will enjoy good health. To a diseased spirit, happiness is no more possible than to an ailing body. Can the unjust man be happy? The question itself is ridiculous, says Plato, and needs no answer.

But man does not live in a vacuum, and for his proper functioning he needs a favorable environment. The wise man may find himself in a community of fools who will prevent him from playing the part rightfully belonging to him in the larger life of the commonwealth. If, therefore, the ordinary individual stands in need of correction, how much more pressing is the necessity of reform for the state! And so Plato, with the same ardor, the same sense of mission which had characterized his master, set himself the task of rescuing the polis. His effort took the form of the finest of his imaginary conversations, the *Politeia* (*Republic*), in which we have the first Utopia, or ideal society, in the history of Western political thought. The *Republic* is universally acknowledged to be Plato's masterpiece, a work written with such gusto and evident devotion that it dispels all final doubts regarding the interest of its author in the practical concerns of life.

Now the form and character of any ideal society will be determined largely by the current ideas of the age in which this Utopia is conceived. Plato's Republic will therefore be a Hellenic city-state and will bear more than a passing resemblance to its prototype. It will therefore not be amiss to recall once more the typical features of the Hellenic polis which distinguish it from the modern national state. In its essence it is a completely integrated society in which the efforts of the individual citizens are co-ordinated to effect a common end, which is the survival and well-being of the state. Naturally such an ideal was never completely realized, but Sparta and Periclean Athens have furnished us with remarkably close approximations to it.

When, therefore, we begin to examine Plato's picture of the ideal state, we are not surprised to find it at bottom an elaboration, in explicit terms, of the trends and tendencies implicit in the actual Greek state. In fact, Plato's Republic is both the *apotheosis* and the *reductio ad absurdum* of the Hellenic polis.

Plato opens with the axiom that the city-state is only the sum total of its citizens, "man writ large," to which he adds as a second proposition that, like its individual constituents, it is an organism, with a body and a soul. Granted these two premises, the rest follows easily enough under the pressure of Plato's relentless logic. As in the case of the individual soul, happiness is possible only through the perfect co-ordination of the soul's activities, so the well-being of society is contingent upon the complete integration of its components; and since, as we have seen, such co-ordination cannot be effected unless justice be enthroned as the governing principle within the soul, it follows that *the true end of society or the state is justice.* This is the rock upon which Plato has built his ideal state.

Now any society will naturally be composed of men of varying characters and aptitudes. Plato roughly classified them under three headings, corresponding to the three parts of the soul.

First there will be those in whom the ignoble element of the soul, the appetites and the acquisitive instinct, is predominant; they are the workers, artisans, farmers, traders, bankers, and, yes, the professional men, and form the largest class in the polis. Next comes that smaller class in which love of distinction is the guiding principle of life; they will form the army and represent the spirited element in the state soul. Finally there is that small minority in whom reason dwells supreme; they are those who have gained that inward harmony, and combine steadfastness of character with acuteness of mind. They make up the rational element in the soul of the polis. The virtue belonging to the first class, again, is temperance; to the second, courage; to the third, wisdom. A state will be temperate, brave, and wise in the degree that these virtues are present in the respective classes which they distinguish; but the justice of the state will depend on the extent to which its three component parts perform their proper functions.

It is not so difficult to see what Plato would consider to be the just distribution of the parts to be played in the communal life by the three classes: the largest class will furnish the material means of life; to the second will be allotted the defense of the state; to the third will fall its government. Such apportionment will strictly accord with the predominant dispositions of each class, the first class desiring wealth, the second honor, the third wisdom. The "lovers of wisdom," therefore, should rule the workers and soldiers; any other arrangement would be a manifest maladjustment and would cause the body politic to sicken and die. The end of the state being justice, — for without this the collective happiness is hopelessly jeopardized, — the means to this end would consist in opening to each the career for which he is best fitted. Plato had in mind a functional society in which the state avails itself to the fullest extent of its human resources. It was exactly the gross waste of these which struck him as the most tragic feature of life in postwar Hellas. The best the Athenians had been able to do with the mind of Socrates was to extinguish it!

But if the wisest in Plato's ideal society were to be entrusted with the complete sovereignty, no private interests of any kind should be allowed to hinder them or to tempt them from the straight course. This led to astounding regulations governing the philosophers' lives. They were not to own private property or even to handle gold or silver. Domestic interests also were denied to the governors: their marriage was to be regulated by the state; their children were to be taken from them, as in Sparta, and brought up under the watchful eye of the state.

Thus Plato intended to safeguard the paramountcy of social interests over the two factors, private property and the family, that most often militate against it. But the communism advocated in the *Republic* was to apply only to the governing class, with the express object of freeing it from any influence tending to impede its complete absorption in its task. It is evident how wide a gulf separates Platonic communism from the contemporary theory. In

Plato's view the higher man rises intellectually and spiritually the more detached he becomes from all earthly possessions; nay, these become a positive hindrance and a burden to him. (What would Socrates have wanted with the wealth of Croesus?) Therefore Plato's legislation concerning the ruling philosophers of his ideal state springs as much from a desire to relieve them of unnecessary burdens as from a fear that the possession of wealth might injure them. Modern communism, on the contrary, originates in the feeling of the dispossessed that they are deprived of their rightful share of the available store of wealth; it springs from a desire for wealth, while Plato's communism has its roots in the disdain of wealth. Furthermore, Plato legislates only for the ruler class; modern communism is all-inclusive, — in fact, aims at benefiting the "masses." But these "masses," according to Plato, are made up of the very people who, because of their ignorance and lack of true insight, find their chief interest in life in the acquisition of wealth. We should first have to educate them until they too became aware of the futility of mere possession as a way to happiness, and Plato despaired of the possibility of raising all men to the level of rational thought; as he puts it, "The world cannot possibly be a philosopher." There are then few who can rise to communism and are worthy of it; but on them Plato laid a heavy task which only a strong sense of duty would enable them to discharge.

There remain a few questions which even in a hasty survey of Plato's *Republic* cannot be ignored. The reader will ask how a caste system such as the philosopher is evidently introducing into his ideal commonwealth is to be reconciled with his equally evident insistence that the state shall fully avail itself of its human resources. And are the women to be accounted among these, or do they remain relegated to their domestic tasks?

In the first place, the three classes are not so rigidly conceived as our first impressions would lead us to think. Plato speaks of them as being made respectively of gold, silver, and iron; but *they have a common origin,* and hence it occasionally happens that golden parents may beget a child of baser alloy and, conversely, that an iron mother may give birth to a golden babe. In such cases Plato has provided for the necessary adjustments; irregularities of this kind will inevitably be discovered in the public schools, which all the young are apparently to attend.

Secondly, Plato would offer women the same opportunities as men. Here he was truly revolutionary; but he did not shrink from the logic of the facts. As to the natural inferiority of women, he shared the common opinion of his country and age. But if a woman has the necessary qualifications, there is no reason why she should not serve the state even in the ruler class; indeed, it is the duty of the governing body to discover talent anywhere and everywhere, and to give equality of opportunity to all alike, for only thus may be achieved that justice which is the true end of the state.

Finally, what is Plato's attitude toward the institution of slavery? No mention is made of any part played by slaves in the co-operative commonwealth; so far as we can discover, slavery has been abolished in the ideal state. If this be true, Plato, in this respect again, was centuries ahead of his time.

As we look back on this new type of human society, the creation of Plato's brain, — this mathematically constructed city-state, so plain, so rational, so sure of its aim, so perfect in its functioning, so beautiful a thing in its orderly simplicity, — we stand in awe and wonder before this fresh product of Hellenic genius. Yet, being human, we cannot help growing a bit uneasy if we reflect upon the practicability of the Platonic vision. For one thing, we have come to regard individual happiness as an end in itself. Plato seems bent upon considering it as only a unit in the organized well-being of the state. We expected it of him; for he was a Greek. But was not the rising individualism of his own time contradicting him? Was he not deliberately closing his eyes to facts that did not fit his theory? Again, we mistrust the introduction of the mathematical spirit into the field of politics. We recall, indeed, the saying of Francotte that Greek legislators go to work "like architects with ruler and compass." Plato did not deviate from the type. But is the assumption on which he acted correct? Must a state be logically constructed in order to endure? The Roman statesmen were not greatly interested in either mathematics or logic, and their constitution was only a crazy patchwork of contradictory elements; but it proved workable. Finally, Plato's ideal state is conditioned, so far as we can tell, by the voluntary surrender of all political power on the part of the more numerous but baser class to the superior minority. Will the day ever come when the ignorant shall have the wisdom to avow their own lack of understanding, — when those who, in Plato's own admission, are blind to their true interests shall recognize that these are best served by entrusting them to the keeping of their betters?

> Until philosophers are kings, or the kings and the princes of this world have the spirit and power of philosophy, and political greatness and wisdom meet in one, and those commoner natures who follow either to the exclusion of the other are compelled to stand aside, cities will never have rest from their evils, — no, nor the human race, as I believe, — and then only will our state have a possibility of life and behold the light of day.[1]

Until philosophers are kings! When will that be?

Nevertheless, we may well pause before summarily dismissing Plato's vision as the foolish dream of an incurable idealist. May not his insistence on the *end* serve as a corrective for our exclusive preoccupation with the *means*? Do the statistics of the economists provide us with a safe index for the well-being of the commonwealth? Or do they, perhaps, leave out of account the most important elements in human life? Is there not more than a grain of truth in

[1] *Republic* (Jowett's translation), p. 473 D.

Plato's assertion that the true wealth of a nation is not in its docks and shipyards and "other such trifles" but in the collective wisdom and virtue of its citizens? And can we afford to ignore Plato's demand for a rational organization of society? Even if it be forever beyond the power of man to convert the ideal into reality, it may steady our sense of direction to have formulated the goal. And was it so fantastic a thought to have made justice that goal? Indeed, it is not too much to say that Plato's definition of the true end of the state as justice will remain a challenge to the political thinkers of all time.

It follows naturally from Plato's conception of the end of the state that he should regard its true function as education. Hence the large amount of space devoted to this subject in the *Republic*, which caused Rousseau to declare that "the *Republic* is not a work upon politics but the first treatise on education that was ever written." In the many pages devoted to its elucidation, Plato is apparently dealing with the training of the two upper classes; but we have no reason to think that he would have proceeded on any other principles in dealing with the lower class, at least in so far as early instruction is concerned.

Plato's theory of education is, in the main, strictly Hellenic. It does not depart greatly, in either objective or method, from Hellenic practice except that Plato took greater pains in defining its aim and that he refined upon its methods.

Hellenic education, as we have seen, aimed at the whole man, and was therefore cultural in essence. Plato wholly approves. For the means, it depended on instruction in "music" to develop the mind, and on "gymnastic" to train the body. Plato adopts this program in substance, with the qualification that gymnastic, in improving the body, contributes to the health of the soul as well. "Mens sana in corpore sano" is a Latin phrase, but it expresses a Greek idea. But Plato is more explicit and articulate than Hellenic practice. He holds the essence of education to be nurture (here we recognize the teaching of Socrates): it is possible to nourish the soul by proper food, but it is equally possible to poison it. After all is said, however, it is the natural endowment of the individual learner which sets the limits to the possibilities of growth. We cannot provide him with an eye; all we can do is to turn the eye to the light and give it the opportunity to see.

Secondly, human beings are by nature imitative; they will seek to make themselves at home in their surroundings by imitating them. Hence the tremendous importance of environment in the training of the young. Special care should be exercised in choosing the sights and the sounds we allow our youths to perceive; for through the eye and the ear impressions reach the youthful mind most easily and most effectively.

> We would not have our guardians grow up amid images of moral deformity, as in some noxious pasture, and there browse and feed upon many a baneful herb and flower day by day, little by little, until they silently gather a festering mass of corruption in their own soul. Let our artists [that is, educators] rather be those who are gifted to discern the true nature of the beautiful and the graceful; then will our youth dwell in a land of health, amid fair sights and sounds, and receive the good in everything; and beauty, the effluence of fair works, shall flow into the eye and ear, like a health-giving breeze from a purer region, and insensibly draw the soul from earliest years into likeness and sympathy with the beauty of reason.[1]

Finally, education should begin with an appeal to the imagination, and not prematurely attempt to awaken a reasoned understanding. Hence the preponderating part assigned, in early training, to the arts. All these arts were grouped together by the Greeks as "music"; they are literature (chiefly poetry), music proper (which includes dancing and singing), and the plastic arts. The true aim of "musical" instruction as defined by Plato is to stimulate and produce sensitiveness to beauty, which, he maintains, will lead to that

[1] *Republic* (Jowett's translation), p. 401 B.

harmony of the soul without which there is no happiness. Of all the arts, music proper is held to be most potent in its influence upon the soul.

> Musical training is a more potent instrument than any other, because rhythm and harmony find their way into the inward places of the soul, on which they mightily fasten, imparting grace and making the soul of him who is rightly educated graceful, or of him who is ill-educated ungraceful; and also because he who has received this true education of the inner being will most shrewdly perceive omissions or faults in art and nature, and with a true taste, while he praises and rejoices over and receives into his soul the good, and becomes noble and good, he will justly blame and hate the bad, now in the days of his youth, even before he is able to know the reason why; and when reason comes, he will recognize and salute the friend with whom his education has made him long familiar.[1]

It has often been observed that Plato assigns a preponderant part to music and has little to say on the plastic arts, whereas the Greeks are pre-eminently known to us as a race of sculptors rather than as musicians. The reason is not far to seek. The arts of painter and sculptor call forth a certain response from the beholder, but they make no direct demand for his active participation. The music, however, of which Plato speaks is music *performed*, not passively enjoyed. This always implies re-creation; hence its greater educational value.

In his discussion of the "musical" material to be placed before the learner, Plato displays an unexpected strain of puritanism in his own self, betraying his moralistic bias. He would banish Homer (with deep regrets to be sure)! For the prince of poets tells many lies about the gods, and this would implant in the young mind totally mistaken notions concerning the nature of the divine. Plato would therefore censor the poetic output of Hellas before admitting any of it into the schools of his ideal state. In fact, not only poetry but all art expresses character (*ethos*) and hence affects character; if it is bad, it can have only a deleterious influence upon the

[1] *Republic* (Jowett's translation), p. 401 D.

soul. Accordingly Plato deals with music as with poetry and will have only such music and such instruments and such rhythms as shall be productive of order and balance in the soul: no wild shrieking of Asiatic flutes, no dizzying clashes of cymbals, no sensuous melodies that will betray the soul into the ways of Lydian luxury and softness. Throughout he shows a marked preference for Dorian austerity and Dorian simplicity. Perhaps the change in the arts which he witnessed in his own time contributed to the sternness of his attitude; but it shows how far Plato was removed from any idea of art for art's sake.

After the training of the imagination through the arts comes the training of the reason. This higher education was apparently reserved for the future rulers of his state. To prepare them for their lifework he prescribed a course in mathematics and related subjects lasting for ten years. Plainly he considered the power of abstract thinking the indispensable prerequisite for the attainment of truth. Only after the mathematical ordeal had been successfully passed — not until the age of thirty — would the philosophers enter upon the last stage of their education, dialectic. Then at last they would be brought into contact with the eternal verities, be initiated into the great mystery, and behold the beatific vision.

It now devolves upon us to attempt to explain the nature of these eternal verities and this beatific vision; in other words, we pass from the ethics of Plato's philosophy to its metaphysics. At this point Plato leaves the guiding hand of his master and sets out alone on his journey into the supersensual world of his imagination. Socrates' faith in the inscrutable power presiding over the world had been great enough to make him leave the pursuit of metaphysics to others. But his disciple, gifted with a more powerful imagination and feeling a more pressing need to answer the arguments of the mechanistic philosophers, would not rest content with his master's assurance that all was well with the world.

Now what was the nature of the problem presenting itself to Plato's mind? He thought that with the aid of his master he had discovered the ethical significance of human life; and he had envisaged a society in which that life might come to full fruition. But what relation was there between man and human fellowship, on the one hand, and, on the other, the greater cosmos which enveloped and conditioned it? If the mechanistic philosophers spoke the truth, what *human values* could prevail in a universe destitute of such? How could the life of man be properly said to have any meaning if there were no discoverable purpose in the greater world of which it was part? Were Justice and Truth and Beauty, then, mere figments of the human brain, meaningless bubbles on the waters of Eternity? To Plato the answer was never in doubt; a man of his moral earnestness and deep religious feeling would intuitively read an ethical significance into the universe. But he had to convince those others; for he admitted that Heraclitus spoke the truth when he showed the phenomenal world to be in essence a thing of Becoming and not of Being. In the eternal flux it was impossible to discover anything abiding; and what knowledge was possible of a constantly changing order? One cannot know that which *is* not.

Granting that knowledge concerning the world of the senses was unattainable, Plato attacked the problem from another angle. His master had not left him without a clue. Keeping in mind Socrates' teaching that the virtues could be defined and known only as general concepts deducible from the particular facts of experience, he set himself to reduce the whole knowable world into a series of concepts, or ideas, that would ultimately admit of being ranged in an intelligible order and allow us to read design and plan into the universe. This is the famous "Theory of Ideas."

He makes mathematics his starting point and puts this question: Does a triangle belong to the world of sense perception or to the world of thought? Is the triangle you draw in the sand a *real* triangle? But if there is no way of presenting the triangle as such to the senses, while you do not doubt its reality as a mental concept, it follows that the triangle is both *supersensual and real.* At least in the field of mathematics, then, it is demonstrable that the quality of knowable reality is confined to the supersensual. Now take Beauty. You do not doubt the presence of beauty in this thing or that, in a human face or figure or in the graceful contours of a vase. Your senses guide you to the discovery of beauty; but do they really apprehend the idea itself? Beauty may be real, but, if it is, its only reality consists in its abstract quality. And what of Man? If we speak of Man and attempt to define him, we do not mean this or that particular man, — not Themistocles nor Pericles nor even Socrates himself. In the eternal flux of things the individual is but a passing phenomenon; as such, reality cannot be predicated of him. But Man is an abstraction, and only as such is he knowable. Had he lived today, Plato might have turned to the scientists, asking them: What of your "laws of nature"? Have you ever tasted or smelled or touched or seen or heard a particular law of nature? Yet you maintain its reality. It is only an idea; and if you believe in its actual existence, it is because that particular idea or "law of nature" appears to fit in with the rest of your scientific ideas. The specific facts on which your law is based are constantly passing away and recurring; but the law behind them, the idea, remains.

And so Plato arrived at the stupendous conclusion that to the World of Ideas, and to this alone, reality belongs, — a quality of being, not subject to change nor affected by time, but perfect forever, whereas the world as apprehended by our senses, forever imperfect and perishable, neither exists nor can be known except in so far as the ideas immanent in its manifestations permit such knowledge. Thus he calls up the vision of a great Concord behind the apparent Discord, — a great Concord in which all the warring elements of the sensuous world are blended into a mystical harmony of Beauty and

Truth and Justice. He urgently invites us to turn our eyes away from the shadows of things and become "the spectator of all time and all existence," even though he knows well enough that man is enslaved by his lower self, a creature of desires and habits, and would rather sit in his dark cave watching the play of shadows than fearlessly look on the light of reason illuminating the real world.

He imagines this world of ideas as another commonwealth, in which all the ideas have their proper place and function, as parts of a final organism which reaches its apex in the ruling Idea of the Good. To understand what he means by this Idea of the Good we must keep in mind that to the Greek the "good" of anything consists in its function, its *ergon*, the purpose which it serves; for, knowing that, we have grasped its meaning. Hence the supreme and final Good which Plato postulates as the key to the understanding of the cosmos — calling it the Sun which lights up the universe — is its functional principle. It is through this informing principle that the ideas will be found to be perfectly coordinated; thus the universe becomes intelligible and akin to the reason of man.

The contemplation of this supersensuous world is the last and the highest task to which Plato calls his future guardians of the state. For "dialectic" means the study of the Ideas. Now it is apparent why ten years of mathematics were thought an indispensable preparation for dialectic; for mathematics also deals with conceptual realities, and by inuring ourselves to dealing with mathematical abstractions we train the mind to attack the changeless realities of the Ideas.

What is to be the end of the philosopher's toil? Will he ever reach the coveted goal, that last and perfect understanding which will enable him to see through the veil of the transitory phenomena and to grasp the fundamental unity and beauty of the real cosmos? Alas, Plato would say, man is but mortal, and he is essaying the part of a god. But if (at least in this life) the full vision is not vouchsafed him, he may strive to gain a fleeting glimpse of the eternal glory; and if its radiance should leave him dazed and half-blinded, this partial revelation would, even so, remain with him as the richest reward that life has to offer man.

It is customary to speak of Plato's "Doctrine of Ideas." But it may be questioned whether the expression fits what is, rather, an inherent trend in his outlook upon life. Let us add at once that it is an attitude shared by all the creative artists and poets of Hellas. Plato's transcendentalism is paralleled by the idealism of Hellenic art; both qualities are the natural result of the union of imagination with the will to perfection. The art of Phidias and Praxiteles, of Pindar and Sophocles, obeys an irresistible inner urge to pass beyond the imperfections of the actual and the temporal to the supramundane beauty of the idea, to capture the vision revealed by the artist's dream, to deny the validity of the passing and to enthrone the abiding. Thus Hellenic art proclaims its kinship to the thought of Plato, whose originality is found, after all, to be grounded in the very spirit of Hellas; indeed, it may well appear that with him Hellenism at last has become articulate.

In another way these Platonic Ideas will be found to be at home outside of Plato's philosophical domain. They are concepts; but the Greek word means the *form seen,* — seen by the mind rather than by the senses; it is the thing in the abstract, stripped of all that is not pertinent to its nature. If we recall the quality of Hellenic art, its emphasis on form and design, we perceive that Plato's insistence on the *form* immanent in all the varieties of sense facts is strikingly paralleled by the incessant search of Hellenic art after the true type, so characteristic of the work of poet, sculptor, and architect alike. Even the humble potter would completely agree with Plato that there is only one "idea" behind each of the varieties of vases he produced: find the exact formula expressing the perfect adaptation of means to end and you have your "idea" of the vase.

The preceding pages contain in no sense an adequate account of Plato's philosophy, nor do they exhaust the topics chosen for discussion. But enough has been said to show the place it occupies in the cultural history of Hellas. It was our object to weave even his philosophy into the variegated web of Hellenism. It was not an alien material which we introduced into that fabric. On the contrary, there is nothing more Hellenic than Platonic thought. If final proof of this is still lacking, let us examine once more the fundamental significance of his teaching and place it side by side with the message of Hellenism.

To begin with the latter, the very essence of Hellenism is in its enthronement of Truth, Beauty, and Justice; this is the Trinity which it worships. Now these three — Truth, Beauty, and Justice — are purely human values. It follows that, at bottom, Hellenism is the evaluation of life in human terms. "Man is the measure of things"; so runs its axiom. It is the natural reflex of that confidence in Man which rightfully belongs to the race that discovered him; it has a Promethean ring to it. We open our Homer, our earliest witness, and the message of Hellenism is there, proclaimed in clarion tones: not only that man stands in the center of the universe but that he has fashioned it after his own likeness, projecting his own self into the world of surrounding nature; he has created his gods after his own image.

We have now reached the last of the prophets of Hellenism. Wherein consists the final significance of his philosophy? Scholars tell us that he introduced design into the structure of the universe — purpose and rational order and just relationship between means and end; and the pattern is the same as that of his ideal state, which, in turn, is man "writ large." In other words, into the cosmos of his creation he projected man's reason and made it human; thus he affirmed the validity of the human values on which Hellenism rests. To be sure, Homer's ways are not Plato's ways; nevertheless, they are close kin. Plato's ideal man, his ideal state, and the transcendental world of Ideas itself are built on the same lines: each has its "Good," its governing principle; each has its inner harmony; each is a living organism, with its just adaptation of means to end. Thus Plato answered the Hellenic demand that man be the measure of things.

We have come to the end of our task. We began with Homer and have ended with Plato. This is altogether proper and as it should be; for these two are the alpha and omega of Hellenism.

SUGGESTIONS FOR READING. The best account of Plato's philosophy for beginners is A. E. TAYLOR, *Plato* (Constable, 1922); see also the same author's *Platonism* (Marshall, 1924). For a short essay on Plato there is nothing better than the admirable introduction of R. DEMOS prefixed to his *Selections* of Platonic writings (Scribner, n.d.). J. M. WARBEKE, *The Searching Mind of Greece* (Crofts, 1930) contains a lucid account of Plato's philosophy and religion.

The reader who, familiar with some of the Socratic dialogues, wishes to extend his acquaintance with Plato, should read *The Republic*. This is a liberal education in itself. JOWETT'S translation is an English classic; more recent versions are those of DAVIES-VAUGHAN (Macmillan, 1882) and P. SHOREY (Loeb Library, 1930–1935). For aid in the interpretation of *The Republic* see R. L. NETTLESHIP, *Lectures on the Republic of Plato* (Macmillan, 1925). R. CHANCE, *Until Philosophers are Kings* (University of London, 1928) is a stimulating book. Indispensable for the historical setting of Plato and his philosophy is G. C. FIELD, *Plato and his Contemporaries* (Methuen, 1930).

In this age of "debunking" even Plato has not escaped. See W. FITE, *The Platonic Legend* (Scribner, 1934).

BIBLIOGRAPHY

The bibliography here appended is supplementary to the suggestions offered in the course of the book. Only such books are listed as would be of interest to the undergraduate student and the general reader.

I. GENERAL WORKS OF AN INTRODUCTORY CHARACTER

GREENE, W. C. *The Achievement of Greece.* Harvard University Press, 1923.
HAMILTON, EDITH. *The Greek Way.* Norton, n. d.
LAVELL, C. G. *A Biography of the Greek People.* Houghton Mifflin, 1934.
STOBART, J. C. *The Glory that was Greece.* Lippincott, 1915. Excellent.

II. THE GREEK GENIUS AND HELLENISM

BURNS, C. D. *Greek Ideals.* Bell, 1917. The opening chapters are most valuable for the interpretation of Greek social ideals.
BUTCHER, S. H. *Some Aspects of the Greek Genius.* Macmillan, 1893.
COOPER, L. (Ed.). *The Greek Genius and its Influence.* Yale University Press, 1917. A collection of essays.
DICKINSON, G. L. *The Greek View of Life.* Educational Edition, Doubleday, Doran, n. d. A classic.
LIVINGSTONE, R. W. *The Greek Genius and its Meaning to Us.* Oxford, 1915.

III. HELLENISM AND THE MODERN WORLD

JAMES, H. R. *Our Hellenic Heritage.* Macmillan, 1927.
LIVINGSTONE, R. W. (Ed.). *The Legacy of Greece.* Oxford, 1921. Excellent.
MAHAFFY, J. P. *What have the Greeks done for Modern Civilization?* Putnam, 1910.
See also the monographs on Greek subjects in the series Our Debt to Greece and Rome (ed. by G. D. Hadzsits and D. M. Robinson) (Longmans).

IV. ETHNOLOGY

JARDÉ, A. *The Formation of the Greek People.* Knopf, 1926.
MYRES, J. L. *Who were the Greeks?* University of California Press, 1930. The most searching examination of the evidence.

V. ARCHAEOLOGY

D'Ooge, M. L. *The Acropolis of Athens.* Macmillan, 1908.

Fowler, H. N., and Wheeler, J. R. *A Handbook of Greek Archaeology.* American Book, 1909.

Gardiner, E. N. *Olympia.* Oxford, 1925.

Gardner, E. A. *Ancient Athens.* Macmillan, 1902.

Marshall, F. H. *Discovery in Greek Lands: A Sketch of the Principal Excavations and Discoveries of the Last Fifty Years.* Cambridge University Press, 1920.

Michaelis, A. T. F. *A Century of Archaeological Discoveries.* Dutton, 1908.

Poulsen, F. *Delphi.* Gyldendal, 1920.

Weller, C. H. *Athens and its Monuments.* Macmillan, 1913.

VI. ECONOMIC LIFE

Calhoun, G. M. *The Business Life of Ancient Athens.* University of Chicago Press, 1926.

Glotz, G. *Ancient Greece at Work.* Knopf, 1926.

Hasebroek, J. *Trade and Politics in Ancient Greece.* University of Chicago Press, 1934. The best treatment of a difficult subject. The author starts from the right premises, namely, that the Hellenic polis is a military state, and the Hellene himself a citizen.

Zimmern, A. E. *The Greek Commonwealth.* Part III. Oxford, 1926.

VII. SOCIAL LIFE

Gulick, C. B. *The Life of the Ancient Greeks.* Appleton, 1909.

Robinson, C. E. *Everyday Life in Ancient Greece.* Oxford, 1933.

Tucker, T. G. *Life in Ancient Athens.* Macmillan, 1906.

VIII. NUMISMATICS

Seltman, C. *Greek Coins.* Methuen, 1933. A fine book; as delightful as it is scholarly.

IX. ADMINISTRATION OF JUSTICE IN ATHENS

Bonner, R. J. *Lawyers and Litigants in Ancient Athens.* University of Chicago Press, 1927.

X. ATHLETICS

Gardiner, E. N. *Greek Athletic Sports and Festivals.* Macmillan, 1910.

XI. LITERATURE

CAPPS, E. *From Homer to Theocritus.* Scribner's, 1901.

Columbia University Lectures on Greek Literature. Columbia University Press, 1912.

CROISET, A. and M. *An Abridged History of Greek Literature.* Macmillan, 1904.

JEBB, R. C. *Greek Literature.* American Book, n.d. Only a primer, but a masterpiece.

JEBB, R. C. *Classical Greek Poetry.* Macmillan, 1893.

JEBB, R. C. *The Attic Orators from Antiphon to Isaeos.* Macmillan, 1893.

MACKAIL, J. W. *Lectures on Greek Poetry.* Longmans, 1911.

MURRAY, GILBERT. *A History of Ancient Greek Literature.* Appleton, 1903.

ROSE, H. J. *A Handbook of Greek Literature from Homer to the Age of Lucian.* Methuen, 1934.

SYMONDS, J. A. *Studies of the Greek Poets.* Harper, n.d.

TYRRELL, R. Y. *Essays on Greek Literature.* Macmillan, 1909.

A most useful handbook on all topics is *A Companion to Greek Studies,* edited by L. Whibley. Cambridge University Press, 1916.

XII. TRANSLATIONS

A good bibliographical survey in F. M. K. FOSTER, *English Translations from the Greek.* Columbia University Press, 1918.

The Loeb Classical Library, a series of classical Greek and Latin texts with parallel English translations, contains versions of all the authors discussed in the chapters on poetry and prose.

Following are some of the better-known translations:

Homer's Iliad: Pope, Bryant, Derby, Way; Lang, Leaf and Myers (prose).

Homer's Odyssey: Bryant, Palmer, Way, Mackail; Butcher and Lang (prose); T. E. Shaw (prose).

Homeric hymns: Shelley, Lang (prose).

Elegiac and iambic poets: in *Greek Elegy and Iambics* (Edmonds, Loeb Classical Library).

Lyric poets: in *Lyra Graeca* (Edmonds, Loeb Classical Library).

Pindar: Myers (prose).

Aeschylus: Plumptre, Morshead, Way, Murray; R. Browning (*Agamemnon*), E. B. Browning (*Prometheus*); Headlam (prose).

Sophocles: Plumptre, Jebb (prose), Way, Murray.

Euripides: Way, Murray; Shelley (*Cyclops*), R. Browning (*Alcestis* in *Balaustion's Adventure*).

Aristophanes: Frere, Rogers.

Herodotus: Rawlinson.

Thucydides: Jowett.

Xenophon: Dakyns.
Demosthenes: Kennedy.
Plato: Jowett; Davies and Vaughan (*Republic*).

Anthologies:

HOWE, G., and HARRER, G. A. *Greek Literature in Translation.* Harper, 1924.

SHOWERMAN, G. *Century Readings in Ancient Classical Literature.* Century, 1925.

A convenient collection of Greek drama: *Ten Greek Plays,* translated by G. Murray and others. Oxford University Press, 1929.

INDEX

PRINTED IN THE UNITED STATES OF AMERICA